Bon Voyage

SARIA /
ENJOU THE
JOURNEY

2023

Bon Voyage

An Around-the-World Adventure

_____

a novel
by Bob Pedersen

Vagabond Publishing Co.
Eugene, Oregon

Published by
Vagabond Publishing Co.
1227 Monroe Street
Eugene, Oregon   97402

Cover Graphics by James Hershiser,
design by R. Wolfgang Turpin
Title Courtesy of Ludmila Shamanskaya-Kremers

Library of Congress Catalging-in-Publication Data
Pedersen, Bob, 1946 -
Bon Voyage, a novel / Bob Pedersen
p.   cm.

ISBN-13: 978-0-9791539-0-7
ISBN-10:   0-9791539-0-5
I. Title

For information regarding the purchase of this book,
please contact Vagabond Publishing at:
vagabondpublishing@hotmail.com
or visit our website at www.vagabondpublishing.com

First Edition
10 9 8 7 6 5 4 3 2 1

"That was before I had you. You satisfied a lot of my desires," he said as he turned the car ignition off and reached over to touch her shoulder. "Look, speaking of desires ... I'm kinda hot and tired. Why don't we go upstairs. We'll take a nap, then I'll take you to daVinci's for dinner."

"I don't want to go to daVinci's," she replied. "And, don't change the subject."

"I'm happy Lynda. What difference does it make?" He was beginning to tire of the direction of their conversation. It went this way many times before, and never ended on anything but a sour note. The argument seemed to be the only thorn in their relationship, and now Jack was feeling many of the same pressures from Lynda as from his first wife.

He'd married very young, just one and a half years out of high school. Marge, his first wife, was his high school sweetheart. Christ, when he thought about it, she was his junior high sweetheart too. It all seemed like so many years ago.

Marge was family minded from the start, with career, (his career), coming up fast on the outside. After graduating from college, she stepped up the pressure on him to forge ahead on both fronts.

It all seemed to come at him so fast. Had she been a little more subtle in her approach, chances are he would have fallen blindly in step with her desires. As it was, he felt trapped and frustrated. He wanted to write a novel, and at age twenty-two and fresh out of college, he felt the task required living in near poverty, drinking most of what he earned, and finding inspiration not in the hour or two after the baby fell asleep at night, but in the three or four hour span between waking and having another drink.

Despite her pressures, the early years of the marriage were good. Marge was fun too. She took a couple of night classes each semester which kept her on the fringe of the college environment. But the fringe proved to be inadequate, and she and Jack slowly drifted, semester after semester, further and further apart.

When he graduated, they took out most of their savings and drove to Yellowstone National Park. He could still recall his feelings on the long journey by car, as well as the tone of the conversation, or rather, lack of conversation. At one time, he thought of counting the miles between words spoken — to make a game out of it — as they moved along the highway.

"Oh, that's pretty," she would say. Or, "Look at that, will you?"

"Uh huh," he'd reply.

And, mile upon mile would drag on.

Once they got to Yellowstone, they made love like it seemed they had forever — quickly, quietly, and then either cleaned up and got up, or cleaned up and went to sleep. Nothing ever varied or changed. It was as routine and exciting as rinsing your mouth out with Listerine before going to bed.

On their way home, Jack remembered something that changed his life, or at least made him wake up to the fact that what he considered living was a far cry from what it should be. By some fluke of nature, Marge and he began to talk. It started with a comment on one of the few married couples they counted as friends.

As they drove along sharing this rare exchange of conversation, the topic swung around to making the decision to marry. Marge commented how a certain couple should have never gotten married when they did, and furthermore went on to add that some people, meaning some men, should never marry at any time. Jack could remember a slight pause in the conversation, and then her asking him, "If we were doing it all over again, you'd marry me, wouldn't you?"

Jack would have gone down in the record books as being one of the wisest men to have ever lived if he, at that very moment and without so much as a millisecond pause said, "Yes Dear." He didn't.

As the pause drew longer and entered into what could be defined as a moment — and then, as the moment lengthened to awkwardness, the future of the marriage was spelled out.

For the next twenty miles Marge cried. He felt bad for her, but they were so distanced from one another that comforting words were hard to come by. As hard as he tried, he could not bring himself to make an excuse, or lie to her. He also could not tell her what a relief it was to finally have the subject broached, something he was scared to death to do.

The marriage lasted another six months, and when Jack announced he was divorcing her, she didn't cry, although he felt she wanted to. He cried, and her lack of effort to console him somehow felt appropriate.

He immediately packed his bags and went to Europe. He was 23 years old, and a couple of weeks by himself was all it took. He never looked back and never regretted getting a divorce. Less than six months after returning from Europe, he held a job with a newspaper, writing about city council meetings and covering one or two high school games on the weekends. And now, seven years later he was still writing for the same newspaper. Personally, he did not see himself in a rut, but knew it wouldn't be difficult for other people to see it that way.

He never got the chance to live down and dirty in the streets like he thought a writer should. He never got the chance to drink all night, write in the mornings as much as possible before the gin, beer, or whiskey kicked in again for another go-around. He never wrote the novel, or even the short story — only getting as far as page twenty-five a half dozen times before giving up for good. For all that Marge wanted, with the exception of children, Jack attained in about six months, a little less than a tenth of the total time they were married.

And now, here he was again, sitting in a car with Lynda and experiencing the same pressure he'd felt from Marge. It was as if the only difference was the names of the women.

"Lynda, I like where I'm working. I know it's not glamorous and all, but it's what I do."

"Yes, but you could do so much better. Instead, you just go through life dreaming about winning the lottery and giving the money away." She was agitated now, and like many times before, it came in torrents like a rainstorm.

"We've talked about taking our relationship to another level, talked about moving in together and getting married sometime in the not too distant future," she went on. "But, you don't seem to be interested in taking your career forward at all. Now, what am I supposed to make of that? How is that supposed to make me feel? More secure?"

"I told you about some offers I've had. Jesus, you make it sound like I'm a bum. I work hard at what I do, and I want to be recognized for that, not for whose ass I've kissed."

"Do you still think that I went to bed with that guy, is that it?" she hissed. "Because, if that's what you think, then maybe we should just stop seeing each other for awhile."

"Baby, don't be like that," he pleaded.

"And don't call me Baby!" she shot back at him.

They sat there in silence for a few moments, not looking at each other.

"Tonight's not a good night," she finally said. "We've got the Thompson trial starting on Tuesday, and it will be very busy at work."

After saying goodbye, Jack drove to his apartment. He knew better than to push the issue. In a way Lynda was correct. He was a dreamer, and winning the lottery held a compelling fascination with him.

Lynda, still angry when Jack telephoned that evening, let her answering machine engage the call. And while her frustration would remain, her anger would eventually subside, for with what she perceived as Jack's laziness and idle day-dreaming, there also came his tender, sensitive side. She knew that sometime tomorrow morning she would receive a beautiful bouquet of flowers from him. The flowers didn't always work an instant magic with her, but over a couple of days time they achieved their purpose.

The next morning however, was no time for floral deliveries or interruptions. Lynda was working with the senior law partner of the firm, preparing for a personal injury trial. Instructions were given to the receptionist that William Hugh Davidson, Lynda and an expert witness from Texas named Wesley, were not to be disturbed.

Lynda was a Legal Assistant for the law firm of Davidson, Talbot, Stritt & Mumphrey. The firm also included twelve other attorneys. William Hugh Davidson was the firm's senior partner, a board member of the California State Trial Lawyers Association, and one of the top personal injury lawyers in the state. Although Lynda previously worked with several of the attorneys in the office, she was now permanently assigned to William, or Bill, as he preferred Lynda and a handful of others to address him.

The initial suit of over twenty-five million dollars, named several different defendants, including a Japanese manufacturer of motorcycles. It was scheduled to go to trial the following morning.

The plaintiff, who was sixteen years old at the time of the accident, had purchased a new motorcycle after a specified date which by law, required all motorcycles to have an automatic "kill" switch located on the handlebars. He had driven the bike up a steep trail and become airborne, the machine eventually coming to rest on top of him.

Visiting the law office once with his grandparents, Lynda thought the boy would have been better off being killed. His quadriplegic body was in a wheelchair, and he was unable to speak. His arms were strapped down to the armrests of the chair, and his head supported and restrained in a headrest.

"Lynda dear, you have everything arranged with his aide?" asked Davidson, in the middle of a discussion of the boy's appearance in court.

"Yes Mr. Davidson," she replied. She would never think to call him by his first name, let alone Bill, when another person was in the room. "They'll be right beside you at the counsel table for every minute of the trial. I've arranged everything, and found the aide to be very capable and meticulous in his preparedness. The very first day, and periodically, he will be in a kneeling position next to the wheelchair when the judge enters the courtroom. He'll remain there, seemingly attending to his patient when the bailiff asks the court to rise. If the judge so much as frowns when the aide doesn't stand, well ... the jury won't be able to discern whether the frown is for the plaintiff or the aide. They'll just naturally look at the plaintiff, and take their displeasure out on the judge or more importantly, the defendants."

Davidson turned to the expert witness, and after a short conversation concerning a technical issue, dismissed him with a few offhand words.

After the door closed, he turned to her. "That was a great move, hiring that aide. You don't think he's going to over-do it, do you? Playhouse fuckin' ninety, try to upstage everybody?"

She wasn't overly fond of Bill's language when just the two of them were together, but she'd become somewhat inured to it.

There were also the subtle, as well as the not too subtle alludes to having an affair with her, and there were times when she might have committed herself to the idea. In fact, depending on one's definition of the word sex, an affair may have already taken place.

When she and Jack were arguing about the usual issues, she sometimes wished Jack was more like Bill. As for the language he used, she was not really offended. Maybe, she thought, she wanted to be offended in an effort to somehow distance herself from him — to be able to tell herself foul language alone was a good enough reason not to get involved with him.

"Is this aide still going to actor's school?"

"I believe so. I had a long talk with him about his theatrics in the courtroom. I mentioned a few clients who are in the Hollywood scene and told him these people would see that he never acted a day in his entire life if he fouled up this role."

"Very well then," stated Davidson. Glancing at his watch, he went on.

"It's almost noon, why don't you and I go have lunch?"

Before she could answer, he continued, "And, we won't talk about the trial. You and what's his name had another fight, didn't you?" He looked at her with a knowing smile on his face.

"Not a fight exactly," she replied. "More like a spat. I'm sure there are flowers on my desk as we speak."

"I really feel that someday the flowers won't be enough," said Davidson, leaning back in his chair. "You deserve more than flowers."

"Listen, I'll go to lunch, but I don't want to talk about my relationship with Jack. Let me go check my messages and we'll go, okay?"

There was a short message on her voice mail from Jack, saying he was sorry, and that he still had the name of the contact at the *Times*. He said he'd call the guy, saying what could it hurt to at least have a short meeting or lunch with him. She knew something would come up to prevent him from following through, but that was to be expected with Jack. He didn't exactly lie or lead her on — he merely possessed a nature which looked at each day as a day to be lived only for the moment. He never looked back. But then, he never looked ahead either.

Meeting Davidson in the lobby, she questioned the receptionist about any floral deliveries. The receptionist seemed embarrassed there were none, and turned her head away momentarily as Lynda became aware she already knew the answer to her own question.

Her lunch with Bill went through the usual niceties about how much he valued her assistance at work, and what a help she was. They talked about the upcoming trial, as she knew they would even though he said they wouldn't, and then he turned to her, surprising her with, "Lynda, why don't you and I run over to Palm Springs for three or four days after this trial is over. We could stay at my second home there. There's a pool, privacy, quiet ... it would be good for both of us."

"And, what about Jack and Mrs. Davidson?" Lynda asked, not even looking up from her plate.

"Listen, you know all about my marriage, or should I say, lack of marriage. I mean, we hardly even speak. I have the apartment in Malibu, and I stay there ... I don't even go home half the time. She doesn't give a shit, nor do I." He paused, taking a bite before going on with his plea. "And as for your situation, it's about the same ... a non-relationship if I ever saw one. Let me guess, there were no flowers on your desk, were there?" he asked.

"No, but he left me a message. I'm surprised he didn't send any," she answered.

"What's that, twice in a row now that he has ... forgot? Or should I say, lost interest?"

She sat back in her chair and looked at him. He was so much different from Jack. How could she be attracted to this man? In her mind she ticked off all of the negatives. He was at least twenty-five years her senior. He was almost bald. He was married, that being a huge negative in itself. Was this a dead end street from the beginning?

She was attracted to him though, and he looked especially good today. He was wearing an expensive black suit that must have cost well over fifteen hundred dollars. He wore a starched, white shirt, so white that in the dim lights of the restaurant it seemed to glow. He was tall and thin. Most likely, he'd never seen the inside of a gym, yet he looked fit. Yes, he was married, balding and twenty-five-plus years older than her, but he was also very good looking, rich and a take charge sort of man.

"Look," Bill started. "I'm married, and no happier about it than you are. But, I can and I will correct that situation in the very near future, and I guess that's my whole point. You have no future with what's his name. He hasn't gone anywhere since you've known him, and he's given you no reason to believe he'll go anywhere in the future. You'll get married, have a couple of kids and a mortgage hanging over your fucking head like a black cloud. He'll continue to go nowhere, and you'll wake up one morning wondering how in the hell you ever let yourself get into such a mess. And, don't tell me I'm wrong, because I know I'm not."

She picked some more at her salad, her interest in eating all but gone. She said nothing, and did not pull her hand away when Bill reached over and took it in his.

"You talked with Henny Willis a few weeks ago, didn't you?" Bill asked.

She looked up at him and nodded her head. Willis was a client of the law firm, and an Associate Editor at the *Los Angeles Times*. Willis was involved in some sort of property or contract dispute, and Lynda created an opportunity to speak privately with him each time he came into the office. Laying on what probably was an excess of womanly charm, she spoke of Jack and what she imagined to be his desire to work for the *Times*.

"And, what was that all about, or do I have to ask?"

"I asked him for a favor for Jack," she said, knowing where the conversation was going and how stupid she'd been for thinking her efforts would be acted upon.

"At Jack's insistence, or was this your idea?" questioned Bill.

"It sounds like you're cross-examining me, Bill. It was all my idea," she sighed. "I thought all he needed was a little push, but I can see now that he needs something more."

They sat quietly now, her hand in his, not moving. Finally, he spoke. "On Saturday, we need to get together to discuss what's happened throughout the week, and prepare for the second week of trial. As you know, I believe the matter may drag on for four or five weeks or more. I'll have Cheryl pack up the briefs Friday afternoon, and Saturday morning I'll get away so I can focus. I'll fly over to Palm Springs and come back Sunday afternoon, and I want you to come with me."

The proposal was a shock to her, but the speed of her response was even more of a surprise.

Immediately after answering, Bill waved their waiter over and asked for the lunch tab. Handing his credit card to the waiter, Bill turned to her, and reading her mind said, "Just tell him staff members on the case are going to Palm Springs. You'll be under no obligations, so it's really not a lie."

Lynda imagined she would feel terribly guilty the rest of the day, and probably all week. She was surprised when, after returning to work, she hardly gave it a thought. After all, she confided to herself, she was going to Palm Springs to work. It was not unusual for her to go out of town now and then on business, although overnight trips were rare. She knew what she was getting into, but felt hopeless and frustrated with her present relationship.

As soon as Davidson returned to his office, he went to work. His first matter of business was to take care of the office receptionist. He rang for her, and a minute later she sat before his desk. She was nervous and intimidated, it being her first time in his office.

Bill stood up and turned his back on her as he gazed out the tenth story office window. "There are many sensitive things that occur in a law office. Some of them you will see. Some of them you will hear. Most of them you will never know about." Turning to face her, he continued. "Everything is on a need to know basis. If you need to know or need to have an explanation, you will be told so. If you do what you're told, and can manage to keep all activities and dealings of this office to yourself, you'll go a long ways here."

The receptionist's name was Brittany, and she had worked for the firm for less than a year. Davidson knew she was attending school at night, but he didn't give a shit what her interests were, what she was studying, or how much longer she remained employed at her current position. He was only concerned with her ability to keep her mouth shut.

Brittany was much younger than the other female employees of the firm, and since her hiring, had remained somewhat removed from the other women's social circle. This fact made Bill more confident, and when he came around the desk to hand her three, crisp one-hundred dollar bills, her reaction did not belie his earlier feelings that the matter was firmly under his control.

She took the bills and quietly folded them in two. "Would you have a plain white envelope, Mr. Davidson?" she asked.

"Yes, very good," he replied, returning to his desk and reaching in a drawer. Handing her the envelope, he asked, "What did you do with the flowers?"

She stood up as she replied, sensing the question was also her dismissal. "I told the delivery boy to give them to his girlfriend, and he obviously had one, as his eyes lit up and he was gone in a flash."

After the receptionist left his office, there was one more matter to address. Taking care of the flowers was a snap. The previous time, it was his good fortune to be in the elevator with the flower delivery boy.

The boy came running up, catching the lift just before the doors closed. When Davidson noticed that the boy saw the lighted, tenth floor button, and then made no effort to select another floor, he casually asked who they were for. The boy looked at the card and told him the name, and Davidson, acting solely on impulse, reached over and pushed the ninth floor button. He'd then handed the pimply-faced kid a twenty dollar bill, and told him to get out on the ninth floor. Davidson felt a need to tell the kid something, so he said he'd ordered them and subsequently changed his mind.

The cancellation today was much more premeditated, and the palm required a little more grease. But, Davidson didn't care. It was only money. Now, he was on the phone to Willis at the *Times*. They chatted for a few minutes before Davidson told Willis his reason for calling. Davidson made sure what they were about to speak of was agreed to be kept in confidence.

"So, if this guy does call you, which I'm pretty sure he won't, just shine him on." said Davidson. "I'd consider it a personal favor. And, when and if your matter goes to litigation, please give me a call. If I know the judge, I may be able to make a call for you."

Davidson, burned by the press a number of times in his career, considered all of them a bunch of liars and pricks. He did not intend to call a judge on behalf of Willis, but it's what the guy wanted to hear.

By the end of the day, Lynda was physically and emotionally drained. Although she did not feel as guilty about spending the weekend in Palm Springs as she imagined she would, the thoughts were still there. And maybe, part of her physical and emotional exhaustion came from the fact that she was feeling guilty about not feeling guilty. She kept telling herself she would be in control, and she could spend a weekend with Bill without getting physically or romantically involved. She kept telling herself that, but in the deep recesses of her mind she knew better.

When she arrived home, the message light on her telephone was blinking. She kicked off her shoes, sat on the edge of her bed, and pushed the playback button on the recorder. After listening to Jack say he was sorry — that he knew with the trial she didn't need the additional stress of being angry with him — she instantly regretted her decision to go to Palm Springs.

Jack was one of the most considerate men she knew. It is what first attracted her to him, his kindness and consideration. Both of their jobs involved deadlines, and early on in the relationship he suggested they not call each other at work unless it was an emergency.

But rarely did a day go by that she did not find an e-mail message on her computer, sometimes in the middle of the day, and sometimes when she first arrived at work. It would never be overly romantic ramblings, but often just, "... I hope you had a good day," or "I missed you today ... how about dinner tonight."

Jack made enough money to pay the bills and have enough left over to enjoy life, even if it were enjoyed on a budget. She never considered herself a material girl, but lately things seem to have changed. She was thinking more about the future.

Maybe it was part of getting older. She was thirty one now, and realized anything not obtained by thirty-five would probably not be obtained at all. She harbored no great desire for children, but she did want to get married some day. God, she thought, all of my college friends are married, and here I am with a guy who dreams of winning the lottery so he can give the money away.

****

It was difficult for Jack to keep his mind on the business of writing a story about over zealous parents at athletic events, and how ugly they could be while pleading, castigating and cheering on their children.

Earlier, he talked with Neal, his editor, and reported on his progress. Saying he'd have something on the little-league parents by the end of the week, Neal responded that there was no urgency, but to simply concentrate on writing quality material. That the only concern was quality was precisely the problem Jack was having. All he could think of as he sat among the parents in the bleachers, was how priorities would be exactly the opposite at the *Los Angeles Times*.

Jack worked for the *South Beach Register*. It was a small-time, rag of a newspaper, with a circulation of one hundred thousand. If one were to take out all of the news about meetings, community notes, upcoming events, traffic tie-ups and the like, little of what could truly be termed, "newspaper journalism," would remain. It was kind of hokey, but Jack liked it that way.

The building he worked out of was remodeled countless times, and in fact, Jack's office had once been a janitors closet. There was a desk, a filing cabinet and a chair. There was not enough space for a visitor's chair, not that one was ever needed.

Lynda's office was palatial compared to his, and her office was adjacent to her sleezeball boss, the eminent William Hugh Davidson. Jack talked with Davidson only once, and that was enough. The guy was an ego-maniac if there ever was one.

Their one and only conversation occurred at one of the law firm's Christmas parties. Lynda wasn't standing next to him when he was introduced to Davidson, and after handshakes, Jack told Davidson who he was and who he was with.

"Oh, you're the news-hound guy," responded Davidson. "I better not say another word, or I'll find it in the paper as something completely different than what I actually said."

Jack had matured and mellowed over the years, otherwise he might have decked Davidson on the spot. Furthermore, he was with Lynda, and that alone seemed to have a rich, calming effect on his life. He didn't feel a need to get upset with anyone or anything. He found a certain peace in being with her, and lying in bed with her made any problems in his life seem irrelevant.

The first time he and Lynda made love was still very vivid in his mind.

They had dated several times before, but he made little effort to show his physical attraction towards her, other than to hold her hand or put his arm around her shoulders as they watched a movie or sat next to each other at a ball game.

Working for the *Register*, he was relegated to reporting on a rag-tag collection of little league, high school, and junior college contests. On that first, intimate night, he obtained some tickets from a writer at another paper in the Los Angeles area. They weren't box seats to the major leagues, but simply good seats on the first base line at a Triple-A club in the valley.

They talked all the way through the game, not standing up when someone hit a home run, nor stamping their feet when the bases were loaded. The innings came and went, fans rushing for the exit like a stampeding herd of cattle the very instant the last out was made.

Lynda and Jack remained in their seats, talking about themselves and their past lives. They didn't notice when they became the only people in the stadium. They absentmindedly watched as the groundskeepers raked the infield as if turning down a bed — getting the field ready to sleep, arise in the morning, freshen up with new chalk lines and clean white bases — ready for yet another day.

They didn't notice as the press crew emptied out of the crows nest at the very top of the covered bleachers, quietly commenting to each other about the couple who remained in their seats on the first base line.

The stadium lights went out, replaced by a clear sky strewn with stars. The weather was warm. Their conversation never skipped a beat.

They sat for two hours after the games conclusion. Jack never felt so relaxed and content with his surroundings and his company. When they finally decided to leave, they started down the tunnel towards the exit. There were a few anxious moments when it appeared they might have to climb over a fence to escape the ballpark, as all of the gates and entrances were locked.

They eventually found a small group of men in the beer garden, probably owners or team management, who were sitting around enjoying a drink. Although none of them said anything, Jack felt the proud embarrassment from what the men were probably thinking — all of this time this man and woman were somewhere in the stands, quietly having sex.

Jack drove them to her apartment. They got out of the car and walked to her door without saying a word. Fumbling with the key, she took his hand, and saying nothing, led him into the dimly lit apartment. They did not pause in the living room, nor did she offer him a drink, but led him directly to the bedroom.

Once there, she lit a candle and told him to sit on the edge of the bed. She slowly and quietly undressed in front of him, silently, with her eyes never leaving his. He realized this woman would be something special in his life, and was excited to have her. More importantly, he felt more complete and content than ever before. Their romance and life together continued to grow from that day on.

While Lynda often wished Jack would show more interest in furthering his career, Jack wished Lynda would be more of a dreamer. He tried to get her to fantasize about things — simple things — things like winning the lottery. There were times when she could, but more often than not, she would only manage a feeble effort. She was far too much the realist, always pragmatic in her approach to life, and she seemed to become more so with each passing day. To Jack, it seemed to be their only subject of dispute.

Trying to get her to dream, he once hypothetically asked her if he possessed a magic wand — if he could wave the wand and give her the ability and talent to be anything in the world she wanted to be — that she only needed to declare her wish — what then would she choose?

"How could that ever be true?" she asked, as a first response to the magical notion.

"Let's just say it's possible," he said as he pretended to wave a wand above her head. They were lying in bed on a Sunday morning. "Just pretend for a moment ... let it be okay," he went on. "You can have the talent, ability, education, knowledge ... anything that is necessary, and you can have it instantaneously. All you have to do is tell me what it is you want to be."

She could not answer him then. She thought the whole idea was silly, that it would be impossible to say. After a lot of prodding, she finally gave him an answer to the effect that she would probably just do what she was currently doing.

Jack often thought the reason for her pragmatism was her job. He knew the work was stressful, and just the very nature of the job itself was not conducive to creative thinking. It was the practice of law. Things were black and white.

Jack lived in a world of fantasy where everything was possible. The lottery, for example, was something he planned to win. He didn't dream he would win. He didn't hope or pray he would win. He just knew someday his winning numbers would appear.

Furthermore, he knew precisely what he would do when he became a lottery winner. He would travel around the world with Lynda. Without a plan, they would while away their days in sidewalk cafes, and waste their nights with long walks on deserted beaches. They would have no worries. There would be no talk of advancing his career or hers. They would have no responsibilities.

****

When William Hugh Davidson buzzed Lynda's extension, it was eight-thirty in the morning. At work for almost three hours by then, she was getting everything ready for the trial. When she first picked up the receiver, she was certain Bill was going to tell her it was time to go.

"Lynda, contact ready-call and the docket clerk ... cancel our spot on this morning's docket. We've got a settlement!" Davidson jubilantly proclaimed. "And, it's a very good one, I might add."

"God!" exclaimed Lynda. "That's great! Did you have any indication this would happen?"

"Well, I spoke with one of their attorneys yesterday afternoon, he asked me how early he could reach me at the office this morning, but other than that, it's all sort of out of the blue. I just got off the phone with them now ... I've been negotiating since six-thirty this morning."

"Well, congratulations. This is good news!"

The client's parents were deceased, and he was raised by his grandmother and grandfather. Lynda thought of them now, and how the settlement would be a relief. They had worried about the trial being hard on their grandson, and rightfully so.

"I'll bet the kid's grandparents will be happy to hear this news," she voiced.

"Yeah, I suppose I'd better call them now. Hopefully, I can get them before they leave for the courthouse. Would you come into my office for a moment, please?" Davidson asked.

She hung up the telephone and went immediately to Davidson's office. He was a stickler about always having his office door closed, and so after knocking, entering, and closing the door behind her, she turned to see Davidson standing before her. He put his arms around her and kissed her on the cheek. He was very happy, and she was anxious to know how much the settlement was for.

"This is wonderful news," she said. "I was not looking forward to weeks of litigation."

"Yes, it's fantastic! You don't have any idea how much help you have been on this case. We wouldn't be celebrating if not for you," he said. He turned then, and looking out of his office window, he said, "And, I don't want you to tell anyone we've settled. Let's just say a settlement is in the works without going to trial, but a few loose ends remain to be tended to."

She didn't understand where Bill was going with this. She sat down in the chair while he turned and sat on the corner of his desk facing her.

"I want you to go to Palm Springs with me this afternoon. We'll take a couple of days, lay by the pool and relax. I'll tell the staff some attorneys from the motorcycle company will meet us there to hash out the fine details of the settlement. You can tell your boyfriend the same thing. He won't have a clue."

"Bill, I can't."

She wanted to, and she knew the rest would be good for her. But, she didn't trust herself with this man, and she was not at the point where she wanted to give up completely on Jack.

"Sure you can. You were going this weekend. What's the difference if you go now, or wait until Friday?"

"Listen," replied Lynda. "I'll go on one condition. Absolutely no pressure. I don't want any hugs or kisses, or even any little pecks like the one you just gave me. If I want something I'll ask for it," she said. Then without thinking very much about how it sounded, she added, "Or, I'll initiate it myself."

Davidson threw up his arms. "That's fine by me! I just want you there!"

After she left his office, she made numerous calls covering the cancellation of the trial. Then, she called Jack's office. She was nervous and scared. She felt her voice might betray her, and he would know she was lying. She was therefore relieved when his voice mail engage, and as she explained the trip to Palm Springs, she became more and more confident she was really not doing anything wrong. After all, she told Davidson he could count on nothing from her other than her presence.

She kept justifying her decision well after hanging up the phone, and well into the later hours of the morning. She kept telling herself it would be good for her to relax and lay around the pool for a couple of days.

At noon, she rode the elevator down to the lobby of the building for a quick bite to eat at a deli on the main floor. When she returned to the office thirty minutes later, her heart sank. On the desk was a beautiful bouquet of flowers. Knowing the source, she almost picked up the telephone to call Jack and tell him there was a change in plans — that the Palm Springs trip was canceled.

She bent down, placing her face close to the scent arising from the bouquet of red and white roses. As the aroma arose, so did her feelings of guilt. Christ, what am I doing? she thought. She wanted to get married some day, and an affair with Bill was an affair and nothing more. He was married, and probably would remain so until the day he died.

Gazing out her office window, she knew Bill Davidson was a dead end street. Just the same, she didn't know what was down that street, and her curiosity sometimes outweighed her sensibleness. Then there was Jack. He was not married, and although the road with him might not be a dead end, she was aware of every curve and idiosyncrasy.

As she looked back at the flowers on her desk, she thought the predictability of her relationship might well be the actual problem. Jack's world was set. He was happy doing what he did, making the amount of money he made, and dreaming about things that would probably never be. Jack wanted to travel with Lynda to Italy, and supposedly was saving for such a trip. But, that dream could be like others — just another dream.

She imagined what it would be like to go to Italy with Bill as opposed to Jack. If Bill wanted to go, that would be it. He would just take her by the hand and they would go. There was something to be said for money, drive, and success.

It was then, as Lynda glanced at the card attached to the flowers, that she recognized not Jack's, but Bill's handwriting. In a mixture of guilt and eagerness, she opened the card. He wrote how valuable she was to his law practice, and how happy he was that she was accompanying him to Palm Springs.

2

One of Jack's friends at the newspaper was the first to notice his melancholy mood that morning. Laboriously attempting to write a piece on water rights in the valley, Jack finished but a few sentences in the space of an hour and a half.

"Jack, I've walked by your office three or four times now and never seen you writing anything, just sittin' there, looking at the wall," said Dan. "Maybe we need to bring back the fridge from the good old days."

When Jack first started working at the *South Beach Register*, the newspaper was a pretty loose operation. They became quick friends, Dan a recent college graduate and newly hired reporter as well.

In those days, they shared an office with another writer who'd been with the paper since its inception ten years prior. Hank Huntly, the seasoned news hound, was a better writer on a bad day than Dan and Jack were in their dreams. But, what Hank really taught the two new employees was not how to write, but how to live. Two years later, the old guy retired, but they never forgot the wisdom he imparted.

At the time, four desks faced each other in a square. The vacant desk was used as a table for a printer and supplies. The desk space was partitioned for privacy with some ragged, shag-rug-carpeted dividers. The small cramped room was dirty, dusty, and cluttered with boxes of papers and books.

The day Jack arrived for his first day at the paper was almost his last. He took one look at the office and the cast of characters, and thought immediately about passing on the opportunity of steady employment in his chosen field.

As he walked through the open doorway, he first noticed the absence of a door. It appeared as if someone had literally ripped the door off its hinges and hauled it away. The hinges were still there, along with small bits of the wooden door which refused to be freed.

Hank saw him staring at the door frame and said, "Our glorious fuckin' editor told me I isolate myself too much from him, so I ripped the son of a bitch right off the sill. But not to worry ... the guy no longer works here. He went to work for one of those women's fish wrapper magazines, ya know, the kind that deals with women's issues. Go on, sit down at yer new desk and tell us all about yourself."

There was a basketball hoop on the wall, posters from the Lakers and Angels, interspersed with clippings from other papers, cartoons, and a couple of ersatz, Playboy-like fold outs.

As he took a seat, Hank instructed Dan to pull out some bottles to celebrate the new employee. Located in the center of the fourth, unmaned desk, where a seated person would normally put their feet, was a small compact refrigerator where Dan was now releasing three bottles of Guinness from captivity.

"Please don't tell me you don't drink," begged Hank.

"No, I love beer, but ah, is this okay with them?" Jack asked, nodding over his right shoulder towards the management area of the building where the editors resided.

"To hell with them," replied Hank. "Don't worry kid, the managing editor owes me a lot of money, and as long as you're in the confines of this dumpy office with me, yer safe. Ya see, when the El-A Lambs were still in town, I bet against em every time. Didn't give a shit about the odds or the spread, I mean really ... fuck the odds. The real odds were that they'd stink up the field, which in fact they did, practically every time. I'll tell ya, betting with those guys was like huntin' ducks with a rake."

A bottle opener was passed around, as well as three glasses which were sort of clean. Jack found himself enjoying a beer at nine o'clock in the morning, the very last thing he thought would be happening on the first day of a new job.

They talked for over an hour. Jack discovered what Hank said was true. The management didn't care what the reporters did, as long as quality material was the end result.

Dan, having broken the spell Jack was in, stopped to listen to his response.

"I just can't seem to get anything going today, man. This water rights issue is not the most exciting thing to cover."

"Yeah, I hear you there. I've got a couple of things I'm working on that are pretty boring too."

Dan started to turn, and then said to him, "Say, I've got a couple of tickets to the Angels game tonight. Rebecca and I can't go, so if you and Lynda want them ...."

"Ah thanks, but she's out of town on business, and I don't feel like going by myself."

Dan didn't say anything for a minute, and then stepped through the doorway and into Jack's office.

"You and Lynda aren't on the outs again, are you?" he asked.

"No, everything's fine," lied Jack. "She went out to Palm Springs to work on some case with that asshole, William Hugh Davidson. I just don't like the son of a bitch. I wish she'd find another job, but that's highly unlikely."

Dan's wife Rebecca worked at an office building not far from Lynda's. Although they were friends, they rarely saw each other, and as two couples, the number of times the four got together were increasingly few.

Dan put his head down for a moment and studied the floor. Shuffling his feet, he looked up at Jack. Solemnly he said, "Maybe you two should see other people for awhile. I know you care about her, but it seems like it's always you revolving around her wishes and time schedule. And, this Palm Springs thing ..."

Jack cut him off. "I know, I know. It bums me out, but I trust her. Christ, I have to trust her, what else can I do?"

Hesitating for a moment, Jack went on, "It's funny. When she is away from her job for more than two days, she becomes something completely different. She can laugh, she has a sense of humor, and she doesn't take life so seriously. Then, one day back on the job and everything is pedal to the metal ... all business like, cross those tees, dot those eyes and let's do lunch," he said.

"Well, think about it, pal. Rebecca has this friend ... I think you met her once at one of our Christmas parties ... don't ever say I told you this, but she's interested in you. She's always asking about you."

After Dan left, Jack worked some more on his story, but it was hopeless. His mind was on other things. He put his lap top in a small carrying bag and left the building.

It was a ten minute walk, due west from the newspaper's offices to the beach, where he would often take his laptop and write. At times, it was far too crowded and noisy to get anything done. But now, in the late spring, the summer crowds in their tank tops, roller-blades, and mountain bikes had yet to invade the area.

He walked along the boardwalk for a few minutes before coming to McGrath's, a semi-sleezy English Pub run by an American of Scottish descent, who imagined himself to be Irish. Bobby McGrath was always behind the bar during the day, and was always around pumping flesh and sipping from the profits the rest of the time. The bar attracted an eclectic group of characters, from beach bums to businessmen — from cops to artists.

When Jack entered, Bobby was at the end of the bar surrounded by a few of his cronies, sorting out one or more of the great mysteries of life. The rest of the place was empty. He looked up when Jack entered.

"Jack Gillette, me good man. Come on down here, have a proper pint, and settle an argument for us all."

"Jesus Christ, Bobby. The last thing I want now is an argument," replied Jack, as he walked over to the group, thereby nullifying any protest about becoming involved.

"Jack here is a reporter!" said Bobby, as he introduced him to the four other men at the bar. "He's a of a lot more knowledgeable about current events and history than any of ya blokes will ever be. He'll settle this."

"Really Bobby," said Jack seriously. "You guys go on with your conversation like I'm not even here. I just stopped in for a cup of coffee and a lottery ticket."

One of the guys was dressed as if he were color blind. He wore a pair of salmon-pink, colored slacks with pant legs four inches too short, and a bright, blue shirt. He raised his half empty glass to Jack and said, "Nice meeting ya. And, not knowin' ya at all, well, I'll take whatever you say as the answer. Can't get any more unbiased opinion than that of a total stranger."

"My friend, you're putting a lot more faith in my intelligence and opinion than it deserves," said Jack.

Bobby jumped into the fray as he set a cup of coffee in front of Jack. "What were discussin' here is ... who was the best president in the last fifty years."

"I'll tell ya, I still think it was Kennedy," quipped one of the group.

"Ah, fuck," said Bobby. "All Kennedy ever did was screw Marilyn Monroe. That don't make em a good president, just a questionable lay with a good eye for tits."

"Well, sometimes the best president is someone who doesn't do anything," said Jack. "Sometimes, just leaving things as they are is better than gambling that changes will work, let alone be accepted and appreciated."

"So, who do ya think, Laddy?" asked Bobby.

"Ah, you'll all laugh," said Jack. But, he could see the men had consumed two or three over their limit, and they were all intently hanging on his every word, so he resigned himself to continuing. After all, someone has to be the expert, and they'd pretty much appointed him. "Lyndon Baines Johnson," stated Jack.

There were a few snorts and laughs, but they remained attentive just the same.

"He was instrumental in the passage of the first civil rights bill in nineteen-fifty-seven and nineteen-sixty. The first ever in this country and well overdue. He pushed through Congress an impressive list of legislation in the area of civil rights, anti-poverty programs, and tax reduction. Unfortunately, he was saddled with the war in Vietnam ... something he did not initiate, and something that, quite frankly, I don't think he knew how to get himself out of. Had he known a way, I really believe he would have acted upon it."

Jack was a bit surprised how they all seemed to accept his authority on the matter, but he figured they were glad to see an end to the argument. Free at last from presidential politics, they could now dive into some other topic they thought they knew something about, like sports or women.

Jack finished his coffee and asked Bobby for a lottery ticket. "What's the jackpot now?" he asked.

"I dunno, but I'll look fer ya," replied Bobby. "Jesus Christ, it's over ninety-six million dollars! Ninety-six-five, to be exact."

"That's too much money," said Jack, as he handed over five dollars for his four single plays and one play with selected numbers. "I'd give a bunch of it away."

"Well, give some ta me!" said Bobby, as Jack started to get up off the barstool to leave.

"Bobby, if I win I'll buy ya a new joint in Scotland ... right next to a golf course," said Jack, walking towards the door.

As he started to open the door, Bobby yelled, "Laddy, I'm a-holdin' ya to that promise!"

Jack went back to the office and worked some more on the article that had plagued him all morning. The writing didn't go much better in the afternoon, but he managed to piece together a mediocre effort in time to meet a five o'clock deadline. It wasn't his best work, but it was finished. He told himself tomorrow would be a better day.

At home that night, he considered calling Lynda in Palm Springs. She'd left the number on his answering machine, but he was afraid she might think he was checking up on her.

He crawled into bed early, propped up some pillows, and read a travel book about the Trans-Siberian express. The book he was reading was about a woman who traveled alone from Moscow to Vladivostok, Russia. She traveled in the middle of winter, and at a stop in Irkutsk, the temperature was forty degrees below zero.

The book conjured up images of train compartments bathed in the warmth of international conversations, interrupted by a continuous flow of beer, vodka, breads, and cheeses. There was a story of how a train attendant, or *provodnik*, proceeded to knock ice off of a carriage step with a hammer, only to see the step snap off in the bitter cold and fall to the ground.

Jack read stories of people who traveled to every country in the world, people who set foot in every time zone, and people who biked or drove across one continent or another. However, what really inspired him were the stories of people who roamed the world and mingled with the locals. To stay in a small bed and breakfast or pensioner's hotel — or better yet, in a room above a pub — that is the way he would travel if he ever got the opportunity.

After turning out the bedside lamp, he lay in bed on his back and closed his eyes. In the strange space between daydreaming while awake and the dream world state of sleep, he thought about traveling around the world. He would traverse continents by train. He would see so many places, and meet so many people. He would travel alone. No, he would travel with Lynda. As sleep overcame him, he was back to traveling just as he was sleeping — alone.

****

Jack's hand rested on the telephone receiver well after hearing a dial tone and hanging up. Not wanting to disturb any meetings, he had waited until 10 a.m. to call her. Normally, he could tell how many cups of coffee she'd consumed by the speed of her speech. But, this morning she sounded lethargic and half asleep.

He knew the lawsuit involved a lot of money, and that its success was important to her. She had been absorbed in the case for over a year, and he often found himself choosing words and subjects carefully, so as not to initiate or segue into anything which might lead to a discussion about the case.

As he got up to leave his office for an appointment to have his hair cut, he thought about how glad he would be when the trial was over. Lynda would become more relaxed and easier to be around, and she would probably take a week or two off work. It might be a good time for them to drive up to northern California or southern Oregon. They could find one of those mountain lodges they both loved, and just lie around for a few days.

The barbershop Jack patronized, lay in a small, block-long cluster of older businesses near the entrance to a community college. It was not the kind of shop where you had your hair styled or high-lighted.

Mike was a barber. He cut hair, and much like a good bartender, could carry on an intelligent conversation about sports, politics, or anything else the customer was interested in, or Mike thought they should have an interest in. The shop was old, and nothing ever changed, a fact emphasized by a dusty, faded pin-up of a scantily-clad model hanging above the cash register, it's vintage somewhere around 1955.

"Ya read the paper yet?" asked Mike, as Jack settled into the big, heavy, black cushioned barber chair. Mike whipped the white cloth around after giving it a few quick shakes, and draped it over the front of Jack's chest and lap. Fastening a paper collar around Jack's neck, Mike went on, "But then, guys that work for the paper probably don't even give it a look, do they? I'll bet you don't even read your own paper, do you?"

"I read the *Register* and a couple of others every day," said Jack. "But, I know what you mean. I often wonder if people who do things for a living, also do those things in their spare time. Or, if they enjoy them."

"Well, I'm a barber and I comb my own hair," laughed Mike.

Jack looked up and rolled his eyes. Mike was completely bald, and once confided that the baldness finished its course about the same time Mike completed barber school, some forty years ago.

"Yeah, you're one of those who is on the other side of the charts all right. But, are there guys like gourmet chefs who work all day and then go home at night and cook a gourmet meal for themselves?" asked Jack. "I'd like to think they'd just eat some Dinty Moore right out of the can ... maybe add a couple of Ritz crackers and a bottle of Bud."

"Well anyway, I got the *Times* here if ya want to read it," said Mike, turning on his clippers and getting down to business.

Jack accepted the offer, but read very little, as the newspaper lay folded in his lap while he and Mike talked.

After leaving the barbershop, Jack walked halfway down the block before he noticed the newspaper still tucked under his arm. He stopped and turned to go back to Mike's before deciding someone else would bring a copy into the shop, and besides, Mike mentioned he'd read it.

A small park sat at the end of the block, and with his lap-top in a shoulder bag, he intended to go there, sit on a bench, and write or read for awhile. As he paused on the sidewalk making the decision to return or not return to Mike's, he looked into the window of the shop he stood before. It was a travel agency, and its window display featured travel throughout the world by rail.

There were pictures of the Trans-Australian train, the Indian Pacific, and an advertisement for the Blue Train in South Africa. Someone even placed a small model train at the base of the display, with a brochure protruding from under the track promoting the wonders of the Canadian Rockies.

But, what really caught his eye was the center of the display. For, in the center was a poster framed with souvenirs from Russia and Siberia, and a sign proclaiming the Trans-Siberian Railway to be the "Grand-Daddy Of Them All." He thought it was strange that twice in as many days he encountered something on train travel across Russia.

Unconsciously, he found himself opening the door to the agency and walking in. It was a small office, with only two desks and a small reception counter. There was a small futon-like love seat for patrons to use, presumably to wait for the next available agent, and directly in front of it was a round coffee table, the plane of its table top acting as the axis for a large globe.

A quick glance around the room would quickly dispel any thoughts by a prospective traveler that they would have to wait. An older woman appeared to be the sole agent available, and she now looked up at Jack as he approached the counter.

"May I help you, young man?" she asked. "If you're looking for parking meter change, I'm sorry, but I just gave the last of mine to a young woman about two minutes ago."

"No, I don't need change. I was just looking at your window display, and was wonderin' what it cost to go across Russia by train?"

The woman arose and slowly walked up to the counter where Jack waited. As she got closer, Jack noticed she was wearing earrings which were small, miniature globes. He also noted her age to be even older than he first thought. Her hair was white, and she spoke in almost a whisper.

"Can't really say what a ticket cost," she answered. "You see, most of the trips are taken as part of a package deal, with prearranged stops at specified cities, accommodation at specified hotels, and onward travel on specified dates ... and to be really honest, I've only sold one trip on the Trans-Siberian, and that was a long, long time ago."

"It looks as if it would be a great, relaxing way to travel."

"People aren't interested in relaxing ways to travel anymore," stated Loraine, her name-tag proclaiming her to be the manager, although in essence it appeared the only person she managed was herself.

"People are in a hurry to get where they're going. Then, they're in a hurry to see what they went there to see or do, and then they're in a hurry to get back. I can't remember the last time I sold an international train ticket other than Euro-Rail passes to students. I sell some of those every year towards the end of the school year."

She glanced over at the window now in a lovingly manner and went on, "My husband, Warren, does the window four times a year whether it needs it or not. He's not very imaginative, I'm afraid. He has four basic themes — ski trips in the fall, Hawaii just before Christmas, cruises to the Caribbean around Valentine's Day, and the train thing in the spring. "If ya come back next year at this same time, I'll bet you wouldn't even think he'd changed the display," she laughed. "It all pretty much stays the same."

Jack was in no hurry, and Loraine showed no sign she was eager to get back to her desk.

"I've always wanted to go around the world. I haven't had the chance to travel as much as I'd like, but someday I'd like to do that."

"Don't wait too long, honey. You'll be old and gray like me and unable to do it. I've never regretted it, that's for sure."

"You've traveled around the world?"

"Yeah, I did just that" she stated, surprising him with her answer. "I was so young then. I think about it now and I often wonder how I ever got the nerve to do it. I'll tell ya, I don't think I'd have that kind of blind courage today."

"Did you fly?" asked Jack.

"Oh, you're so kind," she replied. "No, young man, I didn't fly, and in fact in those days, nobody flew. Oh, I suppose some short flights could be taken, but in those days a person was pretty much limited to travel by sea or rail."

"When did you go around the world?" he asked, purposely keeping his part of the conversation short. He wanted to hear all of what this woman had to say, as he was truly interested in not only the subject, but her story as well.

"And, you were being such a kind, young gentleman," she laughed. "I went around the world in nineteen thirty-four. I was all of nineteen years old then."

"Wow, that's pretty neat! Were you scared?"

"Very," she replied. "My parents had died and left me a small amount of money. I'd grown up an only child, so maybe that prepared me in some way for being all alone, as I truly was. I grew up in Nebraska, and although we were one of the few families who did not live on a farm, I felt that in essence, I was a farmer too, or that I'd end up a farmer if I stayed long enough. I hated it, and wanted to get out so.

"I took the train to New York, and caught a freighter bound for Liverpool. From there, I traveled across Europe, Russia, and into China. I was lucky to meet a Chinese gentleman on the train just before entering that country. He spoke very good English, and told me he had a daughter my age. He looked after me all the way to Canton.

"I didn't ever feel like my life was in danger, but I had a small Derringer pistol packed away in one of my suitcases, just in case. By the time I dug it out I'm sure the danger would have passed, but it was reassuring knowing it was there just the same."

"And, you took a freighter across the Pacific as well?" asked Jack.

"Yes, after a fashion. It took me a long time to find a ship in Hong Kong. I spent over three months there, and in fact, that is where I met my husband. He was British, living in Hong Kong and working in the import-export business. Two years after I left, he came out to California. That was just before the war. We've been here ever since."

"The train ride, you enjoyed it?" asked Jack.

"Oh, it was an adventure, to say the least. I'm sure it's much nicer now, but in those days, traveling across Russia and China was a pretty spartan-like experience. I was in western Europe during the winter, and I remember it being very, very cold. And, it was summer time when I traveled through Mongolia and China, and it was very hot. The trains in China, well they wouldn't let you open any of the windows. Oh my God, was it ever hot and uncomfortable."

"Well, some day when I'm rich, and I don't have any worries, I'd like to go around the world like you did."

"When you're rich you'll have a heck of a lot more worries than you do now," Loraine quickly replied. "Besides, I never really went around the world. I never made it back to Nebraska where I started. I only got as far as California. Warren and I drove as far east as Utah once, but that's as close as I ever got."

Jack said goodbye, letting Loraine go back to whatever she was doing, and walked to the park. He found a comfortable park bench in the shade, pulled out his lap top, and wrote for nearly two hours. When it came time to leave, he was surprised at how much he had accomplished, a fact he would have to emphasize to his editor when he returned to the office, since he failed to sign out or tell anyone he was leaving.

As he packed up his computer, he noticed the newspaper from Mike's barbershop still lay folded on the park bench beside him. He paused for a moment to read an article about a child abduction on the front page, then turned to page three to finish the piece.

As his mind and eyes finished the last sentence about a family member being considered a suspect, he simultaneously spotted the column below. He read it once without any thought or real anticipation. He read it again before setting the newspaper down in his lap, and then in one motion, picked the paper back up and read the column a third time.

Jack read it quickly. He stopped, and then read it again slowly.

He sat on the park bench and stared at nothing. A minute or two passed before he picked up the newspaper and read the column yet again.

He thought about where he'd last seen them. He remembered going home. Had he gone anywhere after that? Were they in the pocket of the shirt he'd worn yesterday, or did he take them out and put them on top of his dresser? Could he have taken them out and put them in his desk at the office?

He read the story yet again. He sat and thought about finding another newspaper to verify what he was seeing. After reading the column one more time, he got up from his seat, slung his shoulder bag onto his left shoulder, and with the newspaper firmly in his right hand, started walking back to work.

He passed the travel agency where he met Loraine, and for a moment thought about stopping. For an instant, he desperately felt the urge to tell someone, to confide in someone, to make it either true or some sort of strange mirage.

Another hundred yards or so, he came to Mike's barbershop, and by now the thought of confiding in someone had changed to a desire to keep the secret his and his alone. What if it wasn't true? What if he was getting nervous and excited over something that was a cruel, but unintentional misprint?

Jack returned to the office and had just opened his desk drawer when Dan knocked on the door casing of his office.

"What's the matter?" asked Dan, concern in his voice now as he saw Jack's deer-in-the-headlights-like eyes look up at him while his hands continued to rummage unchecked. "Are you okay?"

"Yeah, I'm fine." He was sweating now, and beginning to worry. "Look, give me a minute or two. I'll meet you down at your desk in just a sec."

"Okay, but just so you know, Neal's pissed off. He's been looking for you most of the day. I don't think he knows you're back in the building, so it might be best if he found out from you first."

"Yeah, right. I'll talk to him in just a minute."

After Dan left, Jack began to look frantically through his desk drawer. As he looked at the blank screen of his darkened computer monitor, the reflection in the screen made him turn in his chair to a small cork, bulletin board behind him. There on the board was the objective of his search — two tickets for the California Lottery.

He checked the date first, then laid them on the surface of the desk. He opened the newspaper to the page where the small article was printed and slowly compared the two.

Turning on his computer, he went to the internet, punched in the information which would take him to the site, and waited. Seconds later, he clicked on the selected icon, and waited another second while the information filled up the screen. He compared that information to the newspaper, and then to the data on his ticket. He switched the order of comparison a few more times before he was convinced that what he saw was true and not merely imagined.

Absentmindedly, he turned the computer monitor off, and then, not knowing why, he reached over and flipped off the light switch to his office. His door was still wide open, and he made no attempt to close it. He folded his arms on the surface of his desk, put his head down, and silently wept.

When Neal, the newspaper's Associate Editor, came to Jack's office, he was intent upon verbally kicking Jack's butt. The paper was operated in a loose manner, and everyone, including Neal, liked it that way. But, just let me know where the hell you are, thought Neal, as he started to turn into Jack's office.

The site of Jack sitting with his head down and the lights turned off stopped him short. And yes, he was crying, almost sobbing.

He quickly and silently did an about-face and headed back to his office, the anger inside him now vented as completely as if he had beaten Jack with a stick. Closing the door, he wondered what was going on. Had something happened to his girlfriend or family? Maybe Dan could shed some light on things, although earlier, when he was searching all over for Jack, Dan professed to have no idea as to his whereabouts.

He was about to call Dan when there was a light tap on his door, and it simultaneously opened. In the doorway stood Jack.

Neal's first thought was how he hated this kind of thing, or anything concerning employee relations. When Neal and his wife had some kind of major blow-up, if she started to cry, he was sunk. He couldn't deal with it. And now, here was one of his employees doing the same thing.

Neal could see that Jack's eyes were red, but the guy appeared to be happier than a three headed cat in a creamery. After taking a seat in a chair in front of the editor's desk, Jack sat back as if he didn't have a care in the world.

"Ya got one of those Altoid mints back there in your desk drawer?" asked Jack.

"Yeah, why?" questioned Neal, confused with Jack's state of mind. He had a thing about his breath. He was always popping the mints in his mouth, and knew of the office joke about his tendency not to share them. He hoarded them like a spoiled child.

"Cause I'd like to have one. I'm kind of in the mood for something refreshing," answered Jack. "By the way, I'm sorry I left the office without signing out. I kinda needed to get away for a bit, and well, I got a lot accomplished, sitting in the park with my laptop." As Neal held the tin container opened before him, Jack went on. "I know how you feel about that, and I just screwed up. Forgive me."

Neal was completely caught off guard. Hoping this was the extent of what his employee was crying about, and hoping he would now go back to his office, he said, "Hey, not a problem. I'm not so concerned about you. It's just that, well, it would be nice if you could set a good example."

Jack sat there, the cool, refreshing mint in his mouth, and a smile on his face. It didn't surprise him that he had broken down and cried. It had finally happened, as he always secretly knew it would. It didn't happen quite the way he pictured it, but realized things seldom happen in real life the way you imagine them in your dreams.

"I want to write some travel articles for the paper," Jack finally declared.

Neal was happy Jack had finally spoken, and was relieved the conversation was swinging back to newspaper business and not personnel management problems or worse yet, the personal issues of one of his employees. Let's just stick to business, he thought as he considered Jack's request.

"Well, as you know, we really don't have a travel section, per se. I've got some new assignments for you, by the way. But, if you can work in some small travel segment, I suppose we could find a place for it in Saturday's edition," Neal acceded.

"Saturday is okay, I guess. But, I want to do something a lot bigger than what you're thinking. And, I won't be doing any other articles except the travel articles." Jack let his words sit there for a moment before continuing. He knew by the look on Neal's face that he was confused about the direction of the conversation.

Jack was the first one to be surprised. When he first stepped into Neal's office, he expected to hear rantings about his failure to check out. Not that it would have made any difference, or then again, maybe it would have changed his response entirely. He really had no idea what he would to say to Neal, the words having come out almost against his will, as if in a dream.

"Ah, Jack ... I don't ..." Neal started.

Jack held up his hand for him to stop. "Listen, I want you to keep a secret for me. It will all come out sooner or later, but for right now I want this to be between you and me."

Neal could feel his stomach tightening up. He had some Rollaids in his desk drawer, right alongside the mints. God, he thought, please don't make me endure a lot of talk about personal woes.

"I'm going away for awhile. Specifically, I'm going around the world." Before he could really think about it, he added, " ... and, I'll never get on an airplane. I'll go by boat and train. All that I want from the newspaper is to keep my health insurance in force until I return. That will be one less thing I have to deal with right now. I guess I'll expect to get paid something for the articles that I send back to you, but the current free lance rate, or even less is fine by me. Hell, you can even replace me if you want. In fact, yes, I want you to replace me."

"You're quitting the paper?" blurted Neal. "I don't understand. Why do you want to quit, and ... and," he stammered ... "Why do you want me to keep that a secret?"

"Yes, I guess I am quitting the paper," said Jack, realizing then as if for the first time what he was doing. He was free-wheeling now, not knowing where his next words would take him.

"I don't want anyone to know that I'm leaving until I'm gone, maybe in two or three days, I dunno."

"Are you in trouble?" What had this guy done, Neal wondered. As much as he did not want to know all of the juicy details of Jack's personal life, he was curious just the same.

"No, I'm not in any trouble at all. I just don't want anyone to know that I'm taking this trip until after I've headed out to sea. Once the freighter leaves the west coast, you can tell anyone you want."

He paused for just a moment, thinking quickly of a plan and how it might work. "I'll leave from somewhere on the west coast and go to Hong Kong."

Pausing again to remember what Loraine had told him, he continued. "I'll travel north through China and Mongolia, and into Russia. I'll cross Russia on the Trans-Siberian train to Moscow. After that, well ah ... I'll just have to let you know what will come next. Possibly, by the time I leave, I'll have the whole itinerary worked out, and I'll e-mail it to you."

"This is insane," said Neal. "What will you do when you get back? I can't hold your job for you ... I mean, you know I can't just go out and hire someone, telling them that when you get back they're out on the street."

Jack recalled what Loraine said about people being in a hurry to travel somewhere, only to arrive and be in a hurry to get back.

"I don't expect you to hold my job, and I've no idea what I'll do or when I'll return." Again, thinking of the old travel agents words, Jack added, "But I will return. And, I'll return to this very spot, this very seat, here ... right before you. That's very important, so please don't let the building burn down while I'm gone."

He told Neal he would write an introductory article about his trip before departure. They discussed the assignments Jack was currently working on, mutually agreeing that Dan should finish the important ones.

The entire time, Neal sat dumbfounded. It wasn't the losing of one of his senior writers that confused him, but instead, it was the abruptness of it all, as well as the uncompromising way it was dictated. Jack had a good, steady job — a career. How could he just drop everything and go?

Did a train really go all the way from Hong Kong to western Europe? Could you just walk down to the docks someplace and get on a freighter? Wouldn't he have to work on this ship, and what the hell did Jack know about freighters? Before Neal could ask him any of these questions, Jack was standing up, getting ready to leave.

"I'll be gone the rest of the day," said Jack, as if the statement was closed to any negotiation. "But, I won't forget to sign out. Oh, and don't forget, you're sworn to secrecy."

He reached back, as he had done numerous times while conversing with Neal, to his left, rear pants pocket. He felt a surge of security and peace, knowing the ticket was there.

As Neal sat in stunned silence, Jack arose and then, stopping at the door, his hand poised on the doorknob, turned back to Neal. "I hope there are no hard feelings here. This is just something that came up very, very unexpectedly. I have to do it, and I have to do it my way. I'm sorry there can't be any discussion or compromise, it's just the way it is. You've been a good boss and a good friend. I hope that doesn't change."

With that, he turned and walked out the door. As he walked past Dan's office door, he stopped. "Meet me for a beer down at Grath's joint."

"Ah, I got some stuff I gotta do," replied Dan. "Hey, did Neal read you the riot act? I saw you go into his office, and after a minute, when you didn't come out, I figured you hadn't told him to go fuck himself."

Jack ignored the question. "It's important, Dan. Very important. Meet me at Grath's at five-fifteen. Please." With that said, he turned and walked away before any protest could be made.

Jack walked back to the travel agency visited only hours before. As he neared the shop, he worried that it might be closed, and was relieved when he pushed on the door and it swung gently inward.

"You again," beamed Loraine. Jack felt he and the elderly woman had formed a quick bond earlier in the day, and knew by her response and smile that his feelings were correct.

"Yeah, I'm back," said Jack. As she started to get up from behind her desk, he stopped her, telling her to stay where she was, that he wanted to take a seat beside the desk and talk with her.

"I've got a proposal for you," he said after getting as comfortable as possible in the hard, unpadded wooden chair. "I very much want you to do this for me. I'll make it worth your while."

Loraine wore bifocal glasses, and she bent her head down to look over the top of the frames, curiously peering at him.

"I want to clear off the desk there," pointing to a desk filled with papers and brochures. "And, I want to use it for a few days. I'll box everything up for you, put it on shelves, do whatever you want. I also want you to book passage for me on a freighter to Hong Kong, as well as train tickets across China, Russia, and Europe."

He paused for a moment, asking if it was indeed Liverpool that Loraine had sailed to from New York so many years ago.

"Could I sail from Liverpool to the east coast?" he asked. When she confirmed this was possible, he continued.

"I work for the newspaper, Loraine," he said, using her name for the first time. "*The South Beach Register.* My name is Jack Gillette, and I need a little work space for a few days until you can find a freighter sailing from somewhere on the west coast. I'll pay you for the office space, and help out if needed. It's important I sail as soon as possible. If I could go in three to five days, that would be great. Should you have any questions concerning my itinerary, we can solve the problem right on the spot. What do you say?"

Loraine said nothing, and for a moment Jack wasn't sure she would respond. "You probably won't believe this, I'm not sure I do either," she finally uttered. "But when you walked out of here today, I had this strange feeling you would someday be on a train across Russia. I sure didn't think it would be this soon, but," she paused .... "My husband's going to think I'm crazy, and the old loon will probably come down to take a look at what the cat's dragged in. Oh, you'll like him, in fact the two of you'll probably get along famously. When do you want to start this crazy thing?"

"Right now. There's a store down the street. I could go down there and get some boxes and start boxing this stuff up right now."

He looked around now, and then said, "It doesn't look like you have a whole bunch of storage space, but all I really need is a clean desk top, and I'm off and running. Oh, by the way," he added. "I need to fly to Sacramento tomorrow, mid-morning sometime. I'll need a round trip ticket to return early evening."

It was just before five when Jack finished clearing off the desk. He found a vacuum cleaner in a storage closet and vacuumed the carpet. Never adverse to housework, he found himself wiping down the front counter and straightening the travel magazines on the coffee table.

During that time she hardly said a word to him, other than to ask if money was an issue. By 5 p.m., she had secured passage on a container ship out of Long Beach. It was not an easy task on such short notice.

"Damn, I've got to meet someone in five minutes," said Jack when he noticed the time of day. "What time do you get here in the morning?"

"I'll be here at nine," she replied. "Bring your passport tomorrow," she added as he rushed out the door.

Jack was ten minutes late getting to McGrath's Pub, and initially thought Dan had not arrived. Then, he spotted him at a far table in the corner. The place was crowded, and Dan did not have a glass of beer in front of him.

"You didn't order?" asked Jack, as he took a seat.

"No. And, I may not. I sure hope this is really as important as you say it is. Rebecca is pissed off that I'm here instead of picking her up like we'd planned. What's up?"

The waitress came by, so Jack ordered them each a pint of Guinness. After she walked away, he leaned over the table so he wouldn't have to talk loud for Dan to hear him.

"What I'm going to tell you, you have to promise not to tell anyone. Oh, I know you'll tell Rebecca, but just make sure she doesn't say anything to anybody, at least not right away." Dan nodded he understood, but kept the irritated look on his face, indicating he thought whatever was so important would probably fall decidedly short.

"I quit the paper," stated Jack. He paused a moment, watching Dan's facial expression change and his eyes widen.

"You what?" exclaimed Dan.

"Just what I said. I quit the paper ... ah, although I'll be sending articles in periodically."

Jack could see the waitress working her way through the crowd with their order. He waited until she had placed the beers on the table and taken his credit card before he went on.

"I'm traveling around the world without ever getting on an airplane. I talked with Neal, and the paper will run articles every other week or so, probably in the Saturday edition."

"When did this all come to your crazy, deranged mind? I've never heard you talk about this kind of thing before, and ...," Dan took a long drink from his glass, "how can you afford to do this?"

"Two promises, my friend. Number one is, not a word to anyone about what I'm doing or that I've quit the paper until I'm safely on a freighter. It looks like it might be as soon as next week, so that shouldn't be too tough for you. Numero dos, and this will come out soon enough, but it too has to remain a secret until after I sail." He paused for a moment, looking Dan in the eye. "This one might prove to be a bit tougher for you."

"As long as it isn't something illegal. Please tell me you're not in trouble." said Dan. He was wild-eyed with amazement.

"No, no trouble whatsoever." Jack leaned closer over the table now, and said, "I won the lottery."

"Don't do this," Dan finally managed to say. Now it was his turn to look directly into Jack's eyes, and he knew with one glance that his friend was telling the truth.

"You won the California lottery? The drawing they had last night?"

Jack said nothing, and the two men just sat there for a moment staring at each other.

"You really won it, ah ... you won the whole thing?" he asked again.

Now Jack felt as dumbfounded as Dan sounded. They both sat there for a few minutes, not touching their beers or looking around.

Finally, Jack broke the silence. "I don't know if I won all ninety-six million or not. I think that's what the jackpot was, but ah, well, I guess someone else could have the winning numbers too. Christ, if I only won a million dollars, that's all I'd ever need."

"What are you going to do?"

"Well, I already told you. I'll travel around the world, the slow, relaxing way. I'll never get on an airplane, maybe take six months or so to do it."

"And, what about Lynda?" said Dan, as he took a large drink of beer to calm the jitters he now had. Quickly realizing one pint would not do the job, he waved his hand at a waitress who was nearby, signaling for two more.

"Well, that's the whole point of keeping this thing a secret. As you know, I've fantasized about winning the lottery for a long time. One of the things I've always thought I'd do was go away for awhile, to sorta let things quiet down, for people to forget or get tired of trying to contact me with offers of investments and all of that kind of shit. My trip will suffice in that respect.

"As for Lynda, I'm getting her out of that law office. When she's away from there, well ... she's just a completely different person. She hasn't ever traveled before, and I think it'll be good for her. She needs to relax and take life as it comes, not be so serious all of the time."

"Do you really believe taking a trip around the world will change all that?" asked Dan, the doubt clearly sounding in his voice.

"No, I don't," Jack replied, either not hearing or not conscious of the concern which Dan implied. "But, how she'll travel is. You see, I'm going to make it a game. She'll get into it, I know she will. A mere month away from her job, knowin' she'll not have to return ... she'll be okay ... trust me." He paused for a moment, and went on. "I know that you and Rebecca don't especially care for her, but ..."

Dan interrupted him. "Hey, we don't dislike her in any way. But, I also have to be honest with you. I just sometimes wonder if the two of you are right for each other."

Jack started to say something, but Dan stopped him again. "Listen, I just want you to have the very best. And, I don't want to see you get hurt. I'm having a real hard time with just believing you won the lottery, much less think rationally about anything else. If Lynda is who you want, then I'm one-hundred percent behind you. But remember, you can't change people, that's all. That's all I'm saying."

"Well anyway, I'm taking this trip. Lynda will follow me, and things will be great after we hook up in Shanghai or Beijing. But, a lot of what I have planned depends upon you keeping the whole thing secret until I'm gone."

They sat quietly for a few minutes, not saying anything to each other, just sitting there enjoying their pints.

"If you won the entire jackpot, what, ah ... what will you do with all the money?"

"Ninety-six million? Jez, I don't know. I know I'll give a lot of it away." Jack raised his glass to Dan, and the two pints clinked together as they made a silent toast. "I'll take care of you pal, don't worry." He paused a moment and said, "You and Rebecca still want to live in Montana?"

Dan nodded yes.

"Well then, maybe I'll buy Montana for you."

3

Later that night, Jack tried to reach Lynda by telephone. There was no answer at seven-thirty, and again at nine. Finally, at ten, she answered. She told him the staff had gone out for dinner to celebrate. He felt a little jealous he was not there, but this was her job and her project.

Unlike Dan, Jack had no doubts Lynda would change. Change was maybe the wrong word, he thought, as he sat on the edge of the bed after talking with her. No, it wasn't change, he concluded. What it was, was becoming again what you were at the start. She was so carefree when they first met, so spontaneous and full of curiosity about the vagaries of life. She was not hung up on what was scheduled to happen tomorrow, just concerned about living for the moment. She used to enjoy life.

He felt some changes occurred in Lynda, but he also believed a good, loving, kindred spirit resided in her inner self. His plan was to get her to revert to that constant, inner person — the woman he'd fallen in love with.

****

The next morning, Jack arrived at the travel office a few minutes after eight. Loraine had said she would not arrive until nine, and he'd fully intended to walk up the street for a cup of coffee. But there she was, sitting behind her desk and staring intently into her computer monitor.

"I didn't plan to be here this early, but if you're going to be out of here on Monday, I've got a lot of work to do," she said as a way of greeting. "I just came in, so why don't you go in the back and make us a pot of coffee," she added, nodding over her shoulder to a back room which served as a small kitchen.

"Sounds good," he replied, stopping to peer over her shoulder to see what was on the screen. "Is Monday the day I'll sail out of Long Beach?" he asked.

"It looks like it. Yeah, it looks like you'll be the only passenger on a container ship bound for Hong Kong. You'll go from Long Beach to Oakland, so you'll have a chance to jump should you have second thoughts and want to abandon this wild adventure." She laughed, and told him how sea sick she was on her first ocean voyage.

"I can still remember," she said. "The ship wasn't even out of sight of land before I started getting sick. When I thought I had nothing more inside me, well, I'd surprise myself and find some more just the same."

Jack worked on his initial travel article for the newspaper, while Loraine tended to his travel plans. They stopped a couple of times to talk, but for the most part worked quietly and independently.

"Hey, I almost forgot!" she cried, shattering a twenty minute silence between them. "You've got a flight leaving for Sacramento at eleven-thirty. It departs from John Wayne. You can make it if you hurry, or I can reschedule."

Jack looked at the clock on the wall. "And I intended to call Lynda this morning too!" He paused for a moment, considering his choices, and went on. "Look, you've got my credit card numbers, use them if you need to purchase any tickets or anything. I'm going to catch that flight, and I'll see you when I get back. Is there anything else you need from me?"

Loraine had him sign a couple of papers, and got the name of his doctor. There were medical waivers which needed to be signed for the two ocean crossings, as well as interim medical and trip insurance policies. Grabbing his laptop, Jack waved a goodbye and headed out the door.

****

"I not know. I only go hotel," said the Asian cabbie as Jack got into the back seat.

"If you don't want to take me, just say so," replied Jack.

Climbing out of the taxi, he could hear the cab driver saying over and over, in his pigeon-English, "I only go hotel. I only go hotel."

The next cab in line at the Sacramento Airport seemed better, yet still promised some sort of adventure, whether desired or not. A gaunt looking, forty-ish year old male, sat behind the wheel.

As Jack slid into the back seat, he looked at the driver more closely. It appeared as if he'd tried to cut his own hair with a pair of scissors, but without the aid of a mirror. Eye glasses with enormously thick lenses, were held in a light tan frame. One of the arms of the frame was missing, and a piece of wire was taped to the frame and looped around his ear.

"Where ya from?" the driver asked, pulling his car out of the line of awaiting cabs.

After Jack told him the Los Angeles area, the guy went on, "I lived down there for awhile. Fancied myself a screenwriter, but things never seemed to work out."

"Is that why you left?" asked Jack. "Because you couldn't make it as a screenwriter?"

"No, I just left that whole life. Ya see, I got hooked on heroin there, runnin' round with the wrong people, doing all the wrong things. I came up here to live with my sister ... ah, I needed someone to take care of me."

"Well, it's good that you could get away from the drugs," said Jack, now noticing the poor complexion and shallowness of the man's face. "Drugs have screwed up a lot of people's lives, that's for sure."

"Yeah, drugs are bad news," the cabbie agreed. "But, nothing compared to booze. When you stop and think about it, there have been a lot more lives ruined by alcohol than there ever was by hard drugs. I was totally unbiased. I did everything."

They talked about several subjects on the long drive, and Jack told him about his upcoming trip. Although his itinerary was not complete, he knew the projected route, as well as many particulars about the countries, sites and cities along the way.

Jack had taken the trip many times before. He'd sat on the train for days as it crossed China and Russia — ferried to Sweden from Finland — trained south through eastern Europe, along the route of the famous Orient Express to Istanbul. He'd sailed across the Pacific and the Atlantic Oceans.

He had taken the trip many, many times — but always, and only in his dreams. Now, as he related certain points to the driver, it had the familiar feel of an old sweater.

"Man, that sounds like one hell of a trip! You should write a book about it!" said the cabbie.

"I plan to. But until then I'll be writing for a newspaper in the L.A area. They have a website, so if you're on-line you could access the stories ... kinda follow me as I go. Do you have e-mail?"

When they arrived at the destination, Jack noticed the building housing the lottery offices, and directed the taxi driver to a location across the street from it. After stopping the cab and paying the fare, they exchanged e-addresses and shook hands.

"If you e-mail me, I'll e-mail you the website address of the newspaper." He paused, and then made an impromptu promise he would later find himself making time and time again, honoring it to the letter. "And, if you e-mail me anywhere along the way, I'll reply. If you want to know more about Moscow, simply drop me a line."

When the taxi was out of site, he started across the street. Just before entering the building, he checked his back pocket for the winning ticket. He had lightly sewn the pocket closed before going to bed last night, and even considered wearing the pants to bed for added security.

With one hand on his back pocket, and the other on the door handle, Jack turned his head to the sound of a car horn honking furiously. It was the taxi driver.

"Hey, ah ... I came back ... ah, because I thought you might need a lift back soon," the driver said, as he simultaneously spoke and noticed the lettering on the glass door proclaiming the entrance to the State's Lottery Offices.

They had introduced themselves when they parted, and now Jack addressed him by name. "Michael, I don't know how long I'll be. If you'd like to wait, that would be nice, but it's not necessary."

"Are you, ah ... are you going in there for the reason I think you are?" asked Michael.

He'd turned off the engine and was leaning both arms out the open window of the taxi's door, a relaxed smile on his worn and tired face. He looked as if he'd just caught a small child with his hand in the cookie jar, but was overjoyed the kid was getting what he wanted.

Jack knew he was caught. Never a good liar, he felt now was not the time to try to break old habits.

"Sorta," he sort of lied. He walked over to the cab and stood before Michael.

"You seem like a good man. Wait here for me. I'll come back and tell you if I don't need a ride. Be discrete, stay off your two-way radio, and remember, good things happen to good people." With that, he turned and walked into the building.

With fears of television news crews jumping out of closets, microphones being shoved into his face from several different angles, and his entire plan of secrecy going down the drain, he walked into the room. The office was quiet, its environment and atmosphere subdued in every respect.

He asked to see the manager, or someone in charge. A woman, who identified herself as Irene Bennett greeted him and asked how she could be of assistance. He struggled with the haphazard basting of his back pocket, his hand finally emerging with the winning ticket.

"I'm not sure what the exact procedure is here," said Jack, nervously laughing a bit as he looked at Ms. Bennett. "Obviously, I've never done this before, but I would very much like to avoid any and all publicity, at least for the present time. Is that possible?"

"Let me scan your ticket first," she said. "Then, I'll be glad to answer any questions you may have."

After running the ticket through a scanner, the machine reading the bar code and validating it as the winning ticket, Irene returned to the front counter.

"I assume you have brought some identification with you?" she asked.

Jack produced his driver's license and a copy of his passport. He had left his passport with Loraine at the travel agency, and now wondered if this fact might possibly complicate matters.

"This whole process takes two to three hours," explained the woman. "It's relatively painless, and we try to make it as easy as possible. I'll need to make a call to the Highway Patrol. They will send someone over to check your identification to make sure you are who you say you are. We also have some questions that we will ask you, all of them to assure you are the legal holder of the ticket. As for your request of anonymity, well ah, that is not as easy as it sounds."

"I don't care if anyone knows. I'd just like to delay the announcement until after Monday morning."

"I understand," she said, as if she did. Glancing at his driver's license, she continued. "By playing the California lottery and having a winning ticket, you subject yourself to the rules of the Commission. We have the legal right to publish the name of the winner, the type of game they played, the date of the drawing, the amount won, and the retail location where the winning ticket was purchased.

"If this were a one or two million dollar winner, I could assure you the media would not be eager to talk with you. Quite frankly, one or two million is old news anymore. However, ninety-six million, five hundred thousand is very big news."

"Do you schedule a press conference ... is that, ah what you do?" he asked.

"Yes. Ah ... look Mr. Gillette, it is a relatively easy process. But, if you try to hide from this, the press will be relentless. They will think you have something to hide, and some story lies buried underneath the surface. They'll tear things apart trying to get at it. We feel it's much better to just get it over with. You'd be surprised how fast people forget about seeing your picture, or reading your name."

He knew this was true, but he was trying to think on his feet. "Listen, how about this?" he asked. "Let's process the ticket today. Go ahead and call the police, or do whatever else you need to do. But, don't schedule a press conference until Monday morning. I mean, ah ... well, tomorrow is Friday, so instead of doing something right away ... you could set it up for Monday. I'll be here at ten o'clock in the morning, and I'll pose for any pictures you want. Would that work?"

After Ms. Bennett indicated that Jack's plan was acceptable, although a little different, they began the processing. He was a little relieved she didn't push the media issue. By the time they gave up waiting for him on Monday, he'd be out to sea.

The Highway Patrol came, the two officers jovial to be meeting someone who'd just won millions of dollars. They fingerprinted him and checked his identification. They asked questions as to where he lived and how long he'd lived there. Periodically, they would go to a private office, presumably to verify the information.

Ms. Bennett also had a few questions, asking him if he had a photocopy of the ticket to save for a keepsake. She also asked him where and when he bought the ticket, and informed him after his answer that the information was included in the bar code on the ticket.

"It's one of the safeguards we have," she explained. "When I first scanned your ticket, it gave me a print out of all the information. If you had no idea where or when you bought the ticket, that would throw up red flags that could delay the process."

Two hours and twenty minutes later, Irene handed Jack a check. Playing the cash option of the game, he received a lump sum of half of the jackpot amount. Ninety-six million, five hundred thousand became forty-eight million, two hundred and fifty thousand.

Next came Uncle Sam. He took 28 percent. Forty-eight million, two hundred and fifty thousand became thirty-four million, seven hundred and forty thousand.

Jack was surprised the State of California did not want its tax share immediately. Sooner or later they would reach their hand out for 9.5 percent, which would further reduce his winnings to thirty million, one hundred and fifty-three thousand, two hundred and fifty dollars.

When income tax time arrived the following spring, the Federal government would again call for up to a maximum of 38.6 percent of all earnings over $307,000. This could reduce Jack's take home to just over 25 million, depending on tax shelters and creative accounting. But for now, he was left holding a check for $34,740,000.

"Would you like to sit down for a moment?" asked Ms. Bennett.

"No, I'll be fine," he said, a dazed look on his face and feeling lightheaded.

They took his picture, and he reiterated his promise to return to the office on Monday morning. "I've got no reason to hide," lied Jack. "I'll be here Monday morning with bells on. And hopefully, I'll still have some money left by then," he laughed.

He was not sure if Michael and his taxi would be waiting for him, nor was he sure he wanted him to be. But, there he was, waiting patiently, and to Jack's surprise, seeing a somewhat familiar face gave him a good feeling. His adrenaline was running at an all-time high, and it was nice to have someone to talk with. He climbed in the back seat, setting his one and only travel bag on the floor between his legs.

"I've been sitting here trying to read, and it's been impossible. I can't stand the suspense anymore. You did win the lottery, didn't you?"

"Yes, Michael. I did. But, I need you to keep this a bit of a secret for three or four days. Not that anyone you would tell would know me, but there is the slight chance you'd have a fare who's in the media business. You have my e-mail address, and it wouldn't be hard to go from there. After Monday, it won't matter, but until then, well please, keep this a secret."

"My lips are sealed," replied Michael. "Jesus Christ, my body is going to hell so fast from all of the drugs, I might not even be alive by Monday. I'm just glad I lived long enough to meet someone who won. Congratulations," he said, reaching his hand back to shake Jack's hand.

"I didn't win that much," he replied, hoping to head off the inevitable question. "Let's head back to the airport, but first, I noticed a Wells Fargo bank up the street. Let's stop there, and I'll go in for a moment."

They didn't talk for a long time after visiting the bank. Jack was lost in his thoughts and his emotions, and at one point he thought he would weep. Michael seemed to sense this, or maybe he too was lost in his thoughts, for nothing was said.

Finally, Jack spoke. "Where would you go if you could go anywhere in the world?"

"Anywhere?"

"Yeah. Anywhere in the whole, wide, wonderful world. Where would you want to go?"

They had stopped at a traffic signal, and Michael sat thinking, one hand on the wheel, the other readjusting the jury-rigged frame of his spectacles. When the light changed and the taxi did not move, a car behind them honked its horn.

"Yeah, yeah," protested Michael. "Can't ya see I'm thinking here? The man has a very serious question," pressing the accelerator down with a sense of protest.

After more silence, Jack responded. "Am I making the questions too difficult?"

"No, it's just that I've never been anywhere, and there's so many places to go," replied Michael. "But I think ... ah, well ... I think if I could go any place in the world, I think I'd like to go to New Zealand. Yeah, I'd go to New Zealand."

"And, why would that be your choice?" asked Jack.

"I read once it was very peaceful there. I also read where they had great trout fishin'. I've not been fishin' in years. I suppose I could go somewhere around here and do the same thing ... but well, I'd like to go fishin' there. I've seen some pictures of the place, and it looks beautiful. Beautiful and peaceful."

Jack let the conversation die, and moments later they were at the airport. He paid the fare and shook Michael's hand. Reaching in his shirt pocket, he took out three, folded up, one hundred dollar bills, put there when he was in the bank. He gave them to Michael.

"I'd hope this money won't be spent on the very thing you are trying to avoid. Be sure to e-mail me, because I want to be in touch with you. And, thank you." Jack turned, and a few seconds later he was lost in the crowd of fellow travelers.

He tried to telephone Lynda from the Sacramento airport. He called the Palm Springs number first, but only got the answering machine. He didn't leave a message. He tried to call her at home, and when her answering machine switched on, he left a message saying he was in Sacramento following up on a story.

He learned his flight was delayed, and after finally boarding, the plane sat for an inordinate time on the runway awaiting clearance for takeoff. By the time he reached his apartment it was well after 11 p.m., and he was physically and emotionally exhausted.

****

Jack arose early the next morning and went to work. After spending some time with his editor and reviewing the plan for his travel articles, he entered his office. Noticing the blinking light on his answering machine, he punched the play button.

It was a message from Lynda. She had returned home that morning, the

Palm Springs trip, like Jack's venture to Sacramento, lasting longer than expected. In answer to his plea of getting together soon, she told him she was very tired. She planned to work for awhile in the morning, and then go home. She asked that he not come over, but wait until tomorrow night so she could get some rest.

After listening to the message twice, he pushed the erase button and sat back in his chair. Soon, he thought, I'll be on a ship, and very shortly after that she'll be on one too, away from the law office, and away from all of the hassles of cases, briefs, writs and subpoenas.

He intended to put at least a week between them. By the time she reached Hong Kong, he would be in Guilin, or possibly Xian. They had watched a PBS special together on Xian and the Terracotta Warriors exhibited there. Lynda seemed fascinated by the story of a simple farmer stumbling across such an important archaeological find. It would have been fun to meet her in Xian and see in person what they had watched together on television.

But, Shanghai or Beijing would be the best place for her to catch up. By that time they would have spent nearly two months apart, but more importantly, Lynda would have spent two months on her own.

Jack smiled to himself when he imagined how she would look and how relaxed she would be. Every morning, she would be able to do whatever she wanted to do. She could have a glass of wine mid-morning if she liked. She could sleep in, or rise early to catch the sunrise over the mountains or the sea. By the time they reunited, all of the irritations and troubles of the last few weeks would be erased.

Jack's thoughts were broken by a voice.

"How's it going?" asked Dan. He stood in the doorway of Jack's office.

"Oh, pretty well, thanks. Let's go have an early lunch, whatta ya say?"

They walked out of the building and down to a small restaurant on the corner. As they slid into a booth and quickly ordered from the waitress, Jack said, "I'll call you this afternoon with a phone number of my second office."

"Second office?" asked Dan, raising his eyebrows.

"Yeah, I commandeered a desk at a travel agent's office. You'd like this woman. It's a one person show, and I think the only reason she stays in business is to have something to do. She went around the world when she was nineteen, all by herself. Shows you the kind of spunk she has."

"What's Neal say about this?"

"Oh, I didn't tell him. I probably won't either. He's about ready to have a heart attack anyway. He can't get over the shock of me quitting the paper and taking this trip. He doesn't know about the lotto winnings, and the suspense of why I want him to keep the whole thing secret is more than he can bear."

"Is he okay with the articles that you intend to send? You do intend to send them, don't you?"

"Oh yeah, I will. Originally, I thought it would be good to send four or five, but Neal and I talked, and he told me he always wanted to have a small travel section, so this might be a good opportunity to test it out. He told me I was putting him at a disadvantage by not being able to tell anyone, but I told him to go ahead and have the ad department push the idea of a travel section to advertisers. They wouldn't have to know anymore than the fact some travel articles will be coming out soon. Besides, after Monday, I don't care who he tells."

"You're leaving that soon?" exclaimed Dan. "You're really serious, aren't you?"

"What? Did you think this was all a bunch of smoke?" Their soup and sandwiches arrived then, and they paused until after the waitress walked away.

"I don't know, Jack. This whole thing has blown me away. Rebecca and I talked about it last night. She kept telling me you were pulling my chain, that maybe you'd won a thousand dollars or something. When I told her about the night I met you at McGrath's, and how I was sorta pissed off because you'd upset my plans, and I thought you might just be screwing around ... well, I told her the look on your face that night spoke volumes and said everything except, 'I'm messing with your head.'"

"Well, it's all true. I flew up to Sacramento yesterday, signed all of the papers, and did the whole deal. By the way, I want you to do something for me. You've told me you always wanted to be a private eye, well ... here's your chance.

"I may or may not get an e-mail from this guy. If I do, I'll e-mail you his name and e-mail address. He's a cab driver in Sacramento, and supposedly an ex-heroin addict. That's about all I know. I want you to find his home address, whether or not he's an ex-addict, current addict, or none of the above. Hire someone, I'll pick up the tab and make it worth your while besides."

"I gotta ask. But, wait. Let me order us a couple of beers first. I don't know about you, but I think I need one," said Dan.

"Damn," said Jack. "It's only eleven in the morning. We're setting a bad precedent here, my friend."

Dan signaled the waitress, and after she set two beers on the table and left, he said, "How much?"

"How much am I going to pay you for being a private detective?" asked Jack, making Dan ask the question again without beating around the bush.

"No ... and I may charge you an arm and a leg, just for that smart-assed remark. No ... how much did you win from the lottery?"

"Ninety-six, five."

Dan sat opened-mouthed for a moment before draining the rest of his beer in one, large gulp. "Ninety-six, as in ninety-six million?" he asked incredulously.

"Ninety-six million, five hundred thousand to be exact. But, I played the cash option, so I only get half of the total jackpot. That brings us down to forty-eight mil and change. Then, there's taxes, and believe me, old Uncle Sam is right there behind the counter. You don't see a measly dime until he's got his.

After the dust cleared, I got almost thirty-five million."

"I assume you have a good accountant. Hey, I don't know what I'm talking about. Is that what you get? Or, do you get a financial advisor?"

"I don't know either. In fact, I don't have a clue. I guess I could talk to the accountant at the paper, but that would necessitate another person sworn to secrecy. And, this has to remain a secret."

After lunch, Jack went to the travel agency. He found Loraine busy working on the details of his trip. He made a fresh pot of coffee for them, and after pouring two cups, pulled his chair up to her desk.

"Well, I hope I haven't been over-working you on this thing," he said.

"No, it's been good for me. My husband Warren wants to thank you. He told me I usually come home with too much energy, and I take it out on him. Since you came along, I've been too tired to give him any grief," she laughed.

She slid a couple of papers across the desk for him to sign. They were waivers for injury and liability aboard ship, as well as trip insurance forms.

"You'll have seven days in Hong Kong before you travel on to Guangzhou from Hong Kong."

He started to protest, but she cut him short.

"You'll need those days in case the ship is delayed in port somewhere along the route."

"But Loraine, I'll have someone following me. If I have to spend seven days in Hong Kong she might catch me," said Jack.

Loraine raised her eyebrows at the statement, and leaned back in her chair as if to say, out with it.

"You're not in a bunch of trouble are you, young man? If you are, well ... well, you've completely fooled me and my impression of the kind of man you are."

"No, I'm in no trouble." He paused a moment. He had not planned to tell Loraine until later, but she was fast becoming too strong an ally to exclude.

"You see, I came into a bunch of money. I have this wonderful girlfriend who is buried in responsibility and all of the serious crap people insist on calling life. I've spoken of her to you. Lynda Turner is her name. Anyway, I'm giving her half of the money. That amounts to about fifteen million dollars. But, I'm not going to give it to her unless she plays the game. Are you with me so far?"

When Loraine answered she was, he continued. "The rules are simple. Lynda has to follow me without getting on an airplane. She has enough money in the bank, so it won't be a strain on her. So as not to make it sound too easy, I'll tell her that if she follows me and never gets on an airplane, I'll give her five hundred thousand dollars. Only if she catches me does she get the fifteen million.

"Of course, I plan to let her catch me in either Shanghai or Beijing, but she won't know that. I'll e-mail her my itinerary, so she'll know the route. And, just to keep her honest, I'll tell her that she has to follow the exact same route ...

no shortcuts even if she does stay on the ground."

"Why don't you just take her with you from the start?"

"Because, I want her to experience the joy of traveling solo as I did when I was in college. I think it brings out the best in people, and allows them to be who they really are. I also want her to shed some of the worries she has, the burdens which cause her to always do the prudent thing, the actions that lessen the liability, and the tendency to take the low risk approach. Her job has made her think the way she does, and it's not who she really is. I want her to dream. I want her to become the dreamer she used to be, the dreamer I know she is."

"You are a strange man, Mister Gillette. And, what if she decides not to follow you at all?"

"Then I may e-mail you and ask you to divorce your poor, old husband." replied Jack.

Loraine let out a laugh and then took another sip of her coffee. "You shouldn't make promises that you can't keep, Mister. And, don't worry about seven days in Hong Kong. She'll have to get her ticket out of Pasadena, and I'll give them a call. The girl I dealt with there for your ticket ... well, we got along real well. I'll explain the situation so as to stonewall Lynda for a few days. Even without our efforts to delay her, she'll have a difficult time arranging everything quickly. We were real lucky to get you out to sea as fast as we did."

"So, I go from Long Beach to Oakland, and then to Hong Kong?" asked Jack.

"Not so fast, young man. Here is what I have so far. You'll sail out of Long Beach on Monday morning. It's always possible they could sail early, so you'll want to be on board by Sunday afternoon at the latest. You'll go from Long Beach to Oakland, a simple overnight trip. You'll sail to Tokyo and Osaka, Japan. After that, it's on to Pusan, South Korea. Then, you'll sail to Hong Kong. That will take you twenty-one days."

"Wow," Jack managed to say.

"From Hong Kong, you'll travel by train. I've got you booked into what is called, soft class sleepers. That's as good as it gets, but I'm afraid at times you'll think it couldn't be any worse. You'll travel from Hong Kong to Guangzhou, to Guilin, to Xian, to Shanghai, and then to Beijing. From there, you'll travel through northern China and into Mongolia. You'll spend a couple of days in a Ger camp outside Ulan Bator, and travel north to Irkutsk, Russia.

"From Irkutsk, you'll go across Russia on the Trans-Siberian railway to Moscow, and then to St. Petersburg. It was called Leningrad when I was there, and a few years before that it was called Petrograd. After St. Petersburg, you'll travel on to Helsinki, Finland. I'm afraid that's as far as I've gotten, and I don't have much time left to do more."

"That's okay," counseled Jack. "You've done so much for me already. You have no idea how you've inspired me."

"Well, I also have your transatlantic voyage scheduled," she went on. "You'll sail out of Liverpool, England and go to Philadelphia. From there, I've booked you on the Amtrak for the trip across the country."

"So, from Helsinki to Liverpool, I'm on my own, huh?"

"Yes, and maybe that's the way it should be. You and your girlfriend can relax and enjoy eastern and western Europe, and then sail home together. Should I book her on the ship out of Liverpool too?"

He thought for a moment. "No. Let's leave it like it is." If she could not accompany him on the ship, they could stay in England until they could book passage together. There would be no schedule to adhere to, so they could wait for months if necessary.

"So, what else needs to be done?" Jack asked.

"Well, I think things are pretty well set. I'll need to get a train pass for you. I think that's the best way to go. You won't have to get in line to buy tickets that way, you can just get on or get off. Of course, I can't get one for Lynda without her passport, but you could always e-mail me and I could Fed-Ex one to her.

"And, I'll have to get some kind of mailing address for you in Helsinki. I won't have the rail passes before you leave on the freighter, but you won't need them until then."

"How about the U.S. consulate in Helsinki?" asked Jack. "Would that work."

"It might," replied Loraine. "But as a member of American Express, it might be best to use their offices. By the way, I'm assuming your girlfriend won't be coming to me for her travel arrangements, or will she?"

"No. I don't think I'll tell her about you. I want this to be a game for her, and I want it to be fun. But, I also want it to be a challenge and an adventure. You may give away something inadvertently, if nothing more than a feeling of confidence in the buying of tickets. I want her to figure it out."

Jack spent the rest of the afternoon getting all of his affairs in order. From a briefcase loaded with records, he wrote checks for his utilities and other bills. He wrote a note to his apartment manager, saying he would be gone for about six months, and authorized a key for Dan in case of an emergency.

He delayed mailing any of the remittances. He still had a check which needed to be cashed, and he wasn't quite sure what to do. Should he put it all in savings, or in some kind of a money market. Lynda would know, but he didn't have her to rely on. Alone, he knew nothing about investments and the financial world. The subject bored him.

Recalling Loraine's comments about American Express gave him an idea. Looking up the address in the telephone book, he drove to the location. It was in a large business complex, unremarkable in its likeness to hundreds of others in the L.A. area.

After telling the receptionist he needed to talk with someone about investments, he was directed to the fifth floor. When he first walked into the lobby on that floor, he noticed a corner office where an older man sat behind a desk. Approaching the front counter, he saw a display of various employees business cards, and quickly spotted a card for a man whose title was listed as Branch Manager.

"Is that Mr. Blackburn's office?" asked Jack, pointing to where the man sat working. When the receptionist indicated it was and then asked if he had an appointment, he lied saying, "Yes I do."

After a moment of listening to one side of the receptionist's discussion, and turning his head once to reidentify himself, he heard Blackburn behind him.

"Sir, I don't believe I have an appointment with anyone."

"Believe me, if you give me just two minutes of your personal time, you'll not regret it."

Blackburn, a short, round figure of a man, removed his glasses for a moment, and then, putting them back on, told Jack to follow him. They walked to a small conference room just behind the receptionist's area. There were windows on all sides, so everyone at the various desks in the room could see them. After Jack sat down, Blackburn took a seat, leaving the door open.

"I would have thought I'd get the royal treatment, you know, your personal office, maybe a glass of champagne, or at the very least a Pepsi or something," said Jack as he slid the check and his American Express card across the desk.

Blackburn sat there for a moment looking at the document. One moment stretched into another as he silently reread the numbers, thirty-four million, seven hundred and forty-thousand dollars.

"Is this real?" Blackburn asked, glancing up at Jack and then back at the check. "I mean, I hope you're not playing some kind of game here." It was clear he really didn't know what to think, say or do.

"The credit card? Yes, it's very real, and so is the check," Jack laughed. "As you can see, it's lottery winnings, not drug money. And, you're more than welcome to verify its authenticity." He paused for a moment, and said, "Listen sir, I don't know a thing about finances and banking. I'm a reporter. But, I have a feeling you can help me."

"What would you like me to do?" asked Blackburn.

"Well, first of all, can you close the door?"

"Why don't we go to my office!" replied a smiling Blackburn. "And, can I get you something to drink, a Pepsi maybe? I'm afraid I don't have any champagne."

They both laughed as they made their way across the room.

After they got settled, he asked for Blackburn's advice on what to do. He told him he was not interested in anything long term at this point, just a means to cash the check and make some provisions for the safety of the money, and yet still have access.

"Well, if you want to do something temporary, it can be done," said Blackburn. "We can convert it into U.S. Treasury notes. It'll only get you three or four percent interest, but for the short run, that should be okay."

Jack told him of his plans to travel around the world, and after asking how long he planned to be away, Blackburn continued, "This will be in the form of a one year note. If you find yourself gone longer than expected, we can roll it over, but it sounds as if you'll be back before that would be necessary. As for your question about cash, we'll give you a checkbook which will allow you to write a check at any of our offices."

"I'd also like to arrange for my monthly balance to be paid off by an automatic withdrawal from my account," said Jack.

Blackburn still held the check which Jack had given him, and had repeatedly looked at it while conversing about its investment.

"Damn, that's a lot of money," he said. "How much was the jackpot?"

4

Bill stopped at his favorite bar for a couple martinis and a bite to eat. It was after 8 p.m by the time he left the office, and his wife had stopped cooking dinner on his demand or whim, and at whatever hour he got home, years ago. If he wasn't home at six, he didn't eat. He would be forced to either go without, or heat up some leftovers. The fucking bitch, he thought to himself.

Her cooking was the shits anyway. God forbid he tell his wife what he thought about it. Years ago, he'd done just that, and she'd thrown an entire bowl of vegetables at him. Thinking back on it now, he should have called the cops and had her charged with domestic assault.

Bill wanted to go to Lynda's place. He wouldn't care if she fixed dinner or not, but she too was being a bitch, saying she felt guilty about Palm Springs. Jesus Christ, he thought, it's not like the first time we've ever fooled around.

He could remember the time he pulled her into a closet at the firm's Christmas party. Although she pretended the next day that nothing happened, he knew beyond a doubt he had his dick in something. She couldn't have been so drunk she didn't feel it between her legs. Another time, he had her spread eagle on his office desk, that not working out so well, as she became pissed off about the time he was starting to pull her panties down.

What's with women and their conflicting attitudes about sex? Several months ago his wife complained that he never showed any interest in having sex with her, except when he was drunk. After an hour and a half of her haranguing him with, "You don't do this," and "You don't do that," she started crying — her direction changing like the wind — crying her eyes out about how she wasn't attractive anymore, sobbing about being ten pounds over weight and sniveling about looking old. Christ, she was old. And, the woman wasn't ten pounds over weight, she was more like fifty pounds overweight.

He would have divorced her a long time ago if he'd figured a way to do it without her taking him to the cleaners. When he first started practicing law, he and his lovely bride bought a bunch of stock together. She contributed money her parents had left her, and they held the assets jointly. It represented a ton of money in today's market, and Bill knew he'd lose at least half of it if he bolted.

He kept hoping she'd find some young stud who was coaching swimming, tennis, or some such crap at the country club where she spent most of her days. Either that, or some clerk at the mall. Bill knew this was all just wishful thinking on his part. What would some young stud want with a fat, cranky, old pig?

And now Lynda was pulling the same shit. Just thinking of her made him hornier than hell, and he thought he could put up with a lot from the woman just to be next to her body and have that kind of wild sex.

Their little escape to Palm Springs had gone just the way he planned. She'd brought this skimpy, little bikini to wear when she laid around the pool, so he'd figured right off that she was either ripe or being the ultimate prick teaser.

They went out to dinner the first night, and she talked a lot about her boyfriend Jack. He'd let it go, thinking she needed to vent, or some such thing. At the end of her going on and on about his good points as well as his bad points, Bill spoke up and told her the guy was probably a prince.

"But, that's all he'll ever be, is just a prince of a guy. He'll live from payday to payday, wishin', hopin' and prayin' that something will fall into his lap. You'll see a painting in an antique shop for a grand. You'll really like it, and you'd deserve it too, but there is no fuckin' way you could just write the check. Lemme' guess, the fucker has only one credit card, right," he'd said.

He was surprised when she told him he had two or three, but it was the only thing she disagreed or contradicted him on.

When the check came, Bill asked the waiter, who was at least fifty years old, how long he had been waiting tables. The guy got kind of defensive at first, asking if everything was satisfactory, but then relaxed when Bill said he was just curious. After he admitted to waiting tables for thirty years, Bill asked him if he enjoyed it.

"Yes sir, I suppose I do. I don't make a great deal of money, but ... I don't know, I guess I just like the lifestyle and the freedom it gives me," the waiter said.

"Another fucking loser that'll never have a pot to piss in," said Bill, after the waiter left. He purposely stiffed the guy, thinking, enjoy that lifestyle, asshole.

When they returned to the house, Bill made a not so subtle play for Lynda. He expected rejection, but felt like he needed to at least give it a try. Besides, the sight of her lying around all day half naked was just about all his hormones could handle.

No muss, no fuss. They went directly to bed in his room. There wasn't a lot of intelligent conversation before, during, or after, which suited him just fine. There was a lot of moaning and heavy breathing, and most of it was hers.

****

When Jack returned to his apartment, he telephoned Lynda. He knew she was at work, but he wanted to make sure she got his message just as soon as she arrived home.

"Hey, it's me," he said, after the beep. "It's Friday night, and I've not seen my favorite girl all week. How about a nice dinner and maybe a movie, or if you'd rather eat in, I'll cook. Let me know as soon as you get home. Hope you had a good day. I love you."

After hanging up, he immediately dialed another number. It was late afternoon, and if he wanted her to get any flowers today, he'd have to act fast. After a bit of pleading, he got the florist to deliver before 5.

At 6:30 p.m., Lynda finally called. She said she was tired, and that it had been a hectic week. Jack was a bit surprised when she didn't thank him for the flowers, but maybe the florist hadn't delivered as promised.

"Let's just go out for something," she said. "I don't think I have the energy for dinner and a movie, so why don't we just have dinner and make it an early evening."

"You know, I'd sure like for us to spend the night together. It seems like ages since we've been together."

"I know, Jack. And, I'm sorry. I've been under so much stress lately with this lawsuit and looming trial."

He didn't want to push it, but the thought came to mind that possibly he would not get to make love with her before sailing on Monday.

They went to one of her favorite restaurants. It was a small, Italian place, intimate, but sometimes a little too noisy when it was busy, and tonight it was extremely crowded. After waiting at least thirty minutes, they finally got a table.

They talked a little about work. Her work was stressful and exhausting, while he was forced to invent things to make his job at the newspaper sound like something more than a waltz in the park. Knowing his job was all but over, made the task even more difficult.

Before their meals arrived, he sensed their conversation was becoming strained. She seemed tired to the point of being angry. He couldn't think of anything he'd done to initiate such a response, so he continued trying to appease her — to make her laugh or smile.

"I'm going to start working on my novel again," he stated, abruptly changing the subject. Before she could respond, he went on. "This time, I'll work on it full time, not just when I have time or when I can squeeze it in."

"I think that's wonderful! But, what about your job? How can you work full time and write full time too? You've always told me it's impossible to do both."

"Well, I'm getting a better position at the paper, and at the same time, they're allowing me to work half time."

"Can you survive working only part time?" she asked skeptically.

"Yes, I think so," he replied, perhaps a bit too confidently. Changing his tone just a bit, he said, "But, you know it would be easier on both of us if there was only one rent payment every month."

Lynda didn't know what to say. She felt incredibly guilty about what had transpired in Palm Springs. But, strangely, she did not at all regret it. Perhaps Bill was right when he told her it might be time for her to move on with her life, and that leaving Jack was the first step in the process.

Bill also talked to her about attending law school. With her undergraduate degree and experience, he convinced her she could succeed. She had to admit that with Bill, and with or without law school, her financial future was much more secure.

However, there was another part of her which made her want to stay with Jack. She really did love him, and knew in her heart she would be extremely hard pressed to find a man who both loved and appreciated her as much as he did. He was the kindest man she had ever met, let alone loved.

"I don't know, Jack. I know we've talked about this a few times, but well ... I just don't know if now's the right time to move in together."

"Maybe we should take a little vacation together. You'll soon be done with the lawsuit ... you could get away. Maybe that's what we need," said Jack. He was treading on dangerous ground. He was not good at keeping secrets, especially those which contained good news. He would have to be careful.

"That might me nice," she replied.

After they finished their dinner and arrived at her apartment, they kissed. When he tried to gently guide her into the bedroom, she resisted, saying she was tired. He'd told her he'd be busy Sunday night, but that he really wanted to spend tomorrow night with her. She was reluctant at first, but finally agreed.

Their evening together had been a roller coaster of emotions. At times, Lynda seemed as though she was on the verge of tears, and then, for no apparent reason, she acted angry. Maybe it was that time of the month, thought Jack, as he turned on his computer after arriving home alone.

There was a lot to do before Monday morning. He needed to write a column for the newspaper, the opening article of his around-the-world adventure. An itinerary needed to be decided upon, although from Long Beach to Helsinki was complete, thanks to Loraine. His immediate task however, was to write an e-letter to Lynda. After a few false starts, his mind and fingers began to work simultaneously, the screen filling up with his thoughts.

My Dearest Love,

And, you are my dearest love, you know. I have never loved anyone as much as I love you.

It is so difficult for me to be away from you for even one day. I shudder to think how difficult the next few weeks or months will be.

You are probably wondering what I am talking about, and why I'm sending you this e-mail. Rather than beat around the proverbial bush and possibly cause you worry, I'll get right to it. "Cut to the chase," as they say in Hollywood.

I won the lottery! You'll probably read about it in the newspaper — it damn well better be in the Register— and, I hope you don't have a heart attack when you read how much I won. I almost did.

I've kept this a secret from you because I want you. I want you as the woman I've known who can dream and is free spirited. Lately, it seems as though we argue more than we used to, and I have to think it's the pressure of our jobs.

Well, that's all in the past because I essentially quit my job, and I'm asking you to do the same. You have always wanted to travel, and I have always told you how I'd like to see you travel by yourself sometime, so you can experience the freedom and inner contentment it naturally brings out in a person.

And so, I give you this proposal. I know you have money in the bank, so financially this should not be a problem for you. When you read this letter, I'll have already sailed.

Bon Voyage

I am going around the world. I will never get on an airplane. You will find my itinerary at the end of this letter. It will list, in order, all of the cities I'll visit. As you can see, in some of those cities I will spend a specified length of time. In others, I'll let the atmosphere and my moods dictate my departure time. I will stay in small hotels whenever possible, preferably at a bed and breakfast, a room above a pub, or a small pensioners inn. I'll hang out at what I'd think would be a favorite sidewalk cafe for both you and me.

If you follow me and never get on an airplane — If you document that you have traveled, following the same exact route I have taken, visiting the same cities and countries — I will give you $500,000.

Your sea route across the Pacific Ocean does not have to exactly duplicate mine. However, you do have to leave from the west coast of the U.S., and you must start your Asian land journey in Hong Kong.

If you can somehow manage to catch me before I completely circle the globe, (and, I'll make you work a little to accomplish that), I will give you half of what I've won. I will give you $15,076,625.00 That is not a misprint. It reads, fifteen million, seventy-six thousand, six hundred and twenty-five dollars. I've estimated the State Tax, and we'll both probably need a Harvard accountant to figure out all of the income taxes come April 15th, but that will be your share.

I know my dreaming has sometimes upset you. You make it so easy for me to dream. You bring to my soul the peace necessary to be able to dream. Come have a wonderful adventure with me. I love you with all of my heart and soul.

All My Love,

Jack.

P.S. If you're still in town next Saturday, read the <u>Register</u>. My first article about the trip will be published then. I don't know when I'll e-mail the next one — possibly from Hong Kong.

Jack vaguely knew where he wanted to go after Helsinki. Of course by then, they would be traveling together, so they could travel with the prevailing wind. But, for the sake of the game and the ruse of not wanting to be caught, he needed to complete the itinerary. Spreading out an atlas of the world and a couple of old travel guides on the kitchen table, he went to work.

He read about the city of Tallinn, Estonia, its cobblestone streets and medieval Germanic architecture. It was a short ferry ride from Helsinki, and from there he could catch another ferry that would take him to Stockholm. He thought Stockholm might be a welcome change from Russia and China, and a short respite before traveling on to eastern Europe.

He would travel south through eastern Europe to Istanbul. From there, he would explore some of the Greek Isles before continuing on to western Europe.

He would go to Venice and Milan.

He'd visit Freiburg, a small town in southern Germany, a place he'd always wanted to see. After Freiburg, he would wander through several cities before making his way to Liverpool, England.

Liverpool to Philadelphia would be accomplished by another freighter voyage. From Philly, he would train across the country to Los Angeles. He paused to wonder how it would feel to be back in the United States after being gone six months or more. How good would it feel to be home again?

To the itinerary he added information from Loraine, listing the names of the hotels and the length of stay in the cities of China, Mongolia, and Russia.

Because independent travel in those first three countries was difficult, Loraine urged him to commit to a planned program. She stressed this did not mean he was to be any part of a tour group, something he detested, but instead simply predetermined his lodging, length of stay, and onward tickets. She also insisted he pay extra for the services of a guide to meet him at the train station upon arrival, take him to his hotel and assist him in getting checked in. The guide would also meet him at his hotel on the day of departure and take him back to the train station.

"Remember, Jack," she had said. "You neither speak nor read the language, and everything will be in either Chinese symbols or the Cyrillic alphabet."

After printing copies of the itinerary, he made a list of things completed and unfinished. Money, passport, tickets, what else would he need? He sat thinking for a moment, realizing that although he'd made no effort to pack, he had everything he needed — money, passport and tickets. He thought about Lynda. He needed her too, and it made him feel somewhat guilty for making her follow him.

Why not just ask her to come along? Why not allow her the thrill of walking out of the lottery office with fifteen million in her pocket like he had done? He dismissed the thought and the fact that he had no immediate answer.

****

The telephone rang at 8 a.m. Normally, Jack was awake by this time, but the stress of yesterday sedated him into sleeping late. Rolling over, he answered on the fourth ring.

"Jack, this is Loraine," she began. "I normally don't work on Saturday's, but I've made an exception for you ... feel privileged. I'm assuming you'll be in this morning?"

"Yes, I will. Didn't we talk about this yesterday?"

"Well, possibly, I can't remember. But, I have everything completed. And, I talked with the shipping company early this morning. They want you on board tonight."

"Tonight!" Jack exclaimed. "I thought the ship was leaving on Monday morning!"

"Well, there's been a change in plans. This is typical for freighter travel. If they get loaded and unloaded, they leave. Apparently, that is the case, because the shipping agency told me they plan to be underway by two, Sunday morning. They want you on board at least three hours before that."

"Look, give me about an hour, and I'll be down. We'll talk about it then."

As he dressed, he realized his date with Lynda would have to be cut short, and any thoughts of a romantic night together was impossible. She would wonder what was so important he needed to end the evening at 9 or 10 o'clock, and he would have to have a good story.

Before leaving the house he called Dan. They talked for a minute or two about the upcoming travel articles he would send to the paper.

"I'll e-mail them to you, and you can forward them on to Neal. Feel free to take a pencil to anything ... you're a much better writer than I'll ever be."

"Flattery will get you anything except," Dan said, "the begging out on the promise you made. Rebecca asked me about it last night."

"What promise is that?" asked Jack.

"Montana! You promised you'd buy us Montana!"

Jack laughed. "Would a small piece of it be okay? I'm looking at this stack of money on the kitchen table, and I think I might be a little short."

"God, you don't have a bunch of cash lying around, do you?"

"No, not too much," said Jack. "I'll take about two thousand in cash. I've read where it helps to have some good, old American green-backs for unexpected situations. If I find I don't need it, I'll just make a deposit at an American Express office."

"What will you do for foreign money?" asked Dan. "Use an A-T-M?"

Jack once heard a tale of some men who went to Scotland to play golf, one of them insisting an ATM machine was the best way to access money, and at the same time, avoid lines of people.

When he first heard of the Scotland group from a colleague, he thought it strange someone would travel thousands of miles and spend hundreds of dollars, only to avoid the customs, and everyday life of the people.

The story had an interesting twist. On one occasion, well after the banks closed, the ATM lover deposited his card in the machine while his friends looked on. They were on their way to a pub, and were anxious to be lifting a pint.

As they all looked on in horror, the machine ate the card! No explanation, and no amount of yelling, punching numbers, or kicking could force the machine to spit it out.

While the other men in the party retired to the pub, the one who swore up and down about the advantages of using an ATM card spent the next two hours on the telephone trying to understand a customer service person with a heavy Scottish accent. Nothing was wrong with the card or the account, and what set off the machine in a wild display of binge eating, remains a mystery to this day.

What kind of hassle would this event entailed had it happened in China, or Mongolia? What communication problems would have existed there?

"Keep your half percent better interest rate," said Jack, as he told Dan the story. "Speaking of money, I've left you a key to my apartment. I've paid all the bills I could think of, so you shouldn't have to do a lot. On my kitchen table at home is a box. All of the bills are there with due dates written in pencil on the back. If you could mail them all a few days or so before the posted date, I'd appreciate it. There is a checkbook in the drawer of my desk at the office and you're all clear to write checks."

"What about your mail?"

"Billy, the apartment manager, will be collecting it. He's in apartment number one ... you'll see it ... right there by the entrance. I told him you'd be stopping by every so often to pick it up."

"And, how do I contact you if there's an emergency?"

"Well, that might be kinda tough. Probably the best thing to do would be to contact Loraine Ward at Sunrise Travel. It's down by the junior college, in the cluster of shops just before the park. She knows who you are, but you might go down and introduce yourself. You'll like her.

"Oh, I almost forgot. I have a new e-mail address. It's a hotmail account ... I figured it would be the best and easiest to use in a foreign country. The address is onecarefreegypsy at hotmail, dot com."

"I can't believe this is really happening," said Dan. "You're really going to do this, and that much, ah, I guess, I don't find so strange. But, are you still going ahead with your crazy plan for Lynda to meet you?"

"Yes, everything is set. I wrote her a letter last night explaining just how, as you think, I'm crazy. I also wrote an itinerary, and sent one to you on my new e-mail account. Oh, and give a copy to Neal too."

Dan told Jack to hold on a moment while he got Rebecca. "She wants to talk to you," he said.

Jack and Rebecca chatted for awhile. She sounded genuinely concerned about him, telling him if he needed anything, even if he needed them to fly over and join up with him for a week or so, that they were both there for him.

When Jack got to Loraine's office, they went to work immediately. There were still forms and papers to sign. They hadn't been working more than thirty minutes when the phone rang. It didn't ring very often at Sunrise Travel.

After Loraine picked up and greeted the caller, she handed the phone across the desk to where Jack sat. "It's for you," she said.

Who had he told that he would be here, he thought, as he tentatively said hello. It was Dan.

"Well, Buddy. Monday might not be any too soon to get out of town! I was reading the *Times* this morning after you called ... well actually, Rebecca saw it first. And, I quote, 'The California State Lottery announced late yesterday afternoon, that Jack A. Gillette, a Newport Beach resident, has won the ninety-six and one half million dollar Super-Lotto Plus game.' It goes on to say there was a record number of players, and that blah, blah, blah, ... further details are not available at press time."

"There isn't a picture of me standing with a couple of lottery people while they hand me the check, is there?" he tentatively pleaded.

"No, just what I told you. But, tomorrow's another day!"

"By tomorrow, I'll be gone."

"Hey, I thought you said you weren't leaving until Monday."

"There's been a change in plans, and maybe it's for the best. The ship is sailing earlier than originally scheduled. I have to board tonight at ten or eleven."

"We were going to, uh, have you and Lynda over for dinner tomorrow night, but I guess that's out now."

"Look, I'll probably not see you before I leave. Thanks for taking care of everything for me. Thank Neal for publishing my stories and for understanding. I'm sure I've confused him with my secrecy."

"He won't be so confused after he reads you won the lottery."

"No, I suppose he won't. I'd like to have been able to tell him ... ah, in fact, tell him that for me ... but I just couldn't let the word get out to Lynda. It would ruin everything."

"How would it really change anything?" asked Dan.

"Had I not kept this a secret, she would have talked me into taking her with me from the beginning. Hell, I probably wouldn't have even brought up the idea of her trying to catch me. The whole thing was really just a spur of the moment idea with me and nothing more. We would have made more plans, and precious time would have gone by. You see, I just want her to experience traveling by herself, experience life ... even get laid if she wants ... I just don't want to hear about it."

"You're a hell of a lot more liberated than I am, Buddy."

"Well listen. Wouldn't Rebecca get a kick out of trying to catch up with you? I mean, I'll let Lynda catch me in either Shanghai or Beijing. She'll probably figure that out on her own, and I'm sure Rebecca would know you'd let her catch you too. Wouldn't Rebecca get into it?"

"I suppose you're right. I just ... I don't know, I guess I just don't see Lynda seeing the humor in all of this. Have you ever thought what you'd do if she just said, to hell with it?"

" ..., Ah, and miss collecting fifteen mil and a chance to go around the world?"

"Go around the world without ever getting on an airplane, my friend. Don't forget that little detail! It's not like this is a trip to Hawaii ... find me on one of the islands of tropical paradise. China, Russia, eastern Europe, it could all be a lot of work especially for a woman traveling alone. I see Lynda as more of a Club Med type of girl."

"But I keep telling you it'll never go that far. We'll be together by then. And besides, I think you're wrong about her. When we first met, she told me one of her dreams was to cross the Sahara desert on a camel caravan. If that's not work, I don't know what is."

"But Jack," Dan pleaded, "How many years ago was that? Things change, priorities change, people change. That was a dream she told you about — this is reality!"

"Have I changed? Have my priorities changed?"

"No, you're still the same goofy shit you always were. And as for priorities, you never had any in the first place."

They both laughed and talked further of when they would see each other again. Dan repeated his wife's promise to drop everything and come running, even if it was just for a week because he was homesick for friends.

After he hung up, he thought about Dan and Rebecca. They were good friends, but sometimes he felt they were not fond of Lynda. They never said anything, of course, and it was just a feeling he came away with whenever the four of them spent time together. He'd wondered if Lynda harbored the same feelings. She never said anything to him however, and so he pretty much wrote it off as something he only imagined. Still, the feeling was bothersome.

****

Lynda was edgy and tense when Jack called. He said he wanted to see her, but was quick to explain he needed to travel to Bakersfield early in the morning to work on a project for the newspaper. She thought he was a little too quick in saying, despite all his wishes to do otherwise, that he would not to be able to spend the night with her.

Did he know? By some chance had he found out about her and Bill? She could not imagine how he could have discovered her fling, but she also knew things like this could not be kept a secret forever.

Lynda had mixed feelings concerning her unfaithfulness. First of all, she really didn't consider it being unfaithful. She and Jack were not married or engaged. They didn't live together, and she wore no ring to symbolize an event like that might occur in the near future.

She loved him, but life with him had become, well, sort of bland. It wasn't pleasantly exciting anymore. It was more like pleasantly predictable.

She didn't think she loved Bill, but thought she probably could. For all of his faults and his age, he was exciting. Then again, she thought, maybe "it" isn't exciting, but doing something she shouldn't, something forbidden — maybe that was the source of the excitement.

As she sat on the edge of her bed after ending her telephone conversation with Jack, a tear came to her eye. God, I'm a mess, she thought, as she brushed away the wetness. Here I have someone who loves me more than anything in the world, and I reward him by sleeping with someone else. And, here's this other man, old enough to be my father, and for all I know, his sole interest in me is sexual.

Maybe Bill was right. If you want something, take it. If you find you don't want it after taking it, throw it back. He conceded that sort of philosophy would leave a long string of broken hearts and disappointed people, but he'd come right back and said to her, "Who's more important, you or some other poor, dumb schmuck?"

And, maybe Jack was right in his thinking, although when he'd voiced his opinion it usually resulted in them having an argument. Jack had said many times that he thought the stress of her job was somehow at the root of their problems as a couple. She knew he didn't like Bill, but knew even more clearly he didn't like the law profession.

Jack would have a heart attack if she told him of Bill's suggestion she enter law school. It would be a fatal heart attack if he knew she remotely considered it. He referred to lawyers as a bunch of vultures, but quite honestly, she could see no difference between the flock of legal vultures sitting around a dead body, and the flock of media vultures circling overhead.

When he told her last night he would be working part-time at the paper and spending the rest of his time working on his novel, it was great news. She knew he was capable — he had the kind of dreamy, crazy, creative mind she imagined most novelists had, or needed to have.

5

Jack spent the afternoon finishing his introductory article for the newspaper. His writing was laborious at first, with thoughts in the back of his mind about Lynda, his anxiety about the huge odyssey he was undertaking and all of the small details he feared he'd missed. He was glad Lynda was the only person he needed to be concerned about. His mother and father both died a number of years ago, and relatives were distant and few in number.

He'd written the introductory article for the paper as an e-mail document. After saving a copy, he clicked on "Send" to Dan's e-address. Dan might change a word here or there, and in fact might leave or create a glaring grammatical error in order to give Neal something to edit. If anyone could ever play an editor, making the person work for you rather than vice versa, it was Dan.

An Around-The-World Adventure

Call it a midlife crisis, or chalk it up as an urge to complete another entry on life's to-do list. My friends call me crazy, and my girlfriend will be convinced of it when she learns of my plans.

Call it anything you wish, but on Sunday morning, the 13th of May, I will sail on a freighter from Long Beach, California, bound for Hong Kong. From there, I will travel across Asia and Europe by train, sail again by freighter from Liverpool, England, to Philadelphia, and then take a train across the United States, arriving back in Los Angeles in mid-October.

I will never get on an airplane.

I have always dreamed of traveling around the world in this fashion. I recently came into some money — a lot of money — too much money. I won the California Lottery. I have decided to get away for awhile, collect my thoughts, and determine how I'll while away the rest of my life. What better way to come to grips with yourself than to undertake a long, slow journey. I trust that my girlfriend — my best friend — will feel the same, but more about that later.

I had a good sense of where and how I wanted to travel, and with some invaluable assistance from Loraine Ward at Sunrise Travel in Newport Beach, plans for the trip came to life.

People travel for different reasons. Some like to travel in groups where there is safety in numbers. Many Americans travel to places to be pampered and waited upon, preferring destinations that are not too "foreign." There are adventure seekers and tourists who want to experience life on the edge. There are the young college backpackers who, like a rite of passage, tour Europe as a culmination of their youthful years.

I travel to foreign lands to observe. I suppose that comes from working as a newspaper reporter, but I travel to see how other people go about the same everyday rituals of living that we do. I am not steadfast in the belief that Americans do everything the best or most efficient way. Americans do some pretty weird things. So do Italians, Brazilians, Moroccans and Australians.

I enjoy people, weird and otherwise. I revel in the colors and aromas of foreign places, the unrecognizable sounds of different languages, the exotic tastes of what is considered everyday food.

The interaction with ordinary people — people going about their ordinary lives — this is what I believe travel is all about.

I am not obsessed with monuments, castles or architecture. I went to Paris a number of times before I saw the Louvre. After 20 minutes of art, I lingered most of the afternoon at a sidewalk cafe, finding several glasses of wine and people watching much more fascinating.

On a trip to San Antonio, Texas, I found the trinket-laden Woolworth's located across the street from the Alamo a much more interesting site than that of Crockett and Bowie's demise.

This is not to say I don't appreciate the sights and the scenery of the world. During my college years, I traveled to Budapest, Hungary, because of an irresistible urge to see the blue Danube. It's not blue, but rather a grayish-brown color.

While traveling, I avoid other Americans like the plague. The last thing I want to do is meet someone from Omaha while I'm in Istanbul. In Istanbul, I want to meet a Turk.

I avoid the Sheratons and the Hiltons too. They, and hotels like them, are hotbeds for tourists, Americans, businessmen and people of responsibility. I have neither responsibilities nor business interests to pursue. I am a traveler, not a tourist.

The Hanjin Amsterdam, a German ship, sails out of Long Beach bound for Hong Kong on May 13th. The German-owned freighter is of Liberian registry. The captain and officers are of German nationality, while the crew is from Kirabati. The ship, at 68,800 gross weight tons, is 917 feet long and 132 feet wide. As of this writing, I am the only passenger.

The ship has scheduled stops in Oakland, California; Tokyo and Osaka, Japan; and Pusan, South Korea. I will debark in Hong Kong on June 9th.

Many freighters discourage older passengers, and some have limits as to the maximum age. There is no doctor on board, and medical help is limited to *basic first-aid. It is not a place for the weak or feeble.*

However, if a person is flexible and able to enjoy their own company without orchestrated activities, a freighter can be an enjoyable method of travel for about $110 per day.

From Hong Kong, I will travel on the Trans-China/Trans-Mongolian railway system with stopovers in Canton, Guilin, Xian, Shanghai and Beijing, before moving on to Ulan Bator and Ulan Ude, Mongolia, where the train becomes known as the Trans-Siberian railway.

From Ulan Ude, I will make stops in Irkutsk, as well as Moscow and St. Petersburg, Russia.

I will continue this rail odyssey from St. Petersburg to Helsinki, Finland, then ferry from Helsinki to Tallinn, Estonia. Another ferry ride will take me to Stockholm, and yet another to Gdansk, Poland. Back on the train, I'll travel to Warsaw and Krakow. From Krakow, I'll head to Budapest, Hungary, and continue south through Romania and Bulgaria to Istanbul, Turkey.

I'll take a ferry from the Turkish port of Bodrum to the Greek Islands of Kos, Siros, Samos, Tinos, and Mikonos. From Greece I'll ferry to Bari, Italy to start a leisurely rail trip northward through western Europe. I'll visit the cities of Venice and Milan, Italy; Nice and Marseilles, France; and Freiburg and Munich, Germany before taking the train to Prague, Czech Republic. From Prague, I'll re-enter Germany to visit Berlin before traveling to Paris, France. I'll ferry from the port of Le Havre to Portsmith, England. I'll then travel north to Liverpool.

Boarding another German freighter owned by the TIM shipping line, I'll sail from Liverpool to Philadelphia.

I will take a train across the United States, arriving in Los Angeles sometime around October 15. The length of the trip is a little more than five months.

During my travels, I will be writing periodically — via e-mail — about my experiences for the <u>Southern California Life</u> section of the <u>South Beach Register</u>. I will attempt to write in such a way that readers will experience the sounds and the smells — the good and the bad — that I'll be experiencing. I hope readers will savor along with me the joy of a pastry and coffee in a taverna in Greece or at a sidewalk cafe in Budapest. Readers may also experience the surly border guard or the rude civil servant, as well as the everyday man or woman on the street who will stop at nothing to show a traveler unbridled hospitality and the finer points of their country and culture.

I will be traveling alone for an undetermined length of time. Remember the first part of this article when I mentioned my girlfriend, my best friend? She has no idea that I am embarking on this trip. I have written her a letter, promising to share my lottery winnings if she follows and catches me. I'll play hard to get at first, and then I may become easier.

I am doing this to give her the gift of experiencing solo travel, which I believe is the greatest experience a person can ever have. It allows you to come to grips with who you are — deep down — in your very soul.

To always have a travel partner is to have someone who speaks your own language and shares your likes and dislikes. Like consorting with other Westerners, traveling with a spouse, friend or lover simply adds to the comfort level and adds insulation from the cultural differences that I'll be spending thousands of dollars to experience. I don't want to end up at a bistro talking about the same things and the same people that I'd be talking about when I'm at home. I want my best friend to have that experience also.

My friend will have a copy of my itinerary, such as it is. The itinerary is simply a list of the cities in the order that I will visit or pass through them. For much of the trip, it will list neither times of arrival or departure, the length of stay, or name of my accommodation. She is required to visit or pass through all of these cities and in the same chronological order as I do, in her efforts to locate me. She is also bound by the same mode of travel that I am, that is, she must travel by rail, car, bus or freighter. She can never get on an airplane.

Once in a city, I'll hang out at sidewalk cafes. She knows me very well, and one look at this cafe or that, and she'll know whether it's our kind of place or not.

It's exciting to be realizing my "dream trip" and my "dream life" all in one, once-in-a-lifetime experience. It is also scary. I am starting a new life, far from the comforts and familiarities of home. There are the uncertainties of travel in China and Russia — the stories of the Russian mafia and the volatile and ever-changing political climates. I neither speak nor read any foreign languages.

While there are advantages to traveling alone, there are also disadvantages. I will have no one to depend upon. I will have no one to consult on a problem. I will also have no one to argue with, and although I may not always win, at least it will be a fair fight.

I will look forward to the challenges of both independent travel and the friendly match of wits with my friend. I'll be sitting in a sidewalk cafe, enjoying a cup of coffee or a glass of wine — I'll notice a beautiful woman approaching from the other side of the street — I'll squint in the sunlight, trying to focus. Is it her, or is it just another dream?

It took Jack a little more than an hour to pack. The most important items, a 35 mm and digital camera, as well as an older lap top computer, went into one bag. The computer was not very reliable, but he figured if he needed to get rid of it, it would be no great monetary loss. When he contemplated that, he laughed at himself. Thirty million dollars, and I'm fretting about throwing away a three hundred dollar, sixth generation lap top.

A small, over the shoulder bag would hold his money, passport and tickets. A third, somewhat larger soft bag contained his clothes. He packed a couple of pairs of pants and three shirts. He started with two pairs of shoes, but quickly decided it was too much. He would not wear socks, and thereby eliminated another item.

Stopping at a used bookstore on the way home, he bought twenty books. A couple were travel books, and the rest were fiction. He placed all of them and a few maps in a box.

After he finished packing he called Lynda. He arranged to pick her up, telling her he'd made an early reservation for dinner. When she asked him where, he told her he wanted to surprise her.

"It's been a long time since we've been here, huh?" he said, after they were seated. They were at daVinci's, a restaurant they both enjoyed, but one that was expensive.

"Yes, it has been a long time. What's the occasion, or is this just a way to soften me up because you have to leave so early?"

She sounded a bit put out by his effort, and it was the opposite reaction he expected. "No. I just thought you and I deserved something a little special. The last few weeks we haven't seen much of each other, and when we have ... well, it hasn't always been a barrel of laughs. I know how stubborn I can be, and I just want to make up for it somehow."

Lynda caught herself. She was not in a good mood. Seeing two men placed a particular strain on her she was neither familiar or comfortable with. At the moment, she was fed up with both of them. But Jack was just being his usual, nice self. There was no reason to rip him for that.

"I know. And, I can be difficult too," she said. "There's a lot of stuff going on with me right now. I love you, but sometimes I don't think I should be in a relationship with anyone."

"Don't talk like that. We've been together for a long time. It hasn't always been perfect, but nothing is. We've always worked things out, haven't we?"

When she didn't respond, he continued, "Lynda, I love you more than anything. You are the most important thing in my life. We're both going through some changes, and believe me when I say I know how difficult things are for you right now. But, I have faith in you, and I'm confidant we'll weather this storm just fine. Trust in me, and know that I love you. That's all I ask."

God, he did know about Bill, she thought. She could feel a trickle of sweat run down her side from her armpit. The waiter appeared, the drinks they ordered on his tray. It gave her a moment to regroup.

For someone who knew she was cheating on him, he was sure acting calm, she thought. "Jack ... ah ..," she started.

He was holding her hand as he thought about what he had said. Be careful here, he said to himself. You'll go and spill the whole story if you keep talking.

But, I should be standing on my chair and screaming to whoever will listen, he thought. I should be screaming that I just won millions of dollars — screaming that I'm taking the trip of a lifetime — screaming that this beautiful woman across the table will be with me. Instead, I'm trying to act sad and disappointed because I can't spend the night with her. It was disconcerting.

"Listen, please don't say anything, he said. I've probably said too much as it is. Let's just have a great dinner and good conversation for a couple of hours. Then, as much as I don't want to, I'll drop you off at home. I'd love to spend the night, but there is just no way that I can."

"What's in Bakersfield?" she asked, eager to change the subject and trying to sound upbeat.

He told her about the article he was working on at the newspaper. It was the same water rights issue he'd been writing about for weeks, and because it was a familiar subject, it was easy to make up valid reasons for traveling out of town.

They enjoyed their meal, and kept the conversation to rather mundane, but safe subject matter. As they were finishing their dessert, he said to her, "Dan and Rebecca are moving to Montana."

"What?" she asked, incredulously.

"I'm not sure when it'll happen, but I'm pretty sure it will," he responded.

"What brought all of this on? I mean, you're cutting back to part time, and Dan's leaving. Who will be left?"

"They've wanted to move to Montana for a long time. He'll probably do the same thing as me ... write a novel, or maybe he'll go back to work at a small town newspaper."

"That's all there is there," said Lynda. "Small towns."

As Jack spoke, he was thinking to himself what fifty or one hundred acres in Montana would cost. It didn't really matter. He wanted to do good things with the money, better the lives of his friends and do something good for perfect strangers.

"There's all kinds of changes happening, aren't there?" Jack asked.

The conversation was coming back to ground Lynda was not comfortable with. The conversation at the beginning of dinner made her order a second drink before the first one was half finished. Now, with the conversation returning to the subject of personal changes she would have liked another.

Originally, she was disappointed that he could not spend the night. Disappointed, yet also a little relieved. A situation once thought of as heavy on the disappointment and light on the relief, was now just the opposite. As he paid the bill, she knew she would break down crying if they spent the night together.

The waiter, a pudgy, middle age guy, asked Jack if everything was acceptable.

"Everything was fine," he replied. "We've not been here for some time, but I think you were our waiter last time as well." He looked briefly at Lynda for her approval before continuing. "The service and the food was excellent then, just as it is now."

The bill, including an inexpensive bottle of wine, came to $132.00. Jack signed the credit card, and just for fun wrote in a tip of $132.00. He wrote the new total as $264.00.

As they got to the door the waiter caught up with them, and with one hand on his elbow, took Jack aside.

"Sir, ah ... you may be confused. Do you realize that you gave me a tip equal to the amount of the bill?"

Jack reached out and shook the waiter's hand. "Yes, I know what I did. Thank you."

"What was that all about?" asked Lynda as they stepped outside.

"Oh nothing. He just wanted to know if there was any chance that a beautiful woman like you could be single." Putting his arm around her, Jack pulled her to him and kissed her. "You know, people ask me that all the time. I'm starting to get a bit tired of it."

****

At 10:15 p.m., a taxi dropped Jack off at the entrance to the port facility of Long Beach. Trucks, loaded with shipping containers the size of full-sized semi truck trailers, entered and exited the facility under the watchful eyes of port guards. One of the guards called a shuttle bus to take Jack to his ship, and he was now waiting for it to arrive.

After a few moments, a rickety, dented van came to a halt in front of him. Entering, he noticed the condition of the inside of the van reflected that of its exterior. All of the seats were dirty, and the floor was littered with trash. The windows of the van were filthy, in keeping with the overall theme.

Jack's first glimpse of his home for the next twenty-one days, was when he emerged from the van directly in front of the gangway. He could not believe it. The ship was huge. In fact, it loomed over him so high that he could not see either end of the ship or its vast super-structure.

Halfway up the gangway and struggling with his luggage, a Philippine steward met him. Although only half the size of Jack, he insisted upon carrying all of the bags, including the heavy and cumbersome box of books. Jack finally relented, keeping only his small shoulder bag for himself.

They made their way together, into the center of the ship. There, the steward pushed a button on the wall, and presto, an elevator door opened. The elevator was only four foot square, and would have been a tight squeeze for three people. Two people and baggage acted to the same effect, but he was relieved as he noticed the lights of the upper decks blink on and off effortlessly as they ascended.

The steward's name was Franklin Banyon. He showed Jack his room, the "Owner's Suite," and told him he was to be the only passenger. Very spacious and furnished with a sofa, the room also included a writing desk with a chair, a television and VCR and a small refrigerator. A door led into a room with a full size bed, and another door led to a toilet and shower. Except for the bathroom, all of the rooms were carpeted.

Franklin turned the bed down, and closed the curtains on the porthole windows which faced the bow of the ship. As they talked, there would be intermittent noises and faint movement as the cranes placed more containers on board.

Immediately after the steward left, he opened the curtains to peer out. He watched the loading of the ship for about thirty minutes, all the time expecting someone to knock on his door and ask for his passport and travel vouchers. Nothing happened however, and except for the guards at the gate of the port facility, no one had asked for identification.

While Jack waited for someone to come to his cabin, Lynda quit trying to get Bill to exit her apartment. He unexpectedly arrived twenty minutes after Jack left.

"Are you crazy!" she said to him. "What if he comes back? It wouldn't be the first time he's told me something, and all the time had some sort of surprise to the contrary."

Bill maintained that Jack was not as smart as she gave him credit for, coming into her apartment then, uninvited. She didn't like it, but said nothing. For an hour or so she tried to get him to leave, worrying constantly that Jack might return. His parting kiss and words at her door were very tender and romantic. She knew when he turned to go he had a tear in his eye.

The longer Bill stayed and the more time that elapsed, the less worried she became. Finally, she relented to his constant touching and fondling. Intending to take him to her bedroom, they never made it past the hallway, having sex on the floor. By midnight, it was all over. The scent of sex hung in the air of the apartment. Bill wanted to spend the night, but Lynda was exhausted both mentally and physically.

Two other people had restless nights that night. Dan and Rebecca went to bed at eleven, and after turning out the light, they lay in each others arms and talked. At Dan's insistence, Jack met with an attorney and constructed a simple will, making Lynda and Dan the sole beneficiaries.

But, it wasn't money they talked of. Jack had given Dan his e-mail password, and instructed him to e-mail Lynda a message on his behalf. Jack wasn't sure if he would have the privilege of using the ships communication systems, and he wanted his e-mail sent to Lynda on Monday morning.

"Will you read it?" asked Rebecca.

"No. Would you?"

"Probably not. Oh hell ... yes, I would! How could I resist!" she blurted.

"Well, I already know what it says. It simply lays out the rules of the game, and what he wants her to do," stated Dan.

"I'd still like to know how he puts it ... especially if she accepts his offer."

"So, you still don't think she'll follow him?"

"No, I don't. I think she'll be pissed off. She'll be pissed off because he didn't just give her the money. Then, she could run off with the head of the law firm and leave Jack high and dry."

"You know for a fact she's seeing him?"

"Dan, honey ... seeing someone is like looking at someone. I'm faintly seeing you right now, even though the room is dark. I see people all the time, and so do you. I find it the strangest euphemism ... and, coming from a writer you should be ashamed. No, she is not seeing Bill Davidson ... she is fucking Bill Davidson. And yes, I am sure. Speaking of which ...."

****

Something made Jack awaken from his sleep. The constant hum from the ship's generators remained constant, but a faint vibration could now be felt. There was no great roar of engines such as experienced on an airplane — the revving of the engines much like the flexing of a strongman's muscles prior to performing an athletic feat.

He fumbled for a light switch, and then fumbled again to find his wrist-watch on the nightstand. It was 3 a.m.. He got up, slid on a pair of jeans, and walked out to the sitting room portion of his cabin. The portholes of his cabin faced the bow of the ship, and he could see that the ship was slowly moving down a canal-like area, headed for the bay. It would then turn to starboard and head out to sea.

He stood mesmerized by the entire scene. He stopped to consider that he was doing something he'd dreamed of since childhood. Pinch yourself, he thought. Enjoy this experience and every one that follows for each and every second it exists. Treasure this very moment. Savor it. Drink it in.

He made himself a cup of instant coffee, using hot water from the tap in his bathroom. He wished he'd brought along a small coffee maker for the twenty-one day journey. He could have just left it on the ship when he arrived in Hong Kong, a small price to pay for good coffee. But, this wasn't so bad, he thought, as he opened the door to his cabin.

As he walked down the immaculately clean, tiled passageway to the port side of the ship, he noticed that crew members left their shoes outside their cabin doors. At some doors, two or three pairs, from work boots to casual shoes, would be neatly lined up. He decided to follow the custom while aboard.

He could see Long Beach slowly gliding past as the ship made its way towards the bay, and he thought about Lynda, sleeping soundly in her apart-ment. What would her first reaction be when she received his e-mail?

Jack remained at the rail of the ship for nearly an hour. Although by now well out to sea, lights could still be seen on the California shoreline. He had no idea what time they would arrive in the Port of Oakland, and what's more, found himself not caring. He went back to his cabin, and slept like a baby.

He awoke at 10 a.m. to a bright, clear day. Well out to sea, no land was in sight. He dressed quickly, brushed his teeth, and ventured out of his cabin. No one had explained to him any of the procedures of shipboard life, but he figured he could find the galley on the main deck. He might be able to find the Philip-pine steward there, and he should be able to point him in the right direction.

"Good morning, sir!" beamed Franklin when he noticed Jack standing in the doorway of the galley. "We missed you at breakfast this morning," he added.

"Well, I sorta slept in. What time do I need to be here for breakfast?"

Franklin told him to follow, and led him down the passageway to the dining room. It was a larger room than he had imagined, but then everything about this ship was larger than he imagined. Once there, Franklin showed Jack a framed schedule posted on the wall. It listed the times for breakfast, lunch and dinner, as well as times for both morning and afternoon coffee.

Jack found himself smiling when he realized he was right on time for morning coffee. Maybe this is an omen, forecasting that everything I do on this trip, even when I first think I've made a mistake or an error, will work out, he thought.

There were five round tables in the room, each with seating for four. Covered with white linen, four were set with tableware. There were two men present in the room, but they sat apart from one another.

Franklin led him to a table and indicated a particular seat at which he was to sit. It was obvious the seating was by assignment. Another officer entered, taking a seat directly to Jack's right. He introduced himself as Michael Haussman, the Second Officer. He spoke English with a heavy German accent, and Jack was forced to listen carefully to fully understand.

As Franklin poured coffee, the Second Officer explained some of the ship's procedures. Jack was told he would have to ask permission to go on the bridge, and it was requested he notify an officer before walking on the main deck.

Haussman also informed him that, as Second Officer, he was in charge of the "Slop Chest," a sort of communal non-profit store for the benefit of the crew, and if Jack needed anything, all he had to do was write it down on a request form. With a wave of his hand, the officer indicated the general direction of where the form was located.

When Jack asked what supplies were available, he found the list was extensive, including everything from toiletries to snacks and beer. A small refrigerator was in his cabin, and so he requested a case of beer. Haussman told him the case would cost $6.30, U.S. currency. What a deal!

Jack made a small meal of the cold cuts and cheeses spread out on the table before him, and enjoyed a leisurely cup of coffee. A couple of other officers came and went. They voiced hello's, but offered no real conversation. From what was said, he determined English was definitely a second language, if that.

He returned to his cabin, and was drawn once again to bed. He could not believe how tired he was, nor could he believe how well he slept. The constant and steady drone from the engines and generators was a lullaby to his ears.

****

Lynda slept in that morning also. She was surprised Jack did not call. They both enjoyed one of several small, sidewalk cafes for morning coffee and the newspaper on Sunday mornings.

Lying in bed at 10:30 a.m., she imagined he was probably just as tired as she, but for different reasons. God, this is crazy, she thought. But at the same time, she was kind of enjoying herself. I'm not married to Jack, she kept telling herself — so I'm not breaking any sacred vows.

By early afternoon, she was a little more concerned. He still had not called, and two calls to his apartment only produced a ringing telephone. It was odd, she thought, that he would turn off his telephone answering machine. She could not remember him ever doing so before.

By 6 p.m., she was more than worried. She was concerned about his safety, and worried that by some remote possibility, knew Bill was at her apartment last night. She would worry for several minutes and then convince herself it was impossible for him to know about Bill. However, every time she convinced herself, a telephone call to his apartment produced the same lonely and haunting ringing, and all of her doubts would resurface.

At 7:30, she couldn't stand it any longer. She drove to his apartment and knocked on the door. Then, she knocked again a little harder and a little louder. She stood there for a moment, listening to both the silence of the apartment and her conscience. She knocked again, but thought if she kept doing this, someone would call the police. There was a spare key somewhere at home, but a quick search for it before leaving the house was futile.

"Can I help you?" said a voice behind her.

She turned and recognized the apartment manager. She could live in an apartment for five years and not even know what the manager looked like, but Jack would live somewhere for five days and know the manager as well as many of the tenants by their first name. It was one of the things she admired about him, how he seemed to be fueled by people he did not know.

"Well," she answered, "I'm looking for Jack. I know he had to go out of town last night, and I'm kinda worried cause I've not heard from him all day."

Oh shit, the manager thought. Jack had mentioned his girlfriend didn't know he was leaving. What did he say about it — that she didn't know yet, but would in due time? He didn't feel like this particular moment was the "due time" Jack spoke of, and besides, he didn't want to have to explain something that may be bad news.

"Well ... ah, I haven't seen em all day. Course, he coulda come an gone, but no, I can't say as if I've seen em all day," he said.

She introduced herself, shaking the manager's hand. "I'm kinda worried about him. It's not like him to not contact me either by telephone or e-mail. I hate to put you out and all, but would you mind if I went in to see if he's okay? I have a key, but I couldn't find it at home."

How the hell do I get out of this? he thought. If I say I won't open the door, she might call the cops. Then, I'd have to lie to them or tell the truth in front of her, who I've already sorta lied to. And, if I open the door ... Christ, I don't know what he took with em ... his whole apartment could be empty, and then what would I tell her?

"Well ... ah, I suppose I could go in and take a peek," he said. "But, I really don't think I should let ya in, ya know. Privacy rules an' all ... ya know how sometimes these things can come back ta bite ya."

What an idiot, she thought. It was the downside of Jack's outgoing personality. He would talk with anyone, and only later would he make an assessment. He might even think the guy an idiot too, cultivating the fact and saying, "... yeah, the guy is out there, but he's harmless in small doses."

"Whatever," said Lynda. "I just want to make sure he's not inside and sick, or something even worse."

The manager dug around in his pocket for a moment or so, searching for a key, and then let himself into the apartment. Seconds later, he emerged with a shrug of his shoulders. "Ain't nobody in there, Miss. Everything looks neat an' tidy."

"Does it look like he's been home today?" she asked.

This bitch ain't leaving until she gets in, thought the manager. Jack's a good guy, and he wouldn't give a shit if I let her go in an' poke around, so what the hell. He was more confident now that he'd peeked in the closets and saw all of Jack's clothes. It didn't look like he was on the lam.

"Why don't we both go in together. Ya can look 'round and see fer yerself," offered the manager.

The first thing she noticed was Jack's expensive laptop on the kitchen table. It seemed strange it was there and not with him. The manager was ten feet in front of her as they passed through the kitchen, and for some reason she found herself covertly opening the refrigerator door. Jack was never one to have a refrigerator crammed with food. He was a typical bachelor in that respect, although he was a good cook, and enjoyed cooking occasionally for the two of them.

As Lynda drove back home, she thought about last night and last week. The inner turmoil surrounding Jack's absence was probably just her conscience yelling at her, making her imagine this or that — everything from Jack knowing to Bill's wife knowing. Everything seemed fine, yet there was something in the air.

Why would Jack's refrigerator be empty, except for that one box? Not something you'd normally put in a refrigerator, she had to admit. And, not only that, but the light didn't come on when she opened the door.

Although she came to the conclusion instantly, as she drove home she doubted herself and wondered if it were true that someone had unplugged the refrigerator and set an open box of baking soda in the very center of the top shelf.

6

Jack spent most of Sunday in bed. He awoke for lunch, and later napped away the afternoon. At five, he went to dinner, and it was then that he first met the Captain. Of the seven German officers, only the Captain and three others spoke English fluently, which surprised him. For some unknown reason he expected everyone to speak English.

Early the following morning, something awakened him. Was it a noise? Was the ship still moving? The drone of the engines was so faint that it was difficult to discern between the engines running at speed, and the generators operating while the ship was at rest.

There was the sound again. He switched on the light to look at his watch. It was 5:30 a.m. Dressing quickly, he made his way to the port side rail. When he stepped out on the open deck, he heard the sound again, much louder now, as the atmosphere around him helped to identify the sound. The fog was so thick he could not see the white light positioned at the bow of the ship. The fog horn blared again. It sounded close.

He returned to his cabin, but excitement and anticipation prevented him from sleeping. Two hours later the ship began to move. It was the first light of dawn, yet he still could not see what he was searching for as he peered out from the porthole window of his sitting room. In preparation, his cameras lay on the desk, lens caps off and ready to go.

He was forced to be content with taking photos after entering the bay with the magnificent Golden Gate Bridge behind him instead of in front. By then, the fog had lifted just enough for some decent shots, although it was the thrill of sailing under the bridge that was important to him. It was something he had always wanted to do.

Minutes later, the ship passed the abandon Alcatraz Prison. Sailing under the Oakland Bay Bridge, it made a wide, sweeping turn to port, and entered the Oakland Shipping Terminal.

****

As Lynda drove to work Monday morning, she pondered Jack's absence. She checked her e-mail the minute she arose from sleep, and she would check it again as soon as she arrived at work. She was worried. This was not like him, but as she drove and silently reflected upon recent events, other un-characteristic things came to mind. She wondered why he quit sending her flowers. When was the last time she received some from him? She tried to think of the last time, but could not.

Saturday night at dinner, Jack was strangely melancholy. No, melancholy was not the right word. It was more like he was being reflective about their years together as a couple. Reflective and calm. Yes, maybe that was the key word — calm. Now he was missing, and she was far from calm.

She checked her e-mail and voice mail as soon as she reached her office, but there were no new messages. Fifteen minutes later, she checked again, and still there was nothing.

At fifteen minutes to ten, she saw a new message in her "In Box." She didn't recognize the sender's address, and thinking it was spam, was preparing to delete it when another message popped up. The second message identified the sender as Jack, but strangely listed the same subject as the previous, unidentified one. Who was *onecarefreegypsy @hotmail.com* and what was the subject, "Bon Voyage?" She clicked on Jack's message first.

Lynda went through a range of emotions. She smiled at first, thinking this was some sort of joke, but her thoughts kept returning to the memory of the empty, disconnected refrigerator at Jack's apartment.

As she read further, she wondered if he had in fact, won the lottery. At the sight of five hundred thousand, and later, fifteen million, she became downright giddy. And, when she saw what she would have to do to collect the money she became upset and apprehensive.

She read the letter twice before reading the first message from *onecarefreegypsy*. The message was the same as the one from Jack's regular e-mail address. She read the e-mail over and over, her emotions still ebbing back and forth across a vast spectrum.

She went back to her "In Box" and found another message from *onecarefreegypsy*, listing Jack's itinerary.

When she finally closed the screen and sat back in her chair, she felt light headed. She could picture him in her mind, smiling at the sight of her reactions. She could also picture him walking to the dock in Hong Kong everyday, waiting for her ship to come in.

She wasn't sure how long she sat there, when the intercom sounded. It was Bill, and he wanted to see her. She gathered herself together, wondering if she should say anything to him, or wait until later.

As she entered his office, Bill got up from his seat behind his desk and came around it to meet her. He put his arms around her and started kissing her on the neck.

"What's the matter?" he asked, as she pulled away from him.

"Nothing," she replied, slumping down in one of the overstuffed chairs. "Oh, everything is the matter!" She stood up and returned herself to his arms. "Nothing and everything is wrong. I don't know what to do, and yet I do know what to do!"

"Do you think you could get away with telling what's his name you have to go to Palm Springs again for a few days?" said Bill, ignoring her words and mood. "... or, maybe we could go down to San Diego! We could come up with a good excuse."

She pulled away from him then, and motioned for him to sit down in one of the chairs. She took another one, separated only by a small end table, and reached across to take his hand.

"You're married, Bill," she started. When he started to interrupt, she took her hand away and held it up for him to stop. "You're married, and I'm involved with someone. I care very much for you, but I also care very much for Jack. I don't know if either of you are the right man for me, I'm very confused right now."

"Well, if you need some space, ah ...," Bill started.

"No, I don't need time to think about it. I have plenty of time, and it appears that I'll have even more after today."

"What do you mean?"

"Bill ... oh, I don't even know how to begin. I got an e-mail from Jack this morning. He won the California Lottery, and he's giving me half."

"Jesus fuckin' Christ!" said Bill. "The lottery that was just won by someone? He won that lottery?"

"I don't know which one he won. He's always been a bit obsessed with buying tickets for those things. All I know is he's going to give me fifteen million, seventy-six thousand, six hundred and twenty-five dollars." She smiled at him, liking the way she remembered the exact figure, and pleased with how easily it rolled off her tongue.

"Fuck, are you sure?" Are you sure this guy isn't just yanking your chain? Maybe he came by Saturday night, and he's just saying this to piss you off. Have you thought of that?"

"That was my very first thought, but no, I'm certain this is for real. Jack wouldn't do something like that."

"Well, you'd be surprised what some guys will do when they find they're losing someone," said Bill.

Lynda leaned back in her chair and smoothed her dress out with her hands. She was wearing a light tan dress with a matching jacket, something she bought for the personal injury trial. She'd worn it today in hopes it would bolster her spirits. When she looked over at Bill, she could tell he knew exactly what she was about to say, but she needed to say it anyway.

"Jack's not losing me, Bill. You are." Bill tried to speak, but she held her ground and continued. "I care very much for you. In fact, I think if we gave it enough time ... if you weren't married ... and if I was not involved with Jack ...

well, I think there might be a future for us together. But, the way things are is much different than the way it could, or maybe should be. I don't know."

Bill started to speak again, but again she stopped him. "I get very confused when I think about you versus Jack," she started. "I don't know, maybe I love both of you. But, I do know I have to do what Jack's asked me to do. If I don't ... if I don't take the fifteen million that he's going to give me ... there is no amount of love that will make up for that."

"You have to do something to collect the dough?" asked Bill.

"It's nothing, really. He's gone off on an adventure around the world. He's made a game out of it, and when I follow him, I'll get the money."

"Then what?"

"Well, if you think I'm going to dump him and come running back here ... well, you really don't think that's what I'm going to do, do you?"

"I don't know. Tell me, did he put this in writing?"

She asked him to wait, leaving his office to return a few minutes later with a printed copy of Jack's e-mail. She handed it to him as she returned to her chair.

He read it silently. She could tell he was analyzing it the way he analyzed every document he read. She wondered, as she had before, how he ever managed to read something as everyday as a newspaper without it taking him three days to pour over each and every word.

He handed the paper back to her. "This doesn't sound as easy as you're making it out to be. Those cities are not little one-horse burgs, with a coffee shop and one hotel. How in hell will you ever find him?"

"That's just it," she said confidently. "I don't have to find him. I keep telling you I know him. I know how he thinks and how he dreams. As much as he wants me to experience traveling alone, he'll probably be at the docks in Hong Kong when I arrive!" She thought for a moment, and then continued. "No, on second thought, he won't be in Hong Kong. He'll make me go to one or two cities before he'll be waiting at the train station for me."

"And then what?" asked Bill.

"I don't know. We'll probably get on an airplane and fly to Europe ... spend a few weeks there, and then ... who knows."

"Well, the document is binding. That's one positive," said Bill. "I suppose you have to go, and although I guess I have to admit it, I don't have to like it. I've got a pretty good travel agent, and I'll put you in touch with her. If there is anything I can do, or if you ever want to come back, you know you can."

"That's so sweet of you," she cooed.

They both stood up, and Lynda thought about how much she would miss this man. At that moment, in fact, she was more attracted to him than she was to Jack. She found it all confusing, but not bothersome. As she turned to go, Bill reached out and grasped her arm, turning her around to face him. He didn't have to pull her to him, as she fell into his arms and they kissed.

When the kissing stopped, she knew what she would do and so did Bill.

"Why don't we just go ... get in the car and drive to Palm Springs," whispered Bill, as he kissed her neck and ear. I can call my travel agent from there and get her started on your trip."

"I'll go back to my apartment. Give me an hour," she quickly replied.

She went to her office. She started to make a telephone call to clear up final matters on the newly settled case, but stopped in the middle of dialing. What do I care, she thought. With fifteen million dollars, I'm not going to worry about this crap! She walked out, stopping briefly at the front counter to speak to the receptionist. "I'll be out for the rest of the week," she said.

The receptionist looked up, wondering if a week off meant there was some personal emergency, or if it was related to something else. When she determined Lynda's face held no sign of heartache or disaster, she was relieved, but now was curious.

"What ... ah, do you have a really big, like case, coming up or something?" she asked.

"No, I'll just be out for the rest of the week," she said curtly, turning and walking towards the double doors that led out of the office.

"Slut," the receptionist murmured aloud. She thought nothing more of it until fifteen minutes later when Mr. Davidson appeared.

"Marty will be taking all of my calls for the next several days," Davidson said. "I'll be in Palm Springs, but I left him an e-mail about what's going on, so when he comes in tell him to read my memo."

After Mr. Davidson left the office, the receptionist, Brittany, stopped her mundane job of addressing billing envelopes, and thought about the slut, Lynda, and the prick, Davidson. She didn't much care for either of them.

Brittany was not the smartest girl working at the law firm. In fact, in the entire building, she probably would have been considered in the bottom third of the smartness curve. She knew this and knew what people thought of her. She knew they all looked at her clothes, her flipped up hair style and the tattoo on her wrist with disdain. But, she also knew they didn't know everything.

They didn't know, or at least she tried to hide the fact, that she was a snoop. She absolutely loved poking around for information. In fact, before she was hired, she tried to get a job working for a private detective. In one interview, the investigator blew her off, telling her she didn't know shit about the legal profession, and that it was paramount to working as a PI, or a PI's assistant — talking as if he was some kind of Harvard Law School graduate.

When Brittany was hired by Davidson's firm, she told the office manager she wanted to come in early so she could learn all about the computer. The office manager liked her work ethic, and sensed she was somewhat proficient on computers. What the office manager didn't know was that Brittany was not only proficient, she was an absolute genius.

Most of what she learned about computers was self taught, and if she had stopped right there she would be considered a whiz-kid. But, she met her boyfriend, and it was he who coached her to a higher level.

Her boyfriend was a professional hacker. He stood before a judge one day with his dick in his hand, waiting for the hammer to come down. He could have been sentenced to some serious jail time if the very company he hacked his way into had not come to his rescue. The company president stood up in the courtroom, asking that the judge, in lieu of jail time, put the kid on probation. It was also requested the defendant be required to work for the company as restitution for his crimes and to prevent future episodes of the very hacking he had performed.

It did not take Brittany long to get into Davidson's e-mail. This guy talked like a truck driver, she thought, momentarily distracted by e-mail messages to clients and friends.

She went to the last entry, and there was his e-mail to Marty Williams, another member of the firm. She was bummed the message didn't tell her anything she didn't already know.

"I know you're going out of town, asshole. I just want to know if you're going out of town with her," she murmured softly.

Lynda's e-mail might reveal something more, she thought, as she started hacking her way into the system.

"Oh my God!" she said, a little louder than what she had intended. She looked around to see if anyone heard her, and after finding herself alone and unnoticed, mouthed the words, Oh my God, several times again.

This was just too totally awesome to believe, much less keep to herself. It pissed her off that she did not have a printer at her desk. She would have to go to the copy room where the support people were linked up to two, high speed printers. That was too risky, so she saved, cut and pasted, sending Lynda's e-mail message from Jack to her own e-mail address. She could then access it at home, and print it safely without anyone knowing.

This done, she exited the site, eager to have it off of her screen in case anyone walked by. Brittany couldn't keep this to herself, so she first e-mailed her boyfriend and told him, and then e-mailed her girlfriend.

The boyfriend told his friends at the computer repair shop where he hung out when not working. Brittany's girlfriends likewise spread the news to friends and co-workers. While the boyfriend's nerdy circle of associates thought the news was cool, it was Brittany's circle of friends who found it the most interesting.

Beth was one of those girls on the outer rim of that circle. Hearing the news from a friend of a friend, Beth did not know Lynda or Jack. And, she only knew of Brittany as some distant, unnamed receptionist. She did, however, know Ann, who was a co-worker of Rebecca.

Although Beth had met Rebecca only once, she knew that a woman by the name of Lynda worked at Davidson's law firm, and that woman was someone Ann knew through Rebecca. Furthermore, she knew this Lynda woman was not someone Rebecca was overly fond of, due in part to rumors of her having an inner-office affair.

It was Beth who first told Ann about the probability of Davidson going to Palm Springs with a woman named Lynda. And it was Ann who, months earlier, had told Rebecca of the rumors of Lynda and Bill Davidson's affair.

"You won't believe what I heard!" said Beth. Before Ann could say whether or not she believed her, Beth went on. "That woman that you work with ... well, her friend is getting fifteen million from the boyfriend. She has to follow the guy on some sort of trip to get the money, but she's getting fifteen million dollars! Can you believe that?

"But what's more, she and the old attorney guy are headed off to Palm Springs. Can you believe that? A guy gives you fifteen million and you go off with another guy for a little action!"

Ann could believe it. She and Rebecca had discussed Dan's best friend Jack, and his relationship with Lynda several times. Furthermore, at coffee that morning, Rebecca told her in the strictest confidence what had transpired over the last week.

Ann wondered if she should repeat what she was hearing. Actually, she did not debate for more than a micro-second whether or not she should tell Rebecca, but only pondered how to tell her. Better to just get right to the point.

"You'll love this!" she promised, as they took a seat in a deli on the ground floor of the office building where they worked. Ann stirred her iced latte before continuing. "From a reliable source, and I know it's gospel, because of what you told me this morning about you-know-what. Anyway, that woman who you know that's seeing the old, attorney guy on the side ... well, she went back to Palm Springs today with old Mr. Stud, and this is ... and here's where it gets interesting ... she and the old goat went to Palm Springs AFTER she got an e-mail message from your friend Jack! Ya know, the e-mail you told me about, detailing you-know-what."

Rebecca hated one aspect of sharing secrets with her friend Ann. Ann always referred to the secret as "you know what," and she never hesitated to throw a few "you know what's" into any conversation, even ones including people you didn't want to know about "you know what."

"How do you know it was after she got the message?" asked Rebecca. "I mean, how can you be sure of that?"

"Because ... well, for the same reason we know the flowers sent to her by Jack were either tossed or given to her in the name of the attorney guy. The receptionist woman, the friend my friend Beth knows. She knows everything that goes on there."

"Dan will be upset when I tell him this," said Rebecca.

Ann went on, "And, you know it's all true about the flowers, because you had Dan ask his friend if he was still sending them all the time. If he was still sending them, why wasn't she getting them?"

"But how could this receptionist know the sequence, ... I mean, how could she know the e-mail was read before they went to Palm Springs? If that's true, she is totally cold."

"I don't know exactly," said Ann. "I heard she's some kind of computer freak, an amateur hacker or something. I don't know."

"I hate to hear this," voiced Rebecca. "I really wanted to try to break her and Jack up, but Dan kept telling me to mind my own business."

"Well, if you just rat her out, she'll be out fifteen million. Boy, will she ever be one pissed off woman." Ann started to take a drink before abruptly setting the glass down.

"But wait, how will you tell this Jack guy about her and the attorney without her finding out who told? I don't think I'd want to have someone be out fifteen million bucks because of something I said. You'd better be careful."

Knowing Jack, Rebecca wondered if he would believe her or her husband. He'd probably give Lynda the money anyway, in hopes they could reconcile.

****

While Lynda was waiting for Bill, she made a few calls. She contacted the State Lottery Department to verify a winning ticket was issued. She knew the answer she would get, but she made the call anyway.

Next, she tried to ring Jack's apartment. This time, instead of the telephone just ringing, she heard a recorded message stating the phone was disconnected. This was something else she expected. Jack might be a dreamer, but he also was very thorough. She felt his e-mail message was no joke from the start, but these two calls convinced her.

It was only eleven o'clock in the morning, but she poured herself a glass of Chardonnay. "Why not?" she said aloud to herself. She took a seat at her kitchen table and wondered why she was acting the way she was. She should be running to Jack. He was the best thing to ever happen to her, and that was before the money. She should have just walked out of her office, got on an airplane, and flew to Hong Kong. She could be the one with the silly grin on her face, standing on the pier in Hong Kong. It wasn't too late, she reminded herself.

She reflected upon Bill. She'd had no intention of even hugging him goodbye, but, when he told her he'd help her — that he knew a travel agent who could do all of the leg work for her — well, there was just something that made her want him. She took a sip of her wine, and thought maybe that's all it was. She just wanted one last fling with this guy who would bend over backwards to do things for her.

She admitted that, to a large extent, her attitude and actions were governed by the promise of $15,076,625. With that kind of money she would do any damn thing she pleased, thank you very much, and to hell with anything or any man. However, she wasn't fond of herself when she thought that way. It really wasn't the way she was or wanted to be.

When she heard the knock on the door, she said to herself, go and have a good time for a couple of days while a travel agent does all the work. If you feel different in a couple of days, get on an airplane and fly to Hong Kong, or take the silly boat and play the game. Either way you'll win.

The drive to Palm Springs was long and quiet. The wheels of Bill's luxury sedan were spinning round and round, and so too were the wheels in the heads of both passenger and driver.

What Lynda said in the office that morning about the word "love," upset Bill. He wasn't in love with her, he just liked fucking her! He didn't care if she was in love with Jack, just as long as she would jump in the sack with him from time to time.

He thought of himself as a fair kind of guy, and was willing to share Lynda, all things being equal. However, this 15 million dollar thing was something else. Although there was no way he could have it all to himself, nor was he in the remotest way entitled to any of it, the money was something he was desperately trying to think of in terms of making some portion of it his. That accomplished, he would prefer future sharing be kept to a bare minimum.

While Bill tried to concentrate on driving the car, struggle with the anticipation of getting a piece of ass, and dream up some scam to get a share of the jackpot, Lynda was coping with her own inner troubles.

She quit thinking of the logic in screwing Bill when Jack was going to give her 15 million dollars. Every time the thought entered her conscious mind, she'd push it back into some deep, dark recess where it would rest for a short time before coming out to pester her once again.

She also stopped thinking about what she would do with the money. It would sort its way out in due time. And oddly, she never even considered the possibility, and in fact, completely dismissed any chance that she might fail to catch him before he completed his around the world trip. Five hundred thousand for second place never entered her mind.

Her primary concern at the moment was getting to Hong Kong. If she traveled by air, and was waiting on the pier when Jack's ship arrived, he would be greatly surprised. She was certain he would be very happy to see her. However, she was not sure he would continue to be pleased with her ingenuity, or become upset with her for disregarding his offer to play the game. Bill's words about Jack's e-mail being binding rang in her ears. Binding worked two ways.

She was anxious to read Jack's first travel article for the newspaper, silently hoping it would offer some insight into what she should do. The article would not run until Saturday, five days from today, and if she was to take a boat across the Pacific Ocean and play the game to the letter, it would be prudent to act on Bill's offer to help.

With that in mind, the thoughts of what she was doing — going to Palm Springs to have sex with a man while your steady is out on the ocean with 15 million in his pocket, earmarked out of the kindness of his heart to you — those images would rush back into her conscious mind, make a cold shudder run through her body and cause her to absentmindedly reach to turn down the air-conditioning in Bill's car.

"You need to make a copy of the e-mail and his contract with you," started Bill. He drove on for a moment, awaiting a response from her, and when none seemed forthcoming, he went on. "I'll put it in the safe at work, just in case."

"In case of what?" she asked, turning to look at him now.

Jesus, thought Bill. All women are exactly the same. They start getting some dick, and all of a sudden they're looking at you like everything you say is covered with dogshit.

"Well, in case the fucker decides not to give you fifteen million dollars. What the hell do you think he's doing out there on the fuckin' ocean, fishing?" Bill didn't wait for, or want a reply now. Although ad libing a bit, he plowed forward.

"He's thinking. That's what he's doing. He's thinking about investments, and taxes, and stuff he wants to buy. And, all the shit he's thinking about costs money. With each thought, his share dwindles down a little further. If it goes down too low, maybe he'll think he spoke too soon. 'Yeah,' he says ... 'I'll just cut her share a little bit. She loves me, so she'll understand. Instead of fifteen million, I'll just give her five.'"

Now was when Bill wanted a reply, and he took his eyes off the road long enough to glance over at her. She was looking out the side window, watching the landscape speed past. He forged ahead, wanting now to piss her off a little bit, level the playing field since he was a little pissed off about her attitude.

"Or, let's take the worse case scenario. Let's say he meets someone on the fucking boat or something. Hey, stranger things have happened.

"Let's say he meets some babe and decides he doesn't want to give you shit. You've made some major sacrifices here. You've thrown away an opportunity to go to law school, you've quit a very good job, you've moved out of your apartment and sold most, if not all of your belongings. You've spent a considerable amount of savings ... all of this, just so you could fulfill your part of a written agreement ... something he has now decided not to honor. What do you do then?"

He wanted to add "you uppity bitch" to the last sentence, but he only wanted to piss her off a little, not entirely screw up any chance of getting laid in a little less than an hours time.

Lynda quit gazing out the window now, and was looking straight ahead. They would be in Palm Springs in an hour, and the traffic was not very heavy. However, she did not like the direction everything was suddenly going.

What Bill said was causing her to doubt how well she knew Jack. She wanted to tell him he was completely wrong, and in fact, she considered telling him to turn the car around and take her home. That manic sense of confusion was beginning to come over her again.

"I really don't think Jack would do something like that," Lynda found herself saying, a little surprised the statement didn't sound more positive. "I mean, nothing in the past gives me any reason to believe he'd do that."

"But, it's not out of the question," stated Bill confidently.

"Yes, and no. I suppose he could fall in love with someone else, but I know he'd still take care of me first."

"I think you're dreaming," taking his eyes off the road to look at her. Good, he thought as he saw she was now looking at him, she's starting to listen to me for a change.

"You told me once that he was always fantasizing about winning the lottery. And, do you know what you said then?" He glanced at her again now, knowing she'd be right there looking at him, waiting for him to answer his own question.

"And it pissed you off too. You told me he'd probably give all of it away. He'd see some poor, dumb fuck with three or four kids, standing near the gate to get into the ball game, asking total strangers if they had extra tickets, and he'd buy the guy season tickets, box seats, no less."

"But, I'll see him before he has much of a chance to do anything," she said, a little lamely.

"So, what happens if he gets to China, sees all those poor saps running around on bicycles with no shoes on, and decides he's going to give it all to charity? Better yet, what happens if he's approached by someone who talks him into giving it to charity?"

"Bill, I appreciate you wanting to take care of me, and I think to some extent, you're correct. But he isn't stupid, and he wouldn't let someone talk him out of all the money. Believe me, he would love to travel, write and never have to worry about paying bills again in his life."

She waited for him to say something. She was more confident now and her confusion was gone, at least temporarily. She didn't think he would respond like he did.

Bill was a trial attorney. He was a very good trial attorney. In his own mind he was one of the best trial attorneys in California, although in reality, the jury was still out on the matter. Like all trial lawyers, he had a sense for the dramatic. Instead of replying, he looked for a place to pull off the road.

Seconds later, he spotted it, and abruptly brought the car to a stop on the shoulder of the highway. As the dust from his sharp exit off the pavement momentarily hovered over the car and then quickly dispersed in the wake of a passing semi truck, he turned the key, shutting the engine off.

He turned to look at Lynda, and spoke before she could verbally register the confusion on her face.

"Man wins ninety-five-million-plus dollars. I read about it in the paper. Man gets on a boat to sail across the fucking ocean, headed for Hong Kong. I read about that in the paper too. Let's say, for the sake of argument, I control a big charitable organization, or let's say I just have a dream of some charitable enterprise. I fly to Hong Kong and wait for said individual to get off the boat."

He reached over and put both his hands on Lynda's shoulders. She let him turn her a bit so they were directly facing one another, sitting there in the car.

"Here's the deal, I say to this guy. I know you won all of this money. I know you want to be able to travel and do some other things. I also know you're a good guy, and you want to do some good things for society and live a quiet life yourself.

"I tell him I'll put the money in a trust account. I tell him he'll get a guaranteed income of whatever he needs for the rest of his life. I'll throw in some insurance policies and a money market plan to take care of any heirs when he takes the last stage out of Dodge."

Very slowly, Bill looked Lynda directly in the eye, and said, "You're a down to earth kinda guy. What if we guarantee you an annual stipend of sixty thousand dollars after taxes, with a ten percent cost of living increase every two years?"

She didn't say anything at first. Finally, she managed just one word, "Jesus!"

Bill started the car again, and pulled back on the highway. It was awhile before Lynda spoke.

"Do you think someone would do that?" she asked.

"Christ, I'm thinking about doing that!" shouted Bill.

She had to laugh. Jack would not give Bill the time of day, and in fact, might even calculate how much the lawsuit would cost him if he just punched him in the nose without ever saying a word.

"I don't think you'd have a very good chance of getting him to turn the money over to any charity you controlled."

"Yeah, but he'd turn it over to someone, wouldn't he?"

She had to admit he would, and she told Bill so. She told him she also knew that for Jack, sixty thousand a year would be plenty, and in fact, he'd probably prefer having won sixty thousand for life than ninety-five million. He'd have some justification for it, saying something to the effect that sixty thousand would keep his life in the proper perspective.

As soon as they arrived in Palm Springs, Bill was so happy with the way he orchestrated the little scene out on the highway that he decided to segue right into Act II. So, instead of trying to get Lynda's panties down around her ankles before she was completely in the door, he suggested they go to work.

He explained to her that time was money, and the sooner she caught him, the better. She might very well be only one of a number of people in the race. He could also see she was worried now, and he made her smile before they started making telephone calls.

"This is like the two guys out in the fucking woods," said Bill. "They come across this bear, and it stands up on it's hind legs and roars, or whatever the fuck bears do. The one guy sits down, takes his hiking boots off, and starts lacing up a pair of sneakers."

'Why are you changing into your sneakers?' asks the other guy. 'You can't outrun a fuckin' bear.'

'I don't need to outrun the bear,' said the guy lacing up his shoes. 'I only need to outrun you.'"

Bill telephoned his travel agent, explaining some of the aspects of what Lynda intended to do. He told the woman he would e-mail her a copy of the itinerary, and expressed there was an urgency to his requests. Bill could be very demanding, but also knew how to get things done. Lynda knew this, but the fact was emphasized upon her just before he ended the conversation.

"You've been the firm's sole source of our travel needs for some time now," said Bill. "I want to make it clear this matter is of the utmost importance to me personally. I want my friend on a ship bound for Hong Kong by no later than Friday of next week."

When the woman started to protest, Bill interrupted her and said, "I know, I know, you've already explained that. Work around it. You have my friend's credit card numbers and the cost is not an issue. If she is on a boat by a week from Friday, I want you to bill me personally for one thousand dollars. That's for your pocket, not the agencies, so handle the matter separately and discreetly, any way you please. But, it is imperative she be on a boat by a week from Friday."

7

Eighteen hours after arriving in Oakland, the *Hanjin Amsterdam*, sailed out of the bay and into the Pacific Ocean. The next stop would be Tokyo, Japan. The ship was headed north by northwest in a great arc which would take it near the southern tip of the Aleutian Islands. The voyage from San Francisco to Tokyo would cover 4,536 nautical miles.

It was his first trip on a large ship, and he could not believe how relaxing it was. There was absolutely nothing to do, and relatively no one to talk to. It was heaven. He found himself quickly settling into a routine of nothingness. He would arise early, shower, dress and make his way to one of the open decks. There he would watch the sunrise. After that, he would go to breakfast. Although he envisioned prolific progress on a book, he'd done very little writing since boarding the ship in Long Beach.

Shipboard food was nothing to write home about. It was a strange combination of German and Philippine cuisine. Although all of the officers were German, most of the crew were Kirabati or Philippine. The chef had to keep two entirely different nationalities and cultures satisfied. Jack often wondered how he came up with the strange mixtures he did.

One morning, early in the trip, and supposedly in his honor, the steward announced that the morning breakfast was, "American Cowboy." Normally, Jack would just say "Yes please" or nod an assent, not wanting to hear a detailed description of each meal. However, with the announcement of "American Cowboy Breakfast," he felt compelled to ask.

"It is your beans and tomato sauce," replied Franklin proudly. "Also egg," he added.

Jack thought it best to let it be a surprise. There was plenty of coffee on the table, and it was always excellent. Worse case scenario, he'd be doubly hungry at lunch.

"That will be fine," Jack said.

"How like it?"

"How do I like what?"

"Cowboy eggs," stated Franklin.

He settled on scrambled, and sat back with his coffee waiting for the surprise breakfast surely would be. "American Cowboy" turned out to be pork and beans, toast, sausage and eggs. The sausage was like that served at American breakfast restaurants, and unlike the big German-style sausages served at some of the other meals.

After each meal, he would return to his cabin, lay down on the sofa in his sitting room and read from one of the twenty books he brought aboard.

Three days out of Oakland, California he pulled out his laptop after reflecting on the absence of jet lag on any portion of his trip. After a few false starts, he had what would be the beginning of his first travel article from abroad. He would add something more to the story later, and e-mail the finished product upon his arrival in Hong Kong.

****

It was Lynda's third day in Palm Springs. Bill made telephone calls to his travel agent at least twice a day, sometimes just checking on her progress, and at other times calling only to express the urgency of the matter.

Although she appreciated his take charge approach, she sometimes shuddered when he would harangue the woman, using his normal foul language. It was something which sharply defined the differences between the two men in her life.

Jack had the ability to get people to like him and to get them to laugh and be at ease. He would accomplish this prior to getting down to business, prior to asking for a favor, or making a request. People rarely refused to grant him his every wish, and often times would go out of their way to accommodate him.

Bill was just the opposite. He'd get right to it without beating around the bush. He neither wanted or intended to have any kind of relationship with the person. He intimidated them from the very onset of the conversation, and he never let up. If he were to be refused, which he rarely was, he would depart with words and an attitude which would make an observer assume he actually succeeded in his quest.

Bill had just hung up on the travel agent and was irritated.

"The goddamn bitch!"

"What's the problem?" she asked.

"We gotta go back to L.A., that's the problem!"

Bill was enjoying his Palm Springs sexual romp with Lynda, and was not happy with the interruption. He was also dreading the thought of having to call his wife to give her some lame excuse about his whereabouts and what he was doing there. More often than not, his wife would get all pissy while he was in the middle of some well thought out and rehearsed explanation, and he'd end up hanging up on her. This made him think of why he'd gone to all the trouble of making up an excuse in the first place, and his thoughts were there when Lynda interrupted.

"Why do we have to go back?"

"Your passport is expired," he said.

Lynda explained for the second or third time that it wasn't expired and would not be for another three months.

"Yeah, I know all about that," he continued. "But this travel agent says the passport has to be good for six months after the start of travel. I don't know, it's some kind of stupid, fucking regulation or something. Anyway, we have to go to L.A. so you can sign some papers and get another one issued. You'll also have to take another passport photo."

"Well, when shall we go?" she asked.

"Probably the sooner the better. We'll fly instead of drive, that way we can be back here tonight."

"Maybe I should just stay in L.A. for now. You've done so much already, and things at the office are probably stacking up for you. Besides, I'm sure your wife is probably wondering where you are."

Damn the travel agent, thought Bill. "Look, I have nothing happening at work, and I can guarantee you my wife does not even care that I'm not home. I want to spend time with you while you're still here. If we have to fly to L.A. a couple of times in the next ten days, well then, so be it. But please, stay here with me. I want you. In fact, I want you right now," taking her by the hand and leading her down the hallway to the master suite.

It was late afternoon before they arrived at the Palm Springs airport, and another two hours before they found a flight to Orange County. Bill was half drunk by the time they boarded, so Lynda had to rent the car in L.A., and the travel agency was closed by the time they got there. Bill sobered up a little, they ate dinner, and later went to her apartment for a little more of what made them late in the first place.

Dan and Rebecca went out to dinner that night also. Neither of them drank much more than a glass or two of wine, and they only picked at their food.

"I really don't know what to do," said Dan. "Jack has to know, but I'm sure not looking forward to having to tell him. And, how exactly do I tell him. I have no way of calling him. I don't even know where he'll stay when he gets to Hong Kong. In fact, he told me he was unsure of where he'd stay."

"You could fly to Hong Kong."

"That's a little spendy, don't you think? Besides, it would be difficult to get any time off work now that he's gone."

"Dan, I need to ask you something," said Rebecca, changing the subject. "I know Jack is a good friend of yours, and that he considers you his friend. You know him a lot better than I. But, ah ... I guess what I'm asking here is ... well, is he the kind of guy who will give you anything? Do you really believe he'll buy us property in Montana?"

He started to reply before Rebecca interrupted him. "Really, now," she said. "Think real hard about the kind of guy he is. Do you really think he'll keep his promise, or will it just be conveniently forgotten about?"

"I have no doubt in my mind that he'll do something very nice for us. It's like, I just have this feeling he would never let me down. I know he's never made a promise to me he hasn't kept. What's more, I can't ever remember him making a promise to himself that he hasn't kept."

"Good. It's exactly the way I feel too. I just wanted to hear you voice the same thoughts. So, it really doesn't matter what it costs to fly to Hong Kong. The paper will understand, and if they don't, we'll get by somehow until Jack gets back, or until you find another job. Maybe this is just the thing we need to make us go to Montana. Just go, forget about the money, we'll survive somehow."

Finally, Dan decided he would go and see the woman at the travel agency who helped Jack make his plans. Maybe she could offer some advice on how best to contact him.

Loraine Ward was a little suspicious of Dan, waiting by the travel agency's door when she arrived the next morning, asking how he might get in contact with Jack Gillette, and saying he was from the newspaper. Yeah, but what newspaper? thought Loraine.

"You have to understand Mr. Chambers, I'm very fond of Jack, and therefore a little protective. I saw the article in the paper the other day, and saw where they published the photo of him taken at the lottery office. I didn't think they could do that without his permission."

"He told me he'd given them the okay. He wanted to put them at ease, thinking he'd show up on Monday for the news conference. Boy, I'll bet they were a little peeved when he never arrived!"

"Anyway, now that I know you're the Dan whom Jack spoke of, what's all this about getting in touch with him? I hope nothing's wrong."

"Well, yes and no. Jack spoke very highly of you. In fact, he told me that after spending twenty minutes with you he felt as though he'd known you for twenty years. Said something like, 'Good thing for her that I'm not a younger man.'"

She blushed at the comment, saying, "You and him are exactly alike, smooth talking womanizers." She laughed, and went on. "Tell me, what's going on?"

"Well, it's kind of a long story, but let's just say things concerning Jack's girlfriend are not all what they seem. I feel bad I didn't say something months ago, but I felt like it wasn't my business. Maybe it isn't now either, but I'm kinda angry about it too. So I need to get in touch with him and talk. I'd rather not do this with a letter, or by e-mail, but it looks like it may be my only option."

"The phone may be a tall order. I could reach him on the ship somehow, but only for emergencies of life and death, which this is not. Besides, he'd only get a message, which would be more impersonal than a letter or e-mail."

"What about when he gets to Hong Kong? He told me he did not have a hotel reservation. Is that true?"

"Hong Kong is a possibility. He told me not to make a reservation for him, that he wanted to play it by ear. I do know he was looking at the mansions down in the Tsim Sha Tsui area in Kowloon. I think he may change his mind after going there, but ...."

This meant nothing to Dan. He'd never been to Hong Kong, and knew nothing about it. "What about the American Embassy?" he asked.

"Oh," laughed Loraine. "Everyone always thinks the American Embassies of this world have a staff of hundreds to assist stray American's in trouble. It's far from the truth." She rummaged through Jack's file a little before continuing. "Look, I know he has to pick up his onward tickets at the tour agency in Hong Kong. People will be fluent in English there, thanks to the many years of British presence. I'll e-mail the tour company with instructions for him to contact you by phone. I'll stress that it's not an emergency, but that it is important. I don't want to alarm him too much."

Dan was happy and relieved to have Loraine's help. He had a feeling he would need more of it before this adventure was over. Jack will be okay, he thought. I won't let him hang up until I'm sure he's all right.

****

While Jack was sailing across the ocean on a ship which rode steady in all kinds of weather, Lynda was having a rough time of it. While Jack had the advantage of being weighted down by 4642 containers, each the size of a truck trailer, Lynda was weighted down by Bill and poor planning.

As soon as they arrived at the travel agency things began to go wrong. The agent had contacted a number of different freighter companies, trying to get passage to Hong Kong. The only one she found was an older ship which would first go to Vancouver B.C., then to Vladivostok, and onward to Hong Kong. It would be a journey of approximately 40 days.

With this news, Bill hit the ceiling. As he continually berated the woman, Lynda thought how she would have told him to take his precious account somewhere else. At Bill's insistence, the agent showed them a computer printout which listed freighters accepting passengers, and any sailing to Hong Kong. All of the freighters other than the one sailing to Vladivostok were not scheduled to leave the west coast for another month.

Things were beginning to calm down, when Bill inquired about other passengers.

"Well, no sir," said the agent. "At present, it appears she'll be the only passenger. Of course, that may change, and ...."

"What?" yelled Bill. "You mean she has to be alone on that goddamn tub for 40 days? What's she suppose to do with all her time, fish?"

Lynda couldn't take anymore. She appreciated Bill taking charge of things, but at the moment thought she'd be better off without him. She walked away from the counter and slowly, like a punch drunk fighter, stumbled to a small lobby area, slumping down in an over-stuffed chair. She was still close enough to hear Bill harass and berate the poor woman.

A few minutes later, Bill took a seat beside her. "Maybe, I should just get an airline ticket and fly to Hong Kong," she injected quickly, not wanting to have to hear any more, or give him a chance to start ranting and raving again. He was calm for the moment, and she wanted to keep him that way. "He'll understand," she added, knowing Jack would, but wondering just the same whether she would ever see a 15 million dollar check written out to her.

It would not be unlike him to just write her a check for a couple of million and call it a consolation prize. But what was silently worrying her was that it might take time to write the check. Jack could conceivably procrastinate for weeks or even months. With each passing day, there was the threat of him giving the money away — giving it away at such a rate that when he finally did get around to writing her a check there would not be $50,000 left, let alone two million.

"If you fly, you violate the terms of the agreement," said Bill. His comment came out sounding whiny, and he quickly added, "You'd have absolutely no claim to anything, unless ..." He was thinking now, and most of the time, Bill was good at coming up with a solution. Lynda didn't say anything, but just waited patiently. "The numbers he played? Did he pick them himself, or did the two of you choose the numbers together?" asked Bill.

"No ... I don't know. I don't know what the winning numbers were. He could have won on a quick pick kind of ticket, or ah ... I do know he had some favorite numbers. His favorite numbers had to do with Christmas, his birthday, and the birthday of a dog he had when he was in college. Crap like that. At least that's all I know about it. I wasn't into it that much."

She paused for a moment. "Maybe I should just fly to Hong Kong, and marry him as soon as possible. That would solve everything."

Bill didn't say anything. He didn't want to look at her, so he looked away, trying to give it his best sad, "I've been fucked here," kind of look. He still hadn't found a way to get in the loop for the 15 million, but he wasn't ready to throw in the towel yet. If she got married, the whole she-bang was over and done with. As he waited for her to react to his theatrics, he wondered why he was playing this game in the first place. He didn't really need the money. It wasn't like he was living on the streets, or something.

She reached over and took his hand. "Bill, I'm sorry. This is a chance for me to have all of the things I've ever wanted. I'm not sure what to do here, but I don't want to lose this opportunity. Maybe we should wait until his first article comes out, see if it gives us some idea as to how to proceed."

"You can do whatever you want. But, I feel that time is of the essence here." He was thinking while he was talking, sort of moving on his feet. If she flew to Hong Kong, she'd have to marry the schmuck in order to get control of the money. Regardless, it left Bill on the outside, looking in.

"I think you should take the ticket on the freighter. Tough it out for a month to the tune of five hundred thousand a day. You'll get to Hong Kong and find him rather quickly. I can't imagine him wanting to be away from you for very long ... after a month he'll of had his fill of being without you."

She squeezed his hand a little harder with that comment, and Bill, ad libing, forged ahead. "You'll get the fifteen million, and you won't have to be tied down to marriage. Believe me, it's no fun. In fact, this whole thing has kind of spurred me to do something about my situation. It's always been a money thing. The bitch will try to get every penny I have, that's a fact if there ever was one."

"Maybe you're right," said Lynda, ignoring his future financial woes.

She could imagine herself married to Jack, and often pictured it as something which would be a happy and pleasant experience. She could see the split-level house and the kids, the whole family package. That was before 15 million dollars was stirred into the mix, however. The money seemed to change her entire perspective, and all of a sudden being married to him was not the All-American dream she envisioned.

At the moment, sitting in the lobby with Bill, she could only see herself as Jack's unhappy, unfulfilled wife — stuffing hundred dollar bills underneath the sofa in order to squirrel away some dough before her husband gave it all away.

"Let's go," she said, starting to get up while stilling holding his hand.

At first, Bill thought she wanted to leave the office and go get a drink or something. It would give him a little more time to come up with a solution with some kind of benefit for himself.

"Tell your agent I can either write her a check, or put it on a Visa card," she said.

The woman took her credit card and recorded the numbers. She gave Lynda a receipt and a voucher which stated the name of her ship and its sailing time. She told her she would have everything together by 4 p.m., and instructed them to return at that time.

With the receipt and voucher in hand, they made their way to another office to take care of her passport. It had to be renewed, but could not be processed on such short notice without proof of an onward ticket.

They were both quiet as they drove to the Regional Passport Office on Wilshire Blvd. Lynda was quietly contemplating Bill's assistance throughout this ordeal. Despite all of his help, she now was wondering if there was a way she could ask him to sit in the car while she handled the passport proceedings.

The travel office was the world of private enterprise. The customer was always right, and it was situations like this is where Bill was at his best. He truly believed he was always right.

The passport office was another matter. They were bureaucrats, seeing everything in black and white. Those coming to see them were not haughty, privileged customers, but merely, lowly citizens. She knew how to deal with these people, but somehow she did not see the bureaucrats being bullied by a demanding trial attorney.

Bill was silent for other reasons. He had no idea what he was doing here, driving around L.A., when he should be working. He glanced over at Lynda a couple of times during the drive, and wondered how this woman had somehow seemed to corner the pussy market.

Bill was also preoccupied with thoughts of 15 million dollars, and how he might get a piece of it. He kept telling himself he didn't really need the money, and that the entire escapade was merely a game. The dough would come in handy though, as he would be able, courtesy of the lottery, to file for divorce without fear of being left destitute by his wife's greed.

Bill glanced over at Lynda. He was obsessed with her. He was obsessed with being around her. Christ, he thought, I'm old enough to be her father. The thought didn't have time to linger very long, as he pulled into the parking lot.

There was a gate at the entrance to the lot, and it stood slightly ajar, as though inadvertently left open. Bill simply drove around it and whipped the car into the first parking space available, one reserved for the handicapped.

Lynda was about to say something, but before she could speak and before Bill could turn off the car ignition, a man tapped lightly on the driver's side window. Bill fumbled for the unfamiliar button to lower the window of the rental car, locking the doors with a resounding click, then unlocking them, and finally lowering the window.

"You can't park here, sir," said the security guard.

Unlike many security guards, this guy didn't look like a cheap imitation of a cop. He looked like a real cop. In fact, he looked like a cop who'd been a Marine drill sergeant.

"You need a pass to come through the gate, sir," the drill sergeant-cop added.

"Then why the fuck don't you close the gate!" Bill barked back.

Lynda leaned forward a little so she could see the face of the guard, and hopefully intervene on what might become an ugly standoff.

"Back the car up!" exclaimed the guard. "There's parking on the street, and another lot across the street. "Do it now!"

"Fucking Nazi's," he muttered. "Give em a little power and they think they're the King of fuckin' Siam."

He backed the car up, exited the parking lot with a tiny, protesting squeak of the tires, and parked in the street. She knew Bill was angry. He didn't like to lose an argument or a confrontation. He also believed none of the rules or regulations of everyday life applied to him. She saw her opening and acted.

"Listen, you've been a very good boy today, and I'll give you a nice big reward tonight. But, while I'm inside, why don't you go find yourself a martini. You've not had one all day. The only thing I ask is, don't drink all the gin, save some for me. I'll meet you here in one hour."

"What if you have some problems with them," he asked, a little feebly. He didn't really want to go in and hassle with these assholes, especially if they were anything like the Nazi guard in the parking lot.

"Don't worry. I'll be just fine. Go get yourself a drink, and be back here in a hour," she replied, leaning over to kiss him on the cheek.

The kiss was a spontaneous act which surprised her. She'd never shown affection for him in public, those acts reserved for the bedroom of her apartment and the house in Palm Springs. Even holding hands in a public place made her nervous. As she got out of the car, she wondered if this show of public affection was because Jack was far away at sea, or was it plainly what it was, an act of affection.

Government offices are characteristically staffed by old men and middle aged women with the demeanor of a battleship. As she walked into the office, she prepared herself for dealing with these types of people, and was therefore caught off guard when a man her age approached the counter. He was dressed casually, but neatly, and in many ways reminded her of Jack.

Although there were rules and regulations to follow, the young man was extremely helpful, and by the end of the process, she would not have been surprised if he'd asked her for a date.

"I have to ask," he said. "You stated your trip was not business related ... why the hurry to renew your passport for travel?"

"Do you ever read the *South Beach Register*, a small, south L.A. newspaper? Well, you should pick up a copy on Saturday. I have this friend who has given me a challenge to follow him on a trip, and the challenge requires I never get on an airplane. There'll be an article on it in Saturday's edition. It should explain the whole thing."

"That's so cool. He's a lucky man."

She walked out of the building ready for a martini, and with the promise her passport would be ready to pick up the following Monday. Bill was waiting for her, and although she didn't ask, she assumed he'd never left.

They drove directly to the airport, and were having a drink there before flying back to Palm Springs. Bill could tell something was on Lynda's mind, but he was too busy with his own thoughts to explore it.

"Do you think he knows about us," asked Lynda, out of the blue. She held her martini glass before her mouth, the level of its contents all the way to the rim, and she stuck her tongue out slightly, tasting the gin as it rested against the edge of the glass. After taking a sip, she continued. "I mean, I haven't gotten any flowers from him in a month or so."

Bill was just beginning to take a drink, and for a second thought he might choke. "Um, well ... I don't know. I suppose it's possible, but he sure hasn't heard it from me."

She glared at him for a moment. "You haven't been telling all your lawyer friends about us, have you?"

"No dear, I have not," he replied. In truth, he had told everyone at the country club who would listen, but doubted those people knew someone like Jack, or someone in his circle of acquaintances. "And," he added, "You've been getting flowers, they've just been from me instead of from Jack." He laughed nervously at the remark, something he instantly knew was a stupid comment to make. Lynda was smart, and it wouldn't take much to figure out what Bill had done. Why give her clues, he chastised himself silently.

"I haven't gotten any flowers from you this week."

"I'll buy you some right now." He started to get up, but she touched his arm and laughing, motioned for him to sit.

"I'll buy you anything you want. All you have to do is tell me what it is." He paused a moment, and took a drink. Quickly taking a second shot of courage, he plowed forward. "What would you say if I told you I'm going to divorce my wife?"

"I guess the first thing that comes to my mind is what's taken you so long?"

"No, I'm serious. You have to go and do this game for your dough. But, when you get back, if ... well, if I was divorced by then ..." He let his words tail off there, and when he sensed she was thinking of the possibilities and not quickly dismissing his words, he continued.

"Listen, the bottom line is this. I don't want to lose you. I enjoy your company too much. Maybe, for me ... well, maybe for me it's been too good of a thing. Up until now, I'd see you five days a week at work, and we'd be together there. I probably took things for granted, and so nothing on my side of the personal-life-equation was solved. I just let things be, and probably would have continued being comfortable with a status quo arrangement."

Lynda could easily see where the conversation was headed, but saw no reason for interrupting it.

"I know the money will give you the freedom to do the things you want to do. That's good. You should do anything you want to do." Bill knew his next words could be accepted or flatly rejected. He paused and took another sip of his drink.

"But, you have to do those things with someone, and I know you're not into doing things by yourself. You've already told me the thought of traveling by yourself, especially this crazy trip across the ocean, is not especially pleasing to you.

"I also know you're not the kind who wants to pay someone else's way all the time. And, that's what you'll be doing with ninety-nine percent of all the men you meet. Oh Christ, I know ... they might have a good job and all that shit, but how many guys will have the fifteen million cushion you have."

Bill let his words sink in a bit. And, he knew it was exactly what was happening by the way Lynda was acting. She still hadn't said anything in reply, and hadn't rolled her eyes like she was always doing when she thought he was full of shit.

The cocktail waitress walked by then, acting like they weren't even there. Her big ass almost knocked over Bill's drink, and he was about to yell at her, when Lynda spoke to her softly, telling her to bring them another round. She hadn't asked him if he wanted another, just ordered one for each of them. He saw it as a omen, and a green light to continue.

"Bill," she said, interrupting and waiting just a moment until the waitress was out of earshot. "Bill, I don't know what I'm going to do. With each day I spend with you, I find myself a little more detached from Jack. However, once he and I are together, the opposite may become true. I really do love him, you know."

"I know you do," lied Bill.

"But, I may go off by myself for awhile. Not away exactly, but here in California somewhere. Just do some things for myself. Buy some things, ah, I don't know, maybe even buy a house of my own."

"Those are things you should do. Buy things, go shopping, buy a house and decorate it yourself. You've got a talent for that, I've seen it. When we moved the law office upstairs two years ago, you made the interior design guys look like shit.

"However, the question I'm asking you is who will you be sharing this with, and if it's what's his name, would he appreciate the things you want ... better yet, would he even want the things you want?"

"I'm not as material as you're making me out to be."

"I know you're not. But, you don't want to live on a farm either. Didn't you tell me once that he often fantasized about buying a small farm? I really don't picture you milking cows, and shit like that."

Their drinks came, and they drank and waited for their flight's boarding to be announced in relative silence. Lynda commented on this or that, but essentially, her words told Bill the subject of divorce and the two of them being together was closed.

They had just taken their seats in first class, the only way Bill would ever fly, when she leaned over and kissed him lightly on the cheek. "Get your divorce. If it turns out it's only for your benefit, well then ... it's still a good thing. When I get back, we'll see. I don't know what will happen, and I really don't know how I'll feel."

"That's fine. I can live with that. But, there is one thing I want you to do," he replied.

She looked at him, and he turned in his seat a bit to face her. "I want you to give me a copy of his letter and his itinerary. In fact, I would like you to give me copies of all of his correspondence on this matter. If he tries to screw you out of this deal, we'll ... I want you to be ready for that. As far as I'm concerned, and I believe the court would back me up on this, you have first claim on half of the jackpot. He's promised you that, and you have made sacrifices and compensation in the form of time, money, and career to abide by his instructions. Trust me on this."

****

Jack was comfortable on the *Hanjin Amsterdam*. In fact, he could not have been more comfortable had he been at home in his own apartment. His bed was soft, the entire cabin was carpeted, and there was a desk and comfortable chair to sit in. The ship, built in Korea in 1999, was far from being a rust bucket.

When the designers were putting the finishing touches on the plans for the *Hanjin Amsterdam*, the ship promised to be one of the largest container ships ever built. Construction had barely began when another, even larger container ship was proposed from a competing shipyard. By the time Jack's ship slipped into the water at Pusan, South Korea, it's rating in size was diminished to that of a second tier of gross tonnage ships.

Another ship, tied to a pier in Oakland, California, was inferior to the *Hanjin Amsterdam* in every respect. It was half of the size of Jack's ship, and was built in 1975. Designed to carry a total of four passengers, it rarely carried any.

While Jack was quartered in the Owner's Suite, the ship which would carry Lynda didn't even have such a luxury. The two passenger cabins on the *Santiago Mariner* each had two single bunks, a toilet and shower, a sitting area with a small sofa, a chair and a writing table. There was no elevator. The ship smelled bad. Rust and the fumes of diesel fuel lingered about the passageways and decks.

Given the opportunity to choose between the *Hanjin Amsterdam* and the *Santiago Mariner*, Jack might well have chosen the latter. The nostalgic images of the *Santiago Mariner* would have appealed to him. He would have seen a wonderful, old tramp steamer while most sane individuals would have seen a disaster waiting to happen.

It was fortunate Lynda did not have the opportunity to see both ships side by side, and have a choice of which one she would board. While she may have chosen not to board either, she would have definitely not chosen the *Santiago Mariner*.

As she started up the gang way of her home for the next thirty-three days, she felt she was making the mistake of her life. Although she wanted to turn around and run, she found one foot involuntarily stepping in front of the other. After the ugly, little oriental man who showed her to her cabin left, she abruptly sat on the edge of the small, four-inch thick mattress of the single bunk and cried her eyes out.

Between sobs, she kept telling herself it wasn't too late to get off. She'd walked to her cabin as if in a coma, following the little man like a sheep going to slaughter, and all through a labyrinth of passageways. She could somehow find her way to the gangway and the dock — she could jump in the bay if necessary — anything to get off this dump.

Something however, kept her sitting on the edge of the bed. She knew the voyage was something she needed to do, but at the moment, she estimated she was earning every penny of that fifteen million, seventy-six thousand, six hundred and twenty-five dollars.

There were other things which would make Lynda's trip more spartan and less enjoyable than Jack's. While Jack carried a large box of books and his laptop aboard, Lynda brought nothing other than clothes and toiletries. She could not remember having a concrete reason for including it in her packing, but she also packed a small notebook she normally carried in a briefcase she took to work. It followed her everywhere, from home to work, from work to court, and to all of the meetings with Bill and his clients. It seemed natural to have it along.

While both ships were equipped with an officer's lounge, the one on Jack's was far superior. He made a number of trips to it over the course of twenty-one days, and never once encountered another soul. The lounge had a large television and a VCR. A cabinet nearby was filled with the latest video releases, while a bookcase along one wall was stocked with various fiction paperbacks. It was warm and cozy, the floor covered with a rich carpet.

Lynda's first trip to the Officer's Lounge nearly stopped her from ever returning. It too had a bookcase with paperbacks, but the very first one she picked up was entitled, *Jeff and Mom.* The front cover sported a picture of what was presumed to be Jeff, attempting to breast feed off his mother. While Jeff looked to be around twenty-five years of age, his mother may have been all of twenty-eight. Later trips to the lounge would prove the book was not indicative of the genre available.

Both ships were, in a sense, moving work stations. The officers and crew had little time for chitchat while at sea, and the demands when in port were even greater. Despite the congeniality and politeness of the officers, Lynda put the double locks on her cabin door to good use.

Four hours after she started crying, she felt the ship begin to move. After looking out the small, dirty, porthole window of her cabin for several minutes, she abruptly decided to go outside. This decision was not made for the sake of having a better view, or to take a few memorable snapshots of the Oakland-San Francisco Bay. The sole purpose was to get some fresh air.

Unfortunately, it was an unseasonably warm day in the Bay Area, and there was absolutely no wind. The smell of diesel fuel was everywhere, the lack of a breeze seemed to allow each and every fume to enter Lynda's nostrils, and when she leaned over the rail and peered down at the water, she noticed a steady stream of water gushing from the side of the ship just above the water-line. She heard a seagull squawk angrily as it flew above her.

It was the last thing she vividly remembered before being sick, and simultaneously wondered where the water exiting the side of the ship was coming from, and where exactly was the bird flying over her head. Was it just excess water left over from something? Of even greater concern, was it water being pumped out in response to having gushed in from a leak? At the same time, she fully expected an accompanying splat of warm goo on her head, deposited courtesy of her feathered friend.

She could not tell how long she leaned over the railing, her vomit gently spilling down to mix with the water puking out of the side of the ship, all of it coming together in the bay. It seemed like an eternity. When she finally decided she could somehow stumble back to her cabin without messing up the hallway and her clothes, the ship slowly passed under the Golden Gate Bridge, and began to head out into open waters. The next stop would be Vancouver, British Columbia, and then the ship would churn on to Vladivostok, Russia.

By the following morning, she felt like she could stand up without getting sick, and she even ventured a look through the grimy porthole from time to time. But, that was the limit of her activities.

On the third day at sea, a walk to the open deck felt like being freed from a five year stretch in prison, her small cabin and sickness having taken its toll. She ate a meal quickly that day, and hurrying back to her cabin as fast as she could, was relieved the food stayed in her stomach. She told herself if she got sick again before reaching Vancouver, she would treat it as an omen the trip was not meant to be. She would get off and fly to Hong Kong, taking her chances with Jack being disappointed.

As luck would have it, or more appropriately, as bad luck would have it, she did not get seasick again. The ship tied up to a smelly pier in Vancouver, where no signs of civilization other than those related to industry were visible. Two days later, the heavily loaded and tired *Santiago Mariner* once again made its way to the open sea, and began a long, wallowing, fifteen day journey to Vladivostok.

The sea was very calm on the first, second and third day out of Vancouver. She did not get sick. In fact, she even commented to herself one morning, that she probably had gotten her "sea legs."

She slept a lot. She found some books, and although they were not intellectually challenging, they weren't pornographic. She wasn't particularly happy at this juncture of her life, but she had to admit things looked bright on the horizon.

With each day away from Bill, she found herself feeling more and more independent. She missed Jack, but it was difficult for her to put her thoughts into words, or something she could understand when she thought of him. He was incredibly good to her, and one of her problems was reconciling in her mind just where and when she started to take him for granted.

Lynda awoke rather abruptly in the early morning hours of the fourth day out of Vancouver. Her room was dark except for a dim, night light shining from near the entrance to her bathroom door. At first, she was certain that someone was in her room, and she started to cry out to whoever had pushed her out of bed and onto the floor. She was on her knees, and pushed herself up to a standing position.

She stood for no more than a second before the invisible intruder pushed her back towards the bed, her shin hitting the wooden edge of the small bunk's frame. Her body only momentarily touched the mattress before crashing into the wall on the other side, and falling back to the bed's surface.

The two bunks were anchored to the floor, and on one side, to the wall. A small three-foot space separated the two sleeping units. She grabbed the edge of the bunk, anticipating another attack. She rolled hard against the wall, as the bed seemed to want to throw her in the opposite direction and onto the floor.

"Oh no!" she cried out. "Please God ... no!"

She could have dealt with an intruder. She considered herself reasonably tough, or at least thought she could be if the need arose. She could have kicked him right in the balls, drug him down the hallway — and although it might have been difficult for her to lift him over the railing, she would have somehow managed — thereby dropping the sorry bastard into the sea. But, there was no intruder. Lynda was convinced the ship was sinking.

She noticed how the weather had become colder with every day they put between themselves and Vancouver. Were there icebergs in these waters? She had no idea. Maybe they hit another ship? Whatever it was, she could only hope and pray it was something stationary, like land. Like a big chunk of land. Then, she could just climb off the ship and be done with the whole affair.

But, the ship was not sinking, and in fact was weathering the sea quite well for the rusted, old hulk of a ship that she was. The Captain had made sure everything was tied down securely, and that all of the hatches and doors were tightly closed. He briefly considered mentioning the approaching storm to his one and only passenger, but felt it might only alarm her. He was aware of her sea sickness after leaving Oakland, and had given her some motion-sickness pills when they were docked in Vancouver.

Previous conditions were like sailing on a small sea, with only light swells and gentle winds. This was a sea, the Captain thought to himself as he repositioned himself in the elevated, arm chair that was the Captain's Chair on the bridge.

Lynda wasn't sick, yet. She was too scared to be sick. After a few minutes of rolling around on the bed and holding on for dear life, she realized the ship was still moving, although slowly, and more importantly was still afloat.

She managed to turn on the lights, using the switch located near the head of her bed. That done, she could identify the items of her purse which were scattered on the floor. A tube of lipstick rolled back and forth in the space between the two bunks. She quickly extinguished the garish light as it only seemed to heightened the sense of motion.

The captain had mentioned that everyone gets seasick at some point. He'd laughed and told her he became quite ill one time on a small fishing boat belonging to his brother. His sibling never let his salty, seasoned sailor of a brother forget the episode, the Captain telling her it was an ugly combination of alcohol, food and diesel fumes which instigated the attack.

She remembered his words now, as she lay there praying this was all a bad dream. She also remembered the Captain giving her some pills, and she had the good sense to find them. She moved a plastic waste basket, previously put to use, into a position near her bed.

Lynda found herself shivering, and pulled the covers up around her tightly. She lay on her back, her arms spread out like a child laying in the snow and making an angel's wings with the flapping motions of the arms. She grasped each side of the small bed and held on for dear life. She closed her eyes and tried desperately to think of nice things.

It all lasted fifteen minutes. Then, curled up on the floor, the blankets pulled as tightly as she could over her shoulders and her body braced between the two twin beds, she wretched over and over down the front and side of her pajama top and close to, but not directly, into the waste basket.

****

Sam Bryant would not normally take domestic jobs. The clients were either outraged, paranoid, or a strange combination of both. If they thought their spouse was cheating on them, and hours and hours of surveillance produced no proof of infidelity, you were a shitty private investigator. If you went to the client and told them their spouse was in bed with two, thirteen-year-old's, the client would become incensed, and rant and rave.

"Not my husband!" or, "Not my wife!" they'd scream.

Again, you failed because you were a shitty investigator. It was a no-win, no-win situation.

Sam knew this case was different the minute he picked up the phone. First of all, he wasn't dealing with the client directly. If the client could afford an attorney, they could usually afford an investigator too. Just to make sure, he thought of an excuse as he listened to the opening pleasantries of the lawyer.

He could insist the law firm pay him directly, and not the client. This move in itself was not without flaws, because some attorneys were no better at paying their bills than the deadbeats they represented.

"I got your name from James Gardner, of Crompton, Barkovic and Fairchild," said the attorney, who introduced himself as Charles Rogers. He was getting down to business now that the small talk was completed.

"Mr. Gardner told me you've done a substantial amount of work for him and other members of the firm. He also told me you're discrete, and that you go about your business quietly and confidentially."

Sam thanked him for the compliment, if that's what it was. He didn't consider himself any more discrete than anyone else, but it hadn't been a question, so why answer it like one.

"I have a client who is in a very delicate situation. She does not want to anger the other party in this matter, as she is afraid he may become violent. Therefore, it is extremely important the party under surveillance does not become aware they are being investigated."

He paused a moment for Sam to respond that he understood, and continued. "Both my client and I want proof of infidelity and discrepancies within this marriage. As you well know, the State of California is a no-fault divorce state. We aren't required to have proof of infidelity to file for divorce. However, there is a great deal of money and property involved here, and my client wants to be sure the settlement is fair and that she gets her fair share."

Right, Sam thought. Everybody wants to make sure they get their share. And, God forbid should the settlement not be fair. Life wasn't fair, get over it!

He let the attorney ramble on for awhile, telling him the spouse in question was also an attorney. Sam's ears perked up a bit at this, becoming even more curious when the subject was said to be prominent and well known in the L.A. area.

"You ever watch the Angels games?" Rogers asked. "Well, he's right there in the front row behind home plate."

That conversation took place two years ago. Sam had agreed to take the job, thinking it would be an easy grand or two, and he desperately needed the money. At the time of his first conversation with counselor Rogers, Sam did not mention that his van — his sole means of transportation — was leaking oil and in danger of blowing up the next time he backed out of the driveway. Sam figured he could borrow a car from a friend, and later get his van repaired with the money made on the caper. He probably wouldn't have any dough left over, but wasn't it him who just said, "life isn't fair?"

And so, two years ago, Sam agreed to take the job. He'd checked to make sure his fees would be paid on a timely basis, and literally dropped the phone when Rogers told him they would advance him two thousand dollars, and settle up the account every thirty days.

Sam earned the money. Just two months into the project, he followed the subject to Palm Springs. When the man went to a private residence, Sam became intrigued.

Rogers knew the client's husband had an office in Palm Springs, and was not surprised when Sam had told him where he was. Sam didn't tell Rogers he was at a private residence. Instead, he went to the County Courthouse, and spent the afternoon searching through the property records.

If you tried to reach William Hugh Davidson by telephone in Palm Springs, the phone would ring at the office of Baxter and Edwards. Al Baxter and James Edwards were attorneys of little note or merit. They would tell you their specialty was in the field of personal injury, but in fact, they would take just about any case which came down the pike.

When William Davidson approached them one sunny day with an offer to share their office, they were thrilled to have such a well known personal injury attorney in their midst, and silently hoped a record-setting settlement might come their way as a result of the association.

Davidson was not concerned with the well-being of Baxter and Edwards. He simply wanted a place to hang his hat. Any telephone calls to Davidson in Palm Springs would now be answered by a bona fide secretary for a bona fide law firm.

If someone, (especially his wife), asked for him, the secretary would ask their name, at the same time telling them she was unsure as to whether Mr. Davidson was in the office. She would either transfer the call to Davidson's telephone at his residence, or say he was temporarily unable to take their call.

A smart private investigator would have unearthed this information in an hours time, but Sam was not the brightest star in the P.I. world. It took him all afternoon, and the better part of a six pack of Amstel beer.

He was eager to learn more about the owner of the house where Davidson was staying. Property records identified the owner as George Gorman. While the California Department of Motor Vehicles were of no help, a friend in the San Jose Police Department was.

Apparently, Mr. Gorman was represented by Davidson in several matters, ranging from drunk driving, to fraud and racketeering. When Sam followed up by talking with a few neighbors around the Palm Springs address, he hit the jackpot with his second inquiry.

A talkative neighbor lady, and a good friend of the late Mrs. Gorman, told Sam the house was leased to an attorney who lived in L.A. She went on to tell him that Gorman was heavily indebted to this attorney for keeping him out of jail. She went on some more about how Gorman, despite protests from his poor, sickly wife, gave the house to the attorney on some kind of a long-term, lease option deal.

And, she went on even more about how the attorney used the residence for a whore house. She would have continued had Sam not ended the conversation, backed down the sidewalk, and sped away to the relative peace and quiet of the nearest bar.

Charles Rogers, the attorney, was ecstatic upon hearing the news. Ever since then, Sam rode the gravy train assignment of tailing William Davidson.

He saw a number of women pass in and out of the Palm Springs residence, as well as the apartment Davidson openly leased in L.A. None was finer than the current one, and Davidson had somehow managed to engage in repeat performances, the two of them becoming more brazen with each passing day.

Although Sam was content, and could have continued milking this assignment for years to come, Mrs. William Hugh Davidson was not. Her patience with her husband had grown thin a long time ago. She was out for blood, and ready to deliver the opening punch.

8

On the eighteenth day of the voyage, Jack sat at the writing desk in his cabin and made entries in his trip journal. Past ports of call were Oakland, California; Tokyo and Osaka, Japan; and Pusan, South Korea. In two days, the ship would dock in Hong Kong.

He timed the loading in Osaka, Japan, and found it took an average of one minute for the overhead crane to pick up a container and set it in place on the ship. Increased operating costs dictated the loading and unloading to begin the minute the ship tied up to a dock, whether it be two in the afternoon, or two in the morning.

Loraine spoke of her days in Hong Kong in the late 1930's, and how she watched spindly-legged Chinese men and women carrying large burlap sacks of rice and other goods up a wooden gang-plank and onto a ship. She described the scene as being like a stream of ants, steadily moving on and off of the ship, back and forth, never stopping or slowing down until the task was completed.

Today's world of port loading and unloading is totally different. One, or possibly two men are stationed on the ground, a ground which destroys the image of a creaking, wooden pier, so narrow that carts, wagons, or small trucks must gingerly make their way past each other for fear of tumbling over the edge and into the water. Instead, the area is a vast, paved parking lot that ends at the waters edge, the water abruptly deep enough to accommodate large ships.

Semi-trucks quickly maneuver to a position parallel of the ship, and directly under the crane. The crane either lifts a container off or sets one on a truck. The truck then speeds away to fetch another or deposit the incoming container in a storage area.

There is little, if any time for a passenger to go ashore. The difficulties of customs and passport control compounds the problem, and should a passenger be late returning, they would find themselves standing on an empty pier, watching as the ship sailed silently and without conscience, out of the harbor.

Jack was anxious to meet up with Lynda, thinking his original plan to meet her in either Shanghai or Beijing was too far in the future. He would have three days in Xian, China, which was the sight of the ruins of the Terracotta Warriors.

With luck, she would only be about ten days behind him, and would pick up a few days on him by not having the extended stay he was scheduled to have in Hong Kong.

He opened his small shoulder bag and placed his itinerary on the writing desk. Could she conceivably catch him by the time he reached Xian? He'd paid little attention to the schedule of hotels and train schedules. While he would be bound by a structured itinerary, Lynda would have the freedom to merely pass through the cities sequentially without stopping.

Jack could not have known, but he would be glad he packed an extra copy of the itinerary. After the first copy became dog-eared, tattered, and worn beyond recognition from countless foldings and unfoldings, the reserve would be put to good use. By the time he reached Helsinki, even the second copy would be ragged from wear.

Sunrise Travel
Loraine Ward — Proprietor
Russia - China Itinerary, specially prepared for Mr. Jack Gillette

14 JUNE   Prior to today you must pick up your actual train ticket for Hong Kong to Guangzhou from the local office address provided on the voucher. Make your own way to the Hong Kong train station in good time for the 9:25 AM departure of the day-express to Guangzhou (Canton). On arrival at 11:35 AM, you will be met by an English-speaking guide and taken by private car on a sightseeing excursion around town. Lunch is included. In the late afternoon you will be brought back to the station for the 6 PM departure of the overnight train to Guilin. You have one place in a 4-berth sleeper for the journey.

15 JUNE   Arrive Guilin approximately 7:30 AM. You will be met and transferred to the hotel GUANGUANG to freshen up. Then you will be taken on the Li River cruise excursion.

16 JUNE   Free day until the transfer to the train station for the 4:24 PM departure of the train to Xian. You have 1 place in a 4-berth compartment for the journey.

17 JUNE   Arrive Xian at 8:58 PM. You will be met and transferred by car to the TANGCHENG hotel.

18 JUNE   Full day sightseeing tour including the Terracotta Warriors, Bampo Neolithic Village, Huaqing Hot Springs, and the Big Wild Goose Pagoda. Lunch is included.

19 JUNE   Free day until the transfer to the train station for train #140 to Shanghai, departing at 6:22 PM You have 1 place in a 4-berth compartment for the journey.

20 JUNE   Arrive Shanghai approximately 11:25 AM,where you will be met and transferred to the hotel SHANGHAI.

21 JUNE   Free day.

22 JUNE   Evening transfer to the station for train #14 to Beijing departing at 6:00 PM. You have 1 place in a 4-berth compartment for the journey.

23 JUNE   Arrive Beijing approximately 8:00 AM. You will be met and transferred to the hotel XINQIAO.

24-27 JUNE   Free days in Beijing.

27 JUNE   Early morning transfer to the central railroad station for the 7:40 AM departure of Chinese International train #23. You will cross the border into Mongolia during the night. You have 1 place in a 2-berth compartment for the journey.

28 JUNE   On the train as you traverse the Gobi desert and the Mongolian grasslands. Arriving in Ulan Bator at approximately 1:10 PM, you will be met and transferred to your hotel, the BAYANGOL.

29 JUNE   Today you will be taken into the countryside to the GER CAMP at Terelj where you will spend two nights in a traditional ger, (accommodations may be shared by up to 4 people, or if space is available, you may be on your own).

30 JUNE   Free day at the GER CAMP.

01 JULY   Return to Ulan Bator and one more night in BAYANGOL hotel.

02 JULY   Free day until evening transfer to the train station for the 9:00 PM departure of train #264 to Russia. You have 1 place in a 4-berth compartment for the journey.

03 JULY   On board the train crossing from Mongolia to Russia you will have a chance to view rural life and the fascinating scenery in this remote area.

04 JULY   Cross into Russia and travel along the shores of Lake Baikal into Irkutsk for a scheduled arrival at 8:30 AM local time. You will be met and taken to your homestay accommodations.

05 JULY   Free day on your own to enjoy Irkutsk.

06 JULY   Today you will have an excursion to beautiful Lake Baikal and the fishing village of Listvyanka by private car with your own English speaking guide.

07 JULY   Transfer to the train station in Irkutsk for departure of the Trans-Siberian Express train #1 at 3:23 PM local time. You have 1 place in a 2-berth compartment for the journey.

08-10 JULY   On board the train crossing from Asia to Europe.

10 JULY   Arrive in Moscow at 5:00 PM local time. You will be met and transferred to the downtown hotel INTOURIST.

11,12 JULY   Free days on your own to look around the sights and museums of the Russian capital.

13 JULY   Evening transfer to the train station for the 11:55 PM departure of the famous "Red Arrow Express" to St. Petersburg. You have 1 place in a 2-berth compartment for the journey.

14 JULY   Approximately 8:25 AM arrival in St. Petersburg. You will be met and transferred to the centrally located MOSCVA hotel.

15,16,17 JULY   Three free days for exploring this fascinating city on your own.

18 JULY   Transfer to the train station for the day-sitting train #35 to Helsinki, departing at 5:15 PM and arriving at 9:30 PM local time.
*** End Services ***

There was a myriad of ship traffic as the *Hanjin Amsterdam* entered the harbor of Hong Kong. The harbor scene was all of what Jack imagined and dreamed of. Freighters, with small boats and tugs scurrying around them like flies around the head of a cow, were everywhere. It looked exotic, and even smelled exotic. Everything was right except for the weather.

At first, he thought it must be a passing storm, something out of the ordinary — a freak occurrence of nature. When the Philippine steward, Franklin, brought Jack his final bundle of clean clothes from the ship's laundry, Jack asked about the conditions. He was humored by the man's response, talking as if the answer was common knowledge to everyone.

"It is monsoon season, Mr. Gillette," said Franklin. When a smiled played across Jack's face, and he said nothing, the steward continued, correctly reading Jack's thoughts.

"You did not know, sir? This time of year for monsoons. Do not worry, sir. It rain only for a time, then it stop. It is warm," he added almost as an afterthought, hoping to make Jack happy with the forecast.

It was early morning, with the sun, (if it could be seen through the pouring rain and gray clouds), barely over the horizon. The ship was being slowly maneuvered into position alongside the dock, where once again, the loading and unloading process would begin.

Jack was anxious to go ashore, but knew it was way too early to secure lodging. Had the weather been decent, he could have found a cafe or a place to hang out until mid morning, but with this weather he would be soaked after walking a mere twenty yards. He wondered why he failed to pack an umbrella. He left his room for the galley, and the assurance of finding some hot coffee.

"Franklin, what is the procedure here? Am I suppose to see the Captain before leaving? He still has my passport."

"Oh no, no, no, sir. You just sit. I will serve you breakfast ... very good breakfast for your last meal aboard. Maybe, you wish to stay aboard and have lunch too?" asked Franklin.

"No, I want to go ashore. But Franklin, what do I do? Don't I have to go through customs or something?"

"You not worry so much, sir. I will take care of everything. Man from shipping company will come for you. He take care of every thing. You not worry. More coffee?"

After twenty-one days, Jack should have known better. The ship's officers were constantly looking at their wrist watches for any hint they might be vary- ing their routine, and took life very, very seriously. Franklin, and the mixture of Kirabati and Philippines that made up the crew, were exactly the opposite. Why concern yourself with the weather or when the ship will arrive, as nothing can be done about either.

Jack ate a good breakfast before any of the officers arrived, thanked Franklin for his services and returned to his cabin. Hours later, while gazing out one of the room's portholes at the gray, rainy skies, there was a knock at the door.

"Mr. Gillette? Excuse me for intruding upon you," said a short, pudgy, Chinese gentleman. He looked to be about seventy years old, but seemed very alert and in good health.

Shaking hands, he introduced himself as Mr. Lau. He moved to look around Jack and into the room. "I see you are packed. I have your passport, and if you are ready, I will take you ashore."

"Will all of this be going too?" asked Lau in perfect, unaccented English. He was pointing to a box of books, a small cooler, and two sweatshirts on the coffee table in the center of the sitting room.

"No, they are for the steward. He's been very good to me, and so I'd like to leave him and the crew some things."

As they left the cabin, Lau, who had removed his shoes before entering, now put them back on. Jack noticed they were rubber galoshes over dress shoes, and both were soaking wet. He made a mental note to jokingly tease Loraine for not informing him he would be visiting China during the monsoon season.

Before stepping out onto the gangway and the pouring rain, Lau produced a black umbrella he'd stashed behind some rigging. It was a cheap, black affair, recognizable the world over, and bent in several directions from the wind and countless number of foldings and unfoldings.

The umbrella, controlled by Lau, seesawed its way back and forth over their heads as they walked down the gangway and onto terra firma. Once there, they stopped while Lau waved with his free hand, and seconds later a small, black sedan pulled up.

Riding in the car, Lau explained that he worked for the shipping company on a part-time basis. He told Jack he would take him to a hotel, get him checked in, and then, they would go together to the custom and passport authorities. He asked Jack about his hotel reservation, seemingly not surprised by his answer of having none.

"I don't know, but I read about the Mansions on Nathan Street, and well, I guess I'll give it a try," said Jack.

Mr. Lau said something to the driver in Chinese, and a change of direction could be felt in the back seat as the small sedan turned abruptly in traffic.

"You should be very careful," he said, as he eyed the earmarked page in a travel guide Jack produced from his bag. "Some of these places are not safe."

Jack felt if the place was good enough for students and budget conscious travelers, it was good enough for him. The last thing he wanted was to stay in a Hilton, Sheraton, or Holiday Inn, all of which the guidebooks proclaimed Hong Kong to have. The place he selected was run by an Australian and his Chinese wife. How bad could it be? he thought.

After awhile, they reached their destination. They were on the Kowloon Peninsula, in the *Tsim Sha Tsui* area at the tip of the peninsula. All around them were shops with barkers on the sidewalk, begging and cajoling each and every passer-by to enter and see the great deals they had to offer. He guessed correctly that the area at night would be filled with hookers, and that finding a drink in a bar would not be a problem.

They went into the hallway of a building. It was dark and poorly lit. In the corner, opposite an elevator, was a small booth closed off in the front with metal gratings. Behind the gratings sat a Chinese man, watching everyone who got into or out of the lift.

They rode to the fifth floor, and Jack inquired after the Australian gentleman he had read of. He was informed by a woman who was apparently the man's wife, that he'd traveled to Sydney for a visit, but would be returning at the end of the month. Behind the woman, Jack got a glimpse of a small kitchen, where two young boys of mixed descent sat with a Chinese woman whom Jack assumed was the grandmother.

The room secured, Jack and Lau drove to customs and immigration. As they rode along, Jack wondered how he would have accomplished all of this without the help of the man now sitting beside him. Traveling by airplane, it's just a matter of following the person in front of you. Everything is mapped out, and the passenger proceeds from the protective cocoon of the plane to the insulated cocoon of being in the same circumstances and predicament as a hundred or more other people. The tourists all make their way through the bureaucracy without any independent thoughts or decision making.

They arrived at a small building near the waterfront. A waiting room accommodating about forty people looked to be full. The people waiting were all of Asian descent, and some looked as though they'd been there a long time. Some had a frightened look about them, and Jack wondered what each one's particular story might be.

Lau asked Jack for his passport and instructed him to take a seat. Instead of approaching one of the two counter windows manned by a clerk, Lau went to an entrance which led to the back of the room where several desks were occupied by customs agents. He signaled to one, and the gentlemen arose to meet him.

Jack could hear them speaking in Chinese, and after a few minutes, the agent took Jack's passport and returned to his desk. The man punched information into a computer, and picked up the telephone for a short conversation. A few minutes later, he walked back to where Lau was standing and handed him the passport. The official never looked at, or spoke to Jack. The entire process took no longer than fifteen minutes.

The next morning, Jack left the mansions looking for an internet cafe. He didn't have to go very far, as he found one less than three blocks away. He hadn't slept very well. His room was damp from the high humidity, and noisy from the traffic in the street below.

Jack reasoned he might have about two more days left in him for the "local color" of the Mansions. Lynda would have hated the place, and in fact, probably would have refused to stay there. But had she been with him, he would not have chosen such a hovel in the first place. Simply a curiosity, the name of the place alone incited his imagination.

The internet cafe he found was outfitted entirely with Mac computers. He was surprised to not find P.C's, but it was a welcome sight as it was the system he used at work. He sat down with a cup of coffee and signed in. He punched in his password and the screen came to life. He nearly choked on his coffee when he discovered 91 new messages.

Most were from strangers, readers of the *Register* who'd read his opening article. Although many were from the L.A. area, a few were from people who had read the article on the paper's web site. There were messages from Arizona, Oregon, Utah, and a couple from the East Coast. There were two messages each from Dan and Loraine, and one from Lynda. Jack decided to save those for last.

Nearing the end of the messages, he came across two which made no mention of his trip, his luck or his article. Both were names of people he did not recognize, yet both indicated they knew Lynda. He read each of them a number of times, saving the addresses as well as the messages. He made no reply to either, as he was not sure how to respond. Had there been only one, he would have dismissed it as a sick joke. But, two messages, essentially saying the same thing, made him uneasy and sick to his stomach.

He was still inclined to dismiss them as someone's weird sense of humor, when he read Dan's first message. As he read his stomach became more upset. It was vague and meandering, not the way Dan normally wrote.

... so anyway, things are fine here. Beck and I never heard from Lynda, which we found disturbing.

I know I'm a bit of a pain in the ass sometimes — and maybe I should just mind my own business. But, you are my best friend. I love you like a brother, and I'll never forget how you treated me when I was a young, innocent rookie at the <u>Register</u>. You made it so easy for me to succeed. But, I digress.

I've tried to subtlety tell you this before, and I feel like a complete prick telling you now — telling you this way. But, you're going to find out — I mean, the asshole's soon to be ex-wife even said so, (without mentioning Lynda's name, of course), in an article in the <u>Times</u>. I don't know if Lynda is coming after you or not. I'd like to think positive, that she would be up-front with you and let you get on with your life. But, my friend, Lynda is not what she seems. She is, and has been cheating on you.

Please Jack, don't be angry with me for saying this. I think you've known something was wrong for a long time. I remember last year, right after Christmas, you were in such a depressed funk. Remember, we went to the ball game and got roaring drunk afterwards? Do you remember telling me then of your suspicions? Well, they are true. She and Davidson have been seeing each other.

We've been friends for a long time. I am here for you. Rebecca and I have discussed it, and I'm ready to fly to Hong Kong as soon as I hear from you. I talked with our fearless leader/worthless editor, telling him the situation without giving him any details. He'll be pissed if I take off for a week or so, but he'll get over it.

Please call me as soon as you get this message. Don't worry about the time difference — just call. (Please — Please ... that comes from Rebecca)
Our Love,
Dan & Rebecca

Jack read the message over and over. He then went back to the two vague messages from complete strangers. The first one was short and to the point.

I hope you have a wonderful trip. But, you should be running as fast as you can. Don't let that bitch catch you. She doesn't deserve a penny.

The second message was more subtle.

You and I have never met, although I have met your girlfriend. She would not remember me, as we met in passing.

I don't want your money. I don't want you, as I have a man of my own. I just hate to see or hear of people being cheated on. Believe me when I tell you, I know exactly how it feels. I have been there.

That said, it's hard to tell you to have a wonderful trip, but I really hope you do. Be careful of who you trust and make promises to. Be careful who you love. Don't let the ones who can hurt you into your heart.

Even though we've never met, I know you deserve the best.
Love and Peace Through Jesus,
A Friend

Jack brushed away a tear that began its journey from his eye down to his cheek. That done, he brushed away another from the opposite side of his face.

His chest hurt. He had a feeling inside his stomach as though someone had poured battery acid down his throat. He'd eaten a couple of muffins at the internet cafe as he read and responded to messages. He was glad it was nothing more than muffins. He didn't think he could have held anything else down.

He sat motionless for a few moments, and absentmindedly signed out. He paid his bill in a fog, the money he'd received in exchange for traveler's checks like Monopoly script in his hands.

He began to walk back to his hovel of a room. Before he could go far, his stomach began roiling uncontrollably. He was going to get sick, and could only hope he could get back to his room before it happened. He walked faster and faster, using shorter and shorter strides as he hurried along.

He passed a sign pointing to a downstairs bar. The entire sign was in English, and the stairway, as far as Jack could see down, was well lit and clean. He abruptly turned down the stairs.

Delaney's was a clean and respectable English Pub. He headed straight for the restrooms, thankful they were as clean as the rest of the establishment. He sat and cried. He let his nerves have their way with his body. He would have let himself die there had he possessed a way to just throw a switch, a switch that would somehow cease his innate ability to breathe.

It was some time before he left the restroom. He did not intend to stop in the bar, just drift back aimlessly to his room. But it was close to the noon hour, and the place was filling up. He didn't want to be alone. Even more, he knew that to be alone would be the worst possible thing he could do.

He ordered a Guinness, and then another. With the exception of a couple of the waitresses, everyone in the bar was English, the lunch crowd made up of businessmen grousing about the stock market and the rain falling simultaneously.

Attempting to read the English-language newspaper, the *Hong Kong Standard*, the words drifted by without comprehension.

Jack watched the people enjoying their lunches. He drank another beer, and walked back up to the street. It had started to rain again, so instead of returning to his room, he went back to the internet cafe. He had not read the second message from Dan, nor the message from Loraine. He was afraid to read the message from Lynda.

It was nice to hear from Loraine, as her tone was upbeat. No comment was made of his personal life. Dan's message was simply another plea for Jack to telephone him.

He e-mailed a reply to Loraine. He intended to thank her for all of her efforts, but found himself not stopping there. He considered her a dear friend, and two sentences into the message he poured his heart out to her, explaining what he'd heard and what, even without confirmation, he knew was true.

That done, he went back to the "In Box" of his Hotmail. He clicked on Lynda's message. He took a breath and read the message.

My Dear Jack,

When I first read your e-mail I could not believe it. You always told me you would win — I feel bad that I never shared your faith in luck. You know me, I've never felt like luck played a part in life — that everything you got you worked for — that no one was ever going to give you something for free. Your message essentially put all of my theories in the trash.

I'm getting ready to go to San Francisco to catch a freighter. I'm scared and confused. I know what you are making me do is for my own betterment, and in almost every way I believe you are right. But Jack, I am also a very confused person right now. I don't know what I want, and I feel some of the things I think I want are not in my best interest. I wish you were here to straighten me out.

I know our relationship has not been the best in the last 6 to 8 months. Most of the blame, if not all, rests on my shoulders. I want things to get better for me. I want things to get better for us. I'm so down on myself right now. I could sure use your strength.

I'm not sure when I'll get to Hong Kong. The schedule of the boat is kind of confusing, but I know that I'll be well behind you. I'll look forward to being with you and having someone to talk to and see things with. You know how much I dislike being alone, so expect a good spanking when we meet!!!

Love You Much,
LT

Jack read the message over and over. He wanted to believe the messages from Dan and the two strangers were terribly wrong. He wanted to believe that if Lynda cheated on him it was an isolated and single encounter. He wanted to believe that if he just ignored the whole matter of infidelity, the problem would go away, and that when he and Lynda were reunited, things would be just like they use to be.

In his heart he knew different. Dan was correct in saying Jack knew something was wrong. Jack could sense it when he and Lynda talked, or made love, or simply rode in the car together. Without much thought as to what he would say, he punched the "Reply" icon.

Lynda,

I'm in Hong Kong now, this my second day here. It's raining and very humid, but what can one expect during the monsoon season? I've gotten fabulous response from my first travel article in the Register, *well over 75 responses. (Yes, I know — if I was writing for the* Times *I would have over 500).*

I'm sorry I've made you follow me in such a crazy manner. I planned to let you catch me in Shanghai or Beijing. Maybe I've been too controlling. Maybe, I'm too much of a dreamer for you, or anybody.

I know our relationship has not been at its best lately. I feel we must share the blame for that equally. But, the past is the past. What I am concerned about is the present and our future.

Oh God, I hurt so much right now. It tears me apart that I have to say these things to you. About four months ago, we had a fight about this very subject. I'm sure you remember. We argued about another person in your life and you vehemently denied it. Now, I am thousands of miles away, and the same subject arises yet again. I will not believe what I have heard until I hear it from you.

If you are interested in someone else, or if you are seeing someone else — just tell me. It will be okay — really it will. But please, just tell me the truth.

I will include the e-mail address of my travel agent at the bottom of this letter. When you get to Hong Kong, you can make a decision as to whether or not you want to continue. The travel agent will have a return flight ticket to L.A. ready for you. Of course, I will reimburse any money that you have spent since beginning your trip.

I want you in my life. But, I only want you if you also want me. I feel that we can still work this out. I hope so.

All of My Love,
Jack

He sat quietly and stared at his message. After 5 minutes he reached for the mouse and clicked on the "Send" icon. It was quick and final. In less than four hours his life turned upside down. Much like winning the lottery, it all seemed so final — so suddenly and surprisingly final.

He walked back to Delaney's Pub. He didn't talk to anyone. He just sat in the corner and got drunk. At midnight, he staggered back to his dark, dank, closet of a room to sleep. He tossed and turned all night, never quite falling into the deep sleep which would have given him a few hours of peace.

****

"Why do you look so sad?" asked the young American girl clearing the table next to him.

It was the next morning, and Jack was seated in a Starbucks. It was a small room, crammed with tables and chairs. The rain and humidity fogged the cafe's windows, making it nearly impossible to see a passerby on the sidewalk. Instead, one could only see a shadow of a person and their steady companion — the familiar black umbrella. He consumed two large Danish pastries, and was working on his second cup of coffee when the girl spoke to him. It caught him by surprise.

"Oh, ah ... I don't know. Trouble at home, ya know."

"Yes, I do know," she replied. "I'll be leaving Hong Kong at the end of the month. Going home to Kansas. That'll be a change for sure."

"What brought you out here?" he asked.

"Runnin' away. Just runnin' away. I got here and realized how very, very good I had it. Just remember," she said, as she balanced a stack of plates in one hand and took a final swipe with a wet rag over the table top next to Jack's, "It can always be worse."

By the noon hour, Delaney's began to beckon. After having lunch and talking with the pub's manager, he left to walk around. There were barkers in front of many of the shops selling watches, jewelry, suits, and electronic goods.

Had he done the right thing in accusing Lynda, or should he have waited until they met? He didn't know, and thinking about it only confused him more. Right or wrong, it was done.

Around four o'clock, he came across a small hotel operated in conjunction with a Catholic school. Touring the room available, he found it palatial in comparison to where he was staying. Surprisingly, the price was about the same as the Mansions, and although it was farther away from the center of the *Tsim Sha Tsui* area, it was a straight line down Nathan Road by taxi. He checked in, hailed a cab, and retrieved his bags from the Mansions.

There was a telephone in the room, and after settling in, Jack readied himself to call Dan. It was more communication of the type which could only bring bad news.

****

Lynda would have loved to be able to telephone someone — anyone! She was in Vladivostok, Russia. Because she was without a visa, she was unable to get off the ship. It was a moot point. Standing on the upper decks, she could see nothing but industrial sprawl and large, ugly, cement buildings.

Although a bright blue sky loomed overhead, the smoke from numerous factories pushed skyward in an effort to block the small amount of beauty which did exist. It was cold, and a few minutes on the open deck with only a jacket was all she could endure.

She desperately wanted to talk to someone. Any friend would do, and she showed no preference for either Bill or Jack. Between episodes of being sick, she reflected upon the two men in her life. She was confused as to which one she wanted, but the more she thought about it, the more she tended to believe neither of them were right for her.

In port at Vladivostok for two days, the ship's loading and unloading was progressing slower than usual, and the Captain silently wished Russia would go back to being the Soviet Union. All of the regulations were tighter then, and getting work done was a pain in the ass. But, at least something got done.

The ship was due to sail tomorrow. Officials were aboard soon after they tied up, and they would return again just before the ship sailed. The Captain wondered if they would spend as much time looking at the American woman and her passport as they did on their first visit. Then, they had scrutinized every page, scanning them with some sort of lamp detecting God only knows what, and tried to ask her a myriad of questions — all of them in Russian.

The Captain was tired. He'd been at sea for nearly seven months. The ship was tired also. The storms had taken their toll, as there were numerous leaks and malfunctions. Added to that, upon entering the Vladivostok harbor, a tug rammed against the side of the ship harder than intended, punching a hole the size of a soccer ball in the hull. It was safely above the water line, and the crew made some repairs so they would be able to continue the voyage. The Captain would not trust permanent repairs to the Russians, but instead would wait until they arrived in Pusan or Hong Kong.

9

"Dan, yeah it's me!"

"Oh, yeah ... hey Jack, how are you?" Dan stammered in reply.

"I'm not worth a shit, really. Have I got you out of bed? I have no idea how many hours Hong Kong is ahead of the west coast. It's about five thirty in the afternoon here."

"Don't worry about it," he said, coming awake now as he happily listened to the sound of his friend's voice. "Beck and I looked it up before we went to bed, and it's fifteen or sixteen hours, but who cares. Both of us are glad to hear from you. I assume you got my e-mail?"

"Yes," Jack let out with a sigh. "I'm such a mess. I've just been wandering around all day. I don't feel much like eating, sleeping or anything."

"Look, I can be on a plane tomorrow."

"No, that won't solve anything. All I'd have then is someone to get drunk with, and I know getting drunk is only a short time solution." Jack paused. "No, I really don't want you to come out. This is a trip I've wanted to take since I was a child. I'll complete it, despite the circumstances. There's always the possibility something will happen along the way that will make this matter pale in comparison," his voice trailing off to a murmur.

"I hope you're not mad at me. I didn't want to tell you, but I didn't want you to hear about the whole thing from someone else either. I mean, it's in the paper and everything."

"What happened ... where did I screw up?"

"Don't go blaming yourself. You're a saint, and you know it."

Jack stopped, his mind coming out of the self pity he felt for himself to listen to what he'd just heard.

"You said it was in the paper. What was in the paper?" he asked now.

"Davidson went home to the wife, and she went postal on him. The story said the neighbors heard glass breaking and called nine-one-one. You know how those fancy, gated communities can be ... well anyway, the cops were there in less than five minutes, but it was about a minute too late for Mrs. Davidson."

"He killed her?" Jack asked incredulously.

"No, no. She'd apparently told him she'd had enough, and one thing led to another. According to a friend of mine who's on the police beat at the *Times*, you know Amber, the little spunky chick we see down at McGrath's now and then ... anyway, the lovely Mrs. Davidson apparently started throwing lamps and shit, and he punched her in the face.

"They arrested him for assault and domestic violence. And, while the cops were trying to restrain him, she punched one of the cops who was trying to hold her back. So, they arrested her too."

"Jesus!" said Jack.

"Ah, but that's not all. One of the television crews decided to stick a microphone in Mrs. Davidson's face while her attorney was leading her to a car after making bail ... ya know, ask her if she had in fact dropped one of L-A's finest ... and before her attorney could shut her up she blurted how she'd like to punch out Davidson's legal assistant, ah ... well, the one that he's been seeing, as well."

"When did all of this occur?"

"Almost a week ago. One of the television stations tried to run with it a bit, but essentially it died there ... however, not before everyone knew Lynda was the one in your story for the *Register*."

"Ah shit," protested Jack. "I wanted our game to remain mostly a personal thing."

"I know, I know," sympathized Dan.

"I e-mailed her what I'd heard. I tried not to accuse her, but I'm afraid that's the way it came out. I know this will sound dumb to you and Rebecca, but I can forgive her. I still want her in my life."

"That's your decision. Beck and I will support you in any way you choose. I just don't want you getting all depressed and stuff. You're a good man. You're healthy. You're rich. You're on top of the world. Don't let something like this, something you've no control over whatsoever ... don't let this bring you down."

They talked about the weather and the baseball season. Dan was glad to let the subject change, but knew so much still lingered under the surface — unfinished business which would need to be discussed some day.

"Did they run the story in the *Register*?" asked Jack.

Dan knew at once what Jack was referring to, even though he had abruptly changed the subject.

"No. And, you'll like this. I went to Neal, prepared to kick the shit out of him if he ran anything more than the police response call. He told me to shut the door like he always does, and I was ready to start in on him when he tells me he's not going to print one word of the whole thing. He told me he respected you too much to do so. It really made me proud of you."

Between sniffles, with his voice cracking, he told Dan he had to go. Placing the receiver back in it's cradle, the tears rolled down his cheeks.

Where had he gone wrong with Lynda? Should he have forced the issue of a commitment between them sooner? Had he relented to her pleas to get a better job, would it have helped? How many more times could he have told her he loved her?

He lay back on the bed, thankful to be out of the Mansions, and in a quiet, moisture free room. He lay there asking himself a long list of questions with no answers to any of them.

When he awoke, it was eight o'clock. He was hungry, and realized he'd barely eaten all day. After a shower, he walked out of the hotel and hailed a taxi. It was a mile ride down Nathan Road to the corner of Peking Road, and from there a short walk to Delaney's.

After arriving and finding a seat at the bar, he ordered a pint of Guinness. He'd no more than had a sip of the creamy rich, white foam, when the manager approached him. He had introduced himself to Jack earlier in the day as David Bird.

"Mr. Gillette! Lovely to have ya here tonight, it is. A welcome sight indeed!"

They shook hands, and Jack asked if he could buy him a beer.

"There's nothing more I'd like to have than a bit of Beamish, that's for sure," said Bird. "But, it's crowded, and I've a bit av work to do." He paused, taking time to sit on the bar stool next to Jack. "Did ye not tell me earlier that you were a barman when ya were in school?"

"Yes, I did," replied Jack.

"Well, I hate to be a bother, but one of our lads has a bit of trouble with the misses ... has to run home for a bit. You could work with Ian there for about a hour or so, pour some beer, and have some fun. Afterward, I'll buy ya dinner. Ya'd be helpin' us out a bit, you would. And, you'd look quite smart in one of our Delaney's shirts."

The bar and restaurant staff all wore either dark green golf shirts, or a white shirt with the word "Harps" emblazoned on the front. Jack accepted Bird's offer, and although he was nervous about not having poured beer in such a long time, found the task came second nature. He worked for a little over an hour, and enjoyed the camaraderie with customers and fellow employees.

At closing time, with the bartenders and waitresses insisting he tag along, they all adjourned to a small, nearby restaurant. They enjoyed *Dim Sum* and hot tea until the wee hours of the morning — the windows of the small cafe steaming up as the air from the hot food met the coolness of the rain outside.

The morning wasn't pretty, especially with Mr. Beamish and Mr. Guinness knocking rhythmically on the front door of his skull. Jack somehow made his way to the internet cafe by 10 a.m. An hour later he was transmitting a series of stories for the newspaper. He also e-mailed Loraine with instructions to provide an airline ticket, one-way from Hong Kong to Los Angeles for Lynda.

TO My Editor & Friend
RE: Thank you for your consideration of my private life. I am eternally grateful.

DATELINE: HONG KONG

It's nice to feel as if you've received your money's worth.

Whether buying a new car or making a small purchase at the mall, there's delight in knowing you got the better end of a deal.

As a traveler, I'm always pleased when I stumble upon a small, clean and inexpensive hotel, especially if the staff speaks a little English and a small cafe serving great coffee lies just around the corner.

For the traveler, a good deal also may be found in the form of sunny skies, snowy slopes or uncrowded conditions. It's a matter of getting what you came for, as well as what you imagined.

One of the drawbacks of making detailed travel plans however, is that each failure is magnified by your dreams. So you may understand why I was feeling short-changed after spending five days aboard a freighter in the Pacific Ocean amid calm, placid waters.

The Pacific has been like a lake, not a ripple or whitecap to be seen, with only a slight breeze. Standing jacket-less on the open deck, no salty mists have blown in my face. Even the air has lacked that marine odor of which I have dreamed. There have been nothing but crystal clear nights and warm, sunny days.

Though the food has been excellent since I left Long Beach, California, and Captain Walter Oventrop and his officers have made every effort to accommodate me, something's been lacking. The sailing has been much too safe, much too smooth.

Late this afternoon, though, everything changed. The skies darkened and the wind began to blow. The ocean changed from a tranquil lake into a raging sea. What was once blue water is now a shade of gray, mixed with white foam.

The wind is blowing steadily out of the northwest at 50 knots. Michael Haussmann, the second officer, warns me to stay off the open decks, that conditions will decline through the night. He laughs when I mention that the sea is getting rough. He tells me I have yet to see a true storm.

I can hear creaking and groaning coming from deep within the ship. Every few minutes, gurgling sounds emanate from the toilet. My flask of rum topples over on my desk.

Each roll of the ship seems more pronounced than the last. When the ship lurches downward, great walls of water crash over the bow. As big as it is — with the weight of more than 3,500 containers, each the size of a truck trailer — it is still possible to feel the ship give way to the force of the sea.

I look through the porthole of my cabin toward the bow, but darkness hides what is probably best left unseen. Like a theater patron at a scary movie, I have my hands over my eyes, but I'm peeking eagerly through the cracks of my fingers.

Through all of this, I am happy and content. I feel relatively safe and secure. I am satisfied with the knowledge that I've received what I expected, that I've gotten my money's worth.

Jack knew he was in for some very lonely and sad days, but he also knew things would get better with time. The sooner he got started, the sooner he would somehow recover.

He intended to write about Macau, and if it were to be factual, he needed to travel there. He had one full day before his scheduled train to Guangzhou, and he was determined to make good use of it.

****

"You'll have Judge Williams on the bench this morning," said Paul Stritt. One of William Hugh Davidson's partner's, he would enter a plea on Bill's assault charge. "He's kind of an asshole, but you could do worse," Stritt added.

"Yeah, he and I go back a long way," replied Davidson, the moment of irony missed by both men. "We both clerked together out of law school."

"Well, I talked with Judge King last night. He and Williams are good friends and both members of LaQuinta. We discussed the Feyer matter initially, and later I asked him as a personal favor to quietly talk to Williams. He said he would."

"Fuck, that's great!" perked up Davidson.

Bill was downcast from the moment he and his partner began their meeting. Stritt wanted to have the meeting in his office, but Davidson, the eternal, controlling person that he was, insisted upon using his. Stritt looked at it as just another example of the man insisting he was in control when everyone else knew the opposite.

"Well, you're going to owe me one ... and don't forget to correct your language when you're in court this morning."

"Paul, have you ever witnessed an occasion, or have you ever even heard of an instance where I have erred in my actions or my language in a court of law?"

"Well, no. Ah, I know you have control of your language. It's your temper I'm concerned about. Your wife got a black eye from somebody," Paul Stritt shot back.

"Paul, we are not talking about fuckin' black eyes here! The woman was deranged. Even the cop she decked would have to agree with that. She came at me, and I was afraid for my life. Christ, the fucking pig outweighs me by a hundred pounds or so! I was simply acting in self defense!"

"Yes, yes, I know," conceded Davidson's partner. Damn, he thought silently, this guy is sure becoming a pain in the ass.

Paul Stritt concentrated his law practice on matters of criminal defense. He was very good at what he did, and knew it. He also knew he would have to listen to all of Bill's suggestions about how to handle this matter, listening to lectures on various points of criminal law, something Davidson knew little or nothing about. The problem did not end there.

The week before, Talbot, Stritt, and Mumphrey privately met to discuss the future of a certain law firm, that being Davidson, Talbot, Stritt, and Mumphrey. During the meeting, the three partners discussed the anchor member of the firm, William Hugh Davidson. It was unanimously agreed the anchor was becoming heavier and heavier with each passing year. It was not a situation with an easy answer. It would be a strange coincidence that shortly after the men adjourned, a two round, best of three falls, main event between their partner and his lovely wife would occur at the Davidson residence.

Davidson brought a substantial amount of money into the firm. His specialty, personal injury litigation, was the big ticket item for law firms, and Davidson somehow, despite all his ineptness, had a talent for it. He was the rain-maker, the money machine for the firm. However, with each dollar Davidson brought in, the firm, its partners, and all of the junior lawyers lost a couple of pounds of prestige. Prestige mattered greatly to everyone it seemed, except Davidson.

Bill Davidson was not afraid to call himself an ambulance chaser. Although he was practically a legend in L.A. courtrooms for having the ability to always use the correct words and never utter profanities, the talent seemed to go down the toilet the minute the judge slammed the gavel down, arose, and walked to his chambers.

Out of the courtroom, it was open season. Bill was a legend in that arena for always using profanity and seldom using the politically correct words. Clients, rival attorneys, expert witnesses, television camera men and news people were all fair game.

On one occasion, and it was at the end of a victorious trial for Davidson, he called the mother of his own client a "dumb, fuckin' crack" for failing to follow his instructions, thereby giving a less than superior performance on the witness stand.

"... the dumb, fuckin' crack almost cost her kid a couple of million bucks," said Davidson, standing right in front of a television camera. "... I could carve a better fuckin' woman out of a banana."

Judges were not immune either, and at this very moment, there were probably more than a couple of them, having heard the news of Davidson's domestic demise, wishing they could be the one seated on the bench when Davidson entered his plea.

The situation had worsened in the last few years, and something would eventually have to be done. The law partners all hoped Davidson would decide to retire. Some of the junior members of the firm hoped he would die. A few of the legal secretaries could have easily been persuaded to kill him. And, they all knew his legal assistant and sole loyal ally in the law office, was sexually involved with him.

"And Paul," Davidson went on, "I'm certain you are familiar with the

Bellman case which was tried a couple of years ago."

It was Spellman, but Stritt let it go. And yes, he was familiar with the case, but knew Davidson would refresh his memory anyway.

"Bellman offs' his wife. Hey, all I did was punch out mine! Anyway, ah, Bellman shoots the lovely Misses Bellman in the face one night, and the dumb fuck would have gotten off right there had he not cut up the body and tried to force it down the garbage disposal.

"The point I'm making here is, two nights before he shoots the bitch, the cops come to the house. By the time they leave, the wife is wearing bracelets and facing charges of A and B. Bellman has to do some time for abuse of a corpse, but gets off on the murder charge."

There was a lot more to the story, but Stritt was not about to bring it up. The more he listened to Davidson, the more he was convinced he and his partners could not wait around, hoping the old goat would retire. Bracelets? Why couldn't he just say handcuffs? Jesus Christ, muttered Stritt to himself.

After a few more lectures on case law from Davidson, all of his examples flawed in either substance or facts, Stritt got up to leave. As he was opening the door, he could not help turning to Davidson to leave him with a parting shot.

"I would hope the mistress Lynda is chasing after her boyfriend. Personally, I don't want her in this office again. The last thing we need is your wife coming in here with a gun and blasting away at the two of you. And quite frankly Bill, I could not blame her."

****

Jack was up early the next morning. After checking that everything was packed, he took the elevator to the hotel lobby. The old laptop computer he carried was acting up. The battery would not charge, and the power adapter was hot to the touch. He paid his bill with cash, and donated the laptop to the school. The hotel clerk was delighted with the donation, and told Jack the students would be very happy.

A short taxi ride took him to the train station. After boarding, he found a seat by himself and rode along wondering how much different mainland China would be from Hong Kong. Two hours later he found out.

This was China. Jack saw very few Caucasian people on the train, and even fewer after arriving at the train station in Guangzhou. The English-speaking civil servants he experienced in Hong Kong were absent, and the faces did not seem as friendly. The perfunctory passport check of Hong Kong was replaced with a stern, military style examination of identity papers, passports, and baggage.

After obtaining clearance, he made his way to the front of the station. He quickly spotted a man holding a cardboard sign inscribed with the letters, " USA." They made their way to a car where a driver waited, and the guide informed him he would drop him off at another train station for his early evening departure to Guilin. It was just before noon.

At first, he was not going to protest. But, upon seeing the old, crowded train station where he was to be deposited, changed his mind. His itinerary called for a sightseeing excursion of Guangzhou with lunch. He could not imagine being stuck in the train station for six hours.

After some frantic calls to his office, the guide finally relented. Jack, the driver and the guide went to a large restaurant, where they ate lunch in a private room, removed from the rest of the patrons. It didn't feel special, but instead felt segregated.

The sightseeing excursion consisted of a trip to a souvenir store obviously intended as an island of isolation for westerners. The clerks all spoke perfect English. Mastercard, Visa and American Express were welcome. He may as well have been in San Francisco's Chinatown.

By 3 p.m. they were back at the train station. Five hundred to a thousand people were milling around the front of the station. With the driver carrying his bags and the guide leading the way, Jack was told to stay close behind in a position between the two Chinese men. He would soon understand why.

As they neared the front of the station, the crowd became more dense and harried. The entrance they were to go through was no larger than a regular, single door. Next to this entrance, an old woman stood on a wooden box which elevated her above the crowd by two feet. She was yelling at everyone, and in one hand carried a stick the size of a cane. When the crowd would surge toward the doorway, she would hit those who were not allowed to enter, which appeared to be most everyone.

A few words in Chinese were exchanged between the old woman and the guide, and then they moved forward. Following closely behind the guide, he could see the woman raise her hand, and at first thought he would be struck. Although Jack passed through unscathed, the driver following him was less fortunate, albeit the blows fell harmlessly onto Jack's shouldered luggage.

After speaking with an official, the guide and driver departed, leaving him alone in what appeared to be a First-Class waiting room. All of the announcements through a loudspeaker were in Chinese, without the benefit of an English translation.

The language barrier was not a problem until after the scheduled 6:05 p.m. departure of his train had come and gone. He tried to get some information, but it was impossible. There were no clerks who spoke English. There were no other passengers who spoke English. No information windows existed where an explanation might be found.

7 p.m., and everyone in the waiting room remained seated. 7:30, and the officials in charge were visibly tired of trying to explain in Chinese to an American who only understood English. Finally at 8:15, one of the clerks came into the room and took him by the arm. Pointing rudely, the clerk indicated he go in the direction of his hand. After walking 200 feet, Jack came upon an entrance to a platform. Another train attendant led him to his car and his compartment.

If he thought the confusion and delays were over at this point, he would soon find out otherwise. The adventure was just beginning.

After getting comfortable in the two-place compartment, a middle aged Chinese man entered. They nodded a greeting to each other, both men innately sensing the lack of the other's understanding of their native language. Settling in, they sat across from each other on their respective bunks. Their knees would have touched had they positioned themselves directly across from one another in the clean, compact compartment.

Through a mixture of gesticulation and a guidebook's limited appendix of Chinese symbols, they managed to introduce themselves. It came as a relief when, after pointing to a map, his compartment mate, now known as Pan, indicated that Guilin was his destination also. That will make it easy, thought Jack. When Pan gets off, I'll get off.

The train from Guangzhou to Guilin was scheduled to arrive at its destination at 7:30 a.m. The trip would take a little more than thirteen hours to complete. They departed Guangzhou late, and therefore Jack did not panic the next morning when the arrival time expired, and the train continued to meander through the Chinese countryside.

At 9:30, the train had neither stopped nor passed through any towns. Pan remained relaxed and untroubled, while Jack fretted he was on the wrong train.

At 10:30, Jack's increasing worry forced him to renew communication with Pan. On a piece of paper, Jack wrote the words "Guangzhou" and "Guilin." Placing a dot by both names, he drew a line between the two cities and connected the dots. With a rough outline of the northwesterly rail line as it appeared on a map, Jack then made a show of looking at his watch and placing at "X" on the rail-line, very near the dot denoting Guilin. This new mark represented their current position.

Pan shook his head back and forth. He took the paper from Jack and drew another line from the dot of Guangzhou to the dot of Guilin. This line however, looped far to the northeast. It traveled north of their destination, turned southwest, and then turned due south to connect with the Guilin dot. It made no sense whatsoever.

Their compartment door stood open, and Pan would occasionally gesture to someone passing by in the corridor in a vain attempt to help explain the situation to this hapless American.

Around noon, a man passing by abruptly stopped and peered into the compartment. After speaking with Pan in their native language, he entered and shook hands with Jack. He silently reviewed the array of crude drawings cast about on the two bunks. The two Chinese men conversed further, and with a small, limited amount of English, the visitor tried to explain the situation to Jack.

Apparently, mass flooding due to the monsoon rains washed out bridges and track on what would have been the train's normal route. Therefore, a long, roundabout detour was needed to avoid the flood damage. They were now scheduled to arrive in Guilin at 2:30 p.m. — seven hours later than originally planned.

Jack searched in vain for his guide among the hundreds of people outside the Guilin train station. Approached by a young man, promises were made to deliver him to his hotel.

Americans are not trusting people. Although Jack was thirty days into his trip, he'd experienced little contact with foreigners. He spent the bulk of his time either isolated aboard ship, or forlornly sitting in Delaney's English Pub in Hong Kong. Therefore, it took some fortitude to trust this stranger who was not his guide.

As he traveled, he would find himself trusting strangers more and more. It is one of the requirements of traveling solo and without a plan. As the level of trust increases, so also does an awareness that the majority of people the world over can be trusted.

Soon after arriving at the hotel, Jack's room telephone rang. It was the guide originally assigned to meet him. He spoke flawless English. His name was Li Yimin, and he was waiting for Jack in the lobby of the hotel.

A scheduled tour of the Li River was missed because of Jack's delayed arrival, but Li Yimin was determined to make up for the inconvenience of mother nature. He explained to Jack how they would start early the next morning. Some adjustments were necessary since the river tour encompassed a full day, and his train was scheduled to leave Guilin shortly after 4 p.m.

The next morning Jack ate breakfast in the dining room of the hotel. Full of westerners, the surroundings gave Jack an insulated feeling of not being in China at all. He was on his second cup of coffee when Li came through the door. The car and his driver were ready.

As they rode along, windows down to simulate air conditioning, Li explained his plan. After a brief ride, Jack boarded a tour boat to begin his trip up the Li River.

The Li River is the main attraction of the Guilin area. The river provides miles of breathtaking scenery, highlighted by fantastically shaped limestone peaks with names like, "Waiting for Husband Rock," and, "Camel Crossing River."

One hour into the daylong cruise, the boat suddenly turned towards the shore. People could be seen on the river's bank, and a small village appeared through the trees. As the boat gingerly approached the shore, Jack could see Li and his driver waving to him. Jack made his way to the main deck, and when the boat got close enough to some rocks, nimbly jumped from the deck to dry land, and the outstretched arms of Li and his driver. The tour boat returned to the main channel of the river, a quick diversion that, in America, would have been impossible, as risk managers, unions, and insurance carriers would have all suffered symptoms of massive cardiac arrest at the mere thought of what could go wrong, and who might be liable.

Walking from the shore and through a small hamlet of shacks, Jack was approached by a couple of locals either begging, or wanting to sell something. Li and his driver did not shoo the people off, nor did they admonish them. They simply told Jack he did not have to stop walking, or say anything — that he did not have to listen to their sales pitches or pay them any attention — and in doing so was not being rude.

In essence, Li was telling him he should just ignore the people. It was as if to ignore them and to say nothing would make the entire scene simply cease to exist. It was Jack's first encounter with a part of the Chinese culture which would assert itself again and again as he traveled through the country. If the Chinese people believe or are told something — if the blinders are large enough — then the situation, fact, or event is gospel.

They reached their vehicle and were off on a sightseeing tour. Although at first wishing he could have continued the boat tour, Jack soon found the trip with Li much better. The two men talked of many things, including family, occupations, and their respective countries. The driver occasionally stopped to allow Jack to take photographs, and once pulled over to buy watermelon being sold alongside the road. It proved to be a very relaxing and enjoyable day.

His overnight train journey from Guilin to Xian was uneventful. There were no delays due to flooding or other natural disasters. He was in a four-place compartment, and although he tried, he found it impossible to find any rapport with his non-English speaking, Chinese traveling companions.

A guide met him at the train station as scheduled, and drove him to his hotel. A guided tour of the site where the Terracotta Warriors were unearthed was scheduled for the next day, so he spent the day lolling around the hotel and taking brief walks.

Although the tour of the Terracotta Warriors ruins was interesting, Jack was glad when it was over. The Chinese version of a sightseeing tour is eighty-five percent gift shop and high pressure sales, and fifteen percent actual tour of a monument or site.

Stopping a gift stores along the way, tourists are informed that by being aboard this particular and very special tour bus, they will receive a discount of anywhere from twenty to forty percent. Any interest shown in an item brings the immediate attention of a clerk or salesperson. They all speak flawless English.

Should the proffered discount fail to close the sale, the tour guide from the bus appears with a proposal of a few more percentage points to sweeten the deal. Many times, three or four of these gift shops are visited on the way to and from the intended destination.

After a full day of tourism Jack was worn out. He saw more Terracotta Warriors than he cared to, and repeatedly heard the tale of the farmer who first found them. He could have purchased a book signed by the man, a man whose age seemed a bit young for having been a farmer in 1974, as he sat behind a counter at the on-site gift shop. Playing the role of a tourist, he was eager to get back to being a traveler again.

10

Lynda was a traveler whether she wanted to be or not. There were no tour guides or scheduled itineraries. At breakfast, the Captain told her they would be sailing in the early evening. At 10 a.m. there was a knock on her door, and she answered it cautiously. It was the Captain and three Russian officials.

"They want you to go with them," said the Captain.

"What for?" replied Lynda, a little more terror in her voice than she wished or expected to express. "You have my passport, why would I need to go anywhere with them?"

"I don't know," said the Captain, a look of worry and concern showing on his face. "I've sent for the Second Officer. He speaks a little Russian. Maybe he can figure out what they want."

She thought about slamming the door and locking all the locks, but knew it would be pointless. She retrieved her purse and her jacket and followed the Captain and one of the Russians. The other two followed closely behind. She noticed uncomfortably that the Russians were armed. They also did not look happy.

At the gangway leading to the dock, the Second Officer joined the group. There was a discussion between him and the Russians, a discussion which did not sound as though it was cordial.

"They want you to go with them to their headquarters," Second Officer Froebel said. "They said it is not far, that you can walk. I do not like it, but they say the ship will not sail until you go."

"I don't want to leave the ship," she pleaded. "Please don't let them take me," she begged.

Froebel turned to the Russians and spoke in their language. They went back and forth for a few minutes more before Froebel spoke to the Captain in German. The Captain was visibly angry when Froebel addressed Lynda in English.

"I told them you would not go alone. So now they want the Captain and I to go also."

"What do they want of me?" she cried.

She could feel the tears welling up in her eyes, but had not felt the cold, wet tickle that signaled they were rolling down her cheeks.

"Just be calm," soothed Froebel. "They say it is a matter involving your passport. Something about not having the proper visa to be in Vladivostok."

"But, I'm not in Vladivostok," she stammered. "I haven't gotten off the ship!"

The Russian who appeared to be in charge, gestured for them to proceed off the ship. Frightened to death, she made her way down the gangway behind the irate Captain and in front of Froebel. The two Russian goons trailed behind, while the Russian in charge led the parade.

"They say your visa papers are not in order." They were in a small building now, Second Officer Froebel translating as best he could. It was apparent his command of the language was not complete, as Lynda could hear the Russians repeat the same thing over and over again, trying to go slower each time.

Lynda was not well informed with regards to visas, passports and immigration policies, but the Captain had mentioned in passing that none of the crew could debark because they did not have the proper papers. She assumed he was talking about visas.

Froebel was raising his voice now, waving his arms around. He spoke rapidly to the Captain, who became more animated also.

The Captain kept repeating the words, "Nein, nein," over and over.

Lynda had taken German in high school. She assumed retention so many years later was impossible, but now as she listened carefully to the Captain and Froebel, she was surprised how she began to catch bits and pieces of their conversation.

"Nein, nein, nein," the Captain repeated.

"What's happening?" she inquired of Froebel.

"They want money. If you cannot give them money, then they want money from us. The Captain says no, and I know he will not pay them."

"I have some money, if that will make them let us go."

Until now, she had hated being on the ship. The room they were in was warm, something the ship was not. But standing there, she would have done anything to return to the ugly, cold, but beautiful, *Santiago Mariner*.

"You are too easy Fraulein," said Froebel. "It is best you do not speak. Besides, the Captain would not let you pay them. He knows how to handle them."

The Russians and the two Germans each stood their ground. They argued back and forth, sometimes with the Captain shouting "Nein," before Froebel could even translate. Finally, after almost twenty minutes, the Russians said something to Froebel and left the room.

"They will make us wait awhile now," said Froebel. "Make us sweat."

The Captain muttered something aloud, turning afterwards to apologize. She missed the exact translation, but knew it contained unkind words towards the Russians.

After a one hour wait, three different Russian officials came into the room. Unlike the others, they were not armed, and seemed harmless. They said a few short words to Froebel, and led the party out of the building and back to the ship. As they walked along, Lynda started to say something to Froebel, but he quickly whispered for her to be silent.

Making her way back to her cabin, she took a wrong turn and went onto one of the outer decks. She looked down to see the Second Officer watching over a rail as crew members raised the gangway. It would be another six hours or so before they were scheduled to sail, but it was obvious they were taking no chances.

She returned to her cabin and sat down on her bunk. She wanted to sleep, to forget about this bad dream. But, her adrenaline was flowing, so she moved to the small desk in her room. Taking her inadvertently packed notebook and legal pad, she began to write.

Jack often teased her for taking the notebook wherever she went, and once playfully put it in their bed. When lovemaking took them from the living room to the bedroom and she subsequently discovered it, they laughed together. She remembered the scene now, and smiled at how funny she thought it was at the time, and how endearing it seemed to her now.

She wrote the day's date, and jotted down her location. She sat for ten minutes, wanting to write something, but not having a clue as to what that something might be. Finally, it came to her.

I'm cold. I'm emotionally drained. I was scared, and I still am. I don't think I'm happy. No, I know I'm not happy. But, in the same breath, I'm not unhappy.

Had Jack been here, I don't think I would have been so scared. Had Bill been here, I would have been scared the situation might worsen. No, maybe that's not true. Jack would have been more diplomatic than Bill, that's all.

The important thing is I'm alive. Even more important — I feel alive!

Just before midnight, the *Santiago Mariner* silently slid out of the Vladivostok harbor. Lynda was still awake, a rush of relief coming over her as she felt the huge engines of the ship come to life, several decks below her. Forty minutes later, she heard a slight tapping on her door. What now?, she thought.

"Yes, who is it?" she said.

"Second Officer Froebel," came a voice from the corridor. "I have a gift from the Captain."

She cautiously opened the door. Froebel, a youngish looking man of about forty, was blushing. He held a small tray in his gnarled, seventy-year-old hands, hands she noticed as something which did not belong to his youthful face.

On the tray was a small shot glass, filled with a clear liquid. Next to it stood a liter size bottle of beer — its bright, blue label that of some unrecognizable foreign brand. An empty glass completed the trio.

"The Captain sent this with his compliments. He says he is very proud of you for not crying in front of the Russians. He says you are very brave for an American woman."

She took the tray, and was about to ask what was in the shot glass when Froebel spoke. "Is very good schnapps. German schnapps!" And, with the tray in her hands, Froebel reached out for the door, bowing his head as he closed it.

She sat at her desk with the beer and the schnapps. Although she was glad the ship was moving, she knew seasickness followed in its wake. She found she didn't care. If I'm going to be sick, she thought, I might as well be good and sick, and she threw back the single shot of schnapps.

She fumbled for an opener in the desk drawer, the sting of the drink stronger than any schnapps she'd ever tasted. The beer chaser soothed her throat, but her stomach remained warm with the glow of the alcohol.

When she awoke the next morning she had a headache. She found herself checking the area next to her bed for vomit before swinging her bare feet onto the floor. She had not been sick, and now, headache notwithstanding, felt fine. She dressed and made her way below decks for breakfast. She'd eaten very little since being aboard ship, and for the very first time food sounded good.

"It is most probably because we are German," said the Captain, commenting on yesterday's standoff while drinking his coffee at the breakfast table. "The Russians do not like us."

Froebel, having lost his blushing face of the night before, now carried a more serious look. "Had there been problems with your passport, they would have addressed them on their first inspection. They were hoping you would just pull out American dollars for them. They knew that we, as Germans, would never pay."

The rest of the trip was far from what she would term pleasant. The food was very mediocre, and the ship seemed to wallow in the sea even when the waters were calm. From time to time, it would rain, but there were no great storms like the one they encountered after leaving Vancouver. Best of all, she did not get sick again, although at times her stomach felt a little queasy.

They made port in Pusan, South Korea, a stop supposedly to last only two days, but one that stretched to four. Three days after sailing from Pusan, they would be in Hong Kong.

Lynda could not wait to set foot on land again, make some telephone calls and answer her e-mail.

****

"It's not pretty," said Paul Stritt.

He and Bill were in Davidson's office, William Hugh Davidson ensconced behind his throne, a cherry wood desk the size of a small SUV. Paul Stritt sat in one of the uncomfortable chairs reserved for clients, secretaries, and other mindless minions.

"Fuck her, and fuck that sleezeball Rogers!" proclaimed Bill.

"Rogers is a hell of an attorney, Bill. He's no friend of mine, but I've always admired the way he does his homework. He's very thorough."

"You said he knew about my house in Palm Springs?" questioned Davidson.

"Yes, he does. He knows about the dummy law firm you told your wife you were involved with. Those guys won't go out on a limb for you, I can guarantee you that. It's right here in black and white." Paul shuffled through some of the papers on his lap. If he were behind his desk he could at least lay everything out — at least look like he was half-assed organized, he thought to himself.

Davidson sensed the juggling act taking place on his partners lap, but chose to ignore it.

"Paul, I want you to pull out all the stops on this. The fucking bitch will take me to the cleaners if she gets half a chance. Are you with me on this?"

It was a question Paul expected. Davidson always thought he was the only one capable of practicing law. He was also prone to being paranoid, thinking anyone who didn't hang on his every word was instead, out to get him. Quite frankly, Paul could give a shit. He didn't care if Mrs. Davidson got every penny.

While Paul Stritt was thinking of things other than a strategy for his partners upcoming divorce battle, Davidson was thinking of other things as well. He had e-mailed Lynda several times, telling her he was soon to be divorced. He also told her of the fight with his wife, but omitted the part concerning her comments to the press about his sexual involvement with his legal assistant. She would learn of that from one of her women friends, and he wondered if she'd blame him for his wife's comments.

His relationship with Lynda was teetering in the balance, and there was no way of contacting her. If he could just talk to her, he might be able to save the situation. How long does it take a boat to cross the ocean? thought Bill. Earlier in the day, he contacted his travel agent to get more information. Bill insisted she get word to Lynda through the shipping company.

"This isn't exactly a mainstream shipping company. I'll try to contact their agent in Hong Kong, but it's possible they don't even have one," the agent replied.

"Then get one. I don't give a shit if you have to hire some bell boy from the Hilton to go stand on the goddamn dock," said Bill. "Find a way to get it done, or I'll find another agent."

"I'm sorry Paul, what where you saying?" said Davidson, his mind back in the room again and on the subject of divorce.

"Nothing," said Paul. "Look," he added quickly, "I will be working on this all morning. This afternoon, I'll give Rogers a call, sorta see where we stand. Maybe there's a way to wrap it all up, all neat and tidy and without a protracted court battle."

"Well, get ready for court, Paul. I'll not roll over for this bitch, I can tell you that."

As soon as his partner left the room, Bill logged onto his e-mail. His "In Box" held seven new messages. One was from an attorney who wanted his advice concerning a personal injury case, and another was from a porno web site he was continually surfing, looking for even better pictures of a part of the female anatomy that, regardless of the angle it was photographed, or regardless of what was shoved into it, merely remained an aperture in the female body. The remaining five messages were either spam or worthless drivel from the American Bar Association. There was no message from Lynda.

He punched his intercom button, paging his new secretary, Lynda's replacement. A moment later she came in his office, without knocking first, as he had asked her to do, and poured him a fresh cup of coffee.

Susanne had a great body, and that was Bill's only attraction to her. He interviewed her the same morning the agency called, and hired her the next day.

After her interview, he excused her, but asked her to return to the office at 4 p.m. He told her they would have a drink together, that this was part of the interview process — Bill having to determine if his personal secretary could work with him informally as well as in a professional setting. His lines were down pat, all of it sounding polished and sincere. As she left that morning, he added she should dress causally for the one hour meeting over cocktails.

Susanne showed up wearing a pair of black pants and a red, low cut sweater. Bill was careful to not get caught peeking down her chest, into that rich, luscious cleavage. This may be even better than Lynda, he thought, although his stirrings for a piece of Lynda, as well as a piece of the 15 million dollars had not left him in any way.

Susanne was twenty-seven years of age. She possessed a college degree, and once worked for an attorney, as well as a private investigator. She answered all of the questions on the application truthfully, as well as all of the questions Bill asked her in his interview and the bogus interview, where it was evident that all he wanted was to get into her pants. She had spoken when spoken to, and kept her mouth shut otherwise. She knew the legal profession. She knew how to be a competent, professional secretary. She also knew how to handle horny men, old and otherwise.

What Susanne did not tell Bill, until the second day of her employment, was that she was a Christian. She would occasionally have a drink, thinking if Jesus could have wine, surely it was all right for her to have a vodka collins now and then. But she did not smoke, gamble or fool around.

After pouring his coffee and handing him some papers concerning a pending case, she walked back to her office.

Jesus Christ, muttered Bill to himself after she was gone. I'm living in L-A of all places, right fucking next to Hollywood, the pussy capital of the world, and I hire a right wing, fucking full-blown member of the Christian Coalition. Before he could beat himself up anymore, the telephone rang. His calls were supposed to go to Susanne first, and then to him, but some flaws remained in the transition phase from the pagan-like Lynda era to the Christian era, and this call was transferred from the office receptionist.

"You have a call on line one," came this raspy, gum-chewing voice. There was no, "Excuse me sir," or, "Mister Davidson."

As he punched line one, he was thinking he'd have to have a staff meeting before very long to lay down the law about a few basic procedures.

"Mr. Davidson? This is Shirley, from Anaheim Travel."

Mr. Davidson, now that's better already, thought Bill absentmindedly. "Yes, what have you found out?"

"Miss Turner is due to arrive in Hong Kong the day after tomorrow. The freighter's shipping company does not have an office in Hong Kong, but I have located another company that works in a sort of partnership with them. Although they couldn't make any promises, they told me they would try to have an agent contact Miss Turner with a message."

"What do you mean, they can't make any promises?" barked Davidson into the air, his telephone set on the intercom mode and sounding to the travel agent like he was speaking from some vast, empty barrel. "Of course they can make promises. You just have to induce them to. What's their number?"

"Mister Davidson, the man at the shipping agency does not speak very good English," replied the agent. In reality, the man at the shipping company in Hong Kong spoke nothing but English, sounding as though he was calling from the very center of the British Isles, rather than the heart of Asia. But, the travel agent was not about to give the number to Davidson. She'd reached her limit with him and his attitude. In fact, as the owner of the travel agency, she decided that after the client arrived in Hong Kong, she would send a letter to Davidson, Talbot, Stritt and Mumphrey, saying her agency was no longer interested in having their business.

"Mister Davidson. I will call the company again," she answered curtly. "I will tell them we would appreciate them doing this for us. And, Mister Davidson, that is all that I can, and it's all I will do on this matter."

"Hey, let's not get fuckin' pissy! Just ...."

But he stopped there because of the loud, steady hum coming through the small speaker which sat on his desk.

"FUCKIN' BITCH!" he screamed over and over again, to the un-hearing travel agent and dead telephone connection.

Although it was impossible for the travel agent to hear Davidson's screams, there were others who were well aware of his rantings.

Talbot heard the screaming two offices away, knew instantly who it was, and wondered if it was too early to adjourn to his favorite bar for a quiet drink.

Mumphrey — the smartest and most respected member of the law firm, sitting behind the smallest desk in the smallest office — heard it, and so did his client. The client, a wealthy southern California businessman, rolled his eyes and commented matter-of-factly, "Let me guess, Davidson?"

And Stritt heard it too, immediately taking out a note pad and beginning a draft of a letter he would give to his three partners, suggesting the time had come for the law firm of Talbot, Stritt and Mumphrey, sans Davidson.

While the majority of the office staff had heard Davidson screaming many times before, for the new secretary Susanne, it was a first. She sensed this tirade was a precursor of future events, none of them pleasant. She pushed her chair back, lowered her head, and with her hands clasped in her lap, said a small prayer.

She was not praying for Bill Davidson.

She was not praying for the formation of the new law firm of Talbot, Stritt and Mumphrey.

She was praying that the position she'd made a telephone inquiry about, might somehow, by the grace of God himself, materialize by the end of the day. This job, she knew, was a very big mistake.

An hour later, when Paul Stritt buzzed his pain in the ass partner, there was no answer. He checked with the new secretary Suzanne, but she had not spoken to Davidson since before he started his screaming fit.

Paul Stritt made a few more inquiries as to the location of Davidson, each one becoming a little more urgent. Stritt had contacted Rogers, the attorney for the soon to be ex-Mrs. Davidson, and Rogers agreed to meet with them that afternoon at his office. He knew a meeting anywhere other than Bill's private office would piss Davidson off, but Stritt sensed there might be some sort of negotiated settlement on the horizon. If so, that settlement would only be put forth on turf controlled by Rogers, a fact Stritt would have to impress on Davidson.

Bill did not say a word to anyone, including the office receptionist. When she saw him walk out the front door, turning left to go to the elevator, she breathed a sigh of relief. Possibly, just possibly she thought, he's gone for the entire day.

He took the first flight out of John Wayne Airport to Palm Springs, and after renting a car, drove from the airport to a run-down, half residential, half light-industrial area in Palm Desert. He pulled behind an old gas station, converted into a Hispanic Meat Market. A crudely painted sign advertised, "Carnizeria Zamora."

Behind the store was an old shipping container, not unlike those lining the deck of the ship Lynda was now on. It was a rusty hunk of metal, appropriately painted a rusty, red color. In faded blue letters, "K-Line" could be faintly seen through the encroaching oxidation. The door was open at the end of the structure, which Bill took as a good sign.

He stepped out of his rental car cautiously. He was not comfortable around Blacks, Hispanics, or any people who were not Caucasian, Catholic Americans, and nervously imagined he was possibly the only white man within a five mile radius. He noted how his appearance, dressed as he almost always was in a dark, expensive and stylish suit, seemed to make him stand out from his surroundings as he walked from the car to the metal container.

"Buenos dios, Amigo!" said Bill, sticking his head around the door of the container to peer inside. It came out, "ban-hos doze, am-a-go," but it was close enough.

A single light bulb hung from the ceiling, the cord and socket held against the roof with gray, duct tape. A low-wattage bulb emitted a faint glow in sharp contrast to the blaring heat of the container's interior.

"Meister Avidson, my friend," replied a short Hispanic man. He was grinning and sharpening a long machete-like knife.

Normally this would have greatly alarmed Davidson, but he knew this man, and was comfortable around him on a one-on-one basis. Power tools, weed eaters, rakes, and a horde of other garden equipment hung from the walls of the metal container turned workshop. Everything smelled like a mixture of gasoline and grass clippings.

Miguel Diaz Rodriguez was forty-five years old, although he looked much older from the many years of working in the agricultural fields of California, and later, as his own boss in the landscaping business. The skin of his face and hands had an almost baked on appearance.

Miguel started with just one lawn-mower, pushing it around residential neighborhoods, a makeshift sandwich board made of cardboard hanging from his shoulders, proclaiming his desire to mow lawns or weed flower beds for a small price. When he first started his enterprise, he targeted the medium priced neighborhoods of Palm Springs, thinking the police would not bother him there.

After two weeks with no arrests, but several pat-downs and I.D. checks, he moved up to the high rent district, figuring if he was going to go to jail, he may as well do it in style.

Bill Davidson was one of his first regular customers. It was not because of some humanitarian streak in Davidson. In fact, had it been entirely up to Bill, he would have dialed 911 the moment he saw the little, brown savage pushing the mower down the sidewalk in front of his house. But, it was not a decision for him to make. Several weeks before that first encounter with Miguel, Davidson met a photocopier saleswoman.

He met her in a bar, trying to chat her up with boring topics such as 401K plans and negotiated personal injury settlements. She did not listened to a word, other than his name and that of his firm. Two hours later, his receptionist buzzed him, and there she stood in the outer office. She tried unsuccessfully to sell him a copier, and the entire association would have ended there were it not for a chance encounter a week later.

Bill had stopped at a strip club in Anaheim on a whim. He didn't look around a lot before moving to the stage in the middle of the darkened room, taking one of the seats encircling the polished-metal dance floor, and near the shiny, brass pole that arose from the floor and disappeared into the ceiling some twenty-five feet above.

After sitting down, he looked straight ahead, and found himself at eye level with a pair of red, patent-leather, 10 inch heals. He was muttering the words, "Ya gotta like this shit," when the occupant of the 10 inch heals squatted down in front of him. She was naked. In fact, other than the shoes, she was buck naked. She was also the same woman who had attempted to sell him a copier.

Mercedes, (her stage name), was about to whisper a sultry, sexy comment to this expensively dressed new-comer when she recognized his face. Without missing a beat, Maria, (her real name), asked him, "Are you sure you don't want to buy a copier?"

Bill Davidson telephoned the number on the company's business card the very next day. The following afternoon, Maria arrived once again at the offices of Davidson, Talbot, Stritt, and Mumphrey. The firm selected the deluxe model, complete with every bell and whistle available, and much bigger than they really needed. Maria, when Bill had decided on a particular model, said to him winking, "This baby will collate till the cows come home."

Maria knew the sale was not complete without her at least sharing a drink with this man, but figured he was harmless. After sharing a couple of drinks, she found herself kind of liking the old goat. Since she had nothing else going on, and figuring she could do a lot worse, she decided to give it a spin. At the very least it might lead to another sale of the Super-Deluxe 900-C Model copier, a sale which had earned her the Salesperson-Of-The-Month Award and a five hundred dollar spiff.

Maria, although she looked Caucasian, was half Spanish. Her mother was born in Madrid, while her father was from the U.S. And so, it was Maria who first saw Miguel pushing the broken down mower in front of Davidson's pussy pad in Palm Springs. She ran out the door, summoned the man onto the property, and insisted he do both the front and the back lawns.

When Bill told her some "white people" were doing the yard work, saying it right in front of this man who was half like her, Maria essentially asked him if he'd like her to cross her legs permanently.

Miguel did the lawn. Miguel continued to do the lawn, and Bill had to admit the little guy was good. Everything somehow looked greener than before.

A month after Miguel started working on the Davidson property, his mower went on the fritz. He told Maria about it, (she and Bill were now regular Thursday and Friday residents of the house), and she arranged for the three of them to meet at an equipment store in the late afternoon.

Bill went along reluctantly and at Maria's insistence. With more threats of her legs moving to a permanent, crossed and locked position, Bill paid for the new lawn mower.

Miguel promised to pay Bill back in installment payments and with a reduced rate for his labors. It was agreed the payments be put in an envelope and placed under a cement frog which sat in a corner on the backyard deck. The envelope never failed to appear on schedule, the payment always in cash.

Months later, Bill, (Maria having moved on to bigger and better things), was spending the week at the Palm Springs house, working on a stubborn personal injury case. He was alone when there was a knock on the door. It was Miguel with the last payment.

By now Bill was comfortable around him, and so after talking of what to do with a large palm tree in the back yard, Bill asked Miguel why he did not pay with a check. "You know, I could easily have just taken the envelope and told you I never got it. No record of payment, you'd still fuckin' owe me the vig."

Miguel told him he had no checking account, nor bank account. He said he did not trust them, that he liked to have his money in cash. Bill paid Miguel in cash also, but not because he did not trust banks. He did not want any record of the payment, the house remaining a secret from his wife and others.

And so, it was this planned lack of record keeping which made a light go on in Bill's brain. He loaded up Miguel in his car, drove to a Wells Fargo Bank, and opened a savings account. Miguel was unfamiliar with business, banks, signature cards and the English language as a whole. Out of earshot of the teller, Bill explained what Bill wanted Miguel to understand. He would open an account for him, but he could only get money out of this account when Bill was with him. Bill explained how he would put one thousand dollars in the account as seed money. He would pay Miguel his monthly fee for yard work out of this account. Bill was very careful to stress to Miguel that he could not take money out of the account unless he was by his side.

The transactions at the bank always began at an isolated counter area near the front door. There, the two men would sign the withdrawal slip, Miguel always taking the full amount due him in cash. His distrust of banks had not wavered.

Over a seven year period, Miguel had required two loans for equipment and one for emergency dental care for his four year old daughter. As with all transactions, Miguel would sign the card, they would go to the teller together, and with Bill firmly in charge, the money would magically appear.

It was not a joint account. The only name on the account was that of Miguel Diaz Rodriguez. Bill watched the activity of the account closely at first, making sure every penny was accounted for. After he was certain Miguel only went to the bank in his presence, he began making deposits.

Although the account was in Miguel's name, all of the money was Bill's. The total amount represented over seven years of squirreling away cash, and in Bill's mind, he'd found the perfect place to hide money from both his wife and the I.R.S.

Although Bill could never have foreseen or imagined his wife attacking him and a policeman as well, he was not completely blind. He knew divorce loomed in his future, and although he always held onto the remote chance his wife might succumb to some strange disease akin to a bolt of lightning, his intuition told him she would probably outlive him.

Because he could see dark clouds on the horizon, he slowly began increasing the amounts he deposited. He also squirreled away money in a safe, buried below a closet floor in the Palm Springs house. Now he was here to see Miguel, get a signature on the bank withdrawal form, and settle up with the gardener. As far as Miguel would be concerned, the account would be closed.

"I em zeeprised to see you, Meister Avidson," smiled Miguel, putting the knife down on a bench made from an old closet door.

The two men shook hands, Davidson glad the knife was now on the workbench. His comfort level aside, Bill remained wary of Blacks or Mexicans, believing something in their genes could make them turn on a white guy in a New York second.

"Miguel, I have some bad news," he said, getting right into it without beating around the bush. "I've got to pay you your final wages, you see, I've sold my house."

"Maybe I could do zee grass for zee new people," replied Miguel, seeming not caring if Bill sold the house or burnt it down, just a long as the grass remained to be cared for.

"I don't fuckin' know. You'll have to talk to them. But, what I need to do is take you to the bank so I can get the rest of my, ah your money for you." Bill wanted this done, and he wanted it done now, so he added, "And, I've got a bonus for you Miguel. For all of your hard work."

They chatted for a moment or two, Miguel inquiring further about the new owners of the house. Bill had no intention of selling the house, primarily because he didn't hold the deed.

When they arrived at the bank, the two men went through their regular ritual at an isolated counter. After entering the numbers, Bill had Miguel sign the withdrawal form. Together they approached the window, and moments later they were again at an isolated counter.

Bill left eighty-five thousand in the account in case he needed it later. At that time, he'd have to go back to the gardener with another bogus story, but didn't feel the task would be too difficult. He'd think of something.

"That is very much money, Meister Avidson," Miguel said after a long period of grinning silence.

Miguel did not speak very good English. If tested, his English reading ability would have scored somewhere in the range of a normal fourth grader. But, he saw the amount of money pushed across the counter and quickly swept up by Bill and stuffed into his pants pocket. And, he saw the relatively small amount given him as a bonus for all of his work.

Miguel was far from stupid. From the very first visit to the bank with Mr. Davidson, he'd known something besides fish tacos was rotten in Guadalajara. His doubts were confirmed when he spoke with his brother-in-law about the mysterious bank account.

"El esconde el dinero que jode," said his brother-in-law. "No permita que el use su nombre." Translated, his brother had essentially told him he was getting fucked.

Miguel promised his brother-in-law he would confront Davidson, and put an end to the arrangement. But, he never saw a need to, other than to appease his wife and in-laws.

"Yes, it's some money I got out of my account," Davidson lied.

After leaving Miguel, Bill drove to his house in Palm Springs to count the loot. The cash represented years of work, most of it illegal. Anticipating present day events, Bill had skimmed from the law firm for several years.

Placing the money, neatly wrapped in bundles of ten thousand, back in the safe, he turned on his computer to check his e-mail. He knew his partners would be looking for him, especially Paul Stritt.

There were four messages. One was spam, and the other three were from Stritt. He read them absentmindedly, and sat staring at the computer, wondering when he would hear from Lynda. Sitting there, he tried to block out any thoughts of not ever hearing from her.

****

Loraine also checked her e-mail and was upset at what she read. She was fond of this young man. For reasons she was not able to explain, she did not like Lynda even before Jack's fateful e-mail. Now she liked her even less and was worried Jack might forgive and forget, succumb to her charms and regret it in the future.

Jack asked Loraine to provide a return airline ticket for Lynda, but it was apparent he hoped her return to California would not be necessary. It was because of her fondness for Jack and her desire for Lynda to use the ticket that Loraine made attempts to find the location of the promiscuous girlfriend. With a lifetime of contacts and markers not called in, she quickly located the *Santiago Mariner*. She not only knew the day it left Pusan for Hong Kong, but she knew the hour of the day as well.

It was also easy to find the shipping agent in Hong Kong which worked on behalf of the *Santiago Mariner's* shipping company. She spoke to the same man Bill Davidson's agent spoke to, the man an acquaintance of people she knew in Hong Kong. Because of her contacts and their quickly forged relationship, the agent said nothing of Loraine's inquiries to Bill's agent.

Loraine however, was privy to all that transpired with the other agent. She knew a man in L.A. was making life hell for the travel agent, and she figured this must be the "other man." She also knew Lynda's voyage was not exactly a jaunt on the good ship lollipop. She knew of the message the agent was to deliver to Lynda from Bill Davidson, but unlike Davidson or his agent, she was certain the agent would be standing on the dock when the *Santiago Mariner* berthed in Hong Kong.

Loraine also knew the shipping agent would be carrying one, first class ticket — United Airlines flight 003 — to depart the next morning at 9:47 a.m. — one-way to Los Angeles, California.

****

Jack arrived at the station for the overnight train trip from Xian to Shanghai. His guide picked him up at the hotel, drove him to the station, and personally led him to his compartment. It was a four-place compartment, the layout not unlike any other train, with two upper and lower bunks separated by a narrow, two-foot space. No other passengers were in the room.

He slid the door closed and looked around. His guide had indicated he was assigned to one of the lower bunks. After stowing his bags underneath the bunk, he propped up the pillow and half laid and half sat on his bunk.

Passengers were streaming back and forth through the passageway of the rail car, and with each one that passed, he breathed a sigh of relief when they did not open the door. It would be great, Jack thought, if by some chance he would be left with the entire compartment to himself. He badly wanted to be alone.

His breakup with Lynda was beginning to take its toll. At first, he'd been too busy with the excitement of traveling into the interior of China to dwell upon it. Alcohol seemed to heighten his sadness, so he maintained somewhat of a teetotalers existence since leaving Hong Kong.

"Why didn't she just tell me she wanted to see other men?" he mumbled to no one, sitting there on the bunk of the compartment. "Why couldn't she have just told me she no longer loved me? And why, oh why, did she have to cheat on me with that sleezeball Davidson?" When William Hugh Davidson entered his thoughts, his anger with her increased, and his hate for Davidson was laced with secret and unrealistic thoughts of murder. Waste the sleezeball. Society would be well served.

It was the killing Bill Davidson that Jack was thinking of when the compartment door slid opened with a crash. Five, boisterous Chinese men, all around the age of twenty-five to thirty-five, entered the room. They all looked at him, but quickly looked away and continued their loud conversation in Chinese.

Two of the men sat on the edge of Jack's bunk, forcing him to move his legs to protect them from being sat upon. They acted as if he didn't exist. As the men became more comfortable, and as he further moved to accommodate them, the level of his patience lowered. He closed his eyes, trying to shut out the continuous and animated conversation.

The train began to move. He breathed a sigh of relief, thinking at any moment two or more of the men who did not belong in the compartment would leave. It was wishful thinking. One of the men produced a deck of cards, and there was a flurry of activity as the others struggled with a large suitcase to use as a makeshift table. The suitcase barely fit between the bunks, one of the men having to stand on it to force it into place. They began playing cards, a game which seemed more vocal than cerebral.

The train was scheduled to leave Xian at 6:22 p.m. An overnight trip to

Shanghai, the train would arrive at approximately 11:30 the next morning. At 7:30 p.m., the game was still going strong. Jack was upset it was taking place in his compartment, but he tried to think of other things. He tried to think of pleasant things, but all he could think of was William Hugh Davidson.

9 p.m. came and went. The game was still in high gear. With each shout by one of the players, he was reminded of the loud, abrasive, prick, Davidson. Jack was becoming more and more angry, and began to think of the five men as reincarnations of Davidson himself.

Shortly after 10, when he was ready to explode, the card game ended. The large suitcase used as a card table was exiled to an overhead rack. Two of the men repositioned their butts in an effort to make themselves more comfortable on Jack's bunk.

Two of the men left, allowing Jack to relax and believe any action on his part would be unnecessary. He was wrong. Five minutes later, the two men returned. Together, they carried five bottles of beer, each larger than a quart in size. It was the straw that broke the camel's back.

Jack sat bolt upright in his bunk, swinging his legs over the side and onto the floor separating the double-stacked bunks. His feet hit one of the men who had remained sitting on the edge of his bunk, and it made the man jump. With his hands moving about crazily, and in a voice much louder than any of the card players had used in the course of the evening, he went off.

"Goddamn it! I've had it! I've been trying to be patient, let you guys play cards or whatever. I don't know which one of you doesn't belong here, but it's time for this shit to end. If I'd known you were going to bring beer ..." his tirade ending with the word "beer."

In retrospect, he could not have expected any of his words to be understood. There was no indication the men spoke or understood any language other than Chinese. Jack simply hoped his loud voice, it's tone, and his facial expression would convey his message. Like many people who are angry, his vocal outburst was accompanied by wild gesticulations. It was this hand waving and the mention of one English word which abruptly stopped Jack in mid-sentence.

When he uttered the word "beer," his hands were out to each side of his body, palms facing forward, and his arms spread out to convey urgency. At that very instant, one of the large, green bottles was thrust into his open left hand.

"... if I'd known you were going to bring beer ..." his voice stopping abruptly as his head turned to look at the bottle of beer now in his outstretched hand. He was forced to hold onto it, the hand putting it there having been quickly drawn away. He turned to face the five Chinese men, now either sitting or standing across from him. They were all grinning as though they had just found Santa Claus putting toys underneath the tree on a snowy, Christmas morning.

Before he could speak, one of the men said something in Chinese, the other four instantly nodding or shouting approval as the man darted from the compartment and ran down the passageway of the carriage.

Jack had to smile. In an instant, the one who departed returned to the compartment with another bottle of beer to replace the one given to their new found American friend. Jack, gesturing with his hands, urged the men to stop trying to pry the bottle caps off with their teeth, the handle of the coupe's door, or the edge of the top bunk.

Quickly rummaging through his bag, he found his Swiss Army knife, a gift from an old friend prior to his travels to Europe after college. Producing it with a smile, he went around to each man, opening his bottle, finishing with his own. The men waited until he was poised to drink. They said something together, Jack added "Skoal," and the party was on.

He was correct in thinking none of the men spoke English. But, in an unexplainable way, they were still able to converse. Through a combination of charades, hand signs and pictures drawn on the pages of a notebook, the conversation dragged on. The small English-Chinese translation book Jack carried, was practically useless, the phrases forever out of place in the actual conversation the traveler is trying to engage in.

One of the men was sent for more beer. Then, he was sent again.

Food appeared, seemingly from a dining car. Later, as the evening wore on, one of the men ventured out and returned with a bottle of what was translated to be Chinese whiskey. It was a clear liquid, with a strong smell of alcohol and a hint of ginger.

At 2 a.m. two of the men wandered out of the compartment. Jack and his three compartment mates settled down to the business of getting some sleep before the train pulled into the Shanghai Rail Station. It was a sleep brought on by a combination of physical exhaustion and too much alcohol.

Jack slept like a baby, waking up the next morning with only a slight hangover and a major story. The men brought more food to the compartment for breakfast, eagerly sharing it with him. Although in dire need of a shower and a shave, Jack left the train in Shanghai feeling great. He had made five more friends.

As he rode with his guide to the hotel, his thoughts turned to his travel experiences in Europe as a college student. He remembered the people he was forced to meet and engage in conversation because he was traveling alone. He remembered the predicaments that arose where he had only himself to rely on. He remembered the total strangers he trusted, never regretting a single instance — never meeting someone who was intent on harming or cheating him.

He reflected on the past evening, finding it strange that at one point he was ready to physically fight these men, and a few hours later, he trusted them as he would an old friend. It was then that Jack realized why he traveled. It made him a better person. It made him feel happy with the world and alive.

****

Lynda's head hurt. The room was spinning around and around. She felt dizzy and nauseous. Her skin was ashen and clammy, and she felt as if at any moment she would lose what little breakfast she'd eaten. She was not aboard the *Santiago Mariner*, but in room 517 of the Holiday Inn in the *Tsim Sha Tsui* area of Kowloon, Hong Kong.

She sat on the edge of the bed, an envelope containing an airline ticket in her hand. She'd been in a state of shock ever since the shipping agent came aboard the ship. He handed her the envelope and told her to contact her boy-friend in Palm Springs.

The boyfriend in Palm Springs part confused her like a couple of quick left jabs, the right cross to the jaw coming when she opened the envelope. With-out the short note from someone named Loraine Ward, she would have been completely confused, the proverbial light bulb illuminating over her head when she read the word, "unfaithful."

The shipping agent was not very friendly towards her, and she wondered what he knew of the situation. He first took her to immigration, and after show-ing her who to talk with, went outside to smoke a cigarette. After a long wait, the passport and immigration people told her she must have a place to stay before they could process her. At her pleadings, the agent reluctantly came inside, casually informing them she was staying in the Holiday Inn, and then, just as causally, walked back outside to resume his smoke.

With a Chinese man driving the car, Lynda and the agent rode to the Holi-day Inn. Although the agent spoke briefly in Chinese to the driver, he said nothing to her. Finally, pulling up in front of the hotel, he spoke as a bellman opened the car door for her. The aloofness he'd shown was also conveyed in his tone of voice. "You don't have a reservation here, but I say, I doubt there should be any problem. If, in fact there is, you may stroll just down Nathan there. A hotel there may be up to your standards also." She was barely out of the car when it raced from the curb.

As she let herself fall back onto the bed, her eyes searching for meaning from the off-white ceiling of what could be any hotel in the world, the inevi-table tears began to cascade down the side of her face. They tickled slightly as they passed her ears, adorned with her favorite earrings, worn that morning in anticipation of her freedom from a rusty ship. The small diamond earrings were a present from Jack, and she silently hoped he would be the one standing on the dock, not some stranger whom she imagined knew all the sordid details of her personal life.

She awoke as if in a trance. After showering and dressing, she rode the elevator to the Guest And Business Services on the twelfth floor. She logged on her e-mail and read the message from Jack. There was also a message from Bill, but she ignored it for now.

She read a message from Rebecca, the wife of Jack's best friend at the newspaper. From the first few sentences, it was clear Rebecca knew about her and Bill. Rebecca also explained how it was essentially spelled out in the newspaper, with details of the fight between Davidson and his wife, as well as Mrs. Davidson's comments to a reporter. At the end of the message, Rebecca mentioned she and her husband would support both of them in any decision they made. She wrote how she was worried for her, just as she was worried for Jack. It made Lynda feel a little better.

She left the business center and returned to her room. She still had not read Bill's message, she simply lacked the energy. She took another nap, and after waking, telephoned the Palm Springs number. The secretary at the fake-front law firm answered, then transferred her call to Bill's house.

"William Davidson," Bill answered on the first ring.

"It's me, Lynda."

"Goddamn!" Bill said, all excited now. "Where are you?"

"Bill, where do you think I am?" she fired back, not ready for trivial conversation. "I'm in Hong Kong, and I'm coming home, back to L. A."

"You've caught him already?" he said, trying to sound as if it might possibly be true.

"No Bill. Your fight with your wife was in the papers. I got an e-mail message from the wife of one of Jack's friends, a couple of e-mails from friends of mine, and an e-mail from Jack. All of them essentially said the same thing ... that being, you and Bill Davidson are fucking each other."

Bill wasn't quite ready for all of this. He'd just emerged from the shower when the phone rang, the first signs of a woody coming from below his belly as he thought about some of the women he'd cavorted with under the Water-Wonder-Power Spray nozzle he'd shelled out over two hundred dollars for. Lynda was also jumping right into the thick of things, no sobs or crying, just straight out, down to business like.

"I'm sorry the fat bitch sounded off to the media. Believe me, had I been there I would have hit her again to shut her up."

"Hitting doesn't help anything, Bill. Besides, I think it started long before that. From the sound of things, everyone in southern California knew about us. Everyone, it seems, but us."

She sighed, stopping him when he started to speak. "Look, it doesn't matter anymore. It's all over. Jack gave me a ticket to fly back to Los Angeles. It leaves in the morning. I'll be out of work and out fifteen million."

"Now, wait a minute. Listen to me," said Bill, trying to regain control of the situation.

"Bill, I don't blame you," she interrupted. "We created this mess together, but it's over. It's over between you and me, it's over between Jack and I and it's over at the firm. I don't think I even want to stay in L.A. My sister lives in Phoenix, so maybe I'll go there."

"Don't you want the fifteen million?"

When she didn't say anything right away, he plowed forward. "Don't you even want the five hundred thousand? You know, you're entitled to either, depending on whether you catch him or not."

"He doesn't want me, Bill. I doubt very much that he'd be happy if I e-mailed him and told him I was coming after him for the money."

"Who gives a good fuck what makes him happy!" He was pushing the envelope a bit now, and he knew it. He'd have to be careful.

"Here is a story for you. A guy and a girl are together. They get along so-so. She wants nice things, he could give a fuck if he's eating tuna out of a can. She meets another guy. Okay, okay, let's say this other guy is kind of an asshole." Bill didn't hear any laughter coming from the other end of the telephone line, but he didn't hear a dial tone either.

"So anyway," he continued. "This gal and this other guy, they start having fun. They're enjoying life, when the first guy makes this promise. It's a promise he can easily keep, without it affecting him one fuckin' iota. It's a promise that would make this gal's life wonderful and worry free, but he up and decides not to honor his pledge because his gal has found happiness somewhere else."

Bill let the thought sink in for a micro-second, then added, "Now, what is that shit? I can understand him being hurt," he lied. In truth, he couldn't understand how any man with thirty-plus million in his pocket could give a shit if some woman took a walk. Thirty-plus million buys a lot of pussy, but he kept those thoughts to himself.

He tried another tack. "I'll bet he said there was still a chance for the two of you, didn't he?" He didn't get an answer right away, and he wasn't saying anything until he got one.

After a pause, she replied, "Yes, he said he still loves me and hopes we might get back together."

"Yeah, and he'd make your life miserable."

Bill knew the next thing he said was gospel, a person could literally stake their life on it. "Let's say the roles were reversed. Let's say he found someone else, you begged him to come back, and he did. You'd make his life miserable, wouldn't you."

He would have expected a reaction like, "You're fuckin' right I would. I'd make living on this earth, like living in hell." He experienced that world living in the same house as his big, fat, ugly, soon-to-be ex-wife. Instead, he got only silence from Lynda.

"Look, you can do what you want," he said calmly. "But, you're wrong if you think he's being fair. You're wrong if you think you deserve this, that this is some kind of punishment or penance you're required to endure. You're wrong if you think you'll never regret going after him. You're wrong if you think fifteen million won't matter after a couple of years ... that you'll find happiness elsewhere.

"And, I want you to know you're wrong if you think I won't stand behind you. I'll drop everything ... the wife, the firm, everything ... to support you should you want to go after what's been promised ... what's been promised, and is so easy for him to uphold."

There was a pause in the conversation, and he knew instinctively what she was thinking. If she got on that airplane, the whole thing was in the toilet.

"Lynda, I'm divorcing my wife. I've cleaned all the money I can out of the bank, and I'm arranging to dispose of the Palm Springs property today. Just say the word, and I'm on an airplane tomorrow." There was another pause, and for a moment he thought she might have hung up.

"Look, I'll think about it, okay?" she finally replied. "I really don't know what to do, but it's something I have to figure out on my own."

Bill thought changing the subject might be a good move. He was working her, like he worked every conversation, like he was speaking to a jury. He knew you could not beat the subject to death, just plant the seed and nurture it to grow on its own.

"Hey, how was the boat ride?" he enthusiastically implored.

"Fuck, I've never been so cold, miserable and sick in my entire life!" she shot back.

She hardly ever swore, and it caught Bill off guard. "Really, I mean, ah, was it really all that bad?"

"Everything was terrible. I was seasick almost the entire time. I thought for sure the ship was going to sink in this big storm we went through. And, I thought they were going to throw me in one of those Gulags in Russia."

"You went to Russia?" Bill asked incredulously. He couldn't think of any sea route that would take her to Russia.

"Bill," Lynda sighed, "Vladivostok is in Russia. It's one of the ports we sailed to. It's just north of Korea."

"Jesus", thought Bill, still trying to figure out how Russia could even be remotely on the way to Hong Kong.

"So, were there any interesting passengers?" he asked, momentarily forgetting the travel agent had mentioned Lynda would be the sole fare.

"Yeah right." She sounded exasperated now. "The Queen of England was aboard. Her cabin was right across the pool from mine."

"Hey, I'm sorry. I'm just trying to be your friend here!" How in the hell did we ever get on this subject, he thought to himself. He was about to change the subject again and ask what the weather was like, when she said she had to go.

"I'll call you tomorrow morning, before I fly out. I'll think about what you said, but I'm not making any promises. For right now, I just want everyone to leave me alone."

They said goodbye then, Bill feeling his current odds of getting some of the fifteen million were no less now than what they'd been before she called. He had some cash in a cardboard box, stashed in the trunk of his car. He had to find a place to put this and the money from his floor safe where he could easily access it, yet a place where his wife and her attorney wouldn't find it. He knew an attorney in Palm Springs who was willing to rent the house, if his initial plan fell through.

Lynda had her own problems. She was thinking about the fifteen million dollars she'd made a mess of. Losing out on all that money put her in even a darker mood than she'd been before. Bill's last question about the voyage on the *Santiago Mariner*, brought back images of endless retching and misery, and added to her torment.

She slipped on her shoes, thinking a walk might make her feel better. The room, although it was nice enough, was starting to add to her funk.

When she stepped through the doors of the Holiday Inn on Nathan Street, she expected the same partly cloudy weather she'd experienced when she arrived. She stopped dead in her tracks as the automatic doors closed behind her. The livery-clad doorman was asking her if she would like a taxi, his umbrella at the ready to assist her ten foot, rain drenching gauntlet from the protective canopy of the hotel to the relative dryness of the back seat of a taxi. She didn't hear a word he was saying, as she stood there staring at a torrential downpour.

There were people and cars everywhere. The street was a gridlock, set on a virtual river of surface water. People, some with umbrellas and some without, filled the sidewalks. She would have been pushed aside by the stream of people, had it not been for the protective barrier of potted plants jutting out on both sides of the canopy over the entrance to the hotel. A Chinese man, wearing shorts and work boots, but no shirt or hat, pushed a cart through the street, weaving in an out of lanes of traffic as he tried to cross the congested street. It was about 85 degrees.

"Miss, may I be of assistance," said the doorman, moving around in front of her, partially obscuring her view of this sea of madness.

"No, ah ... thank you very much," she said, turning to return to the dry safety of the hotel lobby.

She found the hotel's bar, but decided instead to have a drink in the lobby. It was a vast area, full of overstuffed furniture. It gave her a sense of freedom, the opposite of what she'd had in her hotel room and aboard the freighter. She sat there with a gin and tonic, and after that, another gin a tonic. When the third one arrived, she opened her notebook, at the same time realizing the irony of having the thing with her whenever she turned around.

She began to write.

This legal notebook is like a man. It seems to be there every time I turn around. Sometimes that's good — full of useful information. Sometimes it's bad — full of memories and forgotten promises. I guess it's like all things, good and bad.

Jack owes me. If for nothing else, for the misery of having to ride on that boat. He owes me for being sick. He owes me for putting up with this weather. But most of all, he owes me for jumping through all of these hoops for money. I don't like traveling alone. I hate roughing it, or in his mind, experiencing life like the natives. As far as I'm concerned, quaintness only goes so far.

Bill owes me too. He's part of the reason I'm in this mess.

If I fly home, I'm out the money, unless somehow Jack and I get back

together after he returns. If I follow him and catch him:
    (1) Would he keep his promise?
    (2) Could we really get things back together?
    (3) I'd have to put up with a lot more God-forsaken traveling.
Damn him. Damn him.

After the fourth gin and tonic, she decided she'd better get some food before the gastric experiences of her sea voyage returned to haunt her. She called room service, surprised to find a hamburger as well as some other American sounding items on the menu.

With each drink, she became angrier and angrier with both Jack and Bill. But, despite her alcohol fueled anger, she knew she was dependent on both of them.

The hamburger was terrible. She ate half of it, and returning to the business center, e-mailed messages to a couple of her friends, informing them of her safe arrival in Hong Kong. She wanted to e-mail a short note to Jack.

At first, she sat staring at the monitor, wondering what to say. She thought she loved him, but she wasn't sure of many things right now, love being right at the top of a very long list. She knew she was in love with him at one time, and the memories of their times together made her smile for the first time all day.

Dear Jack

    I really don't know what to say. I'm in Hong Kong, in a state of shock, much like I know you must be. All I can do is be honest with you. I'm sorry I hurt you. Bill Davidson means nothing to me, it was just one of those things that happens. I think I still love you. I know I loved you very much at one time.
    But, I think the question is, whether or not you love me. You won the lottery. I'm happy for you, but why are you making me go through hell to share it with you? I know you want me to experience traveling by myself. I know you want me to be a dreamer. But Jack, I don't enjoy traveling by myself. Why can't I be with you? Why can't I just be me?
    I've had a couple of gin and tonics. It is the only way I've been able to keep my sanity. Yes, I'm mad at you. I feel like I've become your personal puppet. Go here. Do it this way. Now, fly home.
    I've decided I am going through with this. I guess you can run if you want. But, I'm NOT returning to L.A. disgraced AND broke. As mad as it makes me to jump when you pull the strings, it makes me madder to think I have made all of these sacrifices for nothing.
    Lynda

She experimented with various endings for her letter, such words as Love, Love Always, I Still Love You, and With Love. She decided just her name was the best. She clicked on the "Send" icon, immediately wondering if she'd done the right thing and wishing she'd kept a copy to read when she was sober.

She returned to her room, and sitting on the edge of the bed, telephoned Bill.

"Bill, it's me again," she said, surprised to have reached him.

"Hey, this is a surprise! I didn't expect to hear from you again today."

"I've decided to follow Jack. I want what I feel has been promised me, but I want you to tell me straight up now, is the e-mail he sent me a binding contract?"

"You're goddamn right it's binding! I'll make it binding!" Bill said exuberantly. "I'm proud of you. I'm glad you've decided to get what's yours. The guy is such a prick."

"Please. I don't hate Jack, and your saying bad things about him does not support me in any way. If you really want to support me, there is a way you can do that."

"Sure, you just name it," he replied, knowing what she would ask of him even before she said it.

"I'd like you to come over here and help me find him. I want to catch him as fast as possible. I've already suffered enough."

"I'll be on a plane tomorrow or the next day. Where are you staying?" he asked.

"I'm in the Holiday Inn, room five-one-seven in Kowloon. I don't know the address."

"Fuckin' Holiday Inn!" he snorted. "Christ, don't they have any Sheratons or Hiltons in the fucking town? What is it, a motel?"

"It's okay. Not the Ritz, but it's not bad."

"Well, if there's a Hilton or Sheraton close by, check in. Leave a message with the front desk at the Holiday, and I'll find you. You may have to travel by train, but I'll be damned if I'm staying in a fuckin' hovel."

She didn't like the "you" and "I'm" in the last sentence he spoke, but decided not to argue the point. She said goodbye, and hung up the phone.

Lynda didn't need another gin and tonic, however she wanted one. When she started to open the door of her room to leave, she suddenly turned and walked back to the bedside table. She picked up the United Airlines ticket — one way, Hong Kong to Los Angeles, California, departure at 0947, July 5th — tore it in two, then tore it in two again and yet again. She let the pieces fall to the floor, not bothering to pick them up.

That felt good, she thought. "Now, I'm going to have that gin and tonic," she said aloud to no one but herself.

<u>11</u>

Shanghai, full of new skyscrapers and modern infrastructure, is much like Hong Kong. Not indicative of Chinese cities or Chinese life, it's like traveling to Tijuana and telling all of your friends you've been to Mexico.

Jack moved on to Beijing. His transfer from the train station to his hotel went smoothly. The staff at the front desk informed him breakfast was still being served in the dining room, so after a quick shower and shave, he returned to the main floor dining area.

Like the other westerner's hotels in China, the food was served buffet style. The menu featured ham, scrambled and poached eggs, muffins, breads and sweet rolls of all types, and an assortment of fruits and melons. Of the more than thirty different items to choose from, only four or five could truly be considered Chinese cuisine.

After breakfast a walk sounded good, so he passed through the sensor equipped front entry-way, leaving the air-conditioned environment of the hotel. As the doors automatically closed behind him, he stopped dead in his tracks.

Before him, stood a sea of humanity on foot, on bicycles, and in cars. Every vehicle seemed to be piloted by a driver with one hand on the steering wheel and the other on the horn. Pedestrians, bicyclists, and other drivers appeared to be impervious to the noise and motion of each other. But, it was not the sheer number of people which made him stop. It was the air. Within ten seconds of stepping outside, his eyes stung from the smog and the pollution. Los Angeles on a bad day was better than this.

According to a small map he'd found in his room, the street in front of the hotel lead to Tiananmen Square. The map also indicated an internet cafe near the square, and Jack lumbered along, wiping the smog induced tears from his eyes every 50 feet.

The internet cafe was a rather funky place. It was upstairs, in a small two-story building. It was crowded with westerners, and although the polluted air of outside was replaced by cigarette smoke, it was also filled with the sweet recorded sounds of Patsy Cline.

There was a message from Dan, and another from Dan's wife Rebecca.

They both spoke of support and hopes for his safety. He e-mailed replies, which in effect said nothing of how he felt, just vague messages that he was still alive and well.

He also received an e-mail from Loraine, explaining the arrangement of a ticket for Lynda as directed, and that someone would be there to meet her when she stepped off the ship in Hong Kong. Lynda was scheduled to arrive in Hong Kong on July 4th, her return flight ticket scheduled for departure the next day.

Jack sat at the computer, staring at the screen for several minutes. He reached in his shoulder bag and removed the copy of his itinerary. Lynda's arrival in Hong Kong corresponded to his arrival in Irkutsk, Russia. What would she be thinking when she read his e-mail telling her he knew all about her affair, and how would she react to the return ticket?

He immediately wished he'd remained in Hong Kong, confronting her and their problems as a couple, head on. There may have been a slight chance of resolution. In his heart however, he knew his hopes were false, and regardless of how he tried to shape his dreams, he could not imagine a happy ending.

Although Beijing offered many things for a traveler to see or do, only two things interested Jack. Number one on that list was the Great Wall of China.

As many school children have learned, the Great Wall of China is the only man made object visible with the naked eye when looking from the surface of the moon back to earth. It is unclear why a four lane freeway system would not be visible also, but Jack never brought up the point when someone expounded on trivia about The Wall.

He arose the next morning, and after enjoying another American breakfast at the American buffet inside the American-style hotel, he waited in the lobby for the bus that would take him out of the largest city in China.

The bus arrived on time, with only two of the fourteen passengers being of Asian descent. There were two young women from Norway, and a couple from Canada. Two other people were from somewhere in western Europe, a location Jack failed to hear. The remainder were Americans.

The Chinese government likes to keep a close eye on westerners. They prefer visitors make use of tours and guides. There are only certain hotels where an American can stay, and westerners are forbidden to drive a car. On any tour, it appears as though the tour guide is intent on keeping your mind and eyes occupied at all times, save for the brief times when you arrive at a landmark, monument or souvenir shop. Even then, their presence is always known.

Jack made a few notes in his journal, and kept his eyes on the driver as he proceeded in a very unorthodox manner. Like all Chinese drivers, one hand was glued to the horn, and he honked it constantly at whatever moved. He would slowly accelerate — forty, fifty, sixty — until attaining a top speed of sixty-five. Shifting the transmission into neutral, the vehicle would then coast. Sixty-five, fifty-five, forty-five, thirty-five — then back into gear and the whole process would be repeated — all the way to the Great Wall, a three hour trip.

Jack stepped off the bus onto a parking lot filled with tour busses. That he was the only passenger traveling alone weighed heavily on him. The Great Wall was something Lynda had expressed a longing desire to see, and he was saddened they were not experiencing this moment together. A good physical test would clear his mind, so he started off to scale a section of the wall.

He hiked a short distance before stopping to remove his shirt. It was hot, and the steps leading up were of varying heights, anywhere from three inches to two feet. He'd purchased a bottle of mineral water at a souvenir stand where the climb began, and paused for a drink. He noticed another tourist twenty yards ahead of him, leaning over the parapet, and obviously physically spent. He worked his way up to the man, who looked to be an American, and offered him some of his water.

"I came all the way from Idaho to see this," said the man, between gasps for breath and gulps of water. He was about sixty years old and forty pounds overweight. "I don't care if it takes me three damn days to get to the top, somehow, I'll make it."

The man drank the remainder of the water, and then apologized for doing so. Bidding him farewell, Jack wondered why so many people waited so long to see or do the things they dreamed of. They would work and save, work and invest, all for a future that was at best, uncertain. They would wait until they could retire with full, rather than partial benefits, often attaining freedom without the physical ability to enjoy it.

As he passed a rest station, complete with a souvenir shop featuring T-shirts emblazoned in English with the words, "I Climbed To The Top Of The Great Wall Of China," Jack knew the man he'd met would never get to the top. He'd probably buy some bottled water and a T-shirt, wait long enough to make his story believable, and later descend to the parking lot, his wife and friends. He'd tell them he climbed to the top, and embellish the story with each passing year. He would take the secret to his grave. It was sad.

Already fatigued, he estimated he was only halfway to the top. The remainder of the climb found fewer, but hardier people. Just before reaching the top, two young women were descending. As they passed him, he heard one say to the other, "Been there, done that." And that is what it was.

He took a few photos from the top, pausing only a few minutes before making the descent. It was very steep, and in fact, riskier than the ascent. It would be very easy for a person to get moving too fast, not be able to stop, and go tumbling down. No hand railing existed, and no ambulance stood by for the obvious heart attack victim. It was enough to give the average American risk manager a coronary, and his compatriot, slip and fall attorney, a wet dream.

The return trip from the wall included stops at several monuments noted for several different dynasties, as well as four stops at souvenir and gift shops. They also made a stop at a clinic which featured traditional Chinese medicines. In an atmosphere resembling a traveling circus, the "doctors" were able to make a diagnosis by simply taking a patient's pulse. Magical elixirs and an array of herbs were available for every ailment, and of course, Mastercard and Visa were welcome.

The next morning, Jack arose with a mission to visit the another must-see site on his list. He would walk down the avenue in front of his hotel to Tiananmen Square. It was still early morning when he finished breakfast, and he thought the square might be less crowded now than later in the day.

Tiananmen Square, covering 99 acres, is the largest public square in the world. It is the heart of Beijing as well as the Chinese nation. The square includes the Mao Zedong Museum, the Monument To The People's Hero's, and Zhengyangmen Gate. It is flanked by the Great Hall of the People, and the Museum of Chinese History.

Americans equate Tiananmen Square with demonstrations held there in 1989. It was there, that a man stood defiantly before a tank, his hand outstretched as if to stop it by pure will and nothing else. The number of people killed in the demonstration is unknown. Although the man standing before the tank was later identified as Wang Weilin, his fate is also unknown. The Chinese government has stated no man by that name was arrested, charged, or killed in the uprising.

Shortly after arriving at the square, Jack turned to notice two Chinese women. They were both about fifty years of age, and dressed conservatively. He couldn't say what made him turn to notice the two, but shortly after doing so, he saw one of the women extract a small banner from her purse. The sign was in Chinese, the symbols red on a plain white background.

The women held up the sign, and within seconds, a man with a two-way radio approached. One of the women tried to put the sign back in her purse, as her accomplice started to walk in the opposite direction. Other plainclothes officers arrived. A police van surged quickly across the vast expanse of pavement.

The women were grabbed, pulled and dragged to the waiting van. One was thrown into the back — literally thrown, not simply pushed. The other was shoved into the front passenger seat, a seat whose armrests folded down and across her body as a restraint. From thirty feet away, Jack could hear the sound of the mechanism being slammed into place.

At no time did the women protest or fight back against their captors. They never yelled slogans, or even cried out as they were taken away. Jack wondered what fate lay ahead for these women. Would they just disappear like Wang Weilin?

Jack hadn't walked more than fifty yards when he heard another commotion. A young man was running, being chased by yet another plainclothes official. Others seem to materialize out of nowhere, cutting off his escape. The man was grabbed, and with an official on either side and another pushing him from behind, he was escorted to a police van. Just before he was pushed inside, one of the plainclothes men said something to him. He then hit him twice in the face. Like the two women, the man never spoke out in defiance. He never fought back.

The Chinese people and their culture is difficult for an American to relate to. The people themselves, are warm and kind. With the exception of pushing and shoving to get where they want to go, the Chinese people he'd met were polite and courteous.

Their culture looks upon arguing or getting mad at someone in authority or higher stature as losing face. It's not to question, but rather do. They seem to follow like so many sheep, never complaining in public, never questioning or demanding — going about the routine of daily living as if everything around them does not exist.

When Jack first arrived in Beijing and was instantly assaulted by the air pollution, he pondered how the city would ever manage to host the Olympics. After a few days in Beijing, he thought he might have the answer. The Chinese government would simply shut down some of their industry. They might also restrict auto travel to some degree. If a person were a known dissident, they would be relocated, and if a friend or family member questioned the relocation or disappearance, they might be relocated also. In a city of over eight million people, who will miss ten, or even twenty thousand people? Who has ever missed Wang Weilin?

It was the end of Jack's visit to Tiananmen Square, and the end of his stay in Beijing. The next morning, he was picked up at his hotel by a guide and taken to the Beijing Central Rail Station, a station that was a scene of confusion and bedlam.

Most of the passengers crowding and jostling for position near a gate which lead to the train platform, looked to be of Mongolian descent. Different from the Chinese, their facial features are more akin to that of the American Eskimo. Like the Chinese, pushing and shoving seemed to be a part of their culture — the concept of forming a single file line as foreign as a pork chop at a bar mitzvah dinner.

All of the people waiting for the gate to be opened were crowded into a hallway about fifteen feet wide. And, although it was obvious there was no room ahead of Jack and his guide, the fact did not stop people from somehow trying to forge their way past.

The travelers around him seemingly carried everything they owned. There were bundles wrapped in a kind of burlap material, their size larger than a bale of hay. Obese suitcases were everywhere, their hinges and latches straining like the belt of a 400 pound man. Phillipino Samsonite — cardboard boxes wrapped in twine — were stacked here and there.

Every time someone advanced a few inches, like a giant wave, everyone and every package, parcel, bag and bundle moved forward behind them. To not move was to risk having someone push past you in an effort to take the six inch space you failed to reoccupy. Jack's Chinese guide pushed and shoved with the best of them, and they noticed some small progress.

Fifty feet ahead, he saw the large iron gate which sealed off the passageway suddenly open. All hell broke loose as Jack and his guide struggled forward. They were traveling extremely light compared to most, and were thus able to overtake several in the long passageway between the gate and the actual train platform.

They passed one man who was wrestling with his baggage. The man appeared to be alone. One item, the size of a small spinet piano, was entirely wrapped in burlap. On top of it were two large cardboard boxes, taped and roped together in a fashion which would make a UPS worker proud. On top of the two boxes was one of the largest suitcases imaginable. A baby-blue affair, it was duck-taped together, with a lashing of rope for good measure.

The man was trying, (and actually succeeding), to move what appeared to be everything he owned, by sitting down behind the mass, and with his back against the pile, lifting his butt off the floor about four inches and pedaling with his feet, propelling the entire mass down the smooth, tiled floor.

Looking back, amazed the man and mountain of possessions were actually overtaking many who were struggling with their goods in a more conventional manner, Jack nearly missed the turn. The passageway took a sharp right, went forward for another twenty yards, and descended two, long flights of stairs. There was no stopping, and as his guide lead him forward in something slightly under a dead run, Jack was sorely tempted to stop and watch how some of the over-loaded passengers dealt with the stairs.

Boarding, he found the train very clean, though not particularly modern. His guide located the assigned compartment with little trouble. It was the first Chinese train where the car attendants possessed any type of presence. Although conversing only in Chinese, they helped him with his luggage, and stowed it in the overhead bin above his bunk.

The compartment was a two-place coupe. Who would be his compartment mate? What if it was the man with all of the baggage? If so, he was likely trying to collect himself after tumbling down the stairs.

It was not the man with the spinet piano, two huge boxes, and a giant suitcase. Instead, it was another man with three suitcases and a cardboard container which appeared to hold a box spring and mattress. Jack groaned audibly when the young, Mongolian man entered the small room.

Ulzilorshikh "Augie" Jamsran spoke English, which made things easier right from the start. Also, the box, rather than housing a seven piece bedroom set, contained a racing bicycle. Augie often traveled with the bike, and with very little effort stowed it in a common storage area above the door. The suitcases were also handled deftly, and Augie and Jack were both comfortably seated well before the train left the station.

Augie Jamsran, the National Bicycle Champion of Mongolia, was in China for a race. A delightful man, he'd traveled in Asia and eastern Europe, racing his bike. Someday, he wanted to go to America. He also wanted to compete in the Tour de France. When Jack told him he had once met Lance Armstrong, the Mongolian sportsman beamed. He too had met him, and that common bond alone seemed to seal their friendship. They talked and talked as the train lumbered north, slowly eating up the miles and heading for the Chinese-Mongolian border.

****

Jack was fast asleep when the train came to a stop in the dead of night. He was awakened by movement of a different sort than the usual swaying of the train, and noticed Augie was gone. He walked to the end of the car, rubbing the sleep out of his eyes.

At the end of the car, he found the door closed. Turning the handle, the door swung open. They were at some sort of station, and in a daze he proceeded to step off the train. Half asleep, he failed to notice the obvious.

A shout could be heard from someone just as he realized there was nothing in front of him but air. He grabbed the rail on the outside of the car, his ever-present shoulder bag swinging around and out of control. In an effort to keep the bag from hitting the side of the car, he held onto the hand rail with one hand and the swinging bag with the other. It was a losing proposition, and he would have fallen if not for several hands coming to his rescue and helping him down to the safety of the ground. As he straightened himself up and thanked his rescuers, he looked back at the car he'd descended from.

The bottom step of a rail car is normally six to twelve inches above the platform. The step was now six feet above the platform and still rising. A pair of powerful, yellow-painted jacks hoisted the car up and off the rails.

They were at the Chinese border town of Erlian. In the late 50's, when there was a breakdown in Sino-Soviet relations, the Chinese converted their track gauge to a narrower width. It is therefore necessary to change the bogies, or wheel mechanisms under each and every car traveling into or out of the country.

Two men crawl under the train and free the bogie system from the base of the car. Hydraulic jacks slowly elevate the car while additional disconnections are made until the bogie system is free. The track below the car is a system which features both gauges of track, so when the narrower bogie system is rolled out of the way, the wider system can be positioned under the car. The car would then be slowly lowered back down onto the new bogies and fastened into place.

The entire process was repeated with each car, and took place under a brightly lit structure similar to a gigantic carport. After all of the cars were refitted, a new engine was attached. The interchange took over two and one half hours to complete.

While many of the passengers were deposited at a nearby station, Jack stood on the platform and took pictures of the process. The workers seemed delighted to be the center of the photo opportunity. When his car was lowered onto the new bogies, Jack climbed aboard, thanking the workers whose hands rescued him from falling. He wasn't sure they understood him, but they all smiled, bowed and waved.

The train moved back to the Erlian Station, located a few hundred yards away, picked up the remaining passengers and trudged off in the early morning darkness. Without effort, he fell asleep, his last conscious thought being of his destination and how he was about to experience a word familiar to all crossword fanatics.

Clue: 1 Across, Mongolian city

_____ Bator   (Four Letters)

****

Bill wasn't asleep, but his mind was elsewhere when the phone rang. Speaking with the secretary at the ersatz Palm Springs law office earlier in the day, he'd left instructions not to be disturbed. The lone exception being calls from Lynda. Therefore, when the phone rang, Bill thought it was her.

"Where in the hell are you?" came a voice from the other end. "We've got some serious problems here, Bill!" It was Paul Stritt.

"Ah shit, Paul. I needed to get away from the whole goddamn thing for awhile. I'll be back in the office in a couple of days," Bill lied. "We can go see Rogers then."

"Oh, I don't think you need to see Rogers. I saw him myself." Paul Stritt paused for a moment to keep from screaming at his dumb-assed, soon to be, ex-law partner. "Let me just bring you up to speed, Bill. It's ah, well it's kind of like a State Of The Law Firm synopsis of what's going on."

Bill didn't have a clue as to what his partner was getting at, but said nothing. He just wanted the conversation to end so he could get back to thinking about whatever he was thinking about before the phone rang. Whatever that was, wasn't clear at the moment.

"I kept OUR appointment with Rogers! I walked in the door, and there is that sleezeball Bryant. Ya know, the private investigator who seems to get some perverse delight out of serving papers on other attorneys. "Anyway, he says, 'Paul Stritt?' and slaps me with service. Rogers and your wife have hit us with a blanket restraining order, freezing not only your sorry-assed assets, but those of the firm's as well."

Bill started to say something, but Paul cut him off.

"Hear this Bill," he said. "Since Lynda is an employee of the firm, and since she is reportedly having sexual relations with a married partner of the firm, and since she is off chasing some guy for money ... Rogers is afraid that you will spend the firm's money to assist her in her endeavors. Therefore, the firm and it's partners assets have been frozen.

"And I quote, 'The firm and its partners are prohibited of disposition of any assets whatsoever.' Loosely translated Bill, your partners are taking it in the ass on this matter!"

"He's a cocksucker, and she's a cunt," stammered Bill.

"Bill, I hope you're referring to yourself and Lynda, and not Rogers and the soon-to-be, ex-Misses Davidson," Paul shot back. He quickly adjusted his tone, and continued. "Bill, this is all getting to be too much. I've spoken with Mumph and John. We all agree something has to be done. Rogers has set up a hearing requiring you and the firm to account for disposition of all funds for one year to date. We'll do that, but then we're pulling the plug. We all have too much invested here. You're out of control. Plain and simple, you're just out of control."

"Fuck you!" Bill snapped back. He slammed the telephone down in its cradle. "Fuck you!" he screamed again to the innocent looking phone and no one else.

He sat there awhile, waiting for the phone to ring. It would give him the opportunity to tell his law partner how he really felt. But, the phone did not ring, so he dialed a number instead.

"Gorman, you dumb fuck. What the hell is going on with you?" said Bill.

"Well, if it ain't my ol' pal Billy," came a raspy voice from the other end of the line.

"What the fuck are you doing?" Bill asked again.

"I just finished running a marathon, and I'm getting ready to go swim about five hundred laps in the fuckin' pool. What the fuck do you think I'm doing? I'll tell ya what I'm doing," the man named Gorman not pausing a second for Bill to answer the question. "I'm sitting here, a couple of fucking oxygen tubes stuck up my fuckin' nose, waiting to die. Ya happy now?"

"Jesus Christ, ya don't have to get all pissy. I just asked," whined Bill.

Gorman owned the house in Palm Springs that Bill used for a pussy pad. He'd started smoking when he was thirteen because it made him appear a little tougher than the other thirteen year-old boys around him. His voice sounded as if it came out of the muffler of a thirty year-old car, sitting on a beach since the day it rolled off the showroom floor. The doctors had found signs of cancer in his lungs, he had emphysema, and the heart by-pass surgery he needed could not be done because the rest of his body was in such terrible shape.

"I need a favor," said Bill, just laying it right out there.

"Well, tough shit. I'm all fuckin' out of favors for today. I just gave my last one out to a group of Job's Daughters who came to the door. They said they'd blow me for a hundred bucks."

"Hey, I'm serious, and remember if you will, the time you dragged your ass in my office wanting a favor. Without me, you'd not only have bad lungs, you'd have an asshole about six inches wide from being the wife of some buck nigger up at San Quentin. I kept you out of jail, remember?"

"Ya, ya, I know. Hey, those were the fucking days, weren't they? Oh, by the way, I read your name in the paper. It's not one of them coincidences is it, that you need a favor right after you punched out your wife? How is the old bat, anyway?"

Bill ignored the question since Gorman didn't really want to know. "Look, we had a deal where, ah ... I got your house for fifteen years in lieu of, what I would call very reasonable fees for keeping your sex life a heterosexual one. Aye-fuckin'-e, keeping your ass out of jail."

"Ya so?" rasped Gorman.

"Well, I've had it for a little over seven years, and I want to cash out my remaining lease."

It was a while before Gorman stopped laughing, the laugh quickly becoming a coughing fit. Bill could hear him retching, and had to hold the phone away from his ear to keep from being totally grossed out by the sound. Finally, Gorman came back on the line.

"That's the funniest damn thing I've ever heard," he said, still laughing a bit, but desperately trying to suppress it in order to keep from hacking his guts out.

"It's not that funny. Look, I need money. Are you happy now, you heard me say it? I need as much cash dough as I can scrape up. And, I need it quick. I'm leaving for China and fuck knows where, just as soon as I can."

"What the hell, did you kill her?"

"No, but I can't say the fuckin' thought hasn't crossed my mind. I just need money. We had a deal, and now I don't need the house anymore. I suppose I could sublet the joint, but I want all the dough right now. You don't need the house. You could sell it or get a second on it."

"Stop already, will ya?" pleaded Gorman. The conversation was making him tired, and all of a sudden another nap sounded pretty good to him. "Listen, we go way back, don't fuckin' worry. How much ya need?"

"A hundred n' fifty thousand," Bill heard himself say. He would have settled for fifty or even twenty-five grand, but the call was rather spontaneous, and he was shooting from the hip.

Gorman forced himself not to laugh hysterically yet again. "I ain't exactly got it in my wallet, ya know."

Bill was about about to revise the amount of his request, but he heard a relenting sound coming through the hapless, raspy lungs and cigarette scared throat of his friend.

"But, you could raise it fairly quickly?" he ventured.

"Yeah, I can. Ya know this ain't a fuckin' gift. I want the motherfucking money paid back."

"So, how soon?"

Gorman knew from experience Bill's, "How soon," referred to how soon he could get the money, and not how soon Gorman wanted the loan repaid.

"Are you here in Palm Springs now?" asked Gorman, already knowing the answer. When Bill said he was, Gorman sighed. "I'll have Danny O'Neil run the money over to you in the morning. If I were you I'd be sure to be home, because if you're not, O'Neil might end up in Vegas playing some incredibly stupid, fuckin' long shot."

After Gorman hung up the phone, he sat there for a few minutes, the clean, fresh oxygen invisibly making it's way through the small plastic tubes and into his nose from a green tank sitting beside his chair. He had no family and his wife was dead.

"What the fuck," he said aloud to himself. He knew Davidson was chasing pussy, but what did he care. He'd be dead in less than six months.

12

Jack and Augie's compartment was near the end of the carriage, but train attendants were making everyone exit from the opposite end of the car. They had arrived in Ulan Bator, but it appeared it might be some time before they would be able to detrain. Passengers, with all of their bales, bundles and suitcases, were now crowded into the three foot wide corridor ahead of them.

When they finally entered the corridor, they found themselves last in line. Augie Jamsran began chatting with the two train attendants who, like shepherds, were trying to herd their flock slowly through the car.

"I have told them you are with me," said Augie, after nudging Jack.

Jack turned to see what his friend was referring to, and saw that the two smiling attendants intended to allow them to exit the car from a previously locked rear door. As Jack turned, his arms full of his own baggage, he could feel the passengers next to him turning also, in hopes of exiting the car from this more convenient door. Although the attendant spoke in Mongolian, it was clear the people behind Jack would still be required to exit from the far end.

He wasn't sure why they were getting preferential treatment, but he didn't care. It was shortly after mid-day, and it was very hot. The air was rapidly becoming stagnant, with the body odors of thirty hours of train travel impossible to ignore.

Jack was looking down at the steps which led off the car when someone standing on the platform reached out their hand to steady him. There were flashes of light, and he quickly realized this was a planned reception — a planned reception for Ulzilorshikh "Augie" Jamsran, the Mongolian National Bicycle Champion and hero to his people.

After saying goodbye, Jack found his guide, and minutes later arrived at the lovely Bayangol Hotel. A product of Soviet architecture and engineering marvel akin to Cherynobel and the Berlin Wall, the hotel consists of twin, multi-level towers, connected to and separated by a one-level building which houses a restaurant and banquet room. In what may have been a capricious state of creative nomenclature, some genius entitled the towers, Building A and Building B.

The hotel is a colossal mass of ugly concrete. The plumbing only works on a marginal basis, and the floors are uneven. Sitting several feet off the street, the sidewalks leading to and around the buildings are cracked and tilted.

Here, and in many parts of the world, it's as if concrete workers are unable to pour a continuous concrete slab larger than ten foot square. It seems to be imperative that an adjoining slab is constructed to be either four inches higher or lower than the previous one. A slab at a rakish angle may receive bonus points for style and execution. A finished, one-hundred foot long sidewalk is uneven and bumpy. It is difficult to walk on, bone-jarring to ride a bicycle on, and almost impossible to push a baby tram along.

Jack opened his shoulder bag and withdrew his writing tablet and itinerary. Lynda would be arriving in Hong Kong soon, and hopefully they would have a chance to converse via e-mail. Dialog would at least bring him some peace and closure. If they could converse through e-mail, he might be able to settle on one emotion, be it hate, love, sadness or regret.

He read that a guide was scheduled to pick him up at 9 a.m. the next morning, taking him to a someplace called Terelj, where he would spend two nights in a yurt, or *ger* camp.

The next morning, while waiting for the guide, an American strolled through the lobby, pausing for a moment to talk with the desk clerk. Two young Mongolian men in the lobby, dressed in ill fitting and dated sport coats, raised their eyebrows at one another as the American walked out of the hotel. One of the men met Jack's eyes as the American departed. Jack rolled his eyes, and they all shared a smile together and an inner laugh.

Jack learned the other American was from Venice Beach, California. The man was about six foot four, and probably weighed at least 230 pounds. He was tanned and in excellent physical shape. The American carried a small shoulder bag which matched his skirt. His ensemble included a pair of mid-calf height boots, a blond wig which cascaded over his shouldes and a thin sweater, that thankfully was not low cut. He appeared to have breasts.

Being a transvestite in California is one thing. Taking the act on the road to London or Amsterdam is probably something done more often than one would imagine. But, taking it to Mongolia seems downright risky.

There were tales of Mongolians hunting bear by strapping a spike to their chest and allowing themselves to be "hugged" by the bear. What would such a culture think of a man from Venice Beach parading around dressed like a woman. And, the man was most definitely parading.

Goyotsetseg Radnaabazar, alias Goyo, was Jack's guide and source of transportation to the ger camp. They rode together in a mini-van, a van not as old as it sounded or looked. The roads had taken their toll on the vehicle, ruts and potholes now causing the driver to occasionally slow to a crawl in order to navigate through or around the obstacles. It was a long drive, and Goyo told him it would take the better part of two hours.

"Next week I am flying to Bayankhongor, and then driving to Arkhangai,

Zavkhan and Khovsgol ... I will be back on the tenth of July," said Goyo, speaking as if Jack knew of these places.

"That is good," Jack replied, trying to keep the conversation moving while also trying to keep from being bounced out of the bench seat behind the driver.

"Ah ... what do you know about this camp?" A tourist attraction, the camp was not something Jack would have chosen on his own. But he'd left the entire China, Mongolia, and Russian itinerary in Loraine's hands. She assured him she would make it comfortable, but not too comfortable.

"Is very good. You can ride horse there with guides, go in Mongolian countryside. Is very beautiful," replied Goyo.

They rounded a curve at the crest of a small hill, the driver slowing and then abruptly pulling off the road and to a stop. The countryside reminded Jack of Montana. There were hills and broad valleys, with spotted stands of small timber.

The driver and Goyo began to get out, so Jack duck-walked his way out of the upside-down meatloaf pan, shaped van. Jack could see a wide valley ahead of them, with larch and what appeared to be birch trees, scattered along the valley floor. Here and there, were granite rock ridges jutting out of the sides of earthen hills like new molars teething into a developing jaw.

They climbed a small embankment, and at the top was a mound of stones and other objects. At first glance, the uninitiated might say, "What a lovely place for a trash pile."

The stone pile, or *ovoo* is considered an abode of the spirits by Mongolians. They are found at the crest of hills and rises. Circumambulating the *ovoo* three times, and adding a stone with each pass is a custom of the Mongolian people. It is performed out of respect for the dead.

The object placed on the mound can be anything. On this particular *ovoo*, there were a few bottles, an old broken jug, a tin can or two, one crutch, and a wooden lid from a box. The remainder was made up of stones.

The driver picked up three stones as he approached the mound, and had already completed one revolution before Goyo and Jack started. It was a strange custom, but somehow the idea of stopping your journey to walk around and stretch your legs, while at the same time paying tribute to fallen comrades, all seemed somehow refreshing.

When they arrived at the camp, Jack found it to be precisely what it was called — a camp. There were about a dozen *gers*, all spaced well apart from each other, and connected to a large dormatory-like building by a series of wooden walkways. There did not seem to be many people around.

A hostess showed Jack his *ger*. Wooden bed frames, brightly painted a combination of red, blue, white, yellow and green, were arranged around the inside. In the center of the *ger* was a cast iron, wood stove, while a single, bare light bulb hung from the ceiling.

In halting English, the hostess said she would return at sunset to start a fire. She told him the building nearby contained a restaurant and recreational facilities. There was no bathroom connected to the *ger*, the nearest one some 100 yards away.

What would Lynda have thought of this? Jack could imagine the two of them sitting there, staring at each other. Neither may have known in advance what the "Ger Camp" entailed, and both would have agreed it might be a nice diversion from the norm. They would have sat there, next to each other on one of the hard bunks, covered with blankets of scratchy, heavy wool. After a moment of silence, they would have broken into uncontrollable laughter. They would have made do, endured, if for no other reason than to have a great story to tell when they arrived home.

That evening, the hostess returned to start a fire in the stove. When she saw Jack lying on one of the beds reading a book, a small candle flickering nearby in an effort to aid the dim light of a single, overhead bulb, she insisted he move. At the time, he did not understand. Later, after reading about Mongolian culture, it all became clear.

Mongolians are very superstitious. Stepping on the doorstep of a *ger* is an offense to the spirit of the doorframe. Refusing to get on a horse which has been saddled for you is very bad manners. It is also bad luck to unsaddle a horse if it has not been ridden. When *gers* are erected, the door must always face the south, and one must never ride a horse up to a dwelling at full gait. The horse should be walked the final distance, this being a show of friendly intentions.

Lying on the bed to the right of the door, Jack violated a custom of the *ger*. As one enters, the male side is to the left, and the female side is to the right. He laughed to himself when he realized his transgression, but wondered if the transvestite he encountered at the hotel would be staying at a *ger* camp while he/she was in Mongolia. Which side would he/she be relegated to? He doubted Mongolian superstition or customs covered the subject.

Jack spent most of his time reading. There was little else to do. The food in the restaurant was mediocre, and a recreation hall consisted of an old, worn-out pool table. He looked in the room once, and saw several young Mongolian men playing pool, all of them attempting to play at the same time.

****

There were no internet facilities at the camp in Terelj, and back in the lobby of the Bayangol Hotel, Jack was faced with over eighty messages. He answered them all, saving addresses not already saved.

There was a message from Dan, as well as his editor Neal. Other friends were beginning to e-mail him on a regular basis as well. Even though he knew there would be no message from Lynda until she reached Hong Kong in July, he still found himself scrolling down the list and looking for her name.

The following day, Jack was taken to the train station by his guide. Like the train out of Beijing, the amount of luggage carried by passengers more closely resembled that of a group of refugees than travelers or tourists. Most of the people boarding the train appeared to be Mongolians. He looked for some Russians, laughing to himself as he wondered how he would identify one. What exactly did a Russian look like? He had absolutely no idea.

He was assigned a top bunk in a four-place compartment. Soon after getting settled, two women entered the room. Thoughts of the two being Russians were soon dashed.

"Mom, do you want the top or the bottom?" the younger of the two asked.

"Oh, you go ahead and take the top. It's too hard for me to crawl up and down all the time," the other replied.

Jack was standing in the corridor, ducking in and out of the room as other passengers made their way by. He turned and stepped into the doorway. "Hello," he said, extending his hand to the older of the two, a woman about forty years of age.

They introduced themselves as Katy and Zoe England. They were from California, a mother and daughter team traveling from China to Moscow, Russia. The mother, Katy, was a school teacher, while the daughter worked as a flight attendant for a small corporate airline. They proved to be delightful compartment mates.

"Hello, my friend. We meet again," said a voice from the corridor. It was an older couple Jack met at the Bayangol Hotel. Bill and Jean Bullard lived in Seattle, Washington, and both appeared to be in their seventies. Bill was a retired National Park Services employee. It felt like a homecoming of sorts, as all five Americans tried to talk at once. Bill and Jean would be two compartments away, and the subject of compartment mates soon arose.

"We have no one else in our compartment yet," said Jean. "Is it just the three of you in here?"

Before anyone could answer, a man tried to make his way into the room. It was like trying to put ten pounds of potatoes in a five pound bag, and the Bullard's excused themselves, making their way back to their compartment.

The new lodger was from Ulan Bator. He spoke fluent English, and sported a yellow cap, emblazoned with the word "CAT." Tumennasan worked for Catapillar, the heavy equipment manufacturer. He was traveling to Irkutsk on a sixty day assignment to instruct workers on the operation of a new piece of equipment.

"I'm a little concerned," said Jack. The train was moving, and the four occupants of the compartment were enjoying some beer, bread and conversation. "I've heard some strange stories about crossing Russian borders. Have you been to Russia before?" he asked Tumennasan, struggling with the pronunciation.

Zoe started to say something as well, also stumbling to pronounce the Mongolian's name. He was still wearing his "CAT" hat, seated next to Jack on one of the lower bunks.

"I know, we'll call you the Cat Man!" cried Jack. Tumennasan and the

Americans all laughed, agreeing it was better than messing with the tricky pronunciation of his given name.

"Yes, I have been to Irkutsk many times," said the Cat Man. "It is not too
difficult. They not bother you, travelers ... Americans. They check Mongolians
very closely, look for smugglers ... but you, oh no, they not bother you."

Jack asked if he spoke Russian as well as English and Mongolian. The Cat
Man replied that he did, and it would later come as a great relief to Jack and his
tenderfoot, American, traveling companions. Although the Cat Man's friends
and fellow countrymen were on the train, he would spend most of his time with
Katy, Zoe and Jack. For the next two days, they would talk and laugh together,
while eating and drinking their way across Mongolia and into Siberia.

Jack slept well that night, his upset stomach of the day before, slightly
better. He purged his system as best he could before boarding the train, drinking lots of water and eating little, ever conscious of the state of the restroom
facilities on the trains.

So far, only one of the trains had what could be termed a toilet. All of the
rest were equipped with simply a hole in the floor. Urinating was no problem
for a man, but everything else was extremely difficult. The feat — trying to
hold your pants up high enough so they didn't drag in what was on the floor or
what missed the hole, all while maintaining a squatting position in the lurching
and swaying train — was an exercise in flexibility and balance just short of
what was required for a high wire circus act. At least at the circus, the aroma
coming up from below was something not unpleasant, and a slip or misjudg-
ment was punishable by a fall into a soft, clean net.

He looked forward to his stay in Irkutsk. Instead of a hotel, Loraine arranged a "Homestay" experience — lodging in the home of an Irkutsk resident.
Details of the situation were sketchy, the information only saying the location
would be close to city transit facilities with at least one of the residents having
a basic understanding of the English language.

He envisioned a beat-up apartment, with an old man and woman hoping to
supplement their meager income with an occasional traveler. They would have
a grandson or granddaughter living with them, the youngster having marginal
English skills, and acting as a translator for the entire group. The apartment
would be miles away from restaurants or shops, each trip on a trolley or bus a
difficult one due to language and unfamiliar surroundings.

Jack was also curious about his reception at the Irkutsk train station. Several years before, he ran for the office of Mayor of Newport Beach. It wasn't
intended to be a serious election campaign. In fact, his motto had been, "If
elected, I'll demand an immediate recount."

As things progressed however, and as he participated in several local television and radio debates, he found himself taking the election seriously. The
city needed a new public library, but he was opposed to demolishing a building
to erect a new structure simply for the sake of having something new. While he
didn't get a lot of votes, he didn't finish last either. It was a good experience,

and it gave his newspaper articles and editorial opinions a little more legitimacy.

In Hong Kong, he sent an e-mail to the current Mayor of Newport Beach. Irkutsk and Newport Beach were in a Sister City program together, and it was Jack's reason for making contact. Previously reporting on a visit from Irkutsk dignitaries, he thought it might be possible to arrange a meeting with the current mayor or his staff. If so, it could become the basis of an interesting story for the newspaper.

The train pulled into Irkutsk on schedule at 8:30 a.m. He grabbed his bags and was saying goodbye to the two California women and the Cat Man as he stepped onto the platform. Taking but a few steps from the train, he saw a man holding a cardboard sign with "Mr. Gillette" written on it.

As Jack got closer, he saw the man was not alone, and in fact, had several people around him. Jack was smiling, almost close enough to reach out with his hand and greet the man. The sign holder and the other people were all looking at him now, and one man hoisted a large camera, the resulting machine-gun-like flashes of the strobe light temporarily stunning Jack.

This was the reception committee from the Irkutsk City Administration Office. There were introductions and welcomes from Utyasheva Leysan, Olga Serjodkina, Alexander Shumeyev and Ludamilla Kurbatova, all of whom represented the city's administration. Mayor Jakubovsky would have been there also, but there was a tragic air crash near Irkutsk that morning, and his presence was needed at the scene.

With the aid of an interpreter, Jack informed them his itinerary included a guide to meet him at the station. He was about to say he should find this guide before leaving with them when another young man approached the group. This one also held a sign, the gray cardboard sign inscribed with the words "J. Gillette."

The interpreter knew the guide, as they had attended school together. They arranged for the guide to collect his charge later and deliver him to his homestay accommodations. For the next few hours however, Jack was to be the guest of the City of Irkutsk.

The entourage piled into a black Zil limousine, and away they went. First stop, a couple of buildings which housed the local government. Then, it was off to see an old church and a famous statue.

A visit to a museum was next. The museum was closed, but the curator was there to open the doors and personally guide Jack and the city staff through the halls, explaining each and every exhibit. The curator, as well as his hosts, took special pride in one of the last exhibits they viewed. It was a small, but well appointed corner devoted to Irkutsk's hockey team. Season records and history were interspersed between displays of hockey sticks and jerseys.

Irkutsk is the regional center of Eastern Siberia, the city originating as a winter camp for the Cossacks in 1652. Referred to as the, "Paris of Siberia," the term was earned from the wealth of furs, tea, gold and ivory, traded along a route which lead through the Gobi desert to Peking.

The area is rich in natural resources. *Isbas*, or log houses, with richly ornate carved eaves and brightly painted window frames and shutters, are everywhere outside the center of the city. There are many churches and museums to visit, including the Irkutsk Fur Center and the School of Trapping. Irkutsk was also a place of exile in the nineteenth century. Josip Vissarionovich Djugashvili, a.k.a. Stalin, was sent here in the winter of 1903.

But, at this moment in time, at this museum and for a guest from their sister city, the local hockey team exhibit seemed to outshine history. As the group stood around the exhibit beaming, Jack found the atmosphere contagious. He too stood by with a wide smile across his face, feeling the pride swirling around the room.

Jack was not politically inclined, but the experience in Irkutsk made running for mayor worthwhile. He needed a boost at this stage in his life. It was nice to feel somewhat important and special.

****

Jack introduced himself to Nick, his homestay host. Nick had studied and taught at a language institute affiliated with a university in Irkutsk. His home was modest, clean and located near the center of the city. The accommodations were a far cry from Jack's preconceived vision of a worn-out apartment with only a child who could speak marginal English.

After he was shown his room, they sat at the kitchen table together and drank coffee. Nick's English skills were improving by the minute, and he was eager to talk. Although Jack was enjoying himself, he was anxious to get out of the apartment and find an internet cafe. It was July 4th, and Lynda would be in Hong Kong. Nick may have sensed Jack's anxiety, as he abruptly brought the conversation to a close after their second cup of coffee.

He only had to walk a short distance before finding an internet center. Logging on, he found over two dozen messages. His search for something from Lynda was easy. It was right at the top of the list.

Dear Jack

I really don't know what to say. I'm in Hong Kong, in a state of shock, much like I know you must be. All I can do is be honest with you. I'm sorry I hurt you. Bill Davidson means nothing to me, it was just one of those things that happens. I think I still love you. I know I loved you very much at one time.

But, I think the question is, whether or not you love me. You won the lottery. I'm happy for you, but why are you making me go through hell to share it with you? I know you want me to experience traveling by myself. I know you want me to be a dreamer. But Jack, I don't enjoy traveling by myself. Why can't I be with you? Why can't I just be me?

I've had a couple of gin and tonics. It is the only way I've been able to keep my sanity. Yes, I'm mad at you. I feel like I've become your personal puppet. Go here. Do it this way. Now, fly home.

I've decided I am going through with this. I guess you can run if you want. But, I'm NOT returning to L.A. disgraced AND broke. As mad as it makes me to jump when you pull the strings, it makes me madder to think I have made all of these sacrifices for nothing.

Lynda

Jack immediately started to write a reply. Two sentences into it, he stopped, deleted the words, and sat staring at the computer. There were so many things he wanted to say to her, some things said out of anger and some out of love. The two didn't mix.

He intended the trip to be fun, and could remember the Lynda he once knew, as someone who would have enjoyed the game. She would have recognized his proposal as something made out of love for her. She would have instantly realized he had no intention of running.

She said she was sorry. But, as he read and reread the message, with each reading he saw less and less remorse.

"It just happened." Could she have said the same thing the day after she first made love to him — that it just happened? He wondered if there were others.

He tried to reply to her message again, finding the words for how he felt impossible to convey. He gave up, and looked at some of the other messages. There was one from Dan. He clicked on it, desperately wanting to hear from someone he trusted.

Jack,

I hope things are going well. Everything is fine here, and Rebecca sends her love.

John liked what you sent to the <u>Register</u> *and is anxiously awaiting more material. The rest of the staff wants to hear more from you also, so don't be a stranger.*

It's difficult to segue into this, so I'll just jump right out with my size 10 shoe in my mouth. Rebecca has heard by way of friends that Bill Davidson has left his law firm in a flee-by-the-dead-of-night manner.

My first thought upon hearing this was to not tell you. But now, I think you should know.

There is some talk that he may be traveling to Hong Kong.

Jack, I know you want things to work out between you and Lynda. If that's what you want, then I want it too. However, you honestly deserve more than this — especially if BOTH of them are coming after you.

I'm sure you're aware that I read the message you had me send to her the day you sailed. Well, I did a bad thing and told a lawyer friend of mine about it's content and context. He feels that under the circumstances this thing is legally binding.

There's too much to say in an e-mail. Please call me. Rebecca and I were going to go to San Francisco for the Fourth of July, but we're not now. We will stay home so we can talk with you when you call — (and you'd better, or I'll kick your ass when I see you again).

Hope everything else is okay. You'll make it through this, trust me.

Love & Peace,

Dan & Rebecca

He signed out and sat staring at the screen saver endlessly crossing the monitor. It was a picture of a satellite or space capsule of some sort, crossing over the earth, the outline of a snowy Siberia hundreds of miles below.

He didn't feel like returning to the apartment, so he started to walk. He didn't know where he was going and he didn't care.

Walking blindly along, he asked himself over and over how someone you knew and loved could suddenly seem like a stranger? How could someone have such feelings of aloofness about your love for them? Is this what money did to people?

There were so many questions to ask of himself, the biggest being an issue he'd debated since departing Hong Kong. He'd known the answer then, but failed to accept it. There was no getting around it now, and it ceased to be a question. His love affair with Lynda was over. It was finished. It was impossible to save. All he could do now was attempt to save himself.

It was late afternoon when he passed a small garden-like terrace next to the street. A large iron fence separated the area from the sidewalk, with an arched, ivy-covered gate forming the entrance. The gate was open, and a few people were seated about. There was a sign near the gate, but it was in Russian and may as well have been in Chinese. If the place was not a sidewalk cafe, he would soon find out.

Finding a small table, he took a seat. After several minutes without getting served, he arose and walked over to a makeshift counter area where two women stood.

"Beer please," he said.

The two women behind the counter looked at one another before saying something in Russian. All he could understand was that they were asking him a question. Beer bottles sat in a tub full of ice near the women's feet.

"Beer," he said again, pointing to the tub.

Again, one of the women asked him some sort of question. He simply nodded yes to the unknown question, and the woman reached down and pulled a bottle out of the tub. The other woman handed him a glass, and he held out one of the larger denominations of rubles in his pocket.

From his table, he could see the entrance to what was more like a beer garden than a sidewalk cafe. It was nearing 5:00 p.m. He wasn't sure if this wass what he needed at the moment, but he was a believer in fate, and fate he believed, made him stumble into this place.

He looked over and saw a man and a woman come through the entrance. The woman was about forty years old, and she was absolutely breathtaking. Seconds later, two more women came through the entrance. These two were a little younger, stylish, and even more beautiful. It was like sitting next to the runway at a fashion show. Some were alone or with other women. Some were escorted by a male companion. They ranged in age from twenty to fifty, all of them drop-dead gorgeous!

In Jack's short visit, he would be overwhelmed by the number of beautiful women in Irkutsk. There were so many it seemed out of place somehow — like a bus loaded with stunning models was parked out of sight around the corner, and someone like Alan Funt of *Candid Camera* was parading the women past you to merely observe your reaction.

The circumstances made him quit thinking of his problems with Lynda. Glancing at the entrance again, he noticed a couple a women entering. They were both blonde and tall. They were about 30 years old and were looking for a place to sit. The patio-like area had filled up rather quickly with people ending their work day, and the two women were now standing ten yards away and looking directly at Jack and his table of one occupied, and two empty, lonely chairs.

They walked over, and one of them said something in Russian. Jack didn't say a word, but just smiled and spread open his arms indicating the two chairs at his table were vacant and theirs for the asking. He said a quick, silent prayer they would not pick up the chairs and take them to another table to join friends. His prayers were answered. They were both stunning beauties. They smelled wonderful.

After five minutes of private conversation between themselves, one of them turned to Jack and said something.

"I'd really like to answer you, but, I'm ... ah sorry, I only speak English," he stammered, surprised someone so beautiful would speak to him.

"English," said the other one, the word spoken almost in awe.

There followed a quick conference between the two in their native language. The one nearest him, touched his arm. "English," she repeated.

It was obvious "English" was the only word they knew. He reached down and removed one of several small translation books he carried in his shoulder bag. A little larger than a matchbook, the Russian-English version contained such useful phrases as; "Where is the bakery?" and "I have a stomach ache," as well as the ever-popular, "Which way to the beauty parlor?" The book was absolutely worthless for anyone other than a tourist on a cruise ship, but the women moved closer to him so they might look too.

There was another item in his bag that would break the ice and allow them to get acquainted. In the frantic days before beginning his trip he assembled several picture books. Made up of three by five photos, they included snapshots of his apartment, his office and life in southern California. Handing them out, the books brought delightful and appreciative responses. The Chinese and Mongolian people loved them, and now only two remained.

He gave one to each of the women. The wonderful experience of charades and exaggerated gestures followed the turning of each page of the photo album. Jack produced a writing tablet, and pictures were drawn to help in translation.

More drinks were ordered, and despite the differences in language, introductions were made. One of the women was named Tanya. The other was Yelena.

When Jack took Tanya's right hand and indicated the absence of a ring, she made a walking motion with her other hand, using the index and middle finger to indicate her husband had left her. Jack looked at the Yelena with a question-mark-like turn of the head, and her fingers made the same walking motion.

A small combo started to play popular music, but stopped after a couple of songs. Jack wasn't sure what was happening, but he really wasn't paying much attention to the music. A few minutes passed, and all of a sudden there was a flash of light, followed by a loud clap of thunder. Before he could even look to the sky, it began to rain.

Tanya and Yelena took him by the arm, and together they ran down a small alley with all of the other patrons. A nondescript door lead to a basement. The combo was setting up again, and the women talked three other beautiful women into sharing their table.

There Jack was, in the middle of Siberia, sitting with five, very beautiful, Russian women. One of the women sharing the table spoke a tiny bit of English, and seating was rearranged so she could sit next to Jack and translate for the group. She wasn't a great help, but it was better than asking where the beauty shop was, or directions to the bakery.

The band played and he danced with Tanya. When they would return to the table, one of the other women would say something to Tanya, and then, as if given permission, the woman would take Jack's hand and lead him back out onto the dance floor. They ordered food and more drinks. Then, they ordered even more drinks.

When the band took a break, he caught the sound of Tanya humming a popular song. As Jack sat across from her, he started singing the song. With his hand tapping the table top and keeping time, he sang, *Your Song*, by Elton John, to Tanya and Yelena as the other three women looked on with admiring eyes and smiling faces. Finishing, they all applauded while Tanya and Yelena both kissed him on the cheek. It wasn't a stunning performance, but he could carry a tune reasonably well. It was ironic in that it was one of the very few songs he knew all the words to.

When the applause and kisses ended, there was a tap on his shoulder. He turned to see a Russian man standing behind him. He was saying something in Russian, but with words and mannerisms which seemed friendly. The young woman who could translate attempted to, and after a few moments conveyed the message. A member of the band, he was passing by when Jack was singing to Tanya. He wanted Jack to get up and sing the song in English with the band.

When the band met a few minutes later to begin another set, Jack found himself walking up to the small stage and realizing just how drunk he must be. All he could hope for was to not get stage fright and forget the lyrics.

The singer would have been well advised to keep his day job, but the song went off without a hitch. At one point towards the end, he missed a word, and taking his first close look at the audience, found not only Tanya, Yelena and the other three women looking at him, but the entire room. No one was talking, eating or drinking. All of the people were looking directly at him with rapt interest.

There was a second or two of silence after the last note was struck by the band. Then, the entire room stood up and cheered and applauded. There were slaps on the back and hand shakes as he made his way back to the table. All he could do was grin and say thank you to the well-wishers.

He was kissed and embraced. As he took his seat, he notice two waitresses smiling at him while setting small shot glasses down on the table. Already littered with drinks and food, some plates and bottles needed to be moved to make room for the more than thirty shot glasses of Russian Vodka. The dialog never became easier, but the company steadily became more and more comfortable to be with.

It was late when they left, Jack escorting Tanya and Yelena to a street corner where they hitched a ride. As the car turned the corner and disappeared into the night, Jack began to stumble his way back to Nick's apartment. As he walked along, thinking what a wonderful evening it had been, his thoughts came back to Lynda and Bill.

They were both coming after the money. All of a sudden their actions seemed funny to him, and he chuckled to himself as he struggled to put one foot in front of the other. It was laughable, for had she asked, he would have given her the fifteen million without a single condition or obligation.

"Fuck em both," he said aloud. If they want to chase after me for the money, well let them chase. I'll show them how a fox can really run.

He awoke the next morning with a splitting headache. Nick seemed to sense his over-indulgence, making the coffee extra strong. After a small breakfast of fruit, bread and sausage, he left the apartment for the internet center visited the day before. There was a bank of telephones in the shop also, and he desperately needed to talk with someone.

"Dan, it's me, Jack. I hope I haven't gotten you out of bed."

"No, ah ... how are you doing?"

"Well, yesterday I was pretty bummed out, but I went out last night, got drunk and had a great time. When I get back, I'll have to tell you the whole story. But this morning, well ah, well I'm feeling pretty blue. I just needed to talk with someone. I hope you don't mind."

"Jack, for Christ's sake, I'm your friend. That's what friends are for. I assume you've heard from Lynda?"

"Yeah. Yeah, I heard from her all right. I picked up the e-mail message yesterday, hoping for the best, but knowing deep down the whole thing was in the crapper. Why would she want to hurt me like that? I just don't understand."

There was silence on the other end of the line, and he knew Dan did not have any magical answers for him. He also knew Dan was listening intently, waiting patiently for him to release what was on his mind, and so, he went on.

"I mean, we were so good together. Oh yeah, we had our little arguments, but ah, I just felt like I was so much a part of her. It was so comfortable being with her, even when things weren't going well." He caught himself choking up, and felt the first tears forming in his eyes. "She was just so good for me, so right. And, it's not like I took advantage of it, or took her for granted. God, I loved her so very much, and then she does something like this. Maybe I should just give her the money."

As he wiped the tears from his eyes and awaited a response from Dan, he was frightened by how his mood had changed so fast. Dialing the number he felt spiteful towards her, and now after just saying her name he would have done anything to hold her in his arms.

"Jack, I know you're hurting," replied Dan, giving Jack a moment to compose himself. "I don't have an answer for why people treat people the way they do. Christ, if I did, I'd be the Emperor of the World, instead of some hack newspaper writer."

"Yeah, I know. It just hurts so much right now. I was angry yesterday, but now ..." his words trailed off.

"Listen, Beck has a friend, who has a friend, who has a friend ... you know how that goes with women...." Dan paused for a moment. Anyway, she heard through the grapevine that both Bill and Lynda were attempting to catch you. I think I've mentioned that, but ... anyway, I think it's something you need to know."

"Yes, I got your e-mail saying Bill might be with her. She didn't mention it to me in her message, but it doesn't surprise me. She's mad, and says she feels as though I'm making her jump through hoops for the dough. Yesterday, I felt like running, making her run her ass off for every nickel and dime. Now, I just want to get a hotel and wait for her here."

"Where are you?" asked Dan.

"I'm in Irkutsk, Russia. If you look on a map, it's directly north of Ulan Bator, next to Lake Baikal."

"Why roll over for her? I think you should keep moving, but it's your money." People change, ya know. The change isn't always for the best."

"Dan, I know, I know. I know people change, but I've always believed there is something inside a person that is constant. Oh, they might stray away from it from time to time, but I've always felt they'll eventually come back to being the true person they were when they started."

"And so, you think Lynda will change back? If you do, you're a bigger dreamer than I thought you were."

"I don't know what I think anymore. I don't know what to think, or what to do," sighed Jack.

"Keep moving. You've had this dream for a long time."

Neither of them said anything for a moment or two.

"Listen, keep moving on your trip," repeated Dan. "You've got a set itinerary until you get to Helsinki, right? Get that far, and if it's still bugging you, then wait for her there. If that dickhead Davidson is with her, he'll insist on some kind of paper being signed, or some such shit. There are bound to be a lot more English-speaking people in Helsinki than there are in Siberia, and you'll feel more at home. If need be, I'll catch a flight and meet you there."

"I don't know. There are times when I almost wish I'd never won the money."

"Jack, your relationship with Lynda was in the tank well before you won the lottery. You know that, and I think you felt it too. The money only made things rise to the surface. Be glad you didn't marry her, cuz then her and the sleezeball attorney would be trying to get all of it."

"I don't care about the money. I don't care about any of it."

"And, I don't either. Nor does Rebecca. We don't care if you buy us a ranch in Montana, a house in Oxnard, or a pup tent. All we care about is you. We want you to be happy ... ah wait, ah ... Beck wants to talk to you."

"Hi Jackie," said Rebecca, taking the phone from her husband. She always referred to him by that name, and he always found it pleasantly endearing. "I've been standing here listening, my ear against the phone as best I can with my big, lug of a husband in the way." She stopped speaking for a moment, and he could hear her saying something to Dan.

"I just sent him to the kitchen to turn the oven down ... before the baked chicken becomes Cajun chicken." She laughed, and Jack found himself laughing for the first time that morning.

"Jackie, I think you should continue your trip. Just go as you originally planned. I have always admired your ability to dream and fantasize. Make the whole thing a game. Write your stories for the newspaper, and interject little digs here and there about the chase if you like. Have fun with it. If she catches you, well ... so be it. If she doesn't, give her the amount you promised.

"And, If you feel different when you get back, give her more money, or give her less. Whatever, just have fun. You know it's over between you two. You've known that from the time Dan spoke with you in Hong Kong. Just let it be okay. Know that everything happens for a reason. Get on with your adventure, and just let the bad things be okay."

"Maybe you're right," sighed Jack.

"I know I'm right, Jackie. Look, here comes Dan. I'll let you guys talk about stuff in private ... ah ya know, barefoot and ah, in the kitchen ... that's me!"

Dan started to speak, but Rebecca's voice came back on the phone before he could make sense. "And Jackie, my husband is full of shit. We do care about the money. We want the pup tent!"

"Well, what have you decided? asked Dan, coming back on the phone. "I'm not hanging up until I know."

"Well, it's not exactly easy for me to wait here for her, although after last night, it might not be an uncomfortable wait. I'll continue on to Helsinki, and not change my itinerary. I've been getting some e-mail from a friend up in Oregon who has good friends there. They contacted me once in Mongolia, and are excited to meet me. It may turn out to be a good place to rest up for awhile."

"Well, I just hope you don't roll over for her. I know you love her, and I know the money means nothing to you. But, I think you'll regret just giving her the dough."

"Rebecca gave me some good advice," said Jack. "She told me to just make a game out of it, weather it the best way possible. It's kind of what I had always intended to do anyway, it's just that the game is more serious now."

They talked about some of the stories Dan was working on, and how all of the staff at the paper were doing. Knowing dinner was waiting for Dan, he cut the conversation off, telling him he'd call again from Moscow.

Leaving the internet center, he considered returning to his room, but as he walked along, his spirit and energy increased. His mood was turning yet again.

It was a bright, warm day, so instead of turning down the alley to the apartment, he kept on walking. Something made him look up at the position of the sun. He was walking in a westerly direction.

"Go west, young man," he heard himself say aloud.

Go west.

13

After the beverage cart made its first pass, Bill Davidson leaned back in his First-Class seat and relaxed. He relaxed knowing $50,000 in crisp, new bills were stashed in a briefcase in the overhead compartment above him. He intended to use the money to make the chase just as short as possible.

Before leaving Los Angeles, he squeezed as much cash as he could out of everyone who owed him, or who he imagined owed him. He'd left most of the money in a safe at the ersatz law office in Palm Springs, knowing they'd get a subpoena from his wife's attorney, but also knowing they would conveniently forget about the small safe in one of the closets. That stash amounted to nearly three hundred thousand, with another hundred and fifty thousand in the account of his gardener, Miguel.

He'd been unable to find a suitable place to hide all of the money, someplace both safe from auditors and his soon to be ex-wife. He'd therefore returned to Miguel with a cockeyed story about not leaving the area after all, and rehiring him to do the yard work. They made another trip to the bank together, Bill performing his slight of hand bookkeeping out of earshot of the teller.

Now he was flying through the air on his way to Hong Kong. He possessed only a minute knowledge of things apart from the world of law, and knew nothing of life outside the U.S. His wife's favorite vacation spot was Maui. She continually nagged him to take her to Mexico, but he steadfastly refused, saying she could go to Pico Rivera and see all the Mexicans she wanted to.

If he gave it any thought, which he hadn't, he would have imagined having to take a rickshaw from the airport to the Hyatt Regency where he insisted Lynda check in. He knew the Japanese made millions of cars, but would have surmised that, since there were no Chinese cars whizzing down the San Bernardino freeway, there probably weren't very many cars in China. Such was the one-dimensional mind of the man.

When he arrived in Hong Kong, he stepped from the air conditioned First-Class cabin of the wide bodied jet to the air conditioned, slinky, snake-like cylinder which funneled passengers into the air conditioned terminal. With a death grip on his briefcase, he made his way to the air conditioned baggage pick up area and then to the air conditioned queues at customs and immigration. Everything went smoothly, and after clearing customs, he handed all but his briefcase to an eager sky cap, and demanded a taxi.

It therefore came as a shock when he stepped out to the taxi loading area, the skies gray and cloudy, the temperature ninety degrees and the humidity off the charts. It was even a greater shock when the Asian taxi driver addressed him in perfect English, with just a hint of a British accent.

As they drove, the driver prated about the weather and other mindless drivel, all of which Bill ignored. Nearing the *Tsim Sha Tsui* district, it began to rain, the wipers on the taxi struggling to keep the field of vision clear. Although the taxi seemed to have air conditioning, the windows fogged up. When Bill rolled his window down two inches to help matters, he was rewarded with a wave of water from a passing car.

"Jesus Christ," he muttered, rolling the window back up again and wiping the water off his sleeve and pants leg. "You fuckin' people need some more cars and people around here," he said sarcastically, the driver either not hearing or ignoring him, and continuing on with the latest weather forecast.

Bill didn't check in right away, but went to the bar instead. It was full of American tourists, and he immediately felt more comfortable. He ordered a dry martini, hoping the bartender wouldn't screw it up too bad. He'd envisioned Lynda sitting nearby, waiting for him. He'd as much as told her to, but she'd stated a preference to wait in her room before abruptly hanging up the phone.

The martini was great, and he told the waitress to bring him a house phone.

"The house phones are located just over there, near the entrance to the lobby," said the young, oriental girl in perfect English.

"No, you see I have this drink. I want to enjoy the goddamn thing, and want you to bring me the fucking phone."

The conversation may have gotten a little heated after that exchange, were it not for a waiter stepping in while the waitress, shocked and blinking her eyes, took a step backward.

"If it is someone within the hotel you wish to speak with, I may contact them on your behalf," said the waiter.

Bill looked up to see a white guy with an attitude and a pony tail. "Fuck, why fight it," he groused. "Yes, that would be fine. The lady is a guest here, and I am suppose to meet her in the bar. Ring her room and tell her to get down here sometime in the next sixty seconds."

"And the name of the young lady?" asked the waiter.

What a bullshitter, he thought. He has no idea if the lady is young or old, fat or thin. "Lynda Turner," he said curtly, turning his head away and taking another sip of gin.

He was on his third martini when she finally showed up. He saw her walking towards him, and managed somehow to get to his feet. He was tired, half drunk, and needed a shower. His Armani suit was wrinkled from the long plane ride, and the humidity and sweat showed itself on what was at one time a brilliantly-white shirt.

In contrast, Bill thought Lynda looked great. Casual and relaxed, she was wearing a pair of tan, cotton pants and a white, silk blouse. They hugged, and he tried to kiss her, but she turned her head at the last minute so all he got was shot at her cheek.

"The fuckin' weather here is god-awful," said Bill, ordering another martini and a gin and tonic for her. He didn't need another drink, and instantly regretted making the order. If she was receptive, he would have liked to roll around on the bed a little before getting some sleep. He'd packed some Viagra just in case, although her mood and his energy level didn't bode well for an afternoon of wild sex.

"It's been raining ever since I got here, Bill. One of the room attendants told me it's the monsoon season."

"Well, the dumb fuck could have picked a better time to travel, that's for sure!" his drink arriving and his misgivings about having another gone like so much ancient history.

"I don't think you plan when to win the lottery around the changing seasons," she said, rather smugly.

He wasn't real happy with her attitude, or her welcoming. He wasn't sure he should go there right now, but she beat him to it.

"Bill, I think we need to discuss what our goal is here." He started to say something, but she held up her left hand while taking a drink with her right.

"I'm after what Jack promised me. There's a university here, and I've spent the last two days doing some research. I wanted to be up to speed on contracts and binding agreements."

"Ya know, I'm not sliced, fucking ham here. I'm an attorney," said Bill, setting the record straight.

"I know you are. And, you're a good attorney when it comes to personal injury claims. But, you and I are both removed from business law, and I don't want to be running halfway around the world for nothing." She took another drink and went on. "Fifteen million is a lot of money, and quite frankly, I would like to keep it all. However, I can't do this alone."

"That's why I'm here," Bill chimed in.

He sat back in his chair and relaxed, knowing where the story was headed. They were in negotiations, and he was very familiar with the territory. He hadn't expected the topic so soon, but felt it was better to get it out in the open right from the start.

"Frankly, I'm scared to death to step out of the hotel. I tried to go for a walk a few times, and it was either raining, or there were so many people on the street I felt overwhelmed. I can't imagine riding a train all the way across Russia."

"Don't you think we can catch the son of a bitch before that?"

"Not unless he decides to turn around. As we speak, he should be in Irkutsk, Russia, headed for Moscow in a day or so. I've got to document my travel through five Chinese cities and one in Mongolia. Do you have any idea how many miles that entails?"

They sat there for a moment, Lynda finishing her drink and ordering another. Finally, she said, "If you help me catch him, I'll give you two million. I think that's fair."

Bill had his own planned version of the split, something that was close to, if not fifty-fifty. But, he sensed some serious thought went into her offer, and now might not be the time to debate the issue.

"Do you want me to draw up a written contract ... have it notarized and all?" he asked, his tone of voice rather sarcastic.

"No, of course not, Bill. Look, I need you. I need your strength and companionship more than ever. I don't even know if I'm doing the right thing here. There are times when I wished I would have caught the first plane to wherever Jack was, gotten down on my knees and begged for his forgiveness. There are times when I'm very angry with him, and times when I'm sad it has all come to this.

"As far as you and I go, I don't know what will happen. I just know that right now, I need you by my side."

It was exactly what Bill wanted to hear.

"Let's not worry about splitting the dough. Let's focus on catching him as soon as possible. Did you bring your laptop?" Bill asked.

"No, I ah ..." she looked at him confused.

"What we need to do is buy you a lap top. We're close enough to Jap land that the price should be pretty cheap. We need to document every goddamn misery you have to endure, starting with this fuckin' weather. By the time we catch him, I want the record to show how you've been traumatized by the whole ordeal."

She started to dismiss the idea, but he stopped her.

"Anything can happen here. He can get sick and decide to fly home. He still could refuse to pay you, or up and decide to pay you less than promised. Do you have any idea what the winning numbers of the lottery were?" asked Bill. He would have bet anything she didn't, and when he didn't get a quick reply, knew he was correct.

"Two of the numbers were two and twenty-eight. Unless I am mistaken, those are the numbers which correspond to your date of birth, month and day. Am I correct?"

She nodded in agreement.

"I think a sympathetic jury would find for you in this fucking matter," said Bill, speaking a brand of legalese not taught in law school. "The plaintiff was faithfully a part of this man's life for five years. She has put up with all sorts of indignities and inconveniences to abide by the terms for which Mister Gillette set down. She has been severely traumatized by the events. And, ladies and gentlemen of the jury, two of the six winning numbers are directly in reference to her, and her alone. I rest my fucking case."

She had seen the inside of a courtroom too many times to think a legal battle would be easy or stress-free. She also knew the opposing attorney would jump all over Bill's use of the term, "faithful," and that his own personal life would be used against her.

"Not to change the subject, but have you gotten a room yet?" asked Lynda.

"No, I thought you'd taken care of that! Fuck, aren't we sharing a room?"

"Oh calm down," Lynda sighed. I made a reservation for a room right next to mine. They're small, and I need my space right now. However, I think we ought to get you up to your room and into the shower. You smell a bit, ya know. And, you need to get some different clothes. The suit and tie are a little out of place, don't you think?"

"Care to come in and suds me down," said Bill playfully, ignoring her comment concerning his attire and reaching for his drink. He wore a suit everywhere he went. What difference did it make if he was in China?

Moments later, when the elevator doors opened, he prayed the Viagra was packed near the top of his suitcase and somehow, by the grace of God, the shower would have one of those Water Wonder Power Spray nozzles just like the one at his pussy pad in Palm Springs.

****

Bill spent the night in Lynda's room, and the next morning after a breakfast served in her room, they discussed their next move.

Lynda had done her homework in the few days prior to his arrival. She contacted the China Travel Service, (CTS), and prearranged their visa's for travel through China. She also visited the Russian and Mongolian Embassies for travel through those countries. All that remained was to produce Bill's passport. After that, it was just a matter of waiting.

In all of her inquiries, she was extremely polite and understanding. The fact her approach was the same method Jack would have used, entered her mind repeatedly during the process.

They would travel the same route as Jack. While Jack spent two to four days in some cities, they would spend one night. Although she would have liked to keep overnight stops to a minimum, visions of a marathon ride from Hong Kong to Helsinki seemed unfathomable.

While researching law material on contracts, she also browsed a number of travel books and magazines. Jack always left them lying around his apartment, from positions on the coffee table to the top of the toilet tank.

The Terracotta Warriors of Xian fascinated her. She also wanted to see the Great Wall of China. For these reasons, she was thankful for the short layovers in both of those cities. After all, they would be there, and might as well see some of the sights.

Bill was disgruntled at the fact he would have to travel by train also, and suggested he fly ahead to Stockholm and ferret out Jack when he arrived.

"What would you do if you found him?" she asked. "You can't hold him, or make him wait for me. And besides, I don't think it would be in your best interests to walk up to him and start talking about the weather. He never has liked you, and I'm sure he likes you even less now."

"Whatta you mean?" asked Bill, as if feelings were the name of a bad song recorded years ago and nothing more. "You're single and over twenty one."

"Bill, that's not the point. Jack and I had a relationship. I was cheating on him, and it's not like you didn't know about it."

"Well, I don't know why he'd be so pissed off. I don't give a good fuck if my wife screws half of southern California. And, I'm still legally married. The minute he'd said the "M" word, he regretted it. Sure enough, she picked up on it.

"Speaking of which. What exactly is happening with you and your wife? And, what about the firm?"

Two tough questions on top of each other. He was neither prepared, nor did he quite know what the truth really was. "Well, ah she filed for divorce, and we were supposed to get together with her fuckin' attorney a few days before I left."

"Supposed to?" queried Lynda.

"Yeah well, I just said fuck it. Stritt was pulling my chain about the restraining order, and Mumph and Talbot were getting all pissy about it too." He always suspected Talbot might be a closet gay, but had no basis or proof whatsoever. But now, Bill put his hands up by his shoulders, fluttered his fingers, and in a high squeaky voice mimicked the man, "But, how are we going to run a law firm if all of our assets are frozen by a restraining order?"

'So, fuck em. I just walked," he added.

She was drinking a cup of coffee and nearly spilled it trying to quickly set it down on the table. "You just walked away from the entire firm? Are you crazy?" she said, practically shouting now.

She stopped everything she was doing, and was staring at him waiting for an answer. Jesus Christ, it wasn't her law firm, he thought before speaking. "Yeah, I just walked away. They'll be okay, they're all grownups, ya know."

"What about the Davis kid, the one injured at the riding stable?"

"Oh, I forgot about that. Well, someone will take care of it. It wasn't real promising anyway ... dumb fuckin' kid never should have been on a horse in the first place."

"Bill, not real promising? What the hell are you thinking?" She was shouting at him now. "There's a time line on those depositions and some of the other work. Didn't you notify anyone at all about taking over the case. Does Talbot or any of them know you're here?"

God, lots of questions, and more questions! He was having a difficult time. She was standing now, lambasting him for not taking care of business.

"Fuck it! I'm done practicing law."

"You're damn right you are! They'll disbar you," she whined.

"Let em, see if I give a shit," said Bill, wishing he had a drink in his hand and could somehow change the subject.

There were some things concerning the firm he'd told no one. He knew the divorce would open a can of worms the size of a fifty gallon oil drum. There was money siphoned off with the help of the firm's accountant, an employee specifically hired to prevent the very malfeasance that occurred.

The accountant abetting Bill was arrested one night as he sat in his car with a twelve year old boy. Bill threw a lot of money in the direction of judges, cops, and other attorneys he had outstanding markers on. As a result, the charges were quietly dropped. The boy and his parents were paid off in an out-of-court settlement, and the accountant's ass was kept out of prison.

Paybacks are hell. Bill knew that, and now, so did the accountant. However, with the divorce and the blanket restraining order, it was quite possible another CPA firm might be called upon to keep everyone honest. The inconsistencies they would find could send both Bill and the accountant to prison.

Further diggings into where the money went would lead to a trail of mobsters and cheap crooks like his friend Gorman in Palm Springs. There would be charges on top of charges, a plea deal being the only way he might manage to stay out of the "Big House."

Plea deals weren't fool proof either. Plea deals meant giving something to the D.A. they previously did not have. They'd have Bill's balls in their hands, and that meant the only thing to give up would be other names. Gorman and his kind weren't exactly bank robbers and executioners, but Bill had a strange feeling acts such as these were not beyond their scope either.

He wasn't chasing after Jack as much as he was running away from a shady past where the sun was about to go behind a big, dark cloud.

Lynda was still standing there waiting for an answer. The only difference between her and Bill's wife right now was that Lynda was thin and good looking. Also, she wasn't tapping her foot like his soon to be ex-wife, a favorite thing for her to do in these kind of situations.

"Yeah, I just said fuck it. It's been killing me for a long time. I should have gotten a divorce ten years ... no, make it twenty years ago. As far as the firm goes, those guys are all a bunch of righteous assholes. To hell with them and the California State Bar." He let that sit for just a second and then added, "And, well, I wanted to be with you."

"Well, I guess that's sweet, for whatever it counts," she said, sounding exasperated. "Ya know, returning to L.A. might not be so pleasant for you."

"That's another reason I'm here. I find a place that's not full of chinks and spades, and well, ya never know," he said.

"You forgot about Hispanics. Jesus, sometimes your racism is all a bit too much," she said disgustingly.

They sat there for a moment saying nothing. Bill finally broke the silence.

"Hey, why don't we walk down the street and find a bar? Ya know, someplace where the natives hang out."

"You go ahead. I have a feeling it will be awhile before I can take a nice, long bath in peace and quiet. Besides, I'd kinda like to be by myself for a little while."

As he walked towards the elevator, he realized he was okay with the peace and quiet thing too. Having glanced at a brochure next to the television in his room, there appeared to be some titty bars in the area. This might be his only chance to take a peek. Ya, peace and quiet, he said to himself, riding the elevator down to the lobby as the sole passenger ... works for me.

****

Bill looked over at Lynda. They were on a train now, a day tripper from Hong Kong to Guangzhou. For the last hour, they had traveled across a countryside of small farmlands, light industry and housing, a stamp of poverty on it all.

"I still don't understand what the fuck you think is beautiful about all of this shit," he grumbled.

"I didn't say it was beautiful, I said it was interesting, and by being so far from what we are used to, exotic in a sense." She was excited to finally be on the move and out of Hong Kong. It was late afternoon, and although unaware, they were riding the same scheduled train Jack had traveled on a month previously.

"Well, I say it sucks. I mean, look," Bill nudging her now, getting her to look across the carriage out the opposite window. The train had slowed, and some men were working on an adjacent track.

"Look at that, twenty or thirty guys standing around with picks and shovels, every now and then taking a fuckin' jab at the ground. I mean, there's not a piece of motorized equipment within ten fucking miles of these guys."

A man sitting across the aisle was looking now too, as was his wife. They were Americans, and such obvious tourists — they appeared to have just stepped off a tour bus with some doofus travel buff like Rick Steves, his endless litany concerning this monument or that old building guiding their each and every step. They introduced themselves as the Polk's from Kansas at the beginning of the journey, Bill totally ignoring them until Lynda spoke up and responded to their introductions.

"We've been travlin' round China for almost a month now. It's amazing that there is so little machinery to do the work. But, they got lots of people, and I guess the ideer is to keep em all busy," said Mr. Polk, trying his best to stimulate conversation with his American counterparts.

"Well, I don't know about the number of people, but the goddamn AFL-fucking CIO would be proud to have these little bastards working for them. They make fucking off look like an art form," replied Bill.

Mr. and Mrs. Polk both flinched at the language Bill was using, and Lynda nudged him, quietly whispering in his ear to tone down the truck driver's adjectives.

"They spend more time smoking cigarettes and squattin' down like they're taking a shit than they do working," said Bill, speaking in a way that indicated his statement signaled an end to the conversation.

He turned back to Lynda, and with his voice lowered only slightly, said, "Clod busters from Kansas. What the fuck do they know?"

Arriving in Guangzhou, they went through customs without trouble, and found their waiting guide. He rushed to get them to another station, and they had no more than entered their compartment when the train began to move again.

As they settled down in their two-place, soft class compartment, he sensed a coldness from her. She insisted on sleeping alone last night, and now it felt as if she intended to make it two in a row.

After arranging her bunk so she could sleep, she lay on top of the covers with her clothes on. Staring at the ceiling, she said, "Bill, you've got to watch your language a little more. We're not in the States anymore, we're in another country."

"Christ, ninety-nine percent of them don't even understand English. How in the fuck can that offend anybody?" Bill was annoyed. She was in one of her moods about his language. That probably meant no pussy for at least twenty-four hours, and he thought of how the bumping, grinding and swaying motion of the train might benefit a sexual romp. "I don't know what the big deal is," he added.

"The big deal is this!" she snapped. "We are in somebody else's country, just as if we were in someone's home. Act like a guest instead of a prick for a change." She glared at him for a moment before looking back at the ceiling.

Her snappishness was gone in an instant, replaced by a voice that was almost pleading, but not quite. "And, we're here to do one thing, find Jack and get my money. I don't want to screw it up because of something you say to someone, or because of one of your temper tantrums."

He noticed she said, "my" money, and not, "our" money, or even, "the" money. He let it slide. He knew how to handle her when she was having one of her snits. It was best to just back carefully away and wait her out. But, he wondered where she got all this garbage about being a guest in someone's home. Oh well, he thought.

He told her he was sorry, and he'd behave. He was about to add he knew his language was out of control at times, when he glanced over and immediately knew she'd fallen fast asleep.

Since picking up the train tickets, vouchers, and visas, Bill was 0 and 2 in the piece-of-ass category. It was something he intended to correct.

14

Jack's walk took him to a large park near the Angara River, the only river flowing out of Lake Baikal. He was scheduled to visit the lake with a guide the next morning, and after another night in Irkutsk, he would begin the long journey across Russia on the Trans-Siberian Express.

The park was full of kiosks selling food and drink, Jack suddenly hungry for both. He found an empty table and watched all of the beautiful women walk by. He was amazed at how many, on a scale of one to ten, were a solid fifty-two.

He pulled his notebook out of his shoulder bag and worked on a piece he would send to the *Register* later in the day. It was a collection of stories about his experiences and the people he met.

This Just In From Irkutsk

Just a note to let you know that I am still alive and currently in Irkutsk, Russia. Not only did I survive eating some bad yak meat or drinking some tainted mare's milk in Mongolia, I also survived the train trip from hell!

I had a bad stomach when I left Ulan Bator. I felt like I was well-suited to attend an Immodium festival. From Ulan Bator to Irkutsk by rail is about 700 miles. No problem. I can hold my breath for almost that long.

Thirty-seven hours later, I arrived in Irkutsk. That is an average of 19 mph. This train had more stops than a 50-page Western Union telegram. At one point, (around 5:30 am), I awoke to find the train had ceased all forward movement. I stumbled from my bunk, pulled on my pants and half asleep, walked down the corridor. I was surprised no train attendant was present. Furthermore, the door at the end of the carriage was wide open.

"Why not step out and get a little fresh air?" I thought.

I nearly fell over when I saw that, not only were we in a remote settlement somewhere just over the Russian border, but there was no train! Just one car — the one I was aboard.

Four hours later, with no explanation, an engine hooked up to our car and away we went. At least for another 10 miles or so. Luckily, I had some good compartment mates for this leg of the journey. There was Katy and Zoe England, a mother daughter team from California, and luckily for us Americans, a Mongolian gentleman who also spoke Russian. Tumennasan works for a heavy equipment company and was sporting a Caterpillar hat. He is, and will forever be remembered as, the Cat Man.

When a question or a problem would arise, someone would invariably say, "Go get the Cat Man." He was a great guy.

As some of you may know, I ran for mayor of Newport Beach several years ago in a primary election. It was a candidacy spurred by a night of too many Guinness beers at Bobby McGrath's. The ensuing banter between friends and cronies, coupled with a $500.00 wager, ultimately led to a decision to enter the race.

After my trip began, I e-mailed the current mayor and called in a few reluctant markers. The mayor and the city administration informed Irkutsk, (Newport Beach's Sister City), that I would be arriving on July 4. I really had no idea what, if anything, would happen.

Arriving at the train station, I was met by aides for the mayor. I was whisked away on a grand, private tour of the city, complete with photographers and interpreters.

I later met with Mikail Kosheev, vice chairman of the Committee on Townspeople's Deals, and Yulia Kuznetsova, chief specialist in the Foreign Economic and International Affairs Department.

Due to a tragic airplane crash in Irkutsk that very morning, the mayor (doesn't sound like much of a title compared to the aforementioned) was unable to meet me for lunch, as was planned.

Once in a while, it's nice to have VIP treatment. It makes life special. The hospitality that was shown to me was second to none. I was impressed and flattered.

I am off to visit Lake Baikal in the morning, then back to Irkutsk for a day and a night. Lake Baikal has more than 320 rivers flowing into it and only one flowing out. It is said to have taken 400 hundred years to fill. It is the oldest lake in the world.

What I find really impressive is that, if drained of all its water, and subsequently, if all of the fresh water rivers in the world were emptied into it, it would take more than a year for it to refill to capacity. Amazing.

After Irkutsk and Lake Baikal, it's off to Moscow — Red Square — and (last but not least) the one and only golf course in Moscow.

Happy Trails,
Jack Gillette

After making some minor adjustments to the article, he walked around the small park, stopping at several kiosks to enjoy everything from ice cream to sausages.

He wandered past an old church, visited on his tour with the Irkutsk City Administration. He couldn't remember what was famous or unusual about it. It wasn't particularly beautiful or large, it's sole outstanding characteristic being a coppery metal dome which covered a turret-like part of it's structure.

He found himself walking in the direction of the apartment, and came upon the outdoor cafe where he'd met Tanya and her friends. Feeling a rush of excitement as he neared the front gate, he fell back into a mood of resignation when he noticed it was closed.

Arriving at the internet center, he sat down at a terminal and logged onto his e-mail. After answering several messages from readers and friends, he clicked on the "Reply" icon above Lynda's message.

Lynda,

I'm not sure what to say. Not only do I lack the words to explain how I feel right now, I have no idea what kind of response you would like or expect.

I do know that everything I have ever done since meeting you has been done with your happiness at the center of my reasoning. I have never intended to control you or hurt you. I have only wanted to make you happy. I always hoped you would be happy with me. Apparently, that is not the case.

I have heard from friends that you are traveling with Bill. I hope it's not true — you don't need him for anything you want to do, as I know you are capable of anything you put your mind to.

I'm having a difficult time writing this, me the writer, the one whose words are supposed to come so easy. I hurt a great deal right now.

I don't hurt because you are coming after the money and not me. I don't hurt because you are, or are not traveling with Bill. I hurt because I feel lost without the trust we shared — the trust which I would have sworn was something eternal — that it is now gone.

I've always known it was possible you or I might stray. The physical pull from other people is always there, unless we isolated ourselves on an island. That breach of trust hurts, but it is not what is gnawing at my heart right now. The real hurt comes from my belief that you would never intentionally hurt me.

Apparently, I have hurt you. I want you to know that I am sorry for any pain I ever caused you.

And, you have hurt me. It's something I never thought would happen — ever. I trusted you that much.

If you must come after me, that is okay. I'll abide by the conditions which I originally set, though I set them with no intention of us being apart for so long. I'll enjoy a beer in a sidewalk cafe, often saddened because you are not there beside me.

I love you very much. I sometimes think that I have loved you since even before I met you, when you were but a dream to me. It seems as though I will now have to go back there — to my dreams — to the fuzzy, out of focus world where everything seems so close, yet is so very far, far away. Regardless of the

clarity, you will always be there — be there in my heart.
> *Love ,*
> *Jack*

At Nick's apartment he sat talking with his host and wasting time until a guide arrived to take him to the train station. His train was scheduled to leave Irkutsk at 3:30 p.m.

One of Jack's lifelong dreams was to travel on the Trans-Siberian express. With all of the upheaval in his personal life, he'd had little time to think about it — little time to consider a childhood dream was about to come true.

By the time his appointed guide arrived, the sunny day gave way to another of Irkutsk's late afternoon rain storms. The sky had become overrun with dark, dreary clouds. The force and amount of rain falling made him sad and melancholy concerning not only his own personal life, but about leaving Irkutsk as well.

Minutes later the train moved slowly from the station, picking up speed as it left Irkutsk and the rain behind. In a little over 3 days, after traveling 3220 miles, he would arrive in Moscow.

****

Jack sat on his bunk in the two-place compartment and smiled at the old man smiling back at him. The man looked as if he was seventy or eighty years old, his rough gnarled hands, breaking off pieces of bread from a huge loaf sitting on a small table between the bunks. He held out some to Jack, which he accepted.

Nick, his homestay host in Irkutsk, had put together a bag of assorted food for the long journey. Jack pulled the bag out and put the items on the table. Gesturing with his hands, he offered in return his meager collection of food. The Russian fumbled below his bunk for a string bag, which appeared to be the veteran of many Trans-Siberian trips. In it were bottles of beer and vodka. With no words spoken between them, they were communicating. They were to have a feast, both of them contributing equally.

Their impromptu feast was to last for days, ending only when the Russian departed the train in a small town just before reaching Moscow. At each stop, and there were many, they would detrain and rummage among the platform's many vending stands. At some stations, hawkers would come aboard, making their way from compartment to compartment selling everything from furs to pornography.

Although books and articles about the Trans-Siberian railway all proclaimed the trip to be a long, grueling affair, Jack found the trip very pleasant. Perhaps the writers were all embellishing the experience, making it sound more mysterious and adventurous than it really was.

The landscape traversing Russia was pleasing to the eye, and spectacular in its vastness. He enjoyed the ride all the way to Moscow.

****

This was the Soviet Union Jack had read of. He was in the lobby of the Intourist Hotel, just a few hundred yards from Moscow's Red Square. The bureaucracy of simply checking in was an ordeal.

The plumbing wouldn't work in his room, and someone had removed the hot water faucet handle in the shower. Jack notified the front desk, who in turn sent a maintenance technician. The maintenance man arrived with a hammer, a pair of pliers and nothing else. He managed to replace the faucet handle, but the toilet still did not flush properly.

Leaving the hotel, Jack discovered a large, subterranean shopping complex at the edge of the area making up Red Square and the Kremlin. One floor was above ground, the roof serving as a park-like gathering area, complete with benches and fountains.

With a distinctive western flavor, the building was obviously designed as a showcase mall for the Soviet Union. Modern and up to date, the stores offered everything from Gucci handbags to McDonald's hamburgers. As cosmopolitan and capitalistic as the atmosphere was, Jack could not help but think that during the design stages of the structure, one if not all of the architects were thinking, "Bomb Shelter."

At the lowest level he was pleasantly surprised to find an internet center. There were over one hundred monitors and keyboards arranged in neat rows. After checking in and taking a seat, he found the systems lightning fast as well.

There was a message from a Russian woman named Masha. A number of years ago, she had worked at McGrath's, the pub in Newport Beach where Jack purchased his lottery ticket. Masha explained that Bobby McGrath contacted her about Jack's trip. Now residing in Moscow, she wrote how they would love to get together with him while he was in town.

Although he did not know her well, his delightful experience with the city administrators from Irkutsk was fresh in his mind. This invitation may be enjoyable also, he thought. After typing a reply, he began work on another dispatch for the newspaper. The long train ride across Russia gave him plenty of time to edit the piece. He added photos from his digital, the graphics displayed so quickly by the high powered computers, that to blink was to miss the imaging.

Around the World

A LITTLE RECAP: My journey began in Los Angeles, California in mid-May. After leaving Long Beach, and crossing the Pacific Ocean on a container ship, I began a twenty-six day odyssey by train from Hong Kong to Moscow. The route encompassed the Trans-China, Trans-Mongolian and the legendary

Trans-Siberian expresses.

I have traveled more than 8,000 miles by rail.

The trains offer four classes — hard seat, soft seat, hard sleeper and soft sleeper. A hard seat entitles the ticket holder to board the train. The "seat" is optional. If a seat is found, there is no guarantee it will be there should you get up for any reason.

I am not certain, but smoking may be mandatory in this class, while air conditioning is achieved only by opening a window.

The soft-seat class reserves a seat for the passenger. Comfort conditions are only marginally better than that of the hard-seat class. The hard-sleeper carriages consist of several doorless compartments off a main passageway. Each compartment accommodates six people in three bunks on either side.

While access to the top bunk is akin to scaling K-2, the bottom bunk serves as a communal bench, dining table and gathering area. Smoking is allowed in the passageway, and since there are no doors to the compartments and everybody smokes, cigarette fumes are everywhere.

The soft-sleeper class is as good as it gets. Each compartment is fitted with a locking door. Depending upon the train, there are two or four bunks on either side of the small but efficient room. Smoking is allowed only at the end of the carriage.

Food is a big part of a train experience. Although some people eat in the dining car, (if one exists), many bring plastic bags and boxes of food with them, eating in their compartments.

The aromas of some of these foods can be extremely foreign to a Westerner's nose. As there are no showers on the train, and many trips are long, overnight journeys, body odor is also an ever-present olfactory sensation.

And then there are the toilets. The very best facility can only be described as extremely gross. The worst — simply a hole in the floor — is a place where you do not want to go. The stench may be confined to the toilet area or it may permeate throughout the carriage.

These toilets make a call to nature in a modern port-a-potty seem like spending the night at the Ritz.

PEOPLE MAKE THE MEMORIES

The reason I travel is to meet people and forge new relationships. While temples, artifacts and scenery are all pleasant to see, those kind of experiences are best summed up by a comment overheard while scaling the Great Wall Of China.

As I neared the top of this extremely strenuous trek, an English-speaking woman passing on her descent commented to her companion, "Been there, done that."

While the scenery of this rail journey over two continents has been splendid in its extremes, it is the people and the shared experiences that I shall re-

member and cherish.

From Guangzhou to Guilin, China, my compartment mate was a Chinese gentleman by the name of Pan. Amidst a sea of garbage and the reeking odor from a nearby toilet, this supposedly 13-hour ride lasted 20.

With neither a carriage attendant or fellow traveler understanding or speaking English, I was wrought with worry. Did I miss my stop? Am I on the wrong train?

For hours, Pan and I attempted to communicate. Just as I was ready to concede the train was destined for some remote settlement in Kazakhstan, another Chinese gentleman overheard our linguistic standoff, and joined in the fray.

After wild gesticulations, drawings and charades, they finally conveyed that the train was taking an alternate route to Guilin due to flooding. I was on the correct train, but would arrive at my destination seven hours later than scheduled.

The leg of my journey from Xian to Shanghai involved the sharing of a four-place compartment with five boisterous Chinese men. Which two gentlemen did not belong in the compartment was anyone's guess.

Again, English was neither spoken nor understood by my companions.

Beginning in Xian at 6 p.m., their loud, card-playing party went on until 10 p.m. When one of the men left only to return with five large bottles of beer, I felt it was finally time to break my silence and protest.

Neither my protests nor my English were understood. Before I could launch into a full tirade, a bottle of beer was thrust into my hand while one of the men ran off to the dining care for more.

There followed numerous toasts to good health and the sharing of some Chinese whiskey, (a clear liquid with a flavor like a combination of Aqua Velva and lighter fluid). Drinking and vain attempts at conversation lasted until the wee hours of the morning.

There have been other memorable people, from two blushing, 18-year-old Chinese girls to a good friendship with Ulzilorshikh "Augie" Jamsran.

Augie and I shared a compartment from Beijing to Ulan Bator, Mongolia. At the end of this journey, while other passengers crowded to one end of the carriage to debark, Augie insisted that I go with him as the conductor lead us privately in the opposite direction.

Opening the door, we were met at the platform by a television crew and many well-wishers. Augie, it seems, is a member of Mongolia's Olympic cycling team. Returning victorious from an event in China, he is considered a hero by his Mongolian countrymen.

But the best is reserved until last — the Trans-Siberian experience. From Irkutsk to Moscow, Russia, in three days. At each stop — and there were many — the platform was crowded with vendors selling food and drink.

From vodka to beer, from smoked fish to bread and vegetables, it was a sea of gastronomical delight. Some vendors came onto the train, peddling everything from pornography to fur pelts of sable and mink.

When I boarded this train in Irkutsk, I was curious who would share my two-place sleeper compartment. All of the sleeping compartments on trains in China, Mongolia and Russia are coed, which adds an intriguing element to long-distance excursions.

My compartment mate? Alexander Schostokov, a 70-year-old Russian bound for Moscow. He spoke no English, but possessed an international parlance that I understood perfectly.

Alexander drank vodka for dinner and beer for breakfast. Between drinks, we feasted together on roast chicken, black bread, sausage, fresh tomatoes, cucumbers and sweet rolls.

When Alexander ran out of vodka, I produced a flask of American whiskey for a little international flavor.

What a trip! More than 8,000 miles of clickety-clack, good food and drink, great conversation and memorable friendships.

<u>15</u>

"Because, I don't want to go alone!" blurted Lynda. She was sitting on the edge of the bed in a hotel room in Beijing. Bill stood near the window, looking at the street, six stories below.

"Look at all those cocksuckers," stated Bill, speaking as though he'd just discovered something no one else had ever seen. "Cars, bicycles, people ... Jesus, they're all over the fuckin' place!"

"Bill, could you please pay attention for one goddamn minute!" screamed Lynda.

He turned around to look at her, a surprised look on his face. It was as if he was realizing for the first time she was in the room. They had been arguing for twenty minutes. Earlier, Lynda purchased two tickets for a tour of the Great Wall of China. On hearing this, Bill told her he did not want to go, and suggested she get a refund and buy a couple of postcards instead.

"Who the fuck's going to know whether you actually saw it or not?" he'd asked.

She told him she would know, and that was all that mattered.

"Would it really kill you to do this with me?" she now pleaded. "I mean, you haven't seen anything in China, except for the bar in the lobby of a couple of hotels."

"I saw those stupid statues with you," he said, his eyes now returning to the street scene below.

She let herself fall back on the bed. Why does this crap have to happen to me? she thought to herself. She reached for the remote and turned off the television, it's sound muted since their argument began. Bill heard the click of the set turning off, and was about to say something, but quickly thought better.

"Bill, the stupid statues, as you refer to them, were the Terracotta Warriors. They were interesting. Why can't you enjoy something for a change instead of being such an ass?"

"Why can't you enjoy something?" Bill mimicked. He'd had enough of her shit. "I'm the ass, but you seem to have forgotten those two statues you wanted, I bought for you. And, at that fuckin' gift shop full of, what I would call a bunch of junk, I surprised you with those earrings."

She had seen some things she liked but hesitated to buy because of their size or cost. She'd initially passed on the earrings, and was thinking of returning to buy them, when Bill walked up and put them in her hand. She couldn't figure a way to carry the statues, but he found someone who spoke English and could arrange shipping directly to Los Angeles.

"I'm sorry Bill. This is stressful for both of us. The sooner we catch Jack the better. But, I'll never be in China again, and there are a couple of things I'd like to see. I don't want to go to the Great Wall by myself, but if you really don't want to go, I'll live with it."

"Well, I really don't want to go," It wasn't his intention to mimic her again, but that's the way it came out. "I'm sorry too," he reluctantly said. "I didn't mean to snap at you, but damn it, I'm fuckin' tired here. We gotta lot more of this train shit to do, and I'm not looking forward to more clickety-clack with a bunch of Chinks and Ruskies."

She let the racism slide. What was the point? It would do no good to harp about it, he wasn't going to change. She was also feeling a little guilty she had not taken into account his advancing age. He would be sixty-two years old in a couple more months, and it was the first time he'd complained of being tired. Lynda was already beat, and she shuddered thinking of how tired he must be.

"Look, it's fine. I'll just go by myself. I'll be on a tour bus, so it's not like I won't have other people around, or someone directing us where to go. I'll be okay."

Bill turned back to the window. "How many of those little, slant-eyed fuckers do ya think there are in this town, anyway?"

She let herself fall from her sitting position on the edge of the bed, to a prone position, staring up at the ceiling. It was going to be a long trip.

****

The following morning a small bus pulled away from the hotel with Lynda and nine other people aboard. Lynda looked around as the guide, standing next to the driver, tested the microphone. Many of the tourists were couples, much older than herself, and in fact, most were Bill's age. If they could do this, why couldn't he? But, she let the thought pass.

Directly across from her was an attractive man sitting alone. They noticed one another at the same time, and blushing slightly, he introduced himself. He looked as if he were about ten years older than her. He had sandy, blonde hair he kept brushing back with one hand as he spoke.

"Hello, my name is Ian. And you,?" he said, a distinct British accent apparent in just a few short words.

"Hi. My name's Lynda," and she reached over to shake his already extended hand.

As the guide droned on, Lynda and Ian talked the awkward language when conversation is forced by the fact that an absence of conversation would be even more uncomfortable. As they conversed, she became more relaxed, and at Ian's invitation, moved across the isle to the seat beside him.

"What brings you to China?" she asked.

"I've never been here," he replied, matter-of-fact ly. "I was in Hong Kong, and thinkin' bout travelin' to Malaysia. Changed me mind, and er' I am."

"So, you're just taking a vacation?" Lynda asked.

Ian laughed. "Ye are an American, are ye not? And let me guess. This is yer first trip abroad."

"Well yes, it is." She was smiling broadly, partially because Ian was as well, but also because she was enjoying herself.

"Ya see, I'm on holiday. That's what we Brits call it. American is such a strange language. Don't ya think, eh?"

They talked and talked, as the bus lumbered along. Halfway to the Great Wall, they stopped at a large building which housed a gift shop. Lynda and Ian went in with the passengers, but found themselves wandering back to the bus long before any of the others returned. Finding the bus too hot inside, they leaned against one of the front fenders and talked some more.

Ian wouldn't quite say what he did for a living, but it was obvious he was not in any career situation. "I'm not rich, mind ya, although I was born with a bit of a silver spoon in me mouth. Me own father pissed away most of the money before me brother and I were old enough to spit. Luckily, me mum was a proper and thrifty woman, she was. God rest her soul. If it weren't fer er, I wouldn't have a quid in me pocket."

"So, you don't work, or what?" inquired Lynda. They had talked enough by now that the question was not one which would be considered nosy.

"Me brother and I had a pub for a few years. Sold it. Got tired of the behavior the wicked pint brung out. Now we got a garage," he said, the word, "garage," it coming out, "gare-idge."

"Ya see, me brother likes racing those cars round-n-round, the smell of petrol and all. When I'm home, I just go down from time to time for tea, and to see ef Nickie has gotten any of the grease out of es hair."

There was a pause in their conversation. Avoiding the topic of why she was in China, she knew it would arise sooner or later. She wasn't sure what her response would be to this man, but found herself relieved when the subject finally arose.

"And so my dear, what brings you to China? Somehow, I don't feel it's because yer on holiday."

"Well, it's kinda involved," she said, wondering what would come out of her mouth next. She didn't want to tell the whole story, but didn't want to fabricate one either.

"I'm traveling with an older man. Ah, we're traveling to meet another gentleman, probably in Stockholm."

Ian had not been at all reluctant to talk for the last two hours, but now, as they stood next to the bus, the heat and humidity intense, he stood by silently. Lynda could feel herself sweating for the first time, a cold trickle running down from her armpit to where it stopped abruptly at her bra.

She sighed deeply before continuing. "It's a long and complicated story. I've never been anywhere, and I wouldn't be here if I didn't have to."

"Well, thank ya very much, love," he said, smiling, but lowering his head as if saddened.

"I'm sorry. That's not what I meant, and you know it. Quite frankly, this is the first time I've really enjoyed myself since starting this trip. I thank you for that. But, why I am here is very complicated. It's funny, because I'd like to tell you the whole story. I feel a need to tell someone, but not quite just yet. Parts of it are a little embarrassing, I'm coming to believe."

Ian opened a shoulder bag he was carrying. He removed a business card which simply bore his name and an e-mail address.

"I've toured about for years now," he said. "Never had much use for computers and the like, but I have to say this e-mail is lovely. Don't know how I ever got along without it." He handed her the card.

Ian Mickelson was the name printed on the card, and below that was the e-address, *catslandontheirfeet@hotmail.com*. Reading the card, she laughed and smiled. She wanted to give Ian one of her business cards, but they were from a law firm she no longer worked for, and all of the information was meaningless.

"Do you have another card?" she asked.

Ian located a card and handed it to her. She wrote her name and her personal e-mail address.

"We'll have to stay in touch," said Ian, as she handed him the card. "Maybe you can write what you can't seem ta say. You're a mysterious one, that you are, love."

Lynda wanted to just unload on this man, tell him everything about Jack, Bill, and the chase. She had a tremendous urge to tell someone, but at the same time, was afraid how it might sound. She didn't think she was a bad woman, but she didn't think she was exactly an angel either. She was afraid her story would be taken the wrong way, and she would sound like the consummate bitch — especially so with the initial disclosure. With repetition, she was confident it could be explained in such a way to be factual, and at the same time sympathetic of her side.

They later walked up and down the Great Wall together, jointly deciding a walk to the very top was too strenuous a trek. It was hot and muggy, and people all around them were gasping for air as they trudged up and down the steep slope. She bought a tee-shirt for Bill, although she knew he'd probably never wear it.

She found herself getting excited when she saw a table festooned with refrigerator magnets in the shape of the Great Wall. She picked one up which had a tiny thermometer attached to it, before realizing the person who would love to receive such a gift was out of her life. Jack loved these things. They were plastered all over his refrigerator, along with photos dating back to his college days.

"Why don't you buy it, love," said Ian. He had walked up behind her, and for a moment, lost in her own thoughts, she was surprised someone was speaking to her. "It's clear by the smile on your face that ya think it's lovely."

"It just brought back some memories, some good, some bad," she lied. In truth, they were all good. For a fleeting moment, she wondered, did I get tired or did I just get lazy?

"Well love, the bus is going to be leaving straight-away. I bought us a couple of bottles of watt'er for the journey," he said.

When Ian stepped off the bus at his hotel, they made promises to stay in touch. He told her she was welcome at his home in England anytime. His sister lived just down the lane, he explained.

"Ask anyone about Justina, they'll set you right with directions, probably walk ya down to her door. She's a saint, she is, and she'll put ya up proper if I'm not about."

Lynda hated traveling alone. If pressed, she would probably admit to disliking being alone in any situation. She didn't feel she was incapable of functioning by herself, nor did she feel in need of constant company and attention, but now, riding the hotel elevator to her room, she would have given anything to be alone and returning to an empty room.

She would not have brought Ian back here, although he was a nice man, and very comfortable to be around. No, she would like to be returning to an empty hotel room so she could be by herself, so she could be alone with her thoughts. She could take a hot bath, or maybe a nap, or maybe even both.

It had been a long, hot, physically demanding and wonderful day, she thought, as she opened the door of her room and was greeted by the sound of Bill snoring, while the television blared the news in Chinese.

****

Jack's last night in Moscow was a memorable one spent with good friends. It was yet another instance when perfect strangers or mere acquaintances open their doors to a traveler.

Masha and Sasha Shatalina had attended school in the United States. Both were originally from Moscow, and when their university studies were completed, they returned home. Both worked within the international business community. Jack's only connection with Masha was her once having worked for Bobby at McGrath's. Bobby e-mailed her, and she in turn e-mailed Jack when he was in Hong Kong.

She picked him up in front of his hotel. "I am taking you to an Uzbekistan restaurant. I hope that is okay," she told him in perfect English as they sped along the wide boulevards of Moscow. "Sasha will meet us there. It is a very famous restaurant."

A few minutes later, Jack met Sasha for the first time. Once they entered the restaurant, he knew he was in for an experience.

"Beloye Solntse Pustyni" was named after a legendary Soviet film of the same name. Translated, "The White Sun Of The Desert," it is a theme restaurant specializing in Uzbek food. The restaurant's interior is designed to create an illusion of a ship marooned in the desert. There followed a glorious meal with impeccable service. Belly dancers wove their way around the tables throughout the evening.

Returning to the hotel, Jack reflected upon all of the wonderful people he met, and the circumstances of how these new friendships took place. He knew he would not have met some of them had Lynda been by his side. He would have been content with her company. They would have talked together and enjoyed the sites as a couple. There would have been no need for him to reach out to anyone else. What he was experiencing was something unique to traveling solo.

The next day he left Moscow for St. Petersburg. While the trains in China were nothing to write home about, and the Trans-Siberian and Trans-Mongolian only marginally better, this train, speeding along in the dead of night from Moscow to St. Petersburg, was incredible.

The train's interior was ornate, the wood brightly varnished, and the brass fixtures impeccably polished. In his compartment, a bouquet of flowers graced the ever familiar table separating the two bunks. Both beds were turned down, and the pillow's pure-white pillowcases gleamed in the light. At each side of the table were two small boxes containing a croissant, three pats of butter, an apple, and some chocolate. Next to each box was a bottle of mineral water.

This was the famous Red Arrow Express. Departing from Moscow's Leningradsky Vokzal station at 11:55 p.m., Jack was in a two-place compartment in one of the first class carriages.

After stowing his bags he was about to sit down when a liveried steward entered the compartment, offering tea or coffee. Shortly thereafter, his compartment mate entered. The man was dressed in what appeared to be a very expensive suit. Obviously a businessman, he spoke very little English. After a few attempts at conversation, Jack excused himself and walked out into the corridor.

He left for a few moments as a courtesy to the Russian, assuming he intended to sleep, rather than sit up, drink, and play cards like the five Chinese men had done on the train to Shanghai. Carefully reopening the sliding door of the compartment, he could see his assumptions were correct, the man now seemingly fast asleep.

Jack undressed, climbed into the fresh, clean sheets of his bunk, and turned off the night light. The click of the steel wheels hitting the small space separating the end of one rail and the beginning of the next was the only sound he was conscious of as he quickly slid into dreamland. He would have sweet dreams. He would sleep like a baby.

The best part of traveling by train is the night. It often reminded him of traveling in the back seat of the family sedan as a child. Well before the days of toddlers seats and those hideous, yellow, triangle-shaped signs proclaiming a baby on board, Jack would fall into a deep sleep on the back seat. The faint sound of the car's motor and the hum of the tires meeting the road — the unfaltering rhythm as steady and assuring as his father's gnarled hands in his — background music for falling into a deep and happy slumber.

Those sounds then, and the sound of the trains wheels now, were to sleep like foreplay was to sex. It was the best part of traveling by train.

****

"Not in this fuckin' cabin, Jose." Bill was telling an older Mongolian gentleman not to enter their train compartment.

They were at the train station in Ulan Bator, getting ready to depart for Irkutsk, Russia. Much to Lynda's disgust, Bill enticed a guide to alter their tickets, thereby converting a four-place compartment into a two-place one. He paid the man $250.00 up front, and promised another $250.00 after the train got rolling.

"I'll fly back here and kick his Mongolian ass if they make us take on a couple yokels a few miles out of town," he snorted.

Lynda said nothing in reply. In fact, she didn't even look up at him.

"At least we'll be able to have some privacy," he added. He knew she was pissed off. She'd been that way for a long time now, since Beijing or before, and he was getting tired of it. "I mean, wouldn't it be nice to have a little privacy?"

She still did not speak. She was looking out the window, at nothing really, as the view was of a rail yard, full of shunting tracks and what looked to be discarded passenger cars. She was thinking of the poor souls who would love to be able to live in the abandoned carriages, a far cry from living on the streets of Ulan Bator, when Bill yelled at her.

"Answer me, goddamn it!" he screamed.

Lynda jumped, but said nothing.

"When I'm talkin' to you, fucking answer me!" he barked.

"What's to answer?" she yelled back, her shock of him yelling now abated. "What difference does it make if two more people are in this room? Sure, I'd like to ..." She was unable to finish.

"I don't give a good fuck what you think! I'm getting tired of all of these people, and I'd like to be alone. I'm also getting tired of you being such a, well ... so goddamn pissed off all the time. I came here to help you find your asshole boyfriend and pick up fifteen mil. I didn't come here on a National Geographic tour to see yurts, statues, and how the fuckin' locals make a delicious dumpling out of fresh horse-shit."

Lynda desperately wanted to say something, but she was scared. Still, she managed, "Bill, calm down. Let's just try to ..."

He cut her off again. "And another thing. I came here to be with you. It's like all of a sudden I got AIDS or something."

She stood up. She put her hands on his shoulders and gently guided him to a sitting position on the edge of one of the bunks. He started to get up, but hit his head on the bunk above him, lowered by the train attendant before their arrival in anticipation of two more passengers.

"Ah, fuck me," he cried, putting his hands up to where he bumped his head and abruptly sitting back down.

She sat across from him. In a soothing voice, she told him to relax for a few minutes, that everything would be all right. "Bill, I'm sorry. This is very hard on both of us. I'm taking it out on you, and you're taking it out on everyone."

He wanted to say, "No, I'm taking it out on you, bitch," but he didn't.

"Really," she said, "I'm sorry. Let's see what happens here. I just don't want you to get angry and upset if the guide never comes back, and two more passengers are assigned to this compartment."

"That little fuck'll come back. I got two-hundred-fifty waiting for him," he said confidently.

She doubted the guide could change anything, and figured he was miles away from the station by now. That no one had entered their compartment was a moot point, as several had attempted to before Bill ran them off. She kept expecting the sliding door to suddenly and noisily open, the sight of two passengers behind a stern-faced train attendant standing in the corridor.

When the train started to slowly roll forward, there was a knock on the door. She got up and opened it, and there stood the guide. Before she could speak, Bill jumped up and thrust a wad of money past her and into his hands.

"There's a little fuckin' extra in there for ya," said Bill. "But, just remember, we want this cabin all to ourselves, and all the way to Ruskie-dom."

After sitting back down, the train made a slight turn. Through the window, Lynda could see the little Mongolian guide nimbly working his way across the many tracks which ran parallel to the train. He would probably have a party tonight, she thought, the idea of a party so far removed from her thinking.

"What's the date today?" she asked, the guide now out of sight.

Bill could not look at a calendar for days, and still be able to tell someone what the date was. "It's the eighteenth, why?"

"Oh, I don't know. Just wondering." She paused a moment, still looking out the window, and aware of Bill looking at her. "It's Hunter Thompson's birthday," she said, just to be saying something.

"Yeah, and it's also the day that crazy fuck blew all those kids away at the McDonald's in San Ysidro," said Bill.

She didn't want to say anything more. She was wondering what might have been, what could have been, and how things may have been different. A word or action here — another at just the right moment. Possibly just being there at a time when she needed the physical warmth of another person.

She was with a guy who was twice her age, and who scared her when he was angry. She was chasing after a fortune, barely stopping to smell the roses along the way, and catching hell from her companion when she did. She probably burned every bridge she ever crossed, and it was as if she was seeing a huge sign which proclaimed, "No Lane Changes."

July 18th. It was Hunter Thompson's birthday. It was also the anniversary of the tragic day when James Huberty shot and killed 21 innocent people at a McDonald's Restaurant in San Ysidro, California.

July 18th. It was Jack's birthday.

****

Jack received two e-mails from a friend in Oregon. Gene Davis had traveled the world, first as a Marine, and later as an engineer. Reading one of Jack's travel articles on-line, he responded. Jack was glad they still kept in touch, and flattered Gene would seek out his articles.

In his correspondence, Gene mentioned a couple who lived in Helsinki. Close friends, he e-mailed them, telling them of a friend who was on his way from Asia and Russia. The couple, Martin and Ritva Holm, had in turn, e-mailed Jack in Mongolia. They inquired about his arrival date and time in Helsinki, while Jack asked them about accommodation.

The train from St. Petersburg to Helsinki was a day train, the first since travel from Hong Kong to Guangzhou. It arrived in Helsinki at 9:30 p.m. on July 18th.

Jack stepped from the train to the platform of the Helsinki train station. With his bags over both shoulders, he took a couple steps forward so the person behind him could exit. He was standing there when he noticed two people coming toward him.

Martin Holm offered an outstretched hand, and his wife, Ritva, would have done the same. However, carrying a small birthday cake with one candle perched at the top, her hands were full.

"Happy Birthday, Jack!" she said.

"How did you know it was my birthday?" he asked, smiling and truly amazed a couple of complete strangers would be there to welcome him.

"You mentioned it in your e-mail," said Ritva. "You've been traveling a long way, you must be tired," she added.

Martin, taking one of his bags, spoke of lodging at a local university dormitory. "They're on summer vacation now, so all of the rooms are available for travelers, " Martin said in perfect, unaccented English. "We'll take you there and get you settled, and then, if you have no plans for tomorrow, I'll pick you up and give you a tour of the city."

As they walked along, exiting the train station and making their way to where Martin's car was parked, they talked about their mutual friend in Oregon and Jack's trip. They said nothing of the lottery — they either didn't know, or didn't care.

They were talking freely, as if old friends, when they came upon a driveway leading into a parking area. Noticing a car approaching from his right, Jack abruptly stopped. He back-stepped onto the curb, while at the same time the driver stopped. The driver then waved with one hand, directing them to cross in front of him.

Jack hesitated ever so slightly. Crossing a street in China, Mongolia, or Russia was taking your life in your own hands. In the rare instance a "walk" signal was present, it meant little. Adding to the danger, the streets were often wide, two way boulevards, and speed was only restricted by degrees of daring and foolhardiness.

He was struck by a car in Beijing, but able to jump up and come to rest in a sitting position on the hood of the slow moving vehicle. In true Chinese fashion, the driver honked his horn before, during, and after the collision.

Now, as Jack, Martin and Ritva made their way across the lane and in front of the polite and waiting driver, he felt Martin's hand on his arm.

"Welcome to the western world," he solemnly said.

Jack had to laugh. The timing, his hesitation to walk in front of the vehicle, and Martin's hospitality all made the comment profound. It was something Jack would never forget.

Helsinki was wonderful. It really was the western world. There were signs in English, and many of the people he met spoke English. Martin and Ritva took Jack to their summer cabin outside of Helsinki, to their golf club for lunch and to their home for dinner. Without e-mail, the meeting would have been much more difficult to schedule and coordinate. Without good friends, it never would have happened.

After a couple of days, he was ready to be back on the road again. Before going to the ferry terminal, he visited a small cafe with internet access. There were only four computers, and he felt lucky to not have to wait. He had over fifty messages from the newspaper's readership. There were three from Dan, and one from Dan's wife, Rebecca. It saddened him there was no message from Lynda, but thinking about it, what could she possibly say?

He was ready to sign out when the urge hit him. He clicked on Lynda's e-address.

Lynda,

I suppose it's no state secret, so I'll tell you where I am. I'm in Helsinki, getting ready to board a ferry to Tallinn, Estonia. In lots of ways, it's good to be out of Russia, China and Mongolia. It is also good to be traveling without any schedule. I can go as slow or as fast as I wish.

Nothing has changed at my end. I still have periods of deep depression and hurt, but I'm happy to say I'm better. It is evident by the lack of correspondence, (and your failure to even wish me a happy birthday), that you are very angry. *I don't feel there is any reason for you to feel that way — if anyone should be angry, it should be me. I'm not anymore, by the way.*

I've heard through the grapevine that you are traveling with dumbnuts, Bill. (Sorry — you know I've never liked that asshole). If that's what you want, then so be it.

Anyway, I'm writing on an impulse here, with little to really say.

I'll stay true to my word on my offer. If you're not worried about that, I'm sure Bill is. But, I will not just sit and wait for the two of you to show up either. I'm coming to this conclusion as I write, so I have to pause for a second to get my words correct.

I'm moving on. I'll still frequent the small hotels, and hang out at side-walk cafes. But I've only got a couple of months before the ship sails out of Liverpool, so I've got to move fast. I plan to have all of the money when I board my ship to sail home — in other words, I will make the two of you work very hard for what you want.

Remember, it's only a game for me. I don't care one iota about the money. I only wish it could be the same for you. It would fit you so much better.

And, by the way. I still love you.

Happy Trails,

Jack

Jack boarded the ferry just after 10 a.m. A couple hours later he was in Tallinn. True to his word and the message sent to Lynda, he purchased a ticket to Stockholm directly after debarking. He would have a few hours to explore the Estonian city before sailing to Sweden, an overnight voyage.

He was on the move.

<u>16</u>

Arriving in Irkutsk, Russia, Lynda and Bill booked a hotel room prior to catching the Trans-Siberian the next afternoon. A small room in the hotel's lobby provided computer access, but try as she might, Lynda could not get online. She did not expect a message from Jack, but inside her, there was a longing to hear from him.

Their ride across the vast expanse of Russia was a long and tedious one. Lynda found a discarded novel in the hotel lobby in Irkutsk. Luckily it was in English, and that it wasn't some trashy romance novel, even more of a bonus. She spent her time reading and watching the countryside pass by, not at all an unpleasant experience.

When Bill wasn't sleeping, he spent his time grousing about everything from the weather, (which was ideal), to the comfort of the compartment, (which was as good, if not better than trains traveled on previously).

For both of them, the sight of Moscow was therefore a relief. After getting a room and taking a much needed shower, Lynda dressed in a pair of jeans and a white blouse. Bill was just getting out of the shower when he noticed her, getting ready as if she intended to go out. It was 10 a.m.

"Where the hell are you going?" he asked, none to delicately.

"I'm going to go for a walk," she answered curtly. "I'd ask you to go along, but I'm tired of hearing you bitch about everything. The driver said we are only a couple of blocks from the Kremlin, and I'd like to see it."

"Well, aren't we just the little fucking tourist now," said Bill, not being modest in any way, as he stood in the doorway of the bathroom toweling himself off. "You seem to be enjoying this little joy ride, but you better remember that ... well, ah, as ya keep fuckin' round with all this touristy shit, your boyfriend just puts miles and miles between us and our money."

"You mean us and my money, don't you?" she said as she packed a few loose articles in a bag. The laptop Bill purchased in Hong Kong was lying on top of her suitcase and on a whim she put it in her shoulder bag as well. "I mean, our money was probably just a slip of the tongue, right?" She was teasing him now, and not in a playful way. Her voice had an edge which made the teasing more like taunting.

He stopped toweling himself, and just stood there staring at her. He didn't move, and a couple of uncomfortable moments passed, before he said something.

"No, I mean our fucking money. As soon as we're out of Russia the rules are changing a little. So, go ahead a fuck around while you can."

"What do you mean by that?" asked Lynda, uncomfortable now with him staring at her. His voice quivered a bit with his last words, and it scared her. "What do you mean, the rules are going to change?" she asked again.

"Just get the fuck out," he said, turning now to go back into the bathroom. "Have a great time while I take care of all the details. You can thank me later when you're finished being a fuckin' tourist."

She quickly walked out of the room and down to the lobby, glad to be away from him. A man who spoke English without any trace of an accent was behind a small desk marked in both English and what she presumed was Russian for "concierge." After giving her directions, he handed her a small map.

As she departed the hotel, traffic noise and the heat of a summer day greeted her like a slap in the face. It awakened her from a trance-like state, induced by worry and concern over Bill's words of the rules changing. For the present time however, she dismissed any thoughts of him. She didn't want his dark cloud hanging over her head while she went about a tour of the Kremlin, St. Basil Cathedral, and an internet cafe.

Lynda had traveled halfway around the world. She wasn't exactly having the time of her life, but it was much better than the first month or so. She wasn't seasick, and and she wasn't afraid to go out by herself. Maybe Bill will get tired and just decide to fly home, she thought to herself, not believing a word of it, yet determined the impossible could come true.

By mid afternoon she was in high spirits. Playing the part of a tourist, she met a couple from Argentina. South America sounded so far away from Russia, but here they were, a couple her age, traveling all over the globe.

She found internet access in what was a coffee and pastry cafe located on a wide boulevard not far from the Kremlin. There was a message from Jack. There was also a message from Ian.

She returned messages from a couple of girlfriends and a woman who was a secretary at the law firm. Things were a mess there, and the woman inquired about Bill. It was obvious he'd left the firm high and dry.

The two messages she wanted to reply to, she found impossible to do so. Ian's message was brief. He thanked her for their time together, and hoped to see her again. She tried to read between the lines, but found it impossible.

Jack's message was much longer, clear and to the point. She wondered how a man could be abused as much as she abused him, and still proclaim his love for her. She knew if he were sitting here now, and she asked him that very question, he would probably say he was asking himself the same thing. She could not be mad at him anymore. Despite what Bill said about lawsuits, Jack giving the money away, or having to pry the dollar bills out of his clenched fist, she knew he would keep his word.

She signed out and paid for the internet use. At a table near the window of the cafe, she enjoyed a cup of coffee and a pastry whose name she couldn't pronounce if her life depended upon it. A group of young women who may have been college students occupied a table next to her, a second or third generation laptop computer perched between them. At the same time, she noticed the edge of her laptop sticking out of her shoulder bag which lay on her table.

Bill purchased it in Hong Kong, insisting she document all of the things which were traumatizing her as she chased after Jack. She'd entered nothing, but if pressed, would have entered all the crap and abuse endured from her traveling companion.

"Excuse me, ah, English?" asked Lynda.

The girls all smiled, and a couple giggled, child-like.

"I speak little English," said one. "I'm sorry, not good," she added.

"Well, would one of you like to have this?" Lynda said, pulling the laptop out of her bag.

They were all wide-eyed with wonder. Their eyes went from the computer to her, and back to the computer again.

"We could not," said the one. "Is what, this computer?"

"It is a gift. From me to you," she replied, reaching across and placing the laptop on their table. She thought they might think it was stolen, so she added, "I work for a company which makes computers like this one," she lied. "I have too many things to carry, and I am afraid I might be robbed. I would rather give it to you."

She wasn't sure how much of the story the girls understood. She thought suddenly what her reaction might be if someone in California suddenly handed her a two thousand dollar computer while she enjoyed a double latte at Starbucks.

They started to hand it back, but she stood up and held her hand out, palm facing out. "Nyet," she heard herself say. "I want you to have it," she stated, as she quickly gathered her bag and headed for the door.

Walking down the street, she was grinning. Where had the word, *nyet*, come from? She only faintly remembered reading some translated phrases in the back of a guidebook.

It was a long walk back to the hotel, but she didn't care. She'd used a foreign word in a foreign country — speaking to foreigners for the first time. It took her two months and a journey of half the circumference of the globe to do so. She dispensed with some cumbersome baggage, even more than she realized. And, for the very first time she was traveling. More importantly, for the very first time in months she was happy.

*****

Bill wondered a couple times during the day what could be so interesting that Lynda would avoid the comfort and safety of the hotel for so long. He found some postcards at the front desk, pictures of the Kremlin and a bunch of spired churches. Big deal.

He was not overly concerned, as he had his own agenda to deal with. It took him awhile, but he finally got through to Palm Springs on the telephone. A woman's voice answered the telephone. She sounded either sleepy or pissed off, possibly both.

"Who's this?" asked Bill.

"Mary Ann," came the sleepy voice from the other end. "Is this some kind of emergency?"

"No, it's a telephone call," said Bill sarcastically. "Put Gorman on the line."

"Do you know what time it is?"

Questions, questions, questions, thought Bill. Why can't people just do what they're told instead of asking a bunch of questions. "No, I don't have a fucking clue. But before you tell me, put Gorman on the phone!" shouting now to this unknown, sleepy bitch.

Gorman's wife had been dead for years. Bill couldn't imagine who this could be. He was trying to think if Gorman had a daughter or something, when he heard his friend's voice in the background.

"I don't give a shit, just bring me the phone," he heard Gorman say. Actually, what Bill heard was Gorman's voice, rather than his words. The sound came out, "I ..." cough, cough, "... don't give ah," gasp, cough, wheeze. "... shit, just ..." cough, wheeze, pause, cough, "gimmee ...."

"Gorman, it's me, Bill!"

"I should have," cough, hack ... "fuckin' known," replied Gorman.

Bill thought Gorman sounded like shit, but he didn't want to go there. "Hey, who's the fuckin' babe? Whatta ya got over there, some stripper?" he asked excitedly.

"Yeah, I got a whole flock of em out of Vegas..." cough, cough. "You dumb fuck, it's my nurse. I can't get from the bed to the bathroom," cough, wheeze, "... without some help. I had to hire this gal to live-in here. Either that" ... cough, "or go to a fuckin' rest home. And, believe me, she isn't now, nor was she ever a stripper," replied Gorman, the words taking almost five minutes to come out of his mouth along with coughs, sighs, moans and groans.

"So what did you find out?" asked Bill. He contacted Gorman once before from a hotel in Beijing, China. That conversation was a long one, Gorman relating the shit coming down in Los Angeles as a result of Bill leaving town in a hurry, and Bill telling Gorman of the thousands of Chinese running around helter-skelter in the streets. Bill intended to make this conversation much shorter, as Gorman was difficult to understand through all of the coughing fits. He sounded much worse than he had a few weeks ago.

"Hey, you remember Wicks, that faggoty accountant you had on a leash?" asked Gorman, changing the subject. Not waiting for a reply, he went on. "The dumb fuck went an off'd himself."

"What?" exclaimed Bill, curious now. Wicks was the accountant for the law firm of Davidson, Talbot, Stritt & Mumphrey. Wicks concealed Bill's skimming. He was also the one Bill bailed out of a sticky, pedophile matter several years before.

"Yeah, he stuck a pistol in his mouth. According to the word I got, his wife was cooking dinner, and he was sitting in his Lazy-Boy in the living room watching Tee-Vee."

"Why would he do that?" asked Bill, genuinely at a loss as to what was happening in the real world.

"Well, it wasn't cuz the Lakers were losing, I can tell ya that," said Gorman. "The new accountants, under the fuckin' eye of the Feds, opened the books at your firm and a bunch of worms started crawling out ... all of em waving red flags, if ya get my drift. The fuckin' jig was up and Wicks knew it. Probably figured once in the mouth in the Lazy-Boy was better than a hundert-fuckin' times in the ass up at Quentin."

A long pause in the conversation ensued. Gorman spent the time coughing and wheezing, the nurse taking the telephone and telling Bill he'd have to hang on for a moment or two, the sleepiness all out of her voice, replaced by a business-like tone. Bill spent the time reflecting upon his skimming over the years. It didn't seem like much when he looked back at it, but he knew the authorities and his partners would see it much differently.

"Listen, I gotta make this short. I'm fuckin' dying here," sputtered Gorman after coming back on the line. "So, there's a man in Warsaw I got through, ah well, it's not important. Since you're probably going to the big house when ya get back here, the less you know the better. And, by the way, don't think ya can roll over on me. My attorney says I'd get an automatic exemption cuz of my health. In fact, he told me if I ever wanted to kill someone, now would be the time to do it. The most I'd get was house arrest, and that's exactly what I'm doing now." Gorman laughed, and then he coughed for another five minutes before going on.

"So, this guy will slow your man up a bit after he leaves Russia. Don't worry, he won't kill him. Every fucking thing is passive nowadays. Nobody ever takes a gun an shoots a guy in the kneecaps, like it should be. Instead, they hit em with a baton and make em cry, or some such shit. I mean, what the fuck is that?"

Bill said he couldn't explain the sorry state of the world any better than his pal could. "How much do I need to pay the guy, and how do I contact him?" asked Bill.

"You don't see, talk to, or even know this guy. It's all taken care of. I'd like to say we'll settle up when you get back, but I doubt I'll be here. As far as that goes, I don't think you'll have any access to cash or favors in the slammer anyway. We're both fucked."

With that, the line went dead. At first, Bill was going to re-dial, but remembered Gorman often ended his telephone conversations in such a manner. You'd be talking, and all of a sudden, without a goodbye or a howdy-do, you'd be listening to nothing but air.

****

Tallinn was great, and Jack enjoyed the old world charm of the city. He took a relaxing ferry ride to Stockholm, and spent a couple of days hanging out. He didn't visit any tourist sites, but rather spent the time eating and drinking in sidewalk cafes.

On a whim, he dyed his hair a golden blonde — the color of Heineken — one of his favorite beers. He was starting to feel alive again.

A train took him from Stockholm to Nynashamn where he would embark on a ferry bound for Gdansk, Poland. While the departure point in Stockholm was in the very center of the city, the ferry terminal at Nynashamn appeared to be out in the middle of nowhere. The terminal offered little in the way of distractions, and the ferry's departure time was a couple of hours away.

A large grassy area in front of the terminal served as a waiting area for passengers. A warm and sunny day, Jack lugged his bags to a shaded spot and stretched out for a nap. He was almost asleep, when he sensed something. It wasn't as if he felt or heard anything, but more a foreboding of something about to happen. Lying on his side and turning his head, he opened his eyes to see a young man reaching for one of his bags.

"Hey goddamn it!" he screamed. He started to sit up, the kick from the man much too telegraphed to be a threat. He rolled the opposite direction to avoid the boot by several inches. "What the hell are you doing?"

He started to get up again, this time intent on grabbing the would be thief, when someone nearby yelled something. Jack couldn't hear what was said, and the voice appeared to be behind him. The thief, never saying a word, turned quickly and ran.

Jack turned, and was surprised to find a man standing directly behind him. He instinctively jumped before realizing the stranger was not a second attacker, but the man who yelled.

"Are you okay?" asked the man.

"Yeah, I'm fine. I don't know what made me wake up, but I'm glad I did."

"My wife and I," said the man in English with only a hint of an accent, "were sitting there." He pointed to the area some fifty feet away.

Jack's first thought, as he looked over to where the man's wife now stood collecting their luggage, was how this man arrived on the scene so suddenly. The entire incident took place in a matter of seconds. He also knew the sound of a second voice yelling was probably the reason the attacker decided to flee.

"Policia," said the man. "I am a policeman in my country," he added, answering the seemingly written concern on Jack's face.

"What country are you from?"

"My wife and I are from Milano, Italia. We were sitting there, and I told my wife I did not care for the way that young man was acting. I was watching him. He was acting very suspicious."

"What was he doing?"

"He was watching you for some time. I saw you come out of the terminal and lay down, and that is when I first noticed him. He walked completely around you from a distance, looking as if he was deciding which way to go after his assault. I am sorry," said the man, "I should have gone for a local officer at that time."

"No, don't be sorry, my friend."

The man's wife was now standing beside him. Jack introduced himself to them, and thanked the man again for coming to his rescue.

"My wife says I do too much," the Italian said, looking fondly at her while she smiled. "It is the policeman in me. It cannot be helped."

After the couple left, Jack sat back down. With the ferries departure time two hours away, he opened his journal and made a notation about the incident, and subsequently dismissed any further thought of it.

****

Bill and Lynda sped through St. Petersburg, Helsinki, Tallinn and into Stockholm. They arrived in the city by ferry on the morning of July 26th. Had they known how close they were to Jack at that moment, they both would have been much happier. Instead, they were lost as to how or where to proceed next. Jack's itinerary was virtually meaningless now, simply a list of cities to be extensively explored or breezed through, all at his discretion.

Their first-class hotel room overlooked the central train station. Looking out the window just hours before, they would have seen Jack crossing the street to enter the station on his way to Nynashamn.

They were tired, and so after a shower, Bill said he wanted to take a nap. Urging her to join him for some pre-nap frolicking, he was disappointed once again when she declined. She told him she was restless, and wanted to go for a walk to collect her thoughts.

Collect her thoughts, Bill muttered to himself after she left the room. She'd better collect something. I haven't been laid in over three weeks, and I have some needs too. He decided to call Gorman. The phone rang several times before the nurse picked up.

"He's resting," she said curtly. Before Bill could yell at her, she added, "and, I'm not going to wake him."

Arguing all day with Lynda left him spent, and he didn't want to do more of the same with some bitchy nurse. "Yeah, well have him call me just as soon as he's done with his beauty sleep. It's a fuckin' matter of life and death."

He rattled off the telephone numbers of the hotel, not letting the nurse get a word in, and repeated how he expected to hear from Gorman in a very timely manner.

"Yes, Mr. Davidson. I'll see he gets the message. But, just so we understand the situation, there is a matter of, as you call it, 'life and death', here also. And since you don't seem to have even the slightest clue, I'll fill you in. Mr. Gorman is dying. If I hear one more profanity out of your mouth again, the next time you speak to him will be in heaven or hell. Somehow, I don't think you'll both be going to the same place, so even that's irrelevant."

Davidson was about to tell her to go fuck herself, but she'd obviously picked up one of Gorman's habits, that being the termination of a telephone call without saying goodbye. He sat on the edge of the bed muttering to himself and listening to a dial tone. Finally, he placed the receiver in its cradle.

He tried to take a nap, but there were too many things on his mind. He'd wished Gorman would have given him a way to contact the man who was supposed to impede Jack's progress. After pacing the room a couple of times, he sat back down and dialed the concierge.

"Yes, I want you to do me a favor," he began. He gave the person his name and room number, prefacing the conversation with a promise of a generous gratuity for services rendered.

"I want you to contact all of the hospitals in Stockholm. This guy's a fuckin' bozo, so he may check into one that's small and personal just to be quaint. Anyway, find out if they have, or have had, a guy by the name of Jack Gillette treated in the last few days. I don't know what the symptoms might be, but would guess that it would be something akin to blunt trauma.

"And listen up here," he added. "I want this all handled very discretely. You don't know me, and I don't know you. You got that?"

He was afraid he'd have to go downstairs and personally see whomever he was speaking with. Foreigners were so stupid. This guy however, sounded as if he knew exactly what Bill was talking about, the subjects urgency as well as its need for confidentiality. Christ, he thought, maybe this kind of shit goes on every day.

He called room service, telling them to send up a couple of sandwiches and some gin. He added that they might include some tonic water too, thinking maybe if he got Lynda drunk, he might — just might, get laid. Two martinis later, she walked in. She'd only been gone an hour.

"Did you collect anything?" asked Bill.

"What? What do you mean?"

"Oh nothing. Forget it. It was a weak attempt at humor." He was about to add, "Something you've been lacking for a month and a half," but decided it was better left unsaid.

She sat down on the bed next to him. It was as close as she'd come to him on her own accord for over a week.

"Listen Bill," she said. "I've been thinking about this whole thing." She looked at him, to make sure he was listening, which he was. "It seems we've lost our opportunity to catch Jack. We needed to get to Stockholm before him, and we didn't."

Bill wanted to say that if she wouldn't have been so intent on being a tourist in every city, they would have arrived in plenty of time. Once again though, he held his tongue.

"We could have been at the ferry terminal to meet him. There's only so many ferries from Tallinn to Stockholm. It would have been a snap." She paused a moment before continuing. "But now, it's back to trains, and we can't hang out at train stations day and night. If, by some means, we could race ahead of him and wait at the train station, there would still be no way to make sure we saw him."

"So, cut to the fuckin' chase, here," said Bill. "What do you think we should do?"

"Obviously, you're not enjoying any of this. There are some things I'd like to have seen in Russia and China that I didn't get to see. I'll probably never go back, so the opportunity is lost. There are a lot of things in Europe I don't want to pass by."

"So, I get you through the tough shit, and now you want to drop me like a hot, fuckin' spud? Is that it?"

"No, it's not," she sighed. "It's not that at all. I'd like you to go with me, say, as far as Budapest. It's just a few more days. Then, you can fly to England, make your way to Liverpool and wait there. You can find the ship he's booked on, find out where it's docked, everything concerning that part of his itinerary. When I get there, we can intercept him."

She sat looking at him. He didn't feel like being looked at so he got up and made them each a drink. Room service had not only sent up a bottle of gin, but a complete bar on a wheeled cart.

Three things were going for him at the moment. She was being civil, he was getting her drunk, (she'd already had one double gin and tonic), and his odds of getting laid were the best they'd been in weeks. He didn't want to jeopardize any of those advantages, but found himself teetering on the edge anyway.

"What if he could get sick or something. That would slow him up long enough for us to catch up," he said.

"Bill," she said. "I know what you're thinking, and I want you to get it out of your mind. If you do anything, anything at all to hurt him, I'll kill you. I mean it."

She was pissed off, just like that. He was glad he'd not blurted out how he'd hired a hit man.

"Hey, I'm just asking here. You keep forgetting, I'm not the bad guy in this story. I don't know what you're thinking, and the only way to find out is to ask."

He was afraid the phone would ring, so he asked Lynda if she wanted to go have dinner. He didn't expect her to say yes, and was even more surprised she didn't insist on eating some sort of weird, ethnic cuisine.

While Lynda inquired at the front desk about restaurants within walking distance of the hotel, Bill quickly made his way to the concierge's desk in the center of the vast lobby. He introduced himself to the man, the guy immediately sensing the clandestine atmosphere and Bill's exigency. Bill handed him four, fresh American hundred dollar notes.

"Any news from the hospital?"

When the concierge informed him no one by the name of Jack Gillette was treated in any area hospital, Bill went on, "Okay, listen closely. Any calls come to my room, you take them. Take a message, tell the guy I'll call him, but that he's not to call me. Got that? Then, and this is important, ask him if he was successful. If he in fact was, tell him I'll be in touch immediately."

Lynda was walking towards them now. He had to hurry. "And, no fuck ups. No blinkin' lights on the phone when I go back to my room. Got it?" He turned and intercepted her just a few steps from the desk.

"What's that all about?" she asked, good natured for a change.

"Oh nothing. I was just thanking Sven, or whatever the fuck his name is, for the bar cart they brought up to the room."

"Sometimes you think of everything," she smiled. "Supposedly, there's a good Italian place just down the street. Does that sound okay with you?"

He replied that it did. He wanted to tell her he'd continue to think of everything, whether she wanted him to or not. But sex loomed on the near horizon for him, and at times like this, getting in the last word was not as crucial as it normally was.

17

The ferry ride from Nynashamn, Sweden to Gdansk, Poland was an over-night voyage. Jack sat in one of the small bars on the ship and got drunk. For the first time since Hong Kong, he wasn't drinking to drown his sorrows. He was happy again, and thankful Lynda and Bill were not standing on the pier when the ferry arrived in Stockholm. Now, traveling at his own pace, it would now be extremely difficult for them to catch him. He wouldn't alter his course or his activities, but simply travel as the wind blew.

In Gdansk, he hurried to validate his eastern European Rail Pass and catch a train for Warsaw. There was no time to spare, as the moment he stepped aboard, the train started to move.

Arriving at Warsaw's Central Station, he made his way from the train to the crowded station lobby. A posting on a large, lighted board offered various levels of accommodation. One, *Dom Literatury*, its name alone enough to spark his interest, was only 5 miles from the station. With only six rooms, all of which were above a pub, it sounded perfect. The hotel took no reservations, so he would be taking a chance, since it was approaching 5:00 p.m.

He didn't know what made him look back at the line of taxi's behind the one he was getting into in front of the station. Like the incident at the Nynashamn ferry terminal, it was some sort of sixth sense. He recognized the man instantly, even from a distance, and despite the fact he was beginning to get into a taxi as well.

"Do you speak English?" asked Jack of his driver after settling into the back seat.

"Yes," he said with a thick accent.

"There is a taxi, two cars back. I think there is a man in that car who is trying to follow me. Is it possible ...?"

"Ah, Americans. Just like in the movies from Hollywood, eh? Am I right? Perhaps a jealous husband, eh.?" he added.

"I don't know. If you could somehow loose him and then take me to a hotel called Dom Literary, ah ... I think it is on, Krakowskie Przediescie Thirteen," Jack read from a piece of paper he removed from his shirt pocket.

He made a spur of the moment decision. "No, on second thought, lose the taxi and bring me back here ... to the train station. I would appreciate it," he said as he offered the driver four, fifty *zlotys*, or about fifty dollars, folded neatly between his thumb and forefinger.

The driver sped off, weaving in and out of traffic and enjoying himself. Within minutes they pulled to a stop in front of Central Station. Certain he'd lost the man, Jack grabbed his bags and went back into the station.

At the platform to the trains, he looked up at the huge reader board listing departures, its slatted louvers turning over in a wave of commotion every few minutes to record trains about to depart. He was lucky. There was a train leaving for Krakow in five minutes. He made his way to the designated platform, and found a first-class car.

One of the advantages of a train pass is the flexibility it gives the traveler. There is no ticket to buy, unless the user should require an overnight berth. On many trains, a reservation is not necessary. The train traveler simply finds a train, selects the class for which his ticket is written, and gets on. A chase scene out of a Hollywood movie notwithstanding, the pass came in handy.

Before long he was out of Warsaw, racing along in a southerly direction towards Krakow. Jack's mind was racing almost as fast as the train. At first, he doubted himself, thinking maybe the man only bore a very strong resemblance to the one who tried to steal his bags and assault him in Sweden. But the more he considered it, the more he knew his recollection was correct.

It was warm in Nynashamn. Now, sitting on a train heading south from Warsaw, he realized what was odd about the man. He was wearing a black leather jacket, zipped or buttoned all the way up — exactly like the man getting into the taxi in Warsaw.

Davidson arranged this, he said to himself. It must be. And, it was something he would definitely do. What he knew of the man was little, but always suspected Davidson was involved in activities that were shady at best.

He thought about Lynda. Would she condone something like this? He tried to believe she wouldn't, but he was dead wrong on another matter concerning her moral fiber. If she could cheat on him, what made him think she couldn't cheat at catching him? Without bags and a passport, or worse yet, laid up in a hospital, he would be very easy to catch.

Some new rules had been introduced. He knew he could travel faster than Bill and Lynda, but he now would have to outrun the man in the black leather jacket as well.

It was dark when Jack arrived in Krakow. Just before entering the city, he saw flashes of lightning and heard booms of thunder announcing the arrival of pouring rain and a weary traveler from America.

He inquired at a kiosk which featured tours and accommodations. Located in one of the tunnels beneath the tracks of Krakow Glowny, the old station was a grand Hapsburg-era building near the center of the city. He located a room at a place called the Hotel Batory, finally settling into a nice, but unremarkable room at 9:00 p.m.

It had been a long day, and he was extremely tired. Still thinking about the man in the black leather jacket, he arose to recheck the locks on the door.

Had he known what would happen while he was snuggled under the cover of a down filled comforter in a small, over-priced, boutique hotel — the rain pouring down, and flashes of lightning diminishing as the storm moved away — had he known, he would have gotten an even better nights sleep than the wonderful slumber he experienced.

****

Jim Gillette, no relation to Jack Gillette, was thirty-four years old. He was born and raised in Chicago, Illinois, the son of a beer truck driver. He bounced around after finishing high school, hitchhiking across the country, somehow managing to stay out of serious trouble.

On a lark, he got married in California, and then just as quickly, got divorced in Nevada. He returned to Chicago and probably would have ended up in trouble if it were not for his mother.

Jim's mother, worried her son's sense of non-direction would eventually send him in the direction of the state prison, enlisted her brother for help. Her brother, Jim's uncle, was a boss for one of Chicago's largest steel fabrication contractors. He built skyscrapers. At her insistence, Uncle Billy took his nephew on as a laborer. Big and strong, the kid took to walking on beams hundreds of feet above the ground like a duck takes to water.

Jim Gillette was not exactly a Rhodes Scholar, but neither was he stupid. Within a year, he enrolled in a community college welding class. Soon afterward, he was accepted into a union-sponsored apprentice welding program. Uncle Billy was happy and Jim's mother was happy. Even Jim thought he was happy.

Jim prospered through hard work. He was more muscular now than he'd been before becoming a steelworker, and that was saying something. He had always been tough, but now he was even tougher.

Despite his relative success, something was lacking in his life. When he would get together with his high school buddies, they would talk of their college days, something he'd missed. His pals from work were all married, and that experience, save for a fleeting couple of drug induced months, had eluded him also.

One day, he went to his mother and father's house after work. They were sitting at the kitchen table eating dinner. After his mom insisted he join them, and after he ate everything on his plate, he informed them he was quitting his job and going to Europe.

"I need to go and see it," he said to them. "I want to go and find myself."

His father, spooning the last bits of his wife's cherry cobbler into his mouth, suggested Jim go to Muncie and try to find himself there. "It would be a hell of a lot cheaper, and you'd only have to take a couple of days off work," he said smugly.

And so, that is how Jim Gillette happened to be in Warsaw, Poland. He arrived two days before Jack's hasty arrival and retreat from the city. On the continent for two months, he figured he had enough money to stay for another four. He wasn't finding himself, but he was having a hell of a good time. He knew he would not want to leave when it came time to pack up and go home.

In Warsaw, Jim checked into an inexpensive hotel, that according to a travel guidebook, was frequented by young travelers from Australia, Britain and the U.S. His room in the sprawling, often remodeled building, was near the back entrance. The room was away from the noise of a group of partying Sydney-Siders, as the Australians from Sydney referred to themselves. Up until the wee hours the night before with his new-found, Aussie "mates," he was thankful for the peace and quiet his isolated room provided.

There was another man in Warsaw that night who was thankful. He was thankful to be out of Sweden, a country he didn't like, full of people he liked even less. He was thankful to be back in Warsaw, the city he'd grown up in and still called home. Checking his sixteenth hotel, he was thankful the J. Gillette registered there was in a room isolated from most of the other rooms. He was thankful he would be able to sleep in his own bed tonight after the completion of a small, but well paying job.

Jim Gillette didn't hear the intruder enter his room. He couldn't be sure he heard him when he stumbled slightly over some clothes laying on the floor of the pitch black, darkened sleeping area. His first thought when the attack began was not why someone would attack him with a baseball bat. He knew he wasn't a saint, and figured he probably had an attack or two coming. No, his first thought was why someone would attack him and not hit him in the head, or at the very least, the knees.

The attacker's first blow was to his left arm as he lay on his side. The second blow was deflected by Jim's hand, and the third blow he caught in mid air as it descended. By this time he was sitting up with his legs partially over the edge of the bed, and with one hand on the chunk of wood the size of a baseball bat, Jim Gillette arose to a standing position.

At six foot three, and a solid two hundred and twenty pounds, he towered over his attacker and outweighed him by fifty pounds. The guy said something in a foreign language which meant nothing to him. He then tried a half-hearted attempt to knee Jim in the groin, and it was about this time that Jim threw the first punch.

It sent the attacker stumbling backward, tripping and hitting his head against the wall as he fell to the floor. The attacker felt himself being lifted up, slammed against the wall, and the pain of three or four sharp blows to his chest. He didn't hear the bones crack, but knew instinctively his ribs were being broken.

He felt the strength go out of his legs, and could taste the blood rising in his mouth from the first punch. He welcomed the feeling of passing out, knowing the average man will quit hitting you once you stop moving. He very much wanted the hitting to stop.

However, his sense of weightlessness was not the first signs of unconsciousness. He felt like he was flying through the air, which in fact, he was. The sound of broken glass accompanied the realization that cuts were occurring in his new, highly prized leather jacket, his face, and his hands. Then, he was flying free as a bird again.

At this point, the attacker was still not unconscious, but by the time he hit the cement surface of the alley behind the hotel, some thirty feet below the closed window he'd just traveled through, he was.

Jim flipped on a light and surveyed the damage. He'd eventually have a nasty bruise from the first blow, but no other signs of injury. Damn, he thought to himself, as he dressed to see the manager and report the incident. What a dumb shit. He should have hit me in the head, instead of the arm.

****

Jack awoke refreshed the next morning. After a small breakfast at the hotel, he checked out and started out on foot to Krakow's Jagiellonian University. Bright and sunny, the thunderstorms of yesterday were gone.

In Stockholm, he'd found information on the internet about the university. It offered lodging, which he thought might be unique. A room there would also afford him the opportunity to be around fellow travelers, instead of tourists.

Another attraction was the history of the institution. Following World War I, writers and artists were drawn to Krakow's liberal climate. Before the first world war, Jozef Pilsudski began recruiting his legendary Polish legions here, and from 1912 to 1914, Krakow became Lenin's base for directing the international communist movement and the production of *Pravda*, "Truth," the official newspaper of the Communist Party of the Soviet Union.

In September of 1939, the Nazis entered the city and began an unprecedented reign of terror. The notorious Nazi governor Hans Frank, moved into the royal castle on Wawel Hill. Many professors from Jagiellonian University were arrested, along with artists, political liberalists and writers. By 1943, the Krakow Ghetto was virtually eliminated, it's Jewish occupants shipped to nearby Auschwitz with those from the university. It was a terrible waste of humanity.

Jack arrived and found a room. Small, with a common bathroom at the end of the hallway, the room's large window overlooked a small plaza. It was perfect.

Students at a reception area gave him directions on how to get to the center of the city. It was a short tram ride, and armed with a map, he set off to spend the day exploring.

What a wonderful city. Despite the terror and horrors inflicted by World War II, there was little physical damage to the city itself. The architecture is dramatic, and in recent years, a restoration program has begun to show signs of progress.

But, the Rynek Glowny is the gem of Krakow. Built in medieval times, the Rynek Glowny is one of the largest squares in all of Europe.

The Sukiennice, a medieval cloth hall, divides the square into east and west sections. Around this central, rectangular-shaped building is the square itself. Surrounding the square is a ring of historic buildings. The Wierzynek Mansion is home to the city's oldest and most famous restaurant, founded in 1364 and claiming an unbroken culinary tradition. The Grey House has many of its Gothic rooms intact. A tall tower is all that remains of the original, four-teenth century Town Hall. And, in the east section of the square is the Mariacki Church.

The Mariacki Church was founded in 1222. It was later destroyed during the Tartar invasions. The current building, built in 1355, is one of the finest Gothic structures in Europe. The taller of its two towers is topped with an amazing assortment of spires. It is accented with a crown and a helmet.

Legend has it that during one of the early Tartar raids, a trumpeter scaled the tower to sound an alarm. Midway into the effort, he was cut down by an arrow through the throat. The legend lives on, as every hour on the hour, a lone trumpeter plays a somber melody, halting abruptly to mark the moment the watchman was slain.

As the buildings ring the square, so do the sidewalk cafes. Separated merely by ropes or a couple of potted plants, it is only possible to distinguish one from another by the different style and design of their outdoor furniture. Sitting in one of these cafes, protected from the sun by large umbrellas, a patron is enter-tained by strolling minstrels, tap dancers and jugglers. Horse drawn carriages slowly move around the central Sukiennice, carrying tourists and the occasional wedding party.

The beer, wine and food were excellent, and Jack found himself moving from sidewalk cafe to sidewalk cafe. For four days he returned to the Rynek Glowny time and time again. He met a woman from France, a couple from Ireland, a chemical engineer from Australia and a wanderer from Scotland. He sat in the sun and reflected on his life. He sat in the shade and wrote.

His first day at the Rynek Glowny included a visit to a small coffee house which was reached by navigating through a labyrinth of passageways. There was only one computer, and he had to wait for two other people before it would be his turn. He didn't mind, and ordered a cup of coffee and a pastry. Classical music came from two speakers mounted at opposite ends of the small room.

After taking his turn at the computer, he read his messages. He answered all of them, leaving two from Dan until the last. To Dan, he wrote:

Dan & Rebecca,
  Congratulations.
  Rebecca slipped a bit when we last talked on the telephone, and I sensed I would be receiving news of her pregnancy.

I'm very, very happy for both of you. You didn't say in your e-mail if it's a girl or a boy. I have no idea when you find out those things — you'll have to keep me posted.

I'm in Krakow now. You'd love it. Great architecture and great food. Yes Dan, they also have great beer!

I'm doing well and slowly getting over Lynda. I have my moments, but all in all, things are fine. The worst of the depression is over. I haven't heard from her, and really don't expect to. I suspect she is closer to catching me than I realize, but I don't care.

After Krakow, I'm heading to Budapest. Tell Neal I'll send another dispatch from there.

Once again, congratulations to both of you on being a future mother and father. Like everything the two of you do, you'll be great at it.

Love,

Jack

He wrote to Lynda next.

Lynda,

I'll make this short. I can't believe you have anything to do with this, or even any knowledge of it. It does not surprise me your friend Bill would think of it.

Plain and simple. Someone tried to attack me. I'm not sure what he was after, as it was interrupted by people around me, and never fully materialized. I saw the man again later, in another city. There, I managed to lose him.

I'll follow through on my end of the promise. But I swear, I'll take all of the money and burn it, before

He stopped writing. What was the use? Nothing would change. Lynda would do whatever she wanted, and so would Bill. Besides, writing might elicit a reply that she knew of the Bill's plan, or even worse, devised it herself. With a sigh, he deleted the message.

His train left Krakow at 10 p.m. A beautifully warm night, a full moon glowed above. He had a sleeper all to himself.

After rolling out of the station, he made his bed and got undressed. Lowering the window, the warm wind blew gently through the compartment. Soon, the train began to slow as it worked it's way into the Tatra Mountains. There were occasional houses, but no towns to speak of. Small farm plots were interrupted by stands of timber. Numerous changes in the sounds of the trains wheels on the rails signaled yet another small bridge crossing a rushing mountain stream.

He fell into a restless sleep, with vivid dreams of falling in love with a complete stranger. The next morning, the dreamy woman's love was replaced by a love for a city first visited after graduating from college. He arrived in Budapest, Hungary.

****

Bill and Lynda took a ferry from Stockholm to Gdansk, and made their way by rail to Warsaw. At Bill's insistence, they checked into an expensive, five-star hotel. Bill's insisting, along with five-star hotels, were things Lynda was starting to tire of. After a shower and a change of clothes, she wanted to be out of the room and away from him.

"I'm going to go look around a bit," Lynda declared.

Bill was sitting on the edge of the bed reading one of the entertainment magazines found in every hotel in the world, informing the occupants where they could go to get away from the luxury they just paid hundreds of dollars for. He didn't look up when she spoke. She hadn't invited him along, and probably wouldn't.

"Did you hear me?" she asked, a bit perturbed.

"Yes, I heard you. I don't know what the fuck you expect to find, other than a bunch of Pollocks. It's like looking for a needle in a haystack now that he has no set itinerary. He could have gone through Warsaw and stopped in some small town thirty miles down the line. How the fuck are we going to know?"

"Listen Bill." She was all pissed off again, just like that. He was thinking he just should have said "Go" and left it at that. "I'll look for him my way, okay?"

"Yes," said Bill, still unable to keep his mouth shut. "And, I'll look for him my way."

"What does that mean?" she asked.

"Ah Christ, I don't fucking know what it means," moaned Bill. "Just go. Knock yourself out. When you come back, I'll be in the bar seeing how bad these guys can fuck up a martini. Hey, there's a joke about some, ah, a Pollock bartender that ...." But she was going out the door now, a small bag over her shoulder she'd purchased in Stockholm after her other one broke.

Bill sat looking at the closed door, unable to hear her footsteps in the carpeted hallway. He thought about her new bag. She also bought a small camera in Stockholm, and the new bag was just big enough to carry it and a few personal items. For a brief moment, he wondered where she packed the computer.

Lynda walked until her feet were tired, and then walked some more. Finally arriving at the Old Town Square, she found the pain in her feet a welcome release for her anger with Bill, Jack, and men in general.

She was glad to be by herself. The Old Town Square was absolutely beautiful, and she didn't have to share it with anyone. She walked around, taking in the sites of the seventeenth and eighteenth-century architecture. Partially destroyed during World War II, the reconstruction job that followed was nothing short of miraculous.

She visited shops, and on a whim passed quickly through a tour of the

Warsaw Historical Museum. Exiting the museum, she saw a *doroski*, the traditional horse drawn cart, clattering down the cobblestone streets and occupied by a touristy-looking couple.

Who'd know, she thought to herself. I'll never be here again. And so, when minutes later she saw another cart, this one empty except for the driver, she approached.

"Excuse me, English?" she asked.

The man looked at her, and then looked about, as if looking for someone. He told her in passable English, but with a heavy accent, that the cart was available for her use. He asked her where her husband was, something repeatedly asked of her since beginning this trip over two months ago. She was tired of lying, tired of making excuses.

"I have no husband. I am traveling alone," she heard herself say.

"You much too beautiful, too beautiful to be alone yourself," he smiled. "Much too beautiful."

The ride was over-priced, a tourist attraction, but she didn't care. The driver let her out in front of a sidewalk cafe, and finding a table, she realized a number of people were looking at her. After all, she was alone, and women traveling alone is at times an oddity.

Jack often told her she should experience traveling by herself. Lynda would argue that it is easier for a man than a woman, and at that, Jack would bristle. He would gently scold her for not only selling herself short, but selling sisterhood and foreigners short as well.

"If foreigners can learn to adapt to a whole bunch of white-legged, Bermuda shorts-clad, middle aged tourists from Omaha — wolfing down McDonald's hamburgers while cameras bob from a strap around their neck — they can adapt to you being by yourself," he often said.

She sat at the cafe with a glass of wine and considered her situation. I'm doing something that — for every time people see another woman traveling alone, it may result in one less stare, one less reaction of disbelief — one less snub of services for the next woman traveler who comes along.

The sunshine in her hair and on her shoulders felt good. When she ordered a second glass of wine, a sleepy-eyed Frenchman invited her to share his table, but she declined. She was enjoying her own company. And — she was thinking of Jack. This is where I'll find him, in a cafe just like this. He'll be sitting here drinking a beer, and probably writing in his tablet.

With those thoughts she noticed a waiter nearby. She motioned for her bill. Fumbling with the unfamiliar currency, the polite waiter helped her out. Wondering if she should catch a taxi or brave the long walk back to the hotel, she didn't notice as she arose from the table, the tears now streaming down her face. Damn, she thought, as she wiped away the salty taste she detected at the corner of her lip. How long has that been going on?

****

Bill got drunk, sobered up, and started again by the time Lynda returned to the Marriott. Gambling in the hokey and dated casino, he thought about talking to the manager — tell him to take a trip to Vegas, see how it's supposed to be done — but he quickly gave up on the idea. Americans did everything in a first-class manner, and despite their attempts to teach or civilize the rest of the world, the foreigners always managed to find a way to come up short. They just couldn't seem to get the lighting right, or the ambiance just so.

He'd had enough of foreigners and Pollocks. Returning to the room, he tried to call Gorman again , but like before, didn't get an answer. That crack of a nurse probably has caller I-D, thought Bill. The thought made him dial again, with exactly the same results.

Bill was thinking of getting off the bed and either taking a piss, or fixing a drink. In the room no longer than what it took to dial Gorman's number twice, he was startled when he heard the bathroom door open. Lynda was standing there with a towel around her.

"Jesus Christ, you scared the hell out of me," said Bill. He was staring at her now, those lusty feelings having moved past his varicose veined legs, and up his thighs. "Why don't you come over here and sit next to Papa?"

"You're drunk," she said coldly. "I'm getting dressed, and then I'm going to get something to eat."

"Hey, that sounds okay too," said Bill. Food wasn't as good as sex, but it was better than nothing. Besides, he just realized he was starving. The trail mix they'd served in the casino tasted like dog shit.

"No Bill. I'm going to eat by myself. You wouldn't like the food where I'm going anyway," she said, turning to re-enter the bathroom.

He was about to speak when the bathroom door closed. He heard her flip the lock, something he thought odd and unnecessary. "So, what the fuck? You going to do Pollock tonight?" he said a little louder than intended. "Screw it," he said to no one.

He got up, grabbed his jacket, and went out the door. As he stood waiting at the elevator door, he wondered what other kinds of food besides trail mix the casino could screw up. At least the martinis were good, he mused, as the doors opened to an empty, worn, and slightly stale smelling elevator cage.

It would be dark before long, so Lynda decided not to walk. At the front of the hotel there was a small line of taxis awaiting fares. With a small guide book and map listing moderately priced restaurants, she entered the first one in line.

She had no idea where she was going — she just wanted to be away from everything she knew, or was familiar with. She wanted to be away from Bill and other Americans. She wanted to be away from hotel restaurants where the menu was conveniently written in English.

Fumbling with a guidebook in the back seat as the driver waited patiently for her to indicate her destination, she attempted the correct pronunciation. "Please take me to Karczma Gessler," she said.

The restaurant was located in the Old Town Square, but the driver seemed lost and confused from the moment they left the hotel. She tried to speak to him, but found him impossible to understand. Through a series of frantic motions and charades, she finally got him to pull over. With the page of the book folded back, she showed him the list of restaurants and her intended destination.

One look at his face and she knew her mistake. It was so simple, yet so easily overlooked. Why would she think he could read English if he could not speak or understand it?

She pulled the book back, and was thinking fast, trying to figure out a way to complete such a simple task. Remembering the map, she shuffled through a few pages and found what she was looking for. The map was also in English, but the intrinsic nature of the streets designs was enough to set the driver straight.

"Ah, ah!" he said excitedly, his finger pointing now to the spot of the map where her index finger rested. He shifted the taxi into gear and set off with a sudden lurch. Moments later, she was being deposited in an area of the Old Town Square which looked familiar. She didn't know exactly where the restaurant was, but found she didn't care. She walked for awhile, finally finding a place which looked interesting, and enjoyed a quiet meal by herself.

The next morning, Bill and Lynda caught a train for Krakow. Bill had a hangover from drinking in the casino until late at night. She was in bed, but awake, when he finally came into the room. Feigning sleep, she was glad he did not try to wake her.

They rode silently through the countryside to Krakow. Once there, they found a hotel, and she was relieved when Bill did not insist on finding a Hilton or a Marriott.

"So, what's the plan?" asked Bill, as the clerk who checked them in and doubled as a bellman, set Bill's four heavy suitcases on the floor of the hotel room. Lynda had thrown away some clothes and useless personal items when she was in Stockholm. She was down to just two small, soft style bags.

"I really don't know. I suppose we could look for him here, but I don't know if it will do any good."

"Are you still pissed off at me?" he asked. He was getting tired of her attitude. He didn't want to push the issue, but was almost to the point of not caring.

"I'm not pissed off, Bill. I'm upset things have gone the way they have. I don't think we have much of a chance of catching him, I mean, he could still be in Stockholm for all we know. It's obvious he never intended for me to follow his itinerary this far. So, I don't know what to do."

"Do you want a suggestion, or do you just want to keep traveling without any kind of plan, other than being a fuckin' tourist?"

"I'd like you to quit talking like a truck driver!" she screamed at him. She threw one of her bags onto one of the two double beds, something she was happy to see after entering the room. "It's getting old. Fuck this, fucking that, jokes about people with slanted eyes. I'm tired of it!"

Bill was about to scream back, but he didn't get the chance. She was madder than he'd ever seen her.

"Ever since we started, all you've done is complain. You have no interest in seeing anything. You alienate everyone we meet, and insult every foreigner we come in contact with. I'm really getting tired of it!" she yelled.

"Well, you weren't too tired of it when I came over to Hong Kong and rescued your sorry ass!" he yelled back. "All I want to do is get our money, but you got this fuckin' desire to look at everything along the way ...."

"Our money? Our money?" screamed Lynda. "It's my money, Bill! Not your money, not our money, but my money!"

It came all of a sudden, neither of them quite expecting it, least of all Lynda. The slap he gave her face was enough to knock her backwards, and make her stumble and fall to a sitting position on the bed. She started to speak, but the taste of blood on her lip made her hesitate for a moment. When Bill tried to come near her, she scurried across the bed to get away from him.

"Hey, I'm sorry, okay? Goddamn it, sit still for a minute," he said, as he moved to the other side of the bed and she once again crawled across it, keeping the bed between her and her attacker.

"Listen, will ya, I got a man on this deal, we may be closer to catching him than you think. Let's not lose our fucking heads now," he pleaded.

"What do you mean, you got a man on it?" She got ready to move across the bed again, but Bill stood his ground.

"Just what I said. I got my pal Gorman in Palm Springs to get a man to slow dip shit up a little, nothing big, no coma or anything, just a little A & B," said Bill, using the police acronym for assault and battery.

"No!" she screamed.

She was hysterical now, and he wondered how the situation had deteriorated so rapidly.

"No, I don't want that!" she repeated. "Get out! Get out of my room! Get out of my life!"

She moved around the bed as she yelled at him to get out, and with a move faster than she thought possible from an old man, he grabbed her by the arm. She could feel his fingernails digging into her bare arm as he pulled her closer, and she looked down at her arm, expecting to see blood spurting out at the source of the pain. With her head turned downward, the blow from Bill's right fist caught her just above the corner of the left eye. She went down hard on her knees, and then flat on the floor.

She struggled to get up, and felt him lifting her to her feet. This time, the clenched fist of his right hand hit her flush on the left side of her jaw and mouth. She went down on the floor again.

She lay there quiet and still, hoping she would not feel his hands on her again. She was hoping he would not touch her, and she was praying that if he did, he would not kill her. God, please, she thought, don't let me die in some hotel room in Europe. At least, let me die in my own country. Her mouth was filling up with blood, but she did not move for fear he'd strike her again.

"I'm going to go get a drink. Then, I'm calling Gorman to find out where fuck-face is, or rather ... what hospital he's in. You and I are going there. We're going to take some pictures of the two former love-birds together, and then draw up a contract for my half. Don't fuck with me here, I know you're conscious, and I know you hear me. And you heard me right ... my half, half as in fifty, fucking percent!"

She could hear him rummaging around in the room. She didn't dare move or say anything. She just wanted him gone.

"And just for a little insurance, I got your passport. So, don't get any ideas about running off to Bumfuck, Egypt without me."

She heard the door close, but remained where she was. After several minutes, she struggled to get up. She was moving towards the bathroom, not overly anxious to see what her face looked like when there was a soft knock on the door. The knock was repeated, and she felt it wasn't the kind of knock Bill would use, if he used one at all. Cautiously, she opened the door. A young woman and man stood sheepishly in the hallway.

"Ga-day love," said the woman. Her eyes were as big as saucers, and Lynda knew right away her face must look terrible.

"Is he ere, love?" asked the man behind the woman. "If ey is, I could fetch a constable," he added.

"No, he's gone for awhile," Lynda heard herself say. "But, he's coming back. He's got my passport!" she added, alarmed with the both the theft and the panic she heard in her voice.

"Come with me," said the woman. She took Lynda's hand, and gently guided her to the room next door, introducing herself as Maggie. "I can't decide for you what to do," said Maggie. "Me husband and I heard you fightin', and he was certain you were hurt. I'll help clean you up, but you don't want to go back there, do you?"

She was in shock. No one had ever hit her in the face, except her mother. Fifteen years old, she deserved everything she got on that one occasion, the slap stemming from the use of a word Bill used in nearly every sentence.

"My passport, my clothes," she stammered.

"Devon, love," Maggie said to her husband. "Can ya still get in er room?" When Devon nodded, Maggie asked him to go back to Lynda's room and retrieve her belongings. "The gent downstairs seemed like a decent bloke," she added. "Tell em what has happened, see if he can help."

"I'm a nurse back in Sydney," said Maggie. "I've seen it all before, an av' heard it all before. We'll get ya cleaned up a bit, get ya a good nights rest in a room of yer own. What ya do tomorrow is up ta you."

"I just want to get away from him," she wailed.

Finally, the tears came to her eyes, a welcome replacement to panic and fear.

"Good on ya, girl," beamed Maggie. "Now stop yer bloody sobbin' so's I can clean up yer face."

An hour later, she was lying in a small bed, in an equally small room. She didn't mind. The room, secured with the help of Devon and the hotel manager, might be small and lack luxury, but it was free of Bill.

Her Australian neighbors, Devon and Maggie, were wonderful. Maggie cleaned up her face with the skill and speed of a doctor. Meanwhile, Devon, the manager and two men employed by the hotel, went to Bill and Lynda's room upon Bill's return. At the door, they demanded her passport, a demand backed with a threat of involving the police if necessary. Bill reluctantly handed over the passport, and just before he told them to all go fuck themselves, was told by the manager to check out of the room first thing in the morning.

The next morning, there was another knock on Lynda's door. She could tell by the gentle knock it was her Florence Nightingale friend, Maggie.

"We've got to catch a train straightaway, so we'll not be round," Maggie said, a tray of food in her hands. "I've brought ya breakfast, love. The manager's wife will be round at midday. She'll bring ya some soup for lunch. I wouldn't be trying to eat anything solid just yet. Anyway, if ya get a knock, it'll be only a woman's voice ya should hear."

She started to thank Maggie, the tears once again running down her swollen face.

"Now love, don't get all girlie on me. Everything's go'in to be fair dinkem, it is. The bully has checked out, and the desk clerk said he caught a taxi for the airport."

"You've been so kind," Lynda sobbed.

"Now, now, get some rest. I've put me e-mail address down on a card for ya there. Let us know if ya need anything, eh? And, stay here for a few days. Give yourself some time by yourself to heal."

It was midmorning before Lynda found the nerve to look in a mirror. It was another three days before she left the hotel room, and that was only for a brief visit to the hotel's small dining room for breakfast. She went early then, to minimize the stares from other guests.

Everyday, the hotel manager's wife brought her *zupa*, or soup. It wasn't until the fourth day that she ate something other than soup, and it was a delight to have fresh trout, *pstrag*, even though it was accompanied by *kartoflanka*, or potato soup.

After a week, she felt well enough to leave the hotel. The swelling had subsided, and it was just a matter of time before the black and blue marks, like a billboard sign announcing her status as a battered woman, would fade also. With some make-up and a scarf she would at least look presentable.

Bill caught a plane from Krakow to Warsaw, and after a brief, alcohol fueled layover, he flew on to Stockholm. Once there, he checked into the same hotel he and Lynda stayed in before. He had no more than tipped the bellman, when he sat down on the bed and tried to contact his pal Gorman.

As the phone rang, he wondered where Gorman could be. He'd tried to call from Krakow, right after the four idiots came to his room demanding Lynda's passport.

He was about to hang up when he heard someone pick up at the other end.

"Yes, who is this?" said a woman's voice, sounding pissed off, but thankfully, Bill thought, a long way off.

"It's me, Bill," He recognized the voice as that of the nurse. "Put fu ... ah, put Gorman on the blower. I gotta talk to him."

"Oh, it's you. I might have known. Listen, I'm sorry ... ah, Mr. Gorman passed away the night before last. He'd been in the hospital for several days, and died peacefully in his sleep."

"Ah, cut the horse-shit and put him on," said Bill.

"Davidson, is that correct?" came a terse reply. Before he could affirm his name, she went on, "Mr. Gorman is dead. If you should need any further information, I suggest you talk to his sister-in-law. She will be here sometime today, to take care of his funeral arrangements, something that I'm sure you don't care about in even the slightest ...."

Bill slammed the receiver down onto its cradle. "There you go bitch! A little of your own fuckin' medicine," he said to no one. Smiling now, he failed to see the connection that it was his friend Gorman, not his nurse, who'd made the hang-up in mid conversation a trademark. He sat there smiling at the silent, black telephone for a few moments before the death of his pal Gorman sank into his thick skull.

He didn't know who to contact to help him find Jack, and didn't know if it would do any good now anyway. Gorman was gone. Jack could be anywhere. He figured Lynda was probably a lost cause too. Any piece of the fifteen million was gone as well. It was the perfect trifecta gone sour, he mused to himself.

Next to the phone sat a magazine guide to drinking and dining out in Stockholm. He absentmindedly picked it up, and turning the first page, saw an add for group sex. He set the magazine on the bed, and rummaging through one of his bags for his bottle of Viagra, thought a couple martini's might help overcome any future inhibitions.

"Works for me," he muttered, as he walked out of the room, closing the door behind him.

18

Jack arrived in Budapest, took a taxi to the Buda side of the Danube River, and found a small hotel. It was inexpensive, yet a large step up from the accommodations of his first trip. Then, he visited merely out of curiosity. The name of the city, the fact it was on the Blue Danube — he could not be sure what drew him to come here the first time.

Buda and Pest were originally two separate cities. Buda's history dates back almost 1000 years, while Pest is but a baby at 500. They were united in 1872.

Down the street from his hotel, he found a bus stop and entrance to the Metro. Terminating his ride at Deak ter on the Pest side of the city, he strolled until he found an internet cafe.

There was a message from a man who was a friend of a couple he'd met in a restaurant in Hong Kong. The American couple, Bob and Brenda Miller, were with their two teen-age daughters, Brittany and Lauren. Telling them of his trip, and the route he would take, he mentioned Istanbul. The entire family became animated, and Bob Miller told him their daughter's swim coach was from Istanbul. After exchanging e-addresses, the Miller family told him they would have the coach contact him. His name was Suha Tokman.

Suha Tokman's message to Jack was like a note from an old, dear friend. There were no awkward formalities, no over-concern with what Jack might have planned, nor empty, insincere distress that he might be intruding. Plain and simple, Suha was from Istanbul. He was a friend of the Miller family, and they were friends of Jack's. Suha's lifelong friend, Feyyaz Abrak, resided in Istanbul. He would contact Feyyaz, give him Jack's e-mail address, and have Feyyaz contact him directly.

Jack wondered how anything could top the hospitality showered upon him by Masha and Sasha in Moscow, or the Holm's in Finland. He found out the very next day. In an internet cafe near his hotel, he found a message from Feyyaz Abrak. Feyyaz inquired of Jack's time of arrival in Istanbul, and like his friend Suha, he openly offered his services.

Jack answered the message immediately, telling Feyyaz he would arrive in Istanbul on August 5th, at 2:00 p.m. He asked if his new-found friend could find him lodging, nothing fancy or expensive, just safe and relatively convenient.

The next day, in the same internet cafe, he got his reply.

My Friend,

I will look forward to meeting you at the train station on 5 August. I hope you will be able to stay for at least a week, as it is impossible for me to show you all of Istanbul in any less time.

A hotel will not be necessary, as you will be my guest at the home of my father and I.

I shall look forward to your arrival.

Feyyaz

Jack's last day in Budapest was spent writing an article for the *South Beach Register*. He didn't feel it was his best work. Sometimes, writing from the heart and soul does not translate very well to the written page. There are times when distance from the subject is best. The piece would keep his editor happy however, and it would let everyone at home know he was alive.

Budapest

I'm in Budapest, Hungary. There is something about this city — it's mad in a way — crazy and sprawled out — but, there is something that pulls at my heart and soul.

Maybe I should say that, "I'm back in Budapest." I came here for the first time many years ago, as a college student, completing a rite of passage by backpacking in Europe following my graduation.

The name of the city drew me here. Or possibly, it was the romantic nature of the blue Danube that was the attraction.

The weather on that first visit was terrible — it snowed one night — and on that visit to the city, the experience was far from Nirvana. I was ripped off by a taxi driver, my accommodations were gross but at a three-star rate and two locals were in the process of trying to rob me when they were interrupted by some other pedestrians.

I also found the "blue" Danube not to be blue, but a rather brownish-gray color. It also smelled like a sewer.

I searched and searched to no avail for a retail shop called Matachek & Company. I wanted to buy one of those musical candy boxes that plays "Ochi Tchornya," (See The Shop Around The Corner, with James Stewart and Margaret Sullavan — the movie on which You've Got Mail was based).

On that previous visit, I did find a great bar that was like something out of a 1920's Bohemian movie. There wasn't an electric light in the place — all the lighting provided by candles. With a veil of European and Turkish cigarette smoke throughout the room, it remains one of my fondest memories.

Despite the negatives of that first visit, I am continually drawn to this city. Here, the sidewalk cafes and bars appear so international — so foreign and romantic. There is great architecture throughout the city, amid beautiful squares and terraces.

Late at night it all happens.

The cafes buzz with activity, great coffees and fabulous desserts. You sit in these cafes, demitasse cups poised in your hand with your little finger extended, and you partake of rich tortes, cakes and pastries.

You people watch, and what a scene it is.

It is not uncommon to see a 60-year-old man in Speedo trunks walking alongside a 35-year-old woman who looks as though she could be a model.

It is 4:00 p.m. as I pen this — I'm going to get a little jump on the cocktail hour. I'll have a couple of drinks, retire to my accommodations, and go out again at 9:00.

An aperitif, a light meal with a glass of wine — I'll finish with a cappuccino and a decadently rich dessert.

I'll watch the people, and dream of what this city was like in the 1930's. I'll relax and enjoy the evening.

The next evening, Jack boarded the Balkan Express for the trip from Budapest to Istanbul. The route would take him through Romania and Bulgaria, and briefly into Greece before arriving in Istanbul. The trip would take two days.

The conductor, who introduced himself as Janos Mereny, beckoned him to the far end of the car, away from a group of young American college students. There, next to Mereny's compartment, he showed Jack a fine, two place coupe. "You'll be much more comfortable here," he said in perfect English. "I'm sure those kids won't be trouble, but just the same, it will be much quieter here. May I make you a cup of coffee?"

"Thank you," replied Jack, appreciating the gesture.

They had coffee together, Janos telling him he was originally from Budapest. They talked about the changes, some good and some bad, since the Soviet Union left in 1989. His friendly relationship with Janos made the long trip wonderful.

The train rolled through Romania and Bulgaria. Much like the Trans-Siberian railway in Russia, there was little to do but watch the countryside. He bought food from vendors on the station platforms at a few of the stops. He read a lot, and wrote even more.

The scenery in Romania and Bulgaria was beautiful. There were rolling hills of farmland stretching for miles. It reminded him of eastern Washington or Oregon, the summer haze and dust, coupled with the bright sunshine, turned the fields into a golden brown color. Before long, the train was pulling into Sirkeci Station on the European side.

"Istanbul, Constantinople, Istanbul, Constantinople ..." Jack couldn't get the lyrics out of his head, as he gathered his belongings and got ready to exit. He was excited, as the city was a place he'd always wanted to visit.

A centuries old meeting place for persons of diverse cultures, Istanbul is the only city in the world that spans two continents. It is divided into European Arupa and Asian Asya sections by the Bosphorus Straits. The Bosphorus connects the Black Sea with the Mediterranean. Bridges and ferries link the two sides.

Reminiscent of Helsinki, Jack took but a few steps from the train before a stout, athletic looking man of about forty approached him.

Jack and Feyyaz greeted each other in the western style by shaking hands. Feyyaz embraced him, their cheeks touching left and then right. Welcome to the eastern world. Together they walked along, their conversation relaxed and easy, as if good friends for years. Through a combination of public transportation, including buses and ferries, they made their way to the suburb of Pendik.

Jack reflected as he stepped off the ferry — the sounds, smells and sights exotic and so very, very foreign — I've traveled from North America to Asia, to Europe, and now back to Asia. Before I leave this city, I will probably travel back and forth from Asia to Europe several times. The thought of all this continent hopping seemed so incredible.

Istanbul was incredible. Feyyaz gave Jack a royal tour of the city. Together, they saw the Blue Mosque and the Grand Bazaar. With Feyyaz's girlfriend, Mine Cetin, they traveled the Bosphorus Strait on a ferry. A trip to a small town on the banks of the Bosphorus near the entrance to the Black Sea offered a view of the entrance to the sea, as well as the landfall of both Asia and Europe. At that point, the two thin peninsulas of land jutted simultaneously out into the Bosphorus as the two continents come within a few miles of touching one another.

The ferry trip was wonderful for other reasons as well. Food was available from a number of different vendors, the smoke and aroma of the food blowing through the ship with the wind as it made its way up the strait. A small combo of musicians played near the aft, the music middle-eastern and so mysterious in its sound.

Everyday at his home, Feyyaz would cook breakfast, lunch and dinner for himself, his father and Jack. His father, Fazil, was a retired doctor. Before his eyesight began to fail, Fazil Abrak was also a classical guitarist of some renown. At times, Feyyaz's uncle would join them for a meal. He'd once been a member of Turkey's National Soccer Team. Although in his seventies, he was extremely fit and athletic looking.

One day, after taking a trip to the European side of Istanbul to see the Grand Bazaar, Jack left Feyyaz at his home and walked a few blocks to the business district of the suburb of Pendik. Earlier, Feyyaz had pointed out an internet cafe, and he was eager to answer and send mail.

One hundred and seven messages greeted him when he logged on. It took him awhile, and he had waded through seventy percent of them, when he came to a message from Lynda. He considered clicking on the letter-shaped icon and deleting the message without reading it. Even though these thoughts were in his mind, he knew in his heart he must read it. He still loved her. He still had loving feelings for her.

Dear Jack,

This is the second day I've tried to e-mail you, and it's about the millionth time, (well, maybe not quite), that I've tried to find the right words.

I'm in Krakow. Lots of things have changed, and then again, some are very much the same.

I'll still try to catch you. I've no idea where you are at this moment, and maybe I shouldn't be telling you where I am. Oh well.

Bill was traveling with me, but no longer.

You and I were once together, and that is gone also. It is for the best, Jack. I really don't think I am capable of love. I may never have been. It's possible, I may never be in the future. Please let that be OK.

I don't really know what I'm trying to say. (In all my other millions of attempts to write this, this is the point where I have hit the delete button). So, I'll just leave it at this: I would like to think you would be happy to know that I am safe. I'm sure it pleases you to know I'm traveling by myself, something you preached, (although that's probably not the right word), to me time and time again.

I'm no longer afraid to be on my own, and although I'm tired, I've spent a number of restful days here in Krakow.

I hope you're having fun, and hope you're enjoying all the sights. (What did you think of the Old Town Square in Warsaw — wasn't it wonderful?).

Lynda

He wanted to e-mail her and say he was in Istanbul and would wait for her there. He was thinking of a landmark other than the train station where they could meet, as he halfheartedly answered the rest of his mail. In doing so, he came across a message from a woman in Vermont. He received a couple of earlier messages from the woman, once in Hong Kong, and again in Russia.

Judith Rhys, a onetime resident of Newport Beach, was now living in Vermont. She kept in touch with the happenings of Los Angeles by reading newspapers on line. One of the papers she regularly read was the *South Beach Register.*

There was something about Istanbul and the Grand Bazaar that was of great importance and interest to Ms. Rhys, and one of her e-mails included an impassioned plea for him to visit the Grand Bazaar.

The Grand Bazaar, thought Jack. What a wonderful, romantic place to meet. Possibly a meeting by the front entrance, a massive stone structure which bears the date 1461.

Jack began to write.

Istanbul, Turkey

I awoke this morning at 5:30 a.m. to the chanting sounds of Islamic morning prayers wafting exotically through the air. I am in Pendik, a quiet residential suburb of Istanbul, Turkey.

For five days, I have been a guest in the home of Feyyaz Abrak and his father. Feyyaz is a lifelong friend of Suha Tokman, a swimming coach in Medford, Oregon.

I was introduced to Suha by Bob and Brenda Miller, also from Medford. A chance meeting with the Millers and their two daughters in a restaurant in Hong Kong began this network of relationships.

New relationships that develop through friends of friends are one of the true joys and rewards of travel. In this manner, I have been fortunate to experience newfound friends in Irkutsk and Moscow, Russia, and Helsinki, Finland.

Feyyaz was on the platform of the railway station to greet me when I arrived in Istanbul from Budapest, Hungary. Since that time, he has been my guide, interpreter, and confidant.

Together, we have traveled by ferry to the Prince Islands of Burgaz and Buyuk, located in the Sea of Marmara. We have toured Istanbul, seen the famous Blue Mosque and other ancient mosques, with their towering minarets reaching up for Allah. We have visited open-air markets and shops.

Accompanied by Feyyaz's girlfriend, Mine Cetin, we ferried from Istanbul to the mouth of the Black Sea. This is the famous Bosphorus Strait, which connects the Black Sea with the Mediterranean.

A constant stream of huge oil tankers compete for the right of way with luxury yachts and fishing boats. Both sides of the Bosphorus are lined with small, picturesque towns and villages that climb the steep shores from the sea.

But today, Feyyaz and I are on a mission to visit the Grand Bazaar. Istanbul is the only city in the world that spans two continents, and after a 20-minute ferry ride, we reached Europe from his Pendik home in Asia.

After a brief walk, we arrived at the Grand Bazaar — and, oh how very grand it is. Built more than 400 years ago, the Grand Bazaar consists of more than 4,000 shops, several banks, restaurants too numerous to count, street vendors and open-air markets.

From silver and gold jewelry to porcelains, rugs, medicines, spices and aphrodisiacs — everything imaginable is here. The uninitiated would find it easy to get hopelessly lost in its winding, labyrinth of passageways.

And, the price of everything is negotiable. The touts and vendors make the typical American used car salesman seem like a novice.

In the purchase of a Turkish rug, I deferred the negotiations to Feyyaz. With an occasional cry of anguish from one or the other, Feyyaz and the seller went back and forth in nonstop Turkish. They finally agreed on a price, but first it would have to meet my approval.

No, I would like a rug of the same design, but bigger. Off went the rug merchant, pleadings thrown over his shoulder for us not to leave. Moments later he returned and the negotiations began all over again.

After some time, a deal was struck and I walked off, the proud owner of a Turkish rug.

But I cannot be distracted, for I have come to the Grand Bazaar for the sole purpose of having a cup of Turkish coffee.

I have a date with a young lady, a dear friend to whom I have made a promise. Yet, I have never met this woman, nor do I have the foggiest notion of what she looks like.

How can this be?

When the <u>South Beach Register</u> published the initial article describing my around-the-world adventure, I was flattered and surprised to receive more than 60 e-mail messages by the end of that first day. Many more followed, most from strangers who related to my sense of adventure.

But one particular e-mail message stood out from all of the rest.

Judith Rhys, a former Newport Beach resident now living in Vermont, described her lifelong desire to visit Istanbul. She made a long, impassioned plea for me to have a cup of Turkish coffee at the Grand Bazaar.

If I would do that and maybe think of her for just a small moment — somehow, that would satisfy her yearning for this distant and exotic land.

So, I gladly lift the cup in a toast to her and all of the other people who have so wonderfully followed me along this journey. Here's to you Ms. Rhys, and all of the other dreamers, future travelers and souls who suffer from terminal wanderlust.

Happy Trails,
Jack Gillette

On his way back to Feyyaz's apartment, he thought of Lynda. He wondered if he should have answered her message, and imagined the different ways he could have responded. He also thought of how, upon his arrival at the apartment, he would tell his friend Feyyaz he would be leaving in the morning.

****

An overnight bus took Jack to Bodrum, Turkey, on the shores of the Mediterranean. He stayed at a hotel built alongside a sandy beach, a beach littered with sunbathers and a shore cluttered, wall to wall with hotels. It could have been Mazatlan, Waikiki or any one of thousand touristy beach resorts in the world.

The next day, he caught a ferry to the Greek isle of Kos, an island hosting what seemed to be a large, high school graduation party. Revelers were everywhere, whizzing around on rented Vespa's like hives of angry bees. Few looked to be experienced riders, and the outpatient care facilities of the local hospital was probably a cottage business in itself.

Traveling on to Samos, he spent a couple of days lolling at cafes and doing next to nothing. Visiting a travel office to look into which island he would visit next, he could find no map of the Greek Islands other than those within the scope of direct travel from Samos. The ferry agents were no help, as they seemed to know nothing about islands other than their own.

He searched for a book store, and then searched to no avail for a book written in English. While he could travel from Samos to Mikonos, could he go from that island to Naxos, where the wine is said to cure a broken heart? Could he possibly go to Crete, an island reported to be beautiful in its mountains and beaches? He finally decided to ferry to Mikonos and let things happen after that as they may.

Incredibly lucky so far, he'd not missed any boats or trains, and all of the people he met were pleasant. With the small exception of getting bumped by a car as he attempted to cross a street in Beijing, everything had gone well. His luck was about to change.

Walking from his hotel to a location where he could catch a bus to the ferry terminal, he was hit by a car. With his largest bag on his left shoulder and blocking his vision of the street next to him, he'd started to cross a small alleyway when a car came around the corner fast. The car hit the soft bag perched on Jack's shoulder and spun him around. His spinning ended with him falling to his knees on the rough, cobblestone street.

As the hit and run driver sped up the hill and out of sight, he lifted himself off the pavement. He was wearing shorts, and his knees were scraped bare. He checked his camera bag, and it appeared to be undamaged. The incident was an omen of more bad luck.

Jack arrived in Mikonos at 1:00 a.m. Debarking the ferry, the transportation available offered rides only to various campgrounds, not hotels. To make matters worse, the ferry deposited the passengers in a remote location, far from any town or facilities.

It wasn't cold, but it wasn't exactly hot either. The wind was blowing a steady thirty miles per hour. He walked along, the weight of his bags aggravating his already sore knee. He finally came upon a boat ramp leading off the road and down to the beach. It provided some shelter from the wind, sand, and grit, so he arranged his bags so he could sit with some degree of comfort, and began to wait out the wind and the night.

He somehow managed until sunrise. Back on the road, the wind still blowing as steady as a fan set on high, he trudged a couple of miles to what was the outskirts of a town. There was another ferry terminal here, and some travel offices. He waited until the offices opened and booked the first room available. It was just up the road, and without a taxi in sight, he set off on foot once again.

A shower worked wonders, and food from an adjoining cafe helped too. But, what he really needed was some sleep and a respite from walking. The pain in his left knee was killing him.

19

A small collection of kiosks were located in front of the train station, near a line of buses of that would take Lynda to Auschwitz and Birkenau. At one, she found a scarf and a beret she liked. They would help hide some of the nasty looking bruises, which were turning a purplish-gray color.

This was her first day out of the hotel since the beating, and her last day in Krakow. Resigned that Krakow would always hold bad memories, she wanted to get out as soon as possible. But first, she wanted to visit the World War II concentration camp — Auschwitz.

She took a seat on the bus, separated from the other passengers. She overheard some tourists speaking English, but she wanted to be by herself.

Arriving at Auschwitz,, she listened while a guide droned on about this statistic and that, not really listening, just anxious to get started. It was soon after beginning the tour that the enormity of the statistics began to hold real meaning.

The place seemed almost collegiate at first — the tidy, red brick buildings and cobblestone lanes lined with trees. But everything was eerily quiet, and regardless of its appearance, Lynda could sense the evil that once ruled here.

Her group came to a gate which frames the entrance to the camp. The sign, *Arbeit Macht Frei*, (Work Makes You Free), spans the top of the gate. She stopped to wonder what deranged sense of irony possessed the Nazis to erect such a sign, and further wondered if any of them ever thought how the world would view them a mere seven years later.

She heard a woman behind her cry, and a few moments later saw a man wipe tears from his eyes.

She saw the wall where prisoners were summarily shot, a group of young school children now laying flowers at its base.

She saw the enormous glass-fronted displays, where boots and children's shoes by the thousands lay.

She saw the piles of suitcases, the mounds of eyeglasses, shaving brushes and hair brushes.

She saw the piles of human hair the Germans used to make the linings of both military and civilian jackets.

She toured a building where she saw the "standing cells," concrete and brick cells the size of a small closet where several people were forced through a small opening at the bottom. Wedged into one of these cells, they were left to suffocate or starve to death — wedged so tightly that death did not allow them the luxury of lying on the floor — they died upright alongside a person who would outlive them by a matter of a few hours, or possibly a day.

She saw the bunks where people slept — seven to nine of them to a single tier no larger than a double bed.

She saw the relentless display of documentary evidence, first at Auschwitz and later at Birkenau.

She took in the entire ordeal silently. She spoke to no one, and no one spoke to her. She never cried, although she did feel her knees weaken several times.

It wasn't until she was on the bus and headed back to Krakow that she broke down. She was sitting in the back of the bus, with the nearest passenger a few rows in front of her. She felt the tears on her cheeks first, then tasted the saltiness of them as several stopped at the edge of her lip. She put her head in her hands, thinking this would stop soon, and it was then that she started sobbing.

How could a human being do something like this to another human being? She could understand hate, but mass hate and rage that went on for years? Children, women, old people — was there no compassion whatsoever in these people?

Why is there not story after story of guards deserting, their conscience not allowing them to continue? Better to be dead, or die while in the act of killing ones pursuers, than to be a part of this hideous, evil and indiscriminate mass murder machine.

The bus was nearing Krakow, and Lynda was staring out the window at nothing when she felt someone sit down beside her. She turned to see who it was.

"Are you okay?" asked a woman, somewhat older than herself.

"Yes," said Lynda. "I'm fine."

"Well, I won't bother you. I just saw you earlier at the camp, and then I heard you crying. I felt like I should at least ask." She started to get up, this woman who was obviously an American.

"No, don't go," Lynda heard herself say. "I mean, ah, if you're not with someone, please stay."

"No, I'm alone, just like you are. But, I know how much I value my privacy, so I'll go back to my seat."

Minutes later the bus pulled to a stop, and Lynda hurried to get off. She only had a couple of hours before her train left for Budapest, and she wanted to see the Rynek Glowny, Krakow's answer to The Old Town Square in Warsaw. Lynda was not hurrying to get to the square however, she was hurrying to thank the stranger for her unsolicited act of kindness.

"Excuse me," she said, catching the woman and placing her hand on her arm. "I just wanted to thank you for what you did back there. That was kind of you."

"Oh, you're welcome," she replied.

They stood there, awkward for a moment as people heading to taxis and trains, filed around them.

"Listen, I don't know if you're interested, but if you've nothing else to do, I wanted to visit the Rynek Glowny before I leave Krakow." Lynda had not planned to ask this woman to join her, but now it seemed like the thing to do. "I mean, maybe you have other plans and all, but I'm alone, and quite frankly, I'd enjoy the company."

"Well, I would too," replied the woman, who introduced herself as Sally. "I would hope that our visit would include a good, stiff drink. I don't know about you, my dear, but I could use one."

Together, they hailed a taxi for the short ride to their destination. Lynda looked at her watch a couple of times, thinking to herself she would have to watch the time closely to not miss her train. Her ticket, purchased that morning for the journey to Budapest, had a scheduled departure time of 10:30 p.m.

Arriving at the square, they walked a short distance before deciding on a particular sidewalk cafe. Lynda didn't think it was possible for anything to be better than her experience at The Old Town Square in Warsaw, but realized right away the Rynek Glowny of Krakow was special.

"This is wonderful!" she cried, as she pulled her wicker chair closer to the table, a wide umbrella blossoming out above them and hiding the approaching night sky.

After ordering a couple of drinks, Sally said, "Yes, I have fallen in love with Krakow, although after today I'll look at it differently knowing that evil place is just a few miles away."

"How long have you been here?" Lynda asked casually, wanting to avoid the subject of the concentration camps.

"Oh, about a week now. I'm just kinda bouncing around. It's something I've always wanted to do, but never found the time."

She'd tagged Sally to be a widowed school teacher. She was surprised when she asked what she did for a living.

"I'm a, or I guess I should say, I was a veterinarian. My parents are both gone, and a year ago my husband decided to run off with his twenty-three year old secretary. We never had any children, the dogs and cats have always been our children.

"Anyway, I just decided to sell my practice and go. The money, the S-U-V, the house, none of it really mattered when I stopped to think about it. Anyway, here I am!" she said, spreading her arms out wide.

"And, how long have you been traveling?"

"Almost three months now. I'm starting to get tired, so I may return to

Paris next week. Paris always seems to make me feel energetic and alive. And, what about you?"

"Well, it's a long story."

"Hey, they always are. I shortened mine considerably. I know this place isn't open twenty-four hours," she said, looking around and laughing.

"Yes, I know," Lynda sighed. "Mine seems to be getting longer and longer. I'm traveling around the world without getting on an airplane," she declared. It was the first time she'd ever said that to anyone. It shocked her a little bit, as it felt as though it fit her more than it should.

"Wow, and I thought I was a liberated girl!" said Sally.

"Well, it's rather strange how it all happened, but that's what I'm doing."

"I can't help it, I have to ask. Even if it's just to have the security of knowing a perfect stranger didn't do that. You were traveling with a man?"

Lynda wanted to turn away, but she didn't. She took a deep breath. "Yes, a man I was with decided to beat me up. I honestly can't say it surprised me. It never happened before, and it will never happen again, with him or anyone else."

"You should have kicked him in the balls."

"Yeah, well, you think of all the things you would do if the situation ever presented itself, but in reality it all happened so fast I didn't have time to think or act. He was bigger and stronger, and after the first two punches, any fight in me was gone. I was just praying he wouldn't kill me."

"He's gone, I hope?"

"Yes, very much so. I'll be okay. I just want to enjoy myself now, and get to Liverpool, England in time to take care of some business."

After a couple of drinks, they decided to share a bottle of wine. Lynda glanced at her watch and realized she would never catch her scheduled train to Budapest. It was just as well. It was good to have someone to talk with, and they both bared a little portion of their souls — Lynda with Bill, and Sally with her ex-husband, Frank. It was quickly established both men were assholes, and with each sip of wine their stock became more devalued.

Lynda discussed missing the train with Sally, and so when it came time to leave, they went as planned to Sally's hotel. It was small and quaint, and within walking distance of the cafe. It was agreed that if the hotel did not have an extra room, they would share Sally's.

They spent the next day together, walking around Krakow, taking a tour of the castle and cathedral at Wawel Hill, having lunch at a cafe in the square, and having a glass of wine in yet another of the many cafes there. It was fun being with someone who wanted to see things and do things. She found it a welcome relief that her friend seemed to also sense when she needed to stop and do nothing. She discovered the act of just sitting and watching people to be enjoyable as well.

"So, when are you leaving Krakow for Paris?" asked Lynda. They were sitting at a small cafe near the train station. It was mid-evening, and Lynda would make her way to the station soon to catch her rescheduled train to Budapest.

"I don't know. I think I may go to a place called Tarnow, answered Sally. "Do you know anything about it?"

When Lynda replied she'd never heard of it, Sally laughed, saying, "It doesn't surprise me. In fact, many of the guidebooks I've read fail to mention it, or only mention it in passing. I know I'll be disappointed, but I'm going anyway."

"Well," Lynda paused to take a sip of her wine, "If you're going to be disappointed, why go?"

"Because it might be there," Sally said matter-of-factly.

"What? What might be there?"

"Him, or possibly someone that I'll go to my grave knowing they were the most unforgettable character I've ever met. Perhaps it will be someone like you, someone who I just happen to meet and spend a little time with.

"It may not even be a person. It may be a sight, a building, a view from a passing train or bus. It may just be a feeling, possibly a feeling I've somehow been there before, perhaps in another life, or maybe it will just be a feeling that I've finally found my home."

"But, you won't know unless you go," said Lynda, making a statement rather than asking a question.

"That's right. I suppose it all sounds pretty weird, huh? But you know, it's life, or at least it's what life should be. I've spent the better part of my life getting up and going to work. Sometimes I feel as if I can't really call my ex-husband an asshole. I was consumed in work and the day to day grind. Of course, so was he, so maybe he's an asshole after all," she laughed.

When Lynda didn't say anything, Sally continued. "I guess my point is, I never wondered what tomorrow might bring. I never looked at tomorrow as an adventure. Two hours from now, this afternoon, tomorrow, next week ... ah, it was just an entry in my day-planner, a schedule of surgery planned or a date when I would take a short vacation. Everything was orchestrated, nothing was left to chance. My life was completely void of spontaneity and adventure."

"You sound like someone I know."

"Let me guess. It's not the asshole who beat you up, is it?" She didn't give Lynda a chance to answer before continuing. "So, if it's not him, it must be the guy you're chasing after."

Lynda had a mouthful of wine, and struggled not to choke.

Sally picked up on her small, but noticeable alarm. "It's okay. I have no idea, nor do I even have to know. But, I do know that somewhere out there is someone who is the exact opposite of mister asshole. Sorry, but it shows all over you."

Lynda didn't know what to say. Sally and she had known each other for a mere twenty-four hours. She didn't consider her a stranger, but neither did she consider her a soul-sister. How could she know these things about her? There was a pause in their conversation, Lynda not knowing whether, or how to react.

"I'm sorry. I probably shouldn't have said that," said Sally with a sigh. "I'm traveling to Tarnow because it's supposed to be an old gypsy town. As a kid, I once told my mother I wanted to be a gypsy. I can still remember it ... the house, the dress I had on, my mother cooking and standing at the stove. I think I was either six or seven years old.

"Anyway, that's what's taking me to Tarnow. You're traveling to Budapest, and then continuing around the world without ever getting on an airplane. Your reasons are your own. I shouldn't have intruded."

"It's okay. It's just something that's hard to explain. I'm a bit confused as to where I'm going, really."

"I know you are, and I guess maybe that's what shows. But, don't let it bother you. I'm confused too. I have no idea at all as to what I'm doing. But the important thing is, I had even less of an idea of what I was doing eight months ago."

Sally took a sip of wine and looked off at the people passing by. "You're traveling around the world, and somehow that's not, well, that doesn't fit you. And yet, in some small way it does. Let's just let it be. You have my address and phone number, as well as my e-address. I keep telling myself I won't go back to St. Louis, but I probably will. Regardless, the e-address will remain the same."

They talked for several minutes more, not really wanting to say goodbye. Two hours later, in a compartment all to herself, Lynda was on her way to Budapest. As she clicked off the light above her bunk to sleep, she felt more alone than ever before.

She wasn't particularly sad. She didn't feel exactly melancholy. She was just alone, halfway around the world from her home, a place she feared she would never be able to call home again. Two minutes later, she was fast asleep.

****

Jack fell asleep to the sound of the shutters over the windows banging in a syncopated rhythm with the wind. He awoke twelve hours later to the same sound.

He pulled the covers back to look at his left knee. It was swollen twice its normal size. After some effort, he managed to get to the bathroom. It was difficult to bend his leg at the knee, and he ended up sitting down on the toilet seat with a resounding thud as he struggled to keep his leg straight.

Intended as an overnight stay, the plan would have to be scrapped. He would end up spending three days in Mikonos, his knee getting only marginally better. During that time, the innkeeper took pity on him, arranging for food to be brought from the small cafe which was independent from the hotel and by giving Jack access to the computer in the office.

The innkeeper was impressed when Jack told him he worked for a newspaper, and as he typed out another article he hoped the man would not ask to read what he had written.

There was no way a traveler could be overjoyed with the Greek Islands after being the victim of a hit and run, being deposited by a ferry on some lonely stretch of beach in the middle of the night, and having to brace against gale force winds.

"Is it always this windy?" he asked the hotel owner.

"Oh yes," he replied. "This is Mikonos!"

He decided to insert a title for the article.

> ### Tourism Information? In The Aegean,
> ### It's All Greek To Them

Ah, Greece! How beautiful and scenic it is.

The beauty of this country has met all of the visual expectations formed in my mind from perusing countless issues of National Geographic and various travel magazines.

But, circumventing the globe in a whirlwind fashion such as mine, I get only small sips of the true tastes of any of my destinations.

Travel destinations are like food — some are an acquired taste. Sometimes, that initial sip may not be to your immediate liking.

I began my Greek island odyssey with buoyant expectations and a ferry ride from Bodrum, Turkey, to the island of Kos. Located near the Turkish mainland, Kos is a popular day-tripper destination for Turks, as Bodrum is for Greek vacationers.

Both Bodrum and Kos are crowded with tourists and hordes of unsupervised children of the same. Kos is additionally fouled with what seems to be a gigantic high school graduation or fraternity party.

I could not wait to get out.

The next stop was Samos. Also crowded with tourists, Samos had the distinction of being the center for the world's craziest drivers. On the day was to leave Samos, I was the victim of a hit and run.

While I choose Mikonos as my next stop, it was a mistake. The ferry arrived in Mikonos at 1:00 a.m., a full two and a half hours later than scheduled. Of the two main ferry ports in Mikonos, I was deposited at the one that, to be described as remote, would be a gross understatement.

So, I'm stuck at this remote ferry outpost where the only lodging touts are for campgrounds. There is not a taxi in sight. I can see the lights of the town, but they look so very, very distant.

And the wind! The next day a local would remark; "Oh, this is Mikonos. It is always windy here, especially this month." Just what I wanted to hear. Dirt, grit and sand is everywhere.

I resort to sleeping on the beach. Believe me, this is not my style. Cold, covered with wind-blown sand and dirt — I'm not a happy camper.

At 7 a.m. I start the long trek to town. Passed by only a few autos, they must think my arms and hands are waving about due to the wind. None stop. None even slow down. I probably look like hell ... no, I do look like hell.

I arrive in town and everyone is still sound asleep. Oh, did I mention the wind? I sit outside a ferry office/mini-market/room booking office to wait for the 9:00 a.m. posted opening.

When the office finally opens at 10:00 a.m. I'm told that I can still catch a ferry today if I hurry back out to the hinterland ferry dock. But I could not face doing anything other than sleeping in a nice soft bed, sans wind and sand.

By 11:00 a.m. I have an overpriced pensione and a ferry ticket for Siros. I get to my accommodation, but ah; "I'm sorry," the innkeeper says. "The people in your room, they dance all night and are now sleeping in. Your room will be ready in two hours!"

The Greek people I have met have been gracious and accommodating. But, I think their school system must eliminate all courses dealing with Greek geography; they seem to possess no knowledge of their own country. If you ask someone about a particular place, they've either not been there or have absolutely no idea what it is like.

I intended to travel to Tinos, but learned of a religious festival taking place there. Men and women, it seems, crawl on their hands and knees from the square, or some such place, to a church. Not to be confused with a pub crawl, it is a celebration of the assumption of the Virgin Mary, when Mary died, and Christ carried her soul to heaven.

No tourist information person I talked with mentioned the juvenile atmosphere of Kos, the religious zealots of Tinos, the wind and sand storms of Mikonos, or said; "By the way, the ferry will dock 15 miles away from any and all forms of civilization."

If I worked in a travel information center in Los Angeles and one mild January day a Greek couple walked in and told me they would like to take a camping trip to Lake Tahoe in the Sierra Nevada Mountains, I'd be a little more forthcoming with information.

"Yes sir, the wife and I would like to go to Lake Tahoe, maybe camp near the lake shore, swim in the lake, and water ski. Ya know, sorta seize the weekend."

Would I omit the fact that you'd have to be brain dead to do such a foolish thing in mid-winter? Would I not mention the word "snow," or maybe, "lots of snow?" Not if Lake Tahoe was in Greece, apparently.

"No problem," I'd say. "Here's two tickets, take a couple of weenies and buns with you — knock yourself out."

But, maybe camping at Lake Tahoe in January is an acquired taste. One thing for sure — it won't be crowded with tourists.

By the time Jack left Mikonos on a ferry bound for Piraeus, he was sick with pain. The swelling in his knee had receded, but walking was extremely difficult. He boarded a bus to Patra, on the Adriatic coast. From there, a ferry would take him to Bari, Italy.

Once in Bari, he would activate his western Euro-Rail Pass and travel a few miles up the eastern coast of Italy to one of many small towns. He would be able to rest for a week or more if needed.

****

At the port city of Bari, Italy, Jack remained in his seat resting his sore knee while most of the ferry passengers hurried towards the exits. A man a few years younger than him sat across the aisle waiting patiently as well. He looked hip and chic in the way some European men appear. A red and blue bandana covered much of his dark hair, do-rag style.

Studying a map of the Adriatic coastline from Bari northwards, the towns of Molfetta and Barletta looked to be on the rail line, and both appeared to be small, seaside towns.

"Excuse me, English?" Jack asked the man.

They were both standing in the aisle now, the other man still picking up his bags. He looked at Jack.

"Excuse me," he repeated. "Do you speak English?"

"Yes, I speak English very well," the man replied confidently.

"Are you from Italy?"

"Yes."

"Well, I was wondering. I'm looking for a small town where I might get some rest for a few days. You see, I was hit by a car in Greece, and my knee is hurting. Bari seems awful big, and I was wondering if you knew anything about these two towns?" Jack showed him the book he held, the page folded back to show a rather un-detailed map.

"Yes," replied the Italian. "What is it you wish to know?"

"Which of these two towns is the quietest, or possibly the smallest?"

"They are both small. But, there is a better town just here," he said, pointing to an unmarked spot between Molfetta and Barletta. "It is a very nice town, both small and quiet."

"Do you know if it's on the rail line?" Jack asked, looking at the map now. The spot the man indicated looked to be about 40 miles away.

"Yes, it is on the rail line," said the Italian, as they started to walk towards the door of the room, a room now virtually devoid of passengers. "The name of the town is Trani. It is where I am from."

Jack introduced himself, and in turn learned the man's name was Cosma Schiaroli. Cosma had traveled to Greece to visit a girlfriend, and was now returning to Italy to see his father in Trani. He lived in Rome. By the time the two were off the ship, it was decided Jack would ride with Cosma and his father to Trani. They didn't have to wait long before Cosma's father roared up in a small, red Fiat.

Cosma worked as the interpreter for the group, introducing his non-English speaking father to Jack, who was crammed into the back seat with all of the luggage, his knee throbbing with pain.

Elio Schiaroli happily talked to his son, his hands in constant animation as he alternated his attention between the road, his son, and Jack. Ten miles out of Bari, he could sense Elio was asking his son a question. Cosma turned and asked, "My father wants to know how long you plan to stay in Trani?"

"Oh, I don't know," replied Jack. "I'd like to rest my knee a bit. Just kind of kick back and do nothing for three or four days."

Cosma turned to his father. Rapid Italian went back and forth for a moment, and the elder Schiaroli turned to look back at Jack. "No problemo, no problemo!"

"My father says he'd like you to stay at his home. I'm staying at my mother's house for a few days before returning to Rome. He says you are welcome."

The old man turned in his seat to look at Jack. With one hand on the steering wheel of the speeding Fiat, he took his free hand and pinched his own cheek with his thumb and forefinger and exclaimed, "Bella bella, bella bella!"

Elio Schiaroli's small apartment was wonderful. It overlooked the Adriatic, with only the street and a small stretch of beach between it and the sea. Although Elio only spoke Italian, they communicated in a loose sort of way.

Cosma's father and mother were divorced, but each night, Cosma, Elio and Jack would all pile in the car and drive over to the ex-Mrs. Schiaroli's home. There, she would have a table set for four, but she would rarely take a seat herself.

Beer and wine came first. Then came food in the form of antipasto. This was followed by a series of meat, fish and pasta courses. Offerings of beer or wine changed to brandy and grappa. One night, after Cosma's mother had set another plate piled high with food on the table and returned to the kitchen for more, Jack leaned over to Cosma. "When does she stop cooking?"

Very matter-of-factly Cosma turned and said, "When we leave."

It was Jack's second experience with the Italian people, his first, the watchful, off-duty policeman in Nynashamn, Sweden. Warm, friendly and gracious — coupled with a lifestyle built around food and wine — it left the visitor thinking what else could be important.

After four days, Cosma was ready to go back to Rome. He offered Jack a ride and hospitality, but Jack declined the offer. Although the pain in his knee had diminished, he felt some sort of significant damage remained — damage which could only be repaired by rest and treatment. All that aside, Venice beckoned to him more than Rome.

20

The train station was crowded. There were back-packers everywhere — college students roaming around eastern Europe. Looking around, Lynda suddenly felt older than her thirty-two years. Her skin wasn't as creamy looking as the girls she saw, many of them relatively make-up free, and clustered around in groups with either their boyfriend or girlfriend traveling companions. Her attire was different as well. Now, standing there, it seemed so matronly and dated.

She needed a hotel, a hot shower and something to eat. Surely, she thought, that would make her feel both younger and better. Bill normally selected the hotel, but now she was on her own. She started towards the terminal in search of lodging information.

A long line of travelers waited near an information booth. She set her bags down on the floor and started to go through her shoulder bag, looking for a brochure listing hotels in various European cities. Not finding it, Lynda was about to get in line when she noticed a very young girl standing a few feet away. She wore black, horn rimmed glasses, the 1957 retro look in both eye wear and clothing. A backpack stood propped against one leg, while she perused a travel guide.

"Excuse me, but ..." started Lynda.

"Yes?" The girl looked up, the thick lenses of her glasses making her already large eyes seem gigantic.

Lynda was thinking the poor girl shouldn't wear glasses of a style that attracted so much attention to the fact she was probably legally blind without them.

"Oh good, you speak English. I don't have a guidebook of any kind, do you suppose you could let me have a quick look at yours when you're finished?"

"Yeah sure," she replied. "Like, you can have it, totally. I'm like, ah ... getting on a train for Milan in a few minutes, and this is for like eastern Europe." She held the book up so Lynda could see the cover.

"Have you enjoyed Budapest?" she asked, as the girl handed her the book.

"Yeah, it's cool," she said, as if it was just ordinary in every way, shape or form. "Not as cool as Paris, but yeah, it's cool."

"I really don't want to take your book. Just give me a minute, and I'll be finished."

"No, go ahead, it's cool. Just ah, just like, leave it on a bench or something. Someone will like, pick it up or something. Besides, it's like weighing me down." With that the girl turned around, and with a quick wave back to Lynda, walked towards the platforms.

Lynda thumbed through the guide. Over sixty percent of the book was marked in the blazing colors of four different colored highlighter pens, in some cases full pages of what Lynda considered trivial information. She found the pages on Budapest, and located the section on lodging. Three places were highlighted in bright orange.

"Sucks," was written in the margin alongside one. "Cool," the girl's favorite word was written beside another, followed by "but $$$$." The third managed to escape the critics pen.

"Why not," she heard herself say aloud.

She picked up her bags and walked to the front of the terminal, found a taxi, and showed the page to the driver. Next to the name of the hotel, was the name written in Hungarian.

The outside of the hotel was in need of repair, and in fact, looked as if it were ready to collapse. A small building next to it was boarded up, but approaching in the taxi she noticed a cafe at a quiet intersection just down the street. Except for the boarded up building, the neighborhood looked respectable.

She opened the door to a small lobby area and registration desk. Furnished with three overstuffed chairs and some end tables, the 1920's style furniture would have sold for a high price in style-conscious Los Angeles. A older man stood behind the counter.

"Mademoiselle, Anglais, ah ... Francais?" said the man.

"English, yes," replied Lynda. "Do you have a room available, a room for one?"

"En suite, Mademoiselle?" questioned the man, his language remaining in French as if he hadn't heard the answer to his first question.

"Yes, I guess." She wasn't sure what he meant, and was about to ask him if she could see a room.

"Ah, I have but one room left. It is a very nice room for Mademoiselle. I think you will find it lovely. For how many days will you be?"

"I'd like to stay at least two days, possibly longer. Could I see the room please?"

"Oui, oui," replied the man. "Let me help you with your bags. I am certain you will like the room. Ah ... if you don't Mademoiselle, it will tear my heart." With that, the man clutched his chest and looked pleadingly towards the ceiling with hopes that God's light would shine on him yet again.

The room was three flights up and there was no elevator. She wanted to tell the man to leave her bags — that she could run up and view the room on her own — but he seemed determine to do things his way. Once at the door, he produced a skeleton key from his pocket and unlocked the door.

There was a large rug in the center of the room. It had seen better days, but it appeared spotlessly clean. The bed was wrought iron and looked like a large cloud, it's snow-white comforter catching the last morning rays of sunshine coming through the window. Antique chairs, tables and accessories accented the room. It was beautiful, like something out of a movie set.

She intended to inquire how much the room was, but found herself softly saying, "Cool."

"Ah, Mademoiselle is pleased?"

"Yes, this will do fine," she replied. She started to leave, to return to the desk to complete any check-in procedure.

"Oh no, Mademoiselle. Everything is well. Stop and get a key when you decide to leave. There is a very nice cafe just down the street. "Je dois partir," said the man, slipping back into French as easy as changing from a pair of slippers to a pair of loafers. "Adieu."

She lay on her back on the bed, sinking down in what seemed like a sea of feathers. She wondered how much the room was, the other half of the scribbled comment in the margin of the travel guide coming to mind, and instantly realized she didn't care.

Lynda showered and dressed with the intention of getting something to eat. She was starving, but she was also tired. She climbed into bed for a quick nap. It was just after noon.

When she awoke, the room was pitch black. She could discern light from behind the curtained window. She fumbled around for a switch, finally finding the small, metal chain which hung from the fixture of the table lamp beside the bed. Pulling it, the room was bathed in a soft light, tinted yellow by a parchment shade. She looked at her watch, realizing her nap lasted nearly seven hours.

When she descended the stairs, the hotelier was still behind the desk. As he stood up to get her key, she smiled when she noticed the Graham Greene novel he placed page down on the small desk. One of Jack's favorite authors, she was struck by how appropriate his stories were for this city and this hotel from a bygone era.

Lynda walked down the street to the cafe, hoping it would be open. Nearing the intersection, the glow from the lights of the cafe spread out over the sidewalk. It was a warm night and people were sitting at tables placed alongside the narrow sidewalk.

She took a seat at a vacant, outside table placed next to the window. She could see in the cafe where all of the tables were full of couples laughing, eating and drinking. Waiters, large white linen napkins draped over their arms, hustled about pouring wine and serving food. She was still looking inside when she heard a voice. She looked up to see a clone of one of the very waiters she'd been observing.

Again the man said something she did not understand. He placed a menu on the table and spoke yet again.

"I'm sorry," said Lynda. "English?"

The waiter just looked at her for a moment, and then said something in his native tongue. A man sitting directly behind Lynda turned in his chair. "Pardon," he said.

She turned around to look at him. He was with a dark haired woman, who was studying him with adoring eyes as he spoke to Lynda in a heavy accent. "Is it what, you would like? I do not speak so good, but perhaps I help you."

She quickly glanced back at the menu on her table. It was written in Hungarian. She looked back at the man, as his companion said something in Hungarian.

"My friend say I order for you. Is good?"

"Yes, I suppose that's fine," she replied.

"Are you hungry?"

"Yes, I'm famished, er ah ... yes, I am very hungry," she said in an attempt to keep her word usage simple.

"Is good." He began to rapidly list what sounded like enough food to feed ten people. "And, drink ... is what you want?"

"A glass of ... no, I'd like a bottle of nice wine. Whatever you think is best," she heard herself say.

Again he said something to the waiter. As the waiter was walking away, the man's companion again said something.

"My friend wants to know from where you are in America."

"I'm from Los Angeles, California," she said.

Again the woman spoke and the man interpreted. "Disneyland, have you seen?" he asked.

Lynda had lived in L.A. for four years before she met Jack. When they first met, he was shocked to learn she had not been to the Anaheim shrine erected by Walt Disney. They went the very next weekend. Jack was so childlike on that visit. He wanted to go on every ride and stop at every kiosk. He bought Mickey Mouse hats, complete with ears, putting them into a sack later when he replaced them with coonskin caps, ala Davey Crockett and his ilk. She adored him then.

"Yes, I have been to Disneyland," she said, recovering from her brief reverie.

"My friend, she would some day like to go."

It was out of character for her to react the way she did. She considered herself a social person, but conversing freely with strangers never came natural to her. Lynda was surprised when she befriended Sally in Krakow, tagging along with her to the Rynek Glowny without any apprehension. And now, she was engaging in a conversation with a man who was difficult to understand.

Furthermore, she completely trusted this stranger to order a meal as well as a bottle of wine for her.

Surprising herself even further, she pulled a card from her bag. With a pen she wrote her home telephone number and hotmail e-address, and handed the card to the man.

"Tell her if she ever comes to Los Angeles to give me a call. I will take her to Disneyland," said Lynda.

The woman's smile grew as she read the card and her friend translated Lynda's message. Lynda turned back to her table and looked at the menu. I wonder what I'll be eating tonight? she said to herself.

It was a wonderful surprise. She thought it might be veal, but she couldn't be sure. Regardless, it was excellent. The bottle of red wine, light, like a petite sirah perhaps, was also very good.

Halfway through the meal, her friends got up to leave. The man asked how she was enjoying her meal, and translated a thank you from his companion. She was wondering how she would react if this woman showed up on her doorstep some day, and was surprised to find herself hoping it would happen.

"Ah, I ordered for you delicious pastry for follow your meal," said the man, before walking away. "With caffe, enjoy."

The meal, dessert and coffee were perfect in every way. She drank the entire bottle of wine, yet another surprise added to a surprising evening. She lingered at the table well after she had finished eating, sipping the last of the wine.

Stumbling up the street to her accommodations, she thought about tomorrow. On the train that morning, she drew out a precise plan as to what she would see in Budapest, and how she would close up what she perceived as a gap between her and Jack. She decided she would throw the entire plan in the garbage. Tomorrow was another day. Tomorrow was another cafe, and possibly she would again find herself doing things she never thought possible — things she never thought characteristic.

She pulled the comforter over her and tried to write the tears off as a product of being drunk. It was a useless effort. She realized what Jack had tried to make her see and experience. It had taken her nine countries and over two and a half months. Wandering truly was a love affair with your very own soul.

She got up early the next morning and ate a small breakfast which was included with her room. Then, she took her shoulder bag and started walking. She didn't have any purpose or direction in mind. She just walked. She was loving her freedom.

She window shopped at several antique shops. She stopped at a cafe for coffee at mid morning, and again for lunch at noon. Around two o'clock, walking in the direction of her hotel, she passed a small cafe. She was merely glancing in when she saw the computers. She walked in, ordered a cup of coffee and logged on.

There were several messages from friends in L.A., and she also had a message from *catslandontheirfeet-@hotmail.com*. She clicked on the icon and read the note from Ian.

Lynda,

Haven't heard from you in awhile. Wondering how you are? Hope you're enjoying your holiday.

I'm back home for a fortnight or two. Me brother broke his arm riding his motorcycle. I told him that if he would have landed on his head he wouldn't have got hurt at all.

Hope to hear from you again. It would be lovely if you could somehow stop by during your travels.

Ian

He was a terrible letter writer, but so what? She sent him a reply, telling him she was fine. She wanted to tell him more, but found her reply as unspectacular as his message to her.

She answered some other messages from friends in L.A., and one from her sister in Phoenix. Then, she sent an e-mail to Jack.

Jack,

I haven't heard from you, so I have to assume you're either terribly angry with me, or hurt and incapacitated and therefore unable to work a keyboard. I hope that it's not the latter. I know I hurt you, but I have to believe you're getting better by now. If it's anger, well I can't blame you. I don't think I could blame you if that anger never went away.

I'm in Budapest. I'm not writing so you will reply. No reply is necessary unless you feel you want to. I just want you to know that I think I found what you always referred to as the joys of being a solo traveler. It took me awhile. I've probably got a long way to go yet, but I just want to tell you that you were right. It truly is a joy. I feel free for the first time in my life.

Lynda

She went to her address book, clicked on the "Send Mail" icon, and wrote another message.

Jill,

I'm in Budapest, Hungary. Can you believe that?

This trip started out terrible. I probably lost 20 pounds by the time I got to China. I'm starting to gain some of it back. 10 pounds would do just fine, but no more, thank you.

I got rid of Bill. That's a story that will have to wait until I get back. I have no idea where Jack is, and for that reason I'd like you to do me a favor. Maybe you could get the firm's PI in on this — you can tell him he owes me a favor, (which he does). I need to know when Jack is scheduled to sail from Liverpool to Philadelphia. Also, I need the name of the ship.

 There are only a few travel agencies that book freighter travel. It shouldn't be that difficult. As cunning as you and the PI are, (Don't tell him I can't remember his name, but for the life of me, I can't), it should be a snap for you. Anyway, do what you can, and e-mail me right back.

 Things are going well, and I'm finally beginning to enjoy myself. Can you believe I'm halfway around the world and all by myself? What's more, I'm glad I am — I can do whatever I want.

 Love Ya,

 L.T.

The next morning, she checked with the desk clerk, informing him of her wishes to stay one more night. Slipping back and forth between French and English, he told her that would be fine.

 She turned, and was starting to go back to her room when she stopped. "Excuse me, pardon s'il vous plait, um ... how much is the room", she said, adopting the man's proclivity of speaking in two languages at the same time.

 "Ah Mademoiselle, the room is sixty-five hundred forints. It is satisfactory?"

 "Yes, everything is fine. Merci," exhausting her small French vocabulary.

 Ascending the stairs she tried to remember how many *forints* were in a U.S. dollar. In her room, she checked the hand-me-down guidebook and found the previous owners, "but $$$$," in the margin equated to a mere thirty-eight dollars.

 Later that morning, Lynda walked back to the same cafe where she posted e-mails the day before. She logged on, and found a message from her friend Jill. Although she never understood Lynda's attraction to William Hugh Davidson, she was a friend. Friends accept other friend's weaknesses and indiscretions.

Lynda,

 I'm envious and jealous. Oh how I'd like to be in Budapest right now. I don't think I could do it alone like you though.

 What's happening with Jack? He's so sweet. Every Saturday morning I buy the <u>Register</u> in hopes of reading another one of his articles. It's exciting reading them, especially when you know the author personally. And, how did he ever find out about you and Bill? I thought that the two of you were just a one or two night fling at best. In fact, I thought that was over some time ago.

 You definitely need to correspond a little more, girl! I worry about you.

 Anyway, Charlie and I went to work for you. (I couldn't help it, I slipped and told him you couldn't remember his name. He said if you'd buy him lunch when you get back and show him all the pictures you've taken, he'll forgive and forget).

 The name of the ship is the <u>Independent Endeavor</u>. It sails out of Liverpool,

England on September 30th. It goes from there to Philadelphia. That's all we could find out. Charlie is still trying to find out a contact number for the ship in Liverpool, and I'll e-mail you as soon as I know something.

Now, I have a favor to ask of you. You remember my friend Gary? We'll, I moved in with him two weeks ago. Things are going okay, and I've always known he's a good man. (Actually, I'm madly in love with him).

Anyway, he's a big Beatles fan, and when I told him what I was doing for you, and the fact that the ship was in Liverpool, well he got all gooey and excited. So when you're there, would you please pick up some kind of Beatles souvenir, something I could give him for Christmas? I'll pay you back when you get home.

Stay safe. I hope things work out for you and Jack. I have a feeling they will.

I Love You,
Jill

Lynda looked inside her shoulder bag, searching for her appointment book, finally finding it at the very bottom. She had not looked at it since Hong Kong, and wondered why she was even carrying it around.

She checked the date. Today was August 21st. Where had the time gone? She studied the current date and her information on Jack's departure from England. She knew the man. He was never late for anything. Something as important and final as a ship sailing would cause him to be there at least a week early.

Her hand-me-down guide book contained some train schedules. She studied those, calculating how many days it would take her to get to England. She didn't have a lot of time.

Some of Bill's whinings of being a tourist rang in her ears, but she dismissed them quickly. She found her hand instinctively touching her face near her left eye. The swelling was gone — the black and blue color rapidly fading away. The pain, although now just a memory, remained so vivid that she felt a shudder go up her spine accompanied by a slight chill running through her body.

She wanted to see Romania, but that would be impossible now. She rummaged through her bag again, finally locating a tattered and creased copy of Jack's itinerary. He only mentioned traveling through Romania and Bulgaria on his way to Istanbul, Turkey. She decided she would do the same.

Glancing back at her guidebook, she studied a map of Europe. Like a divining rod, she let her finger dowse for Jack's location. She sensed he was somewhere in western Europe. She backtracked from Liverpool to narrow the gap. She felt he wouldn't linger in France. Her index finger moved over the page, not touching it. She narrowed her field to two countries. A smile played over her face as she sat there thinking this game is rather fun.

Lynda's finger no more than touched the dot representing Milan when she moved it an inch and a half to the right. Where her finger now rested was a place Jack often spoke of. He traveled there as a college student, describing it as the most romantic place he'd ever been. His statement at the time made her swell with pride, as most men would never refer to a city as romantic.

Venice, Italy.

She signed off the internet, and took a taxi to the train station. She purchased a ticket scheduled to depart Budapest at 8:45 a.m. the next morning, bound for Istanbul.

Back at the hotel, she settled up her bill, smiling at the thought of the dollar sign symbols in the margin of her guidebook. That evening, she returned to the corner cafe where she'd met the Hungarian couple the night before. This time she waded through the menu herself, asking questions of the waiter in English and interpreting the answers as best she could. She drank the wine, feeling good about the taste and the fact she was tasting it without someone's help.

Her departure from Budapest the next day was marred slightly by an incident at the train station. As she sat in her compartment waiting for the train to depart, she noticed several policemen on a platform three or four rows away. An older woman sat dejectedly nearby. Lynda watched for several minutes before she noticed the black body bag lying by the policemen's feet. She assumed it was the woman's husband, although she could not be certain.

"How short life is," came a voice over her shoulder.

She turned to see the conductor standing there, bent over and looking at the scene of a nameless person's exit from this world.

"Yes, how short life is," he repeated, agreeing with himself. "Ticket please."

Unlike the man lying in the body bag, the train made a sudden, spasmodic jerk and came to life. The train rolled through Romania and Bulgaria non-stop. She spent only a day in Istanbul before catching a ferry on to Piraeus, Greece. It was a long voyage which took her out of the Sea of Marmara, through the Dardanelles and into the Aegean Sea.

She read of the Greek island of Naxos, and how the wine there is supposed to heal a broken heart. She hadn't even considered the fact her heart might be broken until she read about Naxos and its wine. The thought put her in a funk for the rest of the day. She would come back to Greece someday, but for now she would have to keep moving.

Lynda awoke early in Piraeus to brilliant sunshine cascading through her open bedroom window. She dressed with plans to bus the short distance to Athens before catching a late afternoon bus to Patra. From there she would travel by ferry to Brindisi, Italy.

In Athens however, she saw none of the attractions she intended to see, lingering in several sidewalk cafes instead. She enjoyed a cup of coffee. Later, she enjoyed a glass of wine. She liked the way the sunshine felt on her face and shoulders. She was content doing nothing.

21

Jack was on a train bound for Venice. His knee felt slightly better, although he still walked with a pronounced limp. His first visit to Venice since college, he was anxious to arrive.

Over the years he'd spoken with people who arrived by air, taking the bus from the airport to the city. He knew people who experienced Venice, arriving first by rental car. He was convinced that to experience Venice at its fullest, a person must arrive by train.

The traveler detrains behind the station, a dead end for all rail traffic. A long walk with other passengers ensues along a covered platform. Entering the back of the station, it is a mere carbon copy of many European train stations. Old, cavernous and noisy, long lines of people wait for tickets and connections.

A walk across the tiled floor of the station follows, stepping around clusters of people, their baggage resting on the floor beside them. From the back entrance to the front entrance of the station is a distance of about 100 feet. You push open the front doors of the station and step through.

The traveler is now standing on the top landing of a series of steps. Ahead is a panorama that cannot be duplicated. It is a visual rush of colors and movement.

From an ordinary train to a cement platform worn and dirty from the shoes of millions of visitors — from there to a train station like every other train station in western Europe — and, through that station to a glass door smeared with the hand prints of those before you. From all of that ordinariness to a city like no other city.

There are streets as wide as boulevards — *piazzas*, or squares, as grand as one could imagine. Serpentine paths lead to squares no bigger than a large living room — with passageways so narrow a person has to turn sideways for others to pass. Amidst all of this is an absence of cars, mopeds, bicycles, and skateboards. Only the occasional low hum of a motor launch may be heard.

Some squares may be home to a sidewalk cafe, while a small, arched bridge nearby tempts the eye for its architectural beauty. Instead of a street performer juggling bowling pins, or a musician playing the accordion, it is not unusual for a woman in a formal dress to be heard singing opera. The smells of food are wonderful. The stillness and lack of traffic is music to a persons ears.

After arriving, Jack found a small hotel not far from the train station on the Lista di Spagna. It was a busy area, but the condition of his knee forced him to accept something which did not entail a long walk.

Leaving the hotel to find a sidewalk cafe, he didn't have to walk far. He sat for over two hours, drinking beer and having a small meal. He chatted with the waiter, a Frenchman, who came to Venice because of a woman.

"She works here as well," the Frenchman explained in perfect English. "She too is from France. I tried to talk to her, have her come to Paris, but no, here is where she wanted to be. So, here I am also."

"There are worse places to be, my friend."

"Oh yes," said the waiter. "And, I have been to some of them. No, this is not bad, but aye, it is not Paris. Paree est un vrai tresor."

After leaving the cafe, he spotted a small internet center. Logging on, he faced 47 messages. He clicked on the first one, answering a message from a member of the newspaper's readership. Six messages down the list, Lynda's e-mail filled the screen. Jack read it several times before abruptly punching the computer mouse on the "Reply" icon.

Lynda,

I'd like to say that I've been too busy having fun to even think of you, but alas, that's not the case.

As for being angry, hurt and incapacitated, I must tell you that I'm a little bit of all three. I got hit by a car in Greece, but it is more of a minor inconvenience than a major injury.

I'm angry with myself for not paying more attention to your needs. And yes, I'm angry with you for not being faithful — an element of our relationship we once discussed as being the most important thing to both of us.

Then there is the hurt. The biggest part of that has subsided. After the hurt followed the loneliness and sadness of being without you. That too has passed. Now, it is just more of an empty feeling for me — an empty feeling I seem to bring upon myself. That too will pass.

I'm glad to hear you are enjoying yourself. I have to admit that I am surprised you are still doing this — that you haven't gone to an airport and flown home.

Where's Bill?

Jack selected the entire text of his reply and pressed the "Delete" key, and began anew.

Lynda,

Yes, I am angry, hurt and filled at times with all of the emotions in between. Things will get better.

It surprises me that you are still traveling, and that you have not just flown home. Maybe something good will come out of this after all.
   Jack

Returning to his hotel room, he tried to read, but found it impossible. Why did she asked if he was incapacitated? Did she expected him to be, or was she simply making a comment about his not replying or trying to contact her?

Jack remained alert for the man in the black leather jacket in Krakow. It was warm there, and wearing the jacket, the man would have stood out like a sore thumb. He didn't look as closely for the man in Budapest, and by the time he arrived in Istanbul, he'd dismissed him from his mind.

Looking back, had the incident in Greece truly been an accident? He never saw the driver of the car, and in fact, by the time he picked himself up off the street, the car was gone.

Lynda also commented that she was beginning to understand the joy of being a solo traveler. Did this mean she was traveling alone, without Bill? Or, had Bill simply flown ahead? Could Bill have been the driver of the car that struck him?

"Christ." Jack said aloud. "I'm getting paranoid about this whole thing."

He turned off the small table lamp and slid down under the covers, pulling them up to his neck. It felt good to be lying on his back with his injured leg stretched out straight before him. He lay there — staring at the ceiling — thinking.

The more he thought of the different scenarios, the heavier his eyes became. Ten minutes later, with wild theories of conspiracies and fantasies about reconciliation, his eyelids fluttered closed. He would have vivid dreams of the man in the black leather jacket jumping out from behind parked cars — running down the sidewalk with his baggage and laughing at him — all while he limped feebly after him.

Although his weariness and the pain in his leg caused him to sleep rather well despite the bad dreams, he would have slept much better knowing the man in the black leather jacket was incapable of fighting, running, or even walking. In fact, he was not even capable of feeding himself, as both of his arms, stiff in their white casts, hung suspended from cables above his hospital bed. One leg also sported a cast, and it too was elevated with a cable. Gone was the black leather jacket, and in its place was a hospital gown. With three of his four limbs dangling from cables, the man looked more like a life-sized puppet than the cheap, two-bit hood that he was.

The next morning, Jack went directly to the internet center he visited the day before. He answered some outstanding messages, and found a message from Dan in response to his e-mail from the day before.

Jack,
   Glad to hear you're alive. I don't have much time right now, so I'll make

this short. Remember the guy who owned McGrath's Pub before Bobby, a guy by the name of Joe Berg? It was before my time, but we met him a number of times there. He's an attorney, but we won't hold that against him.

Anyway, I saw him last night. I stopped by McGrath's with some of the production people to celebrate a birthday, and he asked about you. When I told him you were injured, he gave me the name of a friend of his who's a dentist in Fossano, Italy.

I know, I know, there's nothing wrong with your teeth. But, this guy is an American, speaks Italian, and works in a clinic with a group of other doctors.

He could probably get you some treatment, and Joe said he'd e-mail him to tell him you may show up. I don't know where in the hell Fossano is, but Joe mentioned it was up north somewhere.

Here's the info: Dr. James Matchefts, Fossano, tel: 011390172206391

Everyone at the <u>Register</u> says Hi!

Be safe, and keep me posted. Remember, I can always fly over and help out if you want me to.

Love ya, Dan

Loraine, his travel agent, insisted he purchase trip insurance in California. Initiated solely for its trip cancellation provisions, the policy also included health and accident insurance protection. To take advantage of it however, he would have to document his injury before leaving western Europe. Fossano, Italy was probably as good a place as any.

Sitting at the computer, he thought of something Lynda said in her last message. He began to write, but abruptly stopped. It was a story which would best be written from its source, a type of on-the-scene reporting.

Five minutes later, he sat in a small cafe. It was eleven in the morning, and a beer sounded good. He ordered, got out his notebook and pen, and went to work.

Neal,

Here's another article. All is not a rose garden, lottery or no lottery. I've wanted to write what I feel and not what the reader expects. I've wanted to write what is real. So, here goes.

I have always had a passion for sidewalk cafes.

Whether enjoying a light meal, a cup of coffee or a glass of wine or beer — I can think of no better way to while away the day or night.

Unlike restaurants where the seating arrangements often restrict the view and the ability to interact with people seated nearby, sidewalk cafes offer the ability to watch each and every individual and event that passes before you on the sidewalk or the street.

Sidewalk cafes tend to facilitate interaction with other people seated nearby. As a solo traveler, I find the sidewalk cafe a wonderful place to meet both locals and fellow travelers.

Not compelled to order a full meal, it is a wonderful opportunity to sample small tastes of that country's fare. And, the very essence of these cafes tend to encourage the patron to linger and consume at a slower and more relaxed pace.

I have found it rare to be rushed by a waiter into the ordering of additional food or drink. One is expected to loiter.

Entertainment in sidewalk cafes can vary greatly, depending on the location. While some attract peddlers hawking everything from hot peanuts to flowers, others offer strolling minstrels and assorted entertainers.

The Rynek Glowny in Krakow, Poland, is a square slightly larger than two city blocks. It is ringed with sidewalk cafes and outdoor bars. The beginning of one establishment is the end of another, with only a change in chair or table design distinguishing one from the next.

Only at the very northeast corner of this square is the ring of cafes broken by St. Mary's Church, its twin towers reaching out to the sky. For added entertainment, the clarion of a lone trumpeter routinely sounds from high atop the church, ending abruptly in mid-song, in imitation of the demise of a trumpeter of yore.

Parading around the Rynek Glowny is a never-ending troupe of tap dancers, violinists and trios and quartets of various musicians. All of this occurs with a backdrop of wandering locals and travelers amidst horse-drawn carriages.

Sidewalk cafes in Budapest tend to feature violinists, while the instrument of choice in Germany is the accordion.

But in all sidewalk cafes, I find that the primary entertainment is "people watching." The seaside resorts of Turkey and the Greek islands offer a strange contrast of overweight, older men in skimpy Speedo swim wear and topless bathing beauties.

Irkutsk, Russia, and Prague, Czech Republic, offer an array of beautiful women passing by. The sidewalk cafes of Italy can be like sitting next to the runway at a fashion show — men and women beautifully and immaculately dressed.

I wander from cafe to cafe. I allow my eyes to roam where they will. I linger as long as I want, and I throw all concern for diet and indulgence to the wind. I sometimes cross the street to another cafe simply for a different perspective of the passing parade of people.

But, in all of this gastronomical and visual delight, there is a canker. As all solo travelers know, there are times when the loneliness of such travel grips you at your very heart and soul.

Sometimes, it is merely loneliness for your own native language. You'll meet someone who speaks English, and find yourself latching onto them much as you would a life preserver as you flounder in the sea alongside a sinking ship.

At other times, the loneliness is borne out of a longing for companionship.

When that happens, it can be the worst malady associated with traveling alone. It can strike at any time — in any place.

For me, that loneliness seems to always encroach itself on my heart when I am in a sidewalk cafe in Venice or Paris. Each time I visit these cities, I vow to never visit them again as a solo traveler. They are cities that one needs to explore with a spouse, a lover or a significant other.

Sitting in a sidewalk cafe in Venice, I am not entertained by a juggler or dancer, but by a woman singing opera. Although I have no understanding of opera, her singing brings tears to my eyes. As I sit there, the gondolas silently cruise by, their cargo of young lovers wrapped lovingly in each other's arms.

And Paris, ah Paris! I will sit in a cafe alongside the Champs de Elysees and watch couple after couple stroll up and down the boulevard — arm in arm, hand in hand. Paris is a city made for young lovers.

And sometimes, while sitting there feeling sorry for myself — thinking of what might have been or should have been — I'll overhear a couple at a table nearby arguing in a foreign language. Although I neither speak nor understand any foreign tongue, I can always interpret more than I really want to know.

And so, I move down the street to yet another sidewalk cafe. The beer is cold here also, and although I cannot read the menu, the food that I see on other tables looks good.

I realize I am hungry, as my eyes follow a beautiful young woman walking down the street. I overhear someone speaking English, but for now, I am content in my solitude.

I'll linger as long as I care to. I have nowhere to go — no place I have to be — and if there is an argument about a situation or decision, I'll have only myself to do battle with.

The piece took longer to write long-hand than on a computer, but the exercise was good for his psyche. He felt better.

He walked to the train station to check the schedules for trains traveling from Venice to Milan. He checked his map and located Fossano. His trip would take him from Milan to Torino and then south to his destination. As he made his way back to the hotel, his feelings came to the surface.

Something happened to him while he scribbled the words to the article on sidewalk cafes. It was something dramatic. At first, he wrote off the feelings to the three bottles of Heineken. But, pausing to decide whether or not to send a copy of the article to Lynda, something inside him clicked into a locked and seemingly permanent setting. His relationship with Lynda was over. It was history, and he knew it.

Jack's train left Venezia, Santa Lucia at 7:05 a.m. As it pulled out of the station, he tried in vain to get a last look at the city he loved. If all went according to plan, he would sleep in Fossano tonight. He was traveling to the very southwest corner of the country, a part of Italy he'd never seen before. He knew nothing of its geography or points of interest. It would be an adventure.

****

Lynda was tired. As she lay fully clothed on a bed in an overpriced hotel in Brindisi, Italy, she wondered how she would summon the energy to leave early the next morning. Romania, Bulgaria, Turkey and Greece had all sped past in a blur of trains and ferries. It was 10 a.m. on Monday, September 3rd.

Her plan was to train to Venice in the morning, spend the night, and then travel at a hectic and ruthless pace in an attempt to close the gap between her and Jack. Traveling day and night, she would first go to Milan. Following his itinerary, she would travel north through Switzerland to Freiburg, Germany. She would allow herself a hotel in Freiburg before moving on to Frankfurt and an overnight journey to Prague, Czech Republic. Arriving in Prague in the early morning, she would have but a few hours to spend exploring the city before boarding a midday train to Berlin, Germany. From there, an overnight train would take her to Paris.

She felt a night, or possibly two would be needed in Paris to recuperate from back-to-back overnight train trips. After Paris, it would be an easy train ride to a port on the French coast where she could catch a ferry to England.

Lately, a single worry, not alleviated by money or anything else material, had entered her mind repeatedly. She dismissed it as loneliness at first, but like waves in the ocean, every time she started to build her own little haven of a sand castle, the waves of doubt would roll in one after another — each one erasing past efforts and smoothing out her thought processes until they were, like the flat sand of the beach, unrecognizable.

As she lay there, she was not thinking of the long haul by train through western Europe and the money. She was thinking of Jack.

Here was a man who was so in love with her, and good to the very bone and soul of his body. She cheated on him. She wondered what ever made her do such a thing. Because he loves me, she thought, he gives me half of his good fortune. Not a million dollars, but half of everything he has. And, I seem intent on pissing all of it away.

She was too exhausted to undress and crawl under the covers of the bed. Her hand reached over and grabbed what she could of the bedspread, pulling the lightweight coverlet over a portion of her body. The room and the weather was warm, but she felt cold.

She stared at the ceiling and wondered how things ever got to be this way. She fell asleep dreaming of being wrapped in Jack's arms.

The next morning, Lynda made her way to the Brindisi Centrale train station. As she rode north towards Bologna, she studied her maps and guide books. With an itinerary of night trains and one night layovers in a limited number of cities, she could easily imagine herself arriving in Liverpool by the 15th. It would give her fifteen days to find Jack's ship.

She knew the ship in Liverpool was the key to catching him. As the Adriatic moved steadily by her right shoulder, she figured Jack would also be aware of his vulnerability. She knew he could be cunning and sly, and wondered if he was still mad enough to act that way.

Having determined she was bound to catch him, Lynda had another worry. What would she say or do, and how would Jack react to seeing her? All hopes of reconciliation had been abandoned in her mind, yet in her heart she maintained a weak grasp on a slim ray of a dream.

Lynda arrived in Venice at five o'clock. The weather was overcast and cool, and her initial efforts to locate a hotel were met with profuse apologies for not having any available rooms. She finally found a small hotel with only a suite available. It was expensive, but she didn't care. After all, it was only for one night. She found a restaurant nearby, ate dinner and retired to her room early. Tomorrow was a busy travel day.

Her big travel day started earlier than expected. At four in the morning she traveled from her bed to the bathroom. For the next four hours she made several of these round trips from bed to bath and back again. She needed to be at the train station by nine, but knew at seven she'd never make it. She dialed the front desk and asked if she could have the room for another night.

"Oh, I am so sorry Signorina, but the room is not available," replied the desk clerk.

"Well, do you have another room that I could move to? I am sick, and I cannot travel."

"No, I'm sorry. The entire hotel is full for the next four days."

"Well, can you find me a place?" she asked, in a hurry now as she felt another trip about to begin. "I need a place. As close by as possible," she added rather hurriedly.

"I will see what is available for Signorina."

An hour and a half later there was a small rap on the door. On shaky legs she made her way from the bed, and opening the door, found a young girl standing there.

"My step-father wanted me to come and see you, to see if you are all right," she said in English with no hint of an accent.

Lynda lied and told her she was feeling better, but she was confused.

"And, who is your step-father?" Lynda asked.

"Oh, I'm sorry. He's the guy downstairs, the owner of the hotel."

"At the front desk?"

"Yes. He told me to tell you he is looking for a room for you, but that Venice is very busy right now and he is having trouble finding something."

"Are you an American?" asked Lynda, curious about the lack of any accent.

"Oh yeah. I'm from Seattle, Washington. My mother married the guy who owns this place, and I'm over visiting for the summer. The rest of the time I live with my Dad in Seattle."

Lynda had to go, so she cut the conversation off. "Will you come back and tell me when he finds out about another room?" She locked the door, and quickly bolted for the bathroom.

It was noon before the young girl came back. She helped Lynda carry her bags down the stairs. Her step-father was not around, but her mother was, and said that a room had been found. Since the hotel was located nearby but difficult to find, the daughter would escort her there.

"Lena here will take you to the hotel, she knows the way."

"Is it far?" she asked as she began to feel another rumbling in her stomach. She wasn't sure if she could make it. Her skin felt clammy, and all of a sudden she was cold.

"No, you can both hurry. Lena knows a shortcut, and I'll call ahead so they'll have your room ready. But Lena, I want you to take the long way home. No shortcuts," she added.

They hurried along, Lena taking the heaviest bag while Lynda followed with her ever-present shoulder bag. They quickly covered the distance, the girl obviously enjoying being in charge of so important a task. They eventually rounded a corner, and there it was.

The Hotel Hesperia was a neat looking two story building. Later, Lynda would learn it was across from the Jewish Ghetto in Cannaregio. It was quiet and clean. As they entered, an older woman greeted both her and the girl by name, took her shoulder bag before she could protest, and led her down a short hallway to where the door to the room was already open.

"Go!" she instructed Lynda, gesturing in the direction of the bathroom.

As she walked briskly towards the welcoming bathroom door, she could hear the woman saying they would lock the door on their way out.

She barely made it in time. And, for the next three days, it was one trip after another from her bed to the bathroom. During her stay, the older woman who ran the hotel brought her food and bottled water. Her delayed arrival in Liverpool no longer mattered. All she cared about was getting well.

By the time Lynda checked out of the Hotel Hesperia, she'd spent a total of seven nights in Venice. As sick as she was, she could still see how Jack found the city romantic. Several times, lying in bed during the middle of the day, she heard someone in a building nearby practicing the piano. The pianist was playing something classical, perhaps Bach. The faint sound of the piano gave her Venice experience an almost magical tone, starting, stopping and returning yet again to the beginning.

After waiting in a long line, she bought a ticket for a 10:03 a.m. departure to Milan. She would continue on to Basel, Switzerland and eventually Freiburg, Germany, for an overnight stay in that city.

It would be a long day.

22

Fossano resembled St. Helena, Yountville, or any one of a number of small towns in California's Napa Valley. It was warm, with the air having a sort of agricultural smell to it.

Jack found a small hotel, and the following morning he limped and hobbled his way to the lobby. His knee was hurting badly as he inquired about a taxi to take him to the hospital.

An unmarked, black Mercedes sedan soon appeared on the other side of the large, double glass doors of the entrance. The driver hurried in, saying something in rapid Italian to the desk clerk as they proceded to where Jack sat resting. The word, "hospital" appeared to dictate the two men's rapt concern.

Both men assisted Jack out of the hotel, and into the front passenger seat of the car. With a click of the seat belts locking in place, and a roar of the engine, the late model sedan blasted out of the parking lot. The taxi driver did not speak English, and as they rode along in silence he kept glancing over to look at Jack's leg. With long pants on, there was nothing to see, but the driver kept a watchful eye anyway, as if expecting to see blood gushing out at any moment.

Minutes later, the driver parked behind an ambulance at the emergency entrance of an ancient looking, off-white building. Once again, the driver hurried to assist him. He found it difficult to protest without appearing rude.

Jack looked around, surveying the room full of patients.

An old woman was accompanied by what appeared to be her daughter. It sadly reminded Jack of his own mother in the last year of her life.

A young boy appeared to have fallen. Sitting next to his mother and clutching his immobilized arm, his earlier tears were all but gone, but his fear remained.

An old man looked sick, and nurses were helping him move from a chair to a wheelchair. Jack started to get up to help them as they struggled with the wobbly man and the rolling chair, but was directed by the nurses to stay put. At least that's what he thought they were telling him.

He had yet to hear anyone speak English. No signs were posted in English, the universal pictures and symbols for wheelchairs, no smoking, exits and arrows, his only guiding light.

An orderly handed him a clipboard and a pencil. There was a form in Italian, and he was only able to complete the obvious name and address blanks. Beyond that, he was lost. He sat and waited, and waited some more.

The old woman who reminded him of his mother, was wheeled away on a gurney. The young boy with the injured arm was doted on by his mother and a nurse, and led through a couple of double doors to an examination room.

He waited some more, the room ebbing and flowing with patients being admitted, treated and released.

On an impulse, he reached into his shoulder bag and retrieved his notebook. When he left California, his e-address list amounted to a dozen people. It now contained over four hundred. He decided to send a personal e-mail to those following his travels, telling them where he was and what he was doing. He began to write, putting details in as the day progressed. By the end of his hospital adventure, the piece was complete.

The English Patient II

While traveling in Greece, I tangled with a mini-van. I lost. The collision spun me around and threw me to my knees on the cobblestone street. The van did not stop.

At first, I thought I was uninjured. A couple of days later, my left knee became swollen and sore. Treated with beer and aspirin, my condition only grew worse. The slight limp became a severe one. Finally, in the small town of Fossano in northwestern Italy, "I could walk no more forever." I went to the local hospital.

Ordering food in China, buying a subway ticket in Russia, purchasing laundry service in Turkey — all of those tasks are a snap compared to seeking medical services without the benefit of speaking or understanding the language. I never saw the movie, "The English Patient," but I heard it was overly long and boring. If they ever decide to make a sequel, and should they want it to be even longer and more boring — Boy, do I have the location and script for them!

Now, I've never been to a hospital or a medical clinic where I haven't been subject to an inordinately long wait before being seen by a doctor or a nurse. I know the drill, and I sit there looking at <u>Women's Day</u> magazines ten years out of date, or perusing a <u>Field and Stream</u> article on, "How To Murder A Magnificently Beautiful Bighorn Sheep."

The hospital in Fossano looks as if it were built in the 1920's. Ornate, 30 foot ceilings with coved archways lead to vast and spacious hallways. It's a warm day, and portable fans are placed at strategic locations. Opened windows complete the air-conditioning package, which is an inexpensive and simple solution to a common problem. In America, the wrecking ball would experience "premature pendulation" at the very sight of such a facility. And, that would be a shame. It is a very beautiful and efficient building, albeit old.

And the care is second to none. Although I found no one on the staff who spoke English, the doctors and nurses went out of their way to take care of me.

First, I went to the emergency room. Although a security guard motioned my taxi driver to stop, he proceeded to a parking area seemingly reserved for emergency vehicles. After a wait of 2 hours, I was seen by a nurse, who then sent me to x-ray.

I had written my name and address on a form, but little else was required before receiving treatment. There were no questions about insurance, HMO referrals, or interviews with some non-nurse type asking the inevitable question; "And, who will be responsible for the bill should your insurance fail to cough?"

I went to x-ray, guided through the maze of hallways by a nurse. Three Italian language magazines later, an x-ray of my knee was finally taken. Then, back to emergency for another 2 hour wait. Once again, I had to be led by a nurse because I could not understand the instructions in Italian about where to go and what to do when I got there.

In the emergency room I saw broken arms and numerous conditions related to old age. I saw an old farmer-type guy who looked as if he'd been kicked in the head by his favorite mule, a young boy whose foot appeared to have been attacked by a weed-whacker, and a guy who had tried to power-drill his hand. Exciting stuff!

Then, it's back upstairs, (no elevators here), to wait for something or other — I have no idea. Once again, a nurse led me there, motioning with a palms down gesture to sit and wait, which I obediently did.

Days it seemed, passed before my eyes.

Two hours later, (I was in fact, the last person in the room from an original number of about 30), I am seen by two doctors. Through a mixture of charades and broken English, it is suggested that I make an appointment for some special type of x-ray. Immediately following the x-ray, they will perform surgery.

I tell them I have only one day and to, "hold the surgery." They look at one another, shrugging their shoulders. After a cell phone conversation, I'm off to another room for that oh-so-special x-ray.

I finally collect some paperwork and copies of all of the x-rays and doctor's diagnosis. I pay a bill which totals less than $100.00. After eight hours at the Fossano, Italy Hospital, I am a free man.

I believe the doctors wanted to do something further, but it was 5:00 p.m. and they were seriously cutting into my cocktail hour.

Injuries and ailments aside, dreamers with wanderlust have priorities too!

Happy Trails,

Jack

****

Jack telephoned Dr. James Matchefts that night from the hotel. Although Dr. Matchefts was his sole reason for choosing Fossano as a place to seek medical treatment, Jack had never met the man. In Los Angeles, Dan had conveyed to Joe Berg the details of Jack's injury, and Berg conveyed the message to his friend, Dr. Matchefts.

"Let's get together tomorrow night. We'll go have some dinner," suggested Matchefts. "And tomorrow, why don't you come down to the clinic about two in the afternoon." There is an Orthopedist here, and we'll have him take a look."

As he hung up the receiver, Jack wondered what Matchefts' clinic would be like. James Matchefts was a dentist. Clinics in America are usually specific to the type of care offered. There are dental clinics, eye clinics and women's clinics. Jack could not remember ever being in a dental clinic which also included an orthopedist.

The next day, Dr. Matchefts translated while an orthopedist examined Jack's knee. The diagnosis was torn cartilage. It would require surgery, but would probably hold out until he returned home.

"Don't run," translated Matchefts. "Whatever you do, don't try to run!"

The area surrounding Fossano is beautiful. Rolling hills and valleys with vineyards scattered here and there. At the summit of many of the hills are wineries with restaurants and tasting rooms, and it was at one of these locations that Jack enjoyed a wonderful dinner with his new friend Dr. James Matchefts.

****

Leaving Fossano, a train would take Jack in a southwesterly direction through Cuneo, across the Italian-French border and south to Nice. On the map it looked rather straight forward. He was pleasantly surprised.

Fossano to Nice is a distance of about 85 miles. Thirty miles out of Fossano the train began to weave its way into the mountains. Higher and higher they went, the speed greatly reduced as the locomotive strained with the effort.

Several small towns, their houses featuring steeply angled roofs, slid by as Jack gazed out the window. The towns resembled pictures of the Swiss Alps. This was, in fact, the southern most end of the Alps, a region called the Maritime Alps. The peaks range in elevation from eight to twelve thousand feet.

After visiting Nice, an express train took him first to Genoa, and later to Milan. There was time for a quick beer and a sandwich at the train station in Milan before boarding a train to Switzerland, where he spent the night in the small, Swiss town of Airolo. The following morning he proceeded to Freiburg, Germany.

Jack's imaginary list of places he'd like to visit was endless. Fantasies stirred by books and movies, inspired him to travel. As the train slowed to a stop at the Freiburg station, he knew he could now cross one of those destinations off the list.

Golden Earrings was filmed in 1947. The movie, set in Freiburg, Germany, starred Ray Milland and Marlene Dietrich. It was directed by Mitchell Leisen.

Jack first saw it on television while he was attending college. It was a rather aimless film of a British spy who is hidden by a gypsy girl during the early days of World War Two. There was something about the movie that captivated him and made him watch it over and over. The source of the captivation was Dietrich.

Dietrich had this lusty, dark and intriguing quality. She was highly superstitious. She took life as it came, never wanting much or questioning the hand that fate dealt her. She was a gypsy and a nomad. Jack was in love with her from the very moment he saw the movie.

Jack decided to stay a couple of days. He would find a road sign with the towns name upon it, and put a couple of dots on the sign for young Byrd, the character who was Ray Milland's accomplice.

Freiburg, formally Freiburg im Breisgau, is surrounded by the velvety hills of the Black Forest. A university town since 1457, there is a noticeable number of young people. The cafes, bars, and 200,000 residents radiate a laid back atmosphere more analogous to French life than German.

In the center of the town, Freiburg's *Munster*, or cathedral, is adorned at the ground level with intricate sculptural documentation, depicting scenes from the Old and New Testaments.

Although he was away from his hotel most of the day, Jack spent little time on his feet. He simply moved from a sitting position in one sidewalk cafe to that of another. In between cafes, he located an internet center. He ignored the forty or so messages, scrolling down until he found what he was looking for. Making his selection, Loraine's message instantly appeared.

Dear Jack,

I hope this message finds you well. The last time you wrote you told me of an accident involving a hit and run. I hope everything is all right.

Things here are fine. Warren just changed the front window display to the ski vacation theme — surprise, surprise! He always asks me how it looks, as if it's the first time in all our years of marriage that he's decorated it. Simple pleasures. Sometimes they're the best.

I contacted the shipping company. You should have their number in Germany, but in case you don't, I've included it at the end of this message. Anyway, everything is set for your scheduled departure on 21 September. However, in talking with the company, I was told the ship often leaves a couple of days earlier or later than what is scheduled. Therefore, it would be a good idea to be in Liverpool by the 16th or 17th. You could make contact with them and get up to date information on the actual sailing time.

I'll bet you're having a great time. Continue to do so. Remember, we can always book another ship and another Amtrak ticket for your trip across the

U.S. You'll lose quite a bit of money, but for a rich guy like you, it's pin money!
Warren says hello, and wants to meet you when you return.
Stay safe, and e-mail me more. I worry about you.
Loraine

Jack departed Freiburg in the morning, leaving young Byrd and Ray Milland's character, Captain Dennison, to battle the Nazis. A tear would came to his eye as he left Marlene Dietrich sitting in her gypsy wagon, her horse, Apple, patiently awaiting her command.

His roundabout journey would take him east towards Munich and later north to Nurnburg to connect with a train to Prague. In Prague, he would visit with an old friend.

Grant Podelco was Jack's first boss at the *South Beach Register*. Six months into their working relationship, Grant abruptly announced his acceptance of a position with the Prague based, Radio Free Europe.

They kept in touch via Christmas cards and occasional e-mails over the years. Although it would be a short visit, it would be the first time in over four months that Jack would be talking face to face with someone he knew personally — someone from his own country — someone who spoke his own language.

Jack wasn't sure he'd even recognize his friend, but his face stood out dramatically in the crowd as he walked towards him where he sat in a small cafe inside the station.

"Jesus!" exclaimed Grant, as he hoisted the largest of Jack's three bags onto his shoulder. "You're traveling round the world carrying all of this? I'd have it in one bag!"

"Well, I've picked up my share of tourist trinkets along the way. You know, a man can't have too many refrigerator magnets!" Jack laughed.

They walked together to the metro, Grant pumping in the required coins for their journey back to his apartment.

"Will three days be too much of a burden for you?" Jack asked.

"No, not at all. My wife is back in the States for a short visit, so I'm batchin' it. The company will be nice. I do have to go to work each morning, so we'll have to put a reasonable limit on the number of beers we consume each evening."

He told his friend about the lottery, his letter to Lynda and the turmoil arising from her infidelity. Grant was sympathetic, but not knowing her personally, it was difficult for him to relate to Jack's sadness.

"Oh, I'm pretty well over it. I guess the first time I see her after this is all over might be a little rough. But, I know it's over."

"You'll be fine. Hell, you'll probably meet someone who'll make you look back and think you were crazy to ever be with her in the first place," commented Grant. "But, aren't you at all worried she might catch you?" he added. I'd think it would be pretty easy. All she'd have to do was go around, following your route just as quickly as possible, and wait for you at the docks in Liverpool or Philadelphia."

Jack had to admit the thought of her catching him in Liverpool crossed his mind several times. Liverpool could be a bit tricky, but he'd not even considered the U.S. port of Philadelphia.

They spent the next two evenings drinking and enjoying Prague. They talked of writing and books. They saw some of the landmarks in the city together. Grant loved Prague and the lifestyle of working and living there. There were negatives, like learning the difficult Czech language, but otherwise, he and his wife were adapting well.

Leaving Prague, Jack traveled north to Berlin. Berlin was cold and windy, so he moved on to Copenhagen where it was even colder. After only one night in each of the cities, he headed south for Amsterdam. Although the city was warmer than Berlin or Copenhagen, it was raining. Perhaps Paris would be better, and so after a day in Amsterdam, he took a train to one of his favorite cities in the world.

Paris is a city where a person can easily walk to almost any location. The people are wonderful if the traveler makes an effort to communicate. It is a city full of wonderful cafes and bars. It is a city of romance.

Romance however, was not to be. Paris cafes are not the same when both your knee and your heart ache. He was tired and lonely. He longed to be around people who spoke English. After two days he caught a train to the city of Le Havre, and boarded a ferry to Portsmith, England. Once there, he rented a car and drove to a town 40 miles north of Liverpool.

The small, seaside town of Southport would be his home for a few days before traveling to Liverpool and boarding his ship, the *Independent Endeavor*. The date was September 15th.

****

Lynda left Venice on the morning of September 12th. She saw very little of the water-borne city, with its sidewalk cafes, artisan shops, architecture and splendid piazzas. She experienced only a few of the joys associated with the absence of automobiles, motorcycles and skateboards.

Of even greater consequence, she seriously jeopardized her rendezvous with Jack in Liverpool. She wanted to be in the port city by the fifteenth, but now would be hard pressed to make it before the eighteenth. Train rides through four more countries remained before traveling to England.

Despite all of this, she found herself not caring. From city to city she wandered oblivious to planning. Often times, her decisions were made on the spur of the moment.

In Prague, she detrained with every intention of spending the night. She was tired and badly in need of a shower. Walking along the platform towards the main hall of the station, she looked up at the reader board, it's Venetian blind-like slats flipping around with a noisy clatter like playing cards flapping against the spokes of a child's bicycle. She was mesmerized by the experience, a smile playing over her face as she wondered where the slats would finally come to rest.

When the reader board finally quit twirling, the city at the very top of the long list of destinations was Dresden, Germany. The train was leaving in 5 minutes from platform 7. Lynda stood on platform 9. Hefting her bags off the floor, she began to walk. Instead of turning towards the station area, she turned the other direction. Moments later she was aboard a first-class car bound for Dresden.

There was no reason for her actions, no preconceived notion of what Dresden was or wasn't. She was simply wandering. Most importantly, she was immensely enjoying it.

As she traveled through western Europe she recalled many of the stories and wisdom Jack imparted upon her, things she'd never paid much attention to. On a whim brought to mind by something he'd said, she instructed her travel agent in Los Angeles to purchase a Euro-Rail pass for her upon arrival in Basel, Switzerland. Jack swore by the passes, and it was now facilitating her wandering. There were no tickets to purchase, and no lines to stand in. She simply got on and off the trains as she pleased.

His love of wandering was exemplified by a poem he often quoted. Thinking of the Robert Service poem several times since leaving Venice, she strained to remember it. She laughed at herself, as she often remarked that he failed to listen to her. The shoe was on the other foot now. She was thinking of how they would have laughed together about her failure to listen, and it was then that her memory recalled the opening lines of the poem.

> "There's a race of men that don't fit in,
>   a race that can't stay still;
> So they break the hearts of kith and kin,
>   and they roam the world at will."

Lynda reached Paris on the morning of September 18th. She wanted to linger, but knew there was little time to waste. A midday train took her to the port city of Calais, where she boarded a ferry to the U.K.

It was a beautiful day, and she spent most of the voyage on the outer deck of the ferry enjoying the sea. When the ship shuddered to a stop at the port of Folkestone, she waited until most of the passengers departed before making her way to the exit. She didn't feel like fighting the crowds.

By the time she walked off the ship, there were only a few people ahead of her in the line for Customs & Immigration. She went through the brief formalities, a common-place event for her by this time, and walked to the outside of the terminal.

One of those smart-looking, black, English taxis rolled up to her when she approached the curb. Before she could grasp the rear door handle, the driver was out of the car to assist her.

"Er Miss. Let's put your luggage in the boot, just here," he said in a fine English accent.

The taxi driver was a gray-haired, sort of round man, with a ruddy complexion. Appearing to be eighty years old, he was an image of the quintessential grandfather.

"Lovely weather we're havin' eh ... it tis," he said, converting the statement into a question and then back again. He shifted the car into first gear and pulled away from the curb. "It's been this way for a fortnight, it has. Lovely, it tis."

Lynda told the man she wanted to go to the train station, and that she needed to catch a train to Liverpool.

"Ah. Lovely city it tis, Liverpool. Smartened it up a bit in the last few years, they have."

There was a pub located inside the train station, and Lynda stood at a small dry bar located in the middle of the room enjoying a glass of wine. The room was smoky, but she didn't care. She was happy to merely sit and listen in on people speaking her native language. It had been a long time since she'd heard it, and the lilt of the British accent was music to her ears.

Two days remained before Jack sailed, and her plan was to use her charm and anything else necessary to get aboard the ship. As she considered her options, she missed her intended train to London. She was surprised it didn't seem to matter, her concern being so nonchalant as to barely make her stir.

What had happened to her? Where had all of her pragmatism gone? Sometimes, she felt as though her entire being had changed, and in some ways, the new-found freedom and relaxed attitude scared her.

Things that once seemed important to her now seemed trivial. She was no longer thinking primarily of the money promised by Jack, or even money in a general sense.

She paused to reflect on the fact, and could not remember the exact dollar amount if she caught him. She shuddered, realizing she now considered the fifteen million an "if," rather than a "when." She felt strangely confused and melancholy that the difference between five hundred thousand and fifteen million didn't matter to her.

Another train came along. She rode to London's Victoria Station, and navigated the tube to Kensington-High Street, smiling at the recorded announcement over the intercom while waiting on the tube's platform, reiterating the warning for passengers to "Mind the Gap."

At the station, a young, uniformed woman acting as a guide and hostess, directed her to a nearby bed and breakfast. She changed her blouse and spent the waning evening hours walking aimlessly around the neighborhood.

Her wandering was rewarded when she found a small pub on a quiet street. The hanging, wooden sign above the entry to the pub, proclaimed the place to be, "The Tower of London Pub." The sign, so typical of English pubs, dangled motionlessly above the door in the still, warm evening air.

There was a beer garden in the back of the pub, and she enjoyed a late meal and a pint of beer. Although preferring a glass of wine or a mixed drink to a beer, in this place and at this time, the beer seemed appropriate.

The next morning, Lynda said goodbye to London and boarded a train to Liverpool. She arrived in the city at 1:00 p.m., September 19th. She had the rest of the day and all of tomorrow to find Jack's ship and deceive her way aboard.

23

After four days in Southport, Jack drove the short distance south to Liverpool and returned his rental car. He caught a taxi to the old town section of Liverpool and walked around, the long and winding road ending on Mathew Street and the Cavern Club. He enjoyed a couple of beers at this, the birthplace of *The Beatles*, and bought a few souvenirs at one of the nearby shops.

He found an internet cafe to post the last story before leaving for the United States, a story of an experience during his marriage. Traveling to Australia a week after graduating from high school, the trip was a graduation present from his mother. It was probably the catalyst for the wanderlust he'd felt since. It was the last thing he did by himself before getting married three months later.

Years later, following the death of his father-in-law, Jack and his wife Marge decided to travel to Australia. It was one of the last things they did as a couple.

Southport, England

Whenever I find myself in that part of the world which is, or once was, under British rule, I look for two things. First, I look for a "proper pint," from a friendly Publican. Second, I look for accommodation by a particular name — The Buchanan Hotel.

I have always found the pub without any trouble. Its pint has always been satisfying, the atmosphere always quintessential English. The hotel however, has been much more elusive.

A number of years ago, my lovely bride and I decided to travel to Australia, with stops in Hawaii, New Zealand and Tahiti. I'd been down under before, and never hesitated to extol the beauty and love that I feel for that country.

I had often told my wife how hospitable the Australian people were, how warm the weather was and how sandy and beautiful the beaches were. Living in the Northwest at the time, it was easy to impress upon her that it hardly ever rained in Australia, and that it was always warm.

During the planning stages of our trip, another couple we knew became interested, and so, in the spirit of adventure, we invited them along. They had never been to Australia, and I regaled them with tales of a tropical paradise.

After weeks of planning, it was decided that my wife and I would travel to Hawaii. Four days later, our friends would meet us in Honolulu, and together we would fly to Cairns, Australia.

My wife and I would continue south by air to Brisbane, while our friends traveled around the Cairns area. After a specified number of days, our friends would rent a car and travel south, while we would travel by bus and rail in a northerly direction — two happy couples meeting in the coastal village of Townsville.

Excitement reigned as I told them to be sure to pack the suntan lotion.

But now, the question of logistics. Where do we meet in Townsville? Being an old hand at this, and having once passed through Townsville, I pulled out a tattered but trusty guidebook and proclaimed the place to meet was the Buchanan Hotel. It has a pub and it has accommodation, which is to say that it has it all.

But my fellow travelers were not so well schooled, and were cautious to the extreme. My friend was afraid the Buchanon might not be up to standards, while our wives worried about finding the place.

Now, I doubt Townsville has a population of more than 1,000, and so I told them not to worry. Walk around in the sunshine, find a pub and have a pint, and we'll find you or you'll find us. Reluctantly, they agreed.

Hawaii was sunny and beautiful. Our friends met us as planned, and we landed in Cairns in a torrential rainstorm. My wife and I traveled to Brisbane, where it rained some more.

On the second day, I was helping my wife by carrying one of her bags. Hurrying to get out of the rain, I dropped it. She had failed to tell me of a bottle of red wine packed in the soft-cased bag, that for safety's sake, she had wrapped in a white dress. It continued to rain.

While traveling by train, a woman sitting next to my wife told her she had beautiful legs. When my wife had in turn thanked her, the woman asked if she could kiss her. And, it rained some more.

Making our way north by bus, we were forced to a stop because of engine trouble. After a couple of hours, the bus driver proudly announced he'd fixed the problem, but that the battery was now dead, and the passengers would need to push the bus to start it.

The water on the road was more than ankle deep and there was a steady, but warm rain falling as the passengers got out to push.

To say that my wife was a little put out would be to trivialize the situation. Had we been speaking, I am sure she would have told me exactly how she felt about Australia, our travels and me.

Therefore, it was with much relief when we reached Townsville where we would meet our two friends, share some refreshment and lighten our moods.

My wife and I arrived by bus, (we didn't have to push it very far), and we made our way through the small depot to the front of the building, where sev-

eral taxis awaited new arrivals. It was raining.

    Entering the back seat of a taxi, I was relieved to know safety was only minutes away. The taxi driver, with one arm draped over the back of the seat, turned his head, and with that fine, Australian drawl said, "Er to, mate?"

    I replied with a seasoned traveler's confidence, "The Buchanan Hotel, if you will, please."

    He hesitated a bit and then informed us, "The Buchanan, eh. Well, I can drive ya by, but er's not much to see — burned down four years ago."

    Well, you could see the steam coming out of my wife's ears. I knew my timing was bad, but I found myself laughing hysterically.

    The taxi driver, noting the look on my wife's face and possibly even seeing the steam rise from her rain-soaked head, sat cautiously, not wanting to say anything that might incite a domestic melee.

    Tensions may have eased had I not insisted, much to my wife's disgust, that we actually drive by the site of the hotel.

    "Really mate, er ain't anything to see," said the driver as he worryingly took sideways glances at the future ex-Mrs. Gillette. But I insisted we go. And, it was a wonderful site indeed.

    There were two buildings on either side of a vacant lot. And the lot was as vacant as vacant could be. Not a scrap of wood, a stray brick or a weed taller than six inches could be found. It was as if the building had burned to ashes — and then someone had burned the ashes.

    My wife and I located our friends without much trouble, and tensions eased as we shared a laugh over the events. However, not long after our return to the State of Oregon, my wife filed for divorce.

    And so, I'll always look for a Buchanan Hotel. It must have a pub where I can purchase a proper pint. Accommodation above the pub would be a nice amenity.

    I'll continue to search for the Buchanan, my personal holy grail. Then, I will enjoy a peaceful and solitary pint, and it may possibly be the best one I'll ever have.

****

    Unlike Townsville, Australia, the weather was beautiful in Liverpool. Lynda found a small, quaint bed and breakfast, and after checking in, went for a walk. She passed a pub, but it was rather seedy and smoky looking, so she continued on.

    She found an Italian restaurant and went in. It was Italian, but it's food did not remind her of Italy. After a so-so meal, she contemplated taking a taxi to where the *Independent Endeavor* was moored, but was too tired.

    She would have the entire day tomorrow to find and approach Jack, an encounter destined to be stressful and emotional. It would be well to be alert and rested, so she returned to her room and took a nap. She would dream of reaching the pier just in time to see the ship sail off, with Jack standing on the open deck waving and laughing at her.

After waking in the early evening, she walked a short distance to the old town area of Liverpool. It was dark by the time she left her room, but going out at night alone no longer frightened her. She wanted to see the place where *The Beatles* first performed.

The Cavern Club was great. There were lots of little souvenir shops and clubs nearby capitalizing on "Beatlemania." She found a number of small things to buy, both for herself and her friends. By the time she returned to her lodging it was after 11:00 p.m. Had she fallen asleep instantly — had she revisited the same dream she experienced while napping earlier — that dream would have been a textbook example of extrasensory perception.

As she pulled the covers over her, the *Independent Endeavor* gently slid from the restraint of her mooring lines. Slowly and quietly she edged her way into the Irish Sea and eventually sailed into the North Atlantic Ocean.

Jack Gillette was the only passenger. He stood at the railing on an outside deck, watching the tugs guide the ship, first through a small lock and into the River Mersey, and eventually into the open waters of Liverpool Bay. It grew colder as onshore objects grew smaller and smaller, with landfall eventually disappearing.

Lynda had missed him once again. She'd missed opportunities in Helsinki and Stockholm, places and times which now seemed so far away. As he stood by the railing, he fantasized of being able to go back in time, back to the good days of his relationship with her. As he tried to envision a different ending, his thoughts seemed to blow away with the cold air that now blew around him, standing on the open deck of the ship.

****

There was no telephone in her room, so Lynda used one in the small, informal reception area of the B & B. She'd hung up more than a minute ago, but her hand still rested on the receiver.

The words, "I'm sorry Miss, the *Independent Endeavor* sailed last night at midnight," still rang in her ears.

"Are you sure? Are you sure we're talking about the same ship? It wasn't supposed to sail until the twenty-first! This can't be!" she'd rattled off in protest at the words.

She took her hand away from the receiver and started back up the stairs to her room. As she took the first steps of the stairway, she willed the telephone to ring, a call from the shipping agent saying he was sorry, of how he'd mistakenly read the wrong line on the departure list.

But the telephone did not ring.

She sat down dejectedly on her bed, staring at the wall before her. She knew it was over. The telephone conversation finalized so many issues. There would be no opportunity to reconcile with Jack. Here in Liverpool, he may have listened to her side of the story, lame and weak as she knew it was.

She stood and walked to the window. It had started to rain. As the tears began to dry, she briefly considered booking a flight back to L.A. "No, I'll see this through to the end in my most pragmatic and stubborn manner," she said to no one.

She knew sleep would be good for her. It would be a safe escape. As the weather turned from a sunny yesterday to a dreary, rainy today, and just before she began to doze off, it puzzled her that she was not more upset at losing 15 million dollars.

The weather changed at sea also. Storm clouds loomed above while wind and rain pelted the ship. The *Independent Endeavor*, although smaller than the ship which carried Jack across the Pacific Ocean, was still a very large 680 feet long. Despite its size, it bobbed like a cork in a bathtub as the storm increased.

The ship was following a route which would swing in an arc to the southeast of England and across the Atlantic. According to the Captain, an arc to the northeast would have been preferable, but remnants of a hurricane stood in the way. Any attempt to swing far enough north to avoid it would have placed them in iceberg territory, something which cast an ominous cloud over a voyage originating from the very same departure port of the ill-fated *Titanic*. Further complicating matters, a storm was pushing northward from the gulf stream, catching the ship in a vice between the two weather systems.

****

Lynda rented a car the next morning. Returning to her bed and breakfast, she telephoned her travel agent in Los Angeles.

"I really don't care when it sails, but I would like to sail out of Liverpool," she told the woman. "And, it has to land somewhere on the east coast."

"Well, I'll have to make some calls, ah .., see what's available. All truth be told, your trip to Hong Kong was the first freighter cruise I'd ever arranged. I hope it was satisfactory."

Lynda didn't have the heart to tell her how bad the first trip was, how sick she was and the trouble encountered in Vladivostok. After promising to call the agent back in two days, she hung up.

Entering the rental car, she toiled for fifteen minutes in an attempt to get the car into reverse. Thinking she would have to push the vehicle out of its parking space, she looked up to see the innkeeper standing aside her door. He carried a large umbrella to shield him from the steady rain.

"In a bit of a bother, are ya love?" he questioned.

She explained the problem, and he pointed out a small button, almost imperceptible, molded into the gearshift lever. She felt foolish as she now easily maneuvered the car into reverse. With a wave of her hand she sped off, driving nonchalantly on the wrong side of the road.

Her first reaction to the swerves and honking horns of other drivers was to scream and wonder why they couldn't instantly recognize her as a foreigner. As she continued, she became more comfortable, and was amazed the drivers were so courteous. True, there were looks of bewilderment and confusion, but no one flipped her the middle finger. Try driving down the wrong side of the road in L.A. and see what kind of reaction you get, she thought to herself.

After visiting the Merseyside Maritime Museum, featuring exhibits of the *Titanic*, the famous British luxury liner that sunk in 1912, she drove north through Blackpool and Fleetwood. She stayed along the coastal road A-558 until veering west to Morecombe. On a whim, she followed signs for a ferry to the coastal town of Heysham.

Rounding a corner, a pub came into view. She did not intend to stop, but when she saw a elderly woman enter the front door with her dog, she abruptly changed her mind.

Inside, the pub looked to be 200 years old. Although the rain had stopped, the day still had the flavor of damp and dismal. A fire crackled in a small fireplace. Two men her age were talking soccer, rugby or some such sport at the bar, while three couples shared a late lunch together at a large table. The elderly woman sat alone in a far corner of the room.

She bought a glass of wine and walked over, asking the woman if she could join her and her dog. They were both delighted. Taking a seat, Lynda noticed the menu, printed crudely on a folded table tent. It featured items like, "Cauliflower and Cheese Pasty" for 2 pounds, and "Beans on Toast" for 1 pound, 60.

Lynda inquired about the ferry, and the woman's reply suddenly provoked her decision. In this quaint, old and rustic pub called the Fleece Inn, the words from the woman made her smile.

"Ah, Dear. It's so lovely. I've not been for many years, but it's so lovely. You're young, and ya should go."

"Well, I think I will," she heard herself say.

Lynda finished her wine, said goodbye to the woman and her dog Maxwell, and walked out. She was going to the Isle of Man.

For a reason she could not empathize with, Jack cried when they watched the movie, *Waking Ned Devine*. Filmed on the island, she found it ironic the movies theme, that of someone winning the lottery, mirrored the theme of her life and the circumstances of the last few months. Although the movie left the viewer thinking the lives of the people of the village would not change dramatically, she wondered if her life would ever be the same.

"No," she said aloud to herself, sitting behind the wheel of the car and surprising herself with the sound of her own voice, "My life will never be the same."

Arriving in the port of Douglas four hours later, she immediately traveled south to Port Erin. She found a nice B & B to spend the night. She knew she was acting without a plan or goal, but it did not bother her.

A week later, she returned to Liverpool, and after checking in to the same lodgings as before, she made some telephone calls.

"Where have you been?" the travel agent asked frantically. "I was worried about you! The guy there was hard to understand. He said you checked out, but would be back in a week or so!"

"Well, I went to the Isle of Man for awhile," she said, feeling no other explanation was necessary. "What have you got for me?"

"I'll have to call back and see if it's still possible. But, if it is, you're to sail out of Liverpool the day after tomorrow, the third of October."

Lynda told her to book the trip, and to call her back with the details.

"Don't you even want to know where it goes?" the travel agent asked, bewilderingly.

Three days later, she was aboard the *Nordic Discoverer*, a container ship bound for Richmond, Virginia. She was the only passenger. She never got sick, even when the Captain warned her at breakfast the condition of the sea was still somewhat rough from a storm passing through ten days earlier. She arrived rested and relaxed in Richmond on October 12th.

As she rode the train towards Chicago, she examined her current situation. Unless Jack lingered somewhere along his train route from Philadelphia to Los Angeles, he would have arrived home on October 9th. There was one place he might stop. She would stop there as well, for old times sake as well as the slim possibility of seeing him.

After a brief layover in Chicago, she changed trains and continued west aboard Amtrak's, *Empire Builder*. The route took her through Wisconsin, Minnesota, North Dakota and Montana.

From Montana the train swung southward through Idaho and into the State of Washington. She traveled along the magnificent Columbia Gorge to Portland, Oregon, and then south to Albany. She left the train there and rented a car. It was a short 25 mile drive to where she spent four years in college, and the place where she first laid eyes on a handsome, relatively shy, fellow college student named Jack Gillette.

It was a few years later when she met him again in southern California. He seemed so much more worldly than before, so much more a complete and self-assured man. Yet, he still had an almost childlike approach to life. It was this childlike quality that attracted her to him, and it was the same quality which allowed her to drift away. She found it interesting that the cute, charming and divergent qualities which attract one person to another, through repetition and habit so often become trite, and the object of one's scorn.

Corvallis, Oregon had changed so much she barely recognized it. The Oregon State University campus seemed so small, and the town around it so much larger than before. High tech industry, taxing the infrastructure, added to the urban sprawl.

After a couple of hours however, it seemed like the same old place. "Sleepy and a couple of steps short of today," was the way she always described it to

people. In essence, those traits were what made it a good place to go to school.
Learning was plentiful while distractions were minimal.

A parkway and series of bike paths were built along the river which skirted
the downtown area. She found a small cafe, located a seat outside and ordered
a glass of wine. It was early afternoon.

****

Jack arrived in Philadelphia on September 28th. The Captain invited him
to travel onward to Richmond, Virginia, but he declined. His trip was almost
over, and he wanted to get home.

Unfortunately, his reservation on Amtrak was not scheduled for departure
from Philadelphia until October 4th. He thought of changing the ticket to an
earlier date, but opted instead to just hang around Philadelphia for six days. He
spent his time reading, writing and lolling around the hotel.

Before boarding the train bound for Chicago, he bought a couple of books
to read along the way. He'd seen very little of the United States, and after
several miles on the train, he put the books in one of his bags, content to peruse
the scenery of his own country.

Throughout his around the world trip, delays were few. Even being hit by
a car in Greece was an event which added to his list of good experiences. No
accident would have meant no Fossano, and the wonderful experience of visiting an Italian hospital. If not for the crazy, card-playing Chinese men on the
train ride from Xian to Shanghai, there would have been no experience of
drunken, hospitable camaraderie. Therefore, when he was informed in Portland, Oregon that he would have to take a bus 100 miles south to Eugene because of a derailment, he calculated this as another opportunity to have a strange
and exciting experience on the road.

He was on the bus, seated, with his bags safely stowed like a dog biscuit in
the belly of the greyhound when he changed his mind. The driver seemed to
care less that someone didn't want to ride with him, but the baggage handlers
were a little more vocal.

"Why'd ya get on if yer just goin' ta get off?" asked one, as he handed
Jack's bags back to another man. "If yer thinkin' the trains going to start running before the end of the day, ya got another think a-coming. Shit, it may be a
month before they get the thing on the track again," he laughed.

Jack walked away with his bags, passing through the train station to an
area where a couple of taxis waited. He'd grown up outside of Portland, and
knew the city well.

"Jake's," he told the driver. "No, take me first to the Mallory Hotel. "I
hope it's still there," he said, fearing a repeat of the disaster that befell him in
Australia when he'd told the taxi driver to take him to the Buchanan Hotel.

"Yeah, the Mallory is still there, and so is Jake's," replied the driver, speeding out of the drive and onto the street a little faster than necessary.

It was a short ride, and soon Jack was checked into a room on the fourth floor. He took a shower, put on a clean shirt and walked down the street to Jake's, a classic, landmark bar in downtown Portland.

His plan was to stay in Portland for a couple of days, and later reboard the bus to Eugene. But, after a couple of beers he was bored. He wandered over to Powell's Book Store, and after roaming the myriad of stacks, went back to his hotel.

The next morning he rented a car, leaving Portland behind. He wanted to visit the small town where he attended college. I'll spend the afternoon there, he thought to himself, as he accelerated up a ramp and onto the southbound lanes of Interstate 5. After a short visit in Corvallis, it would be another 60 mile drive to Eugene. He could reboard the train there for the 1000 mile journey home.

That was his plan.

<u>24</u>

Lynda looked over to see a woman pulling a couple of tables together. The after work crowd would soon arrive, as it was approaching 5:00 p.m.

She imagined being home in Los Angeles and sharing a drink with friends. The thought made her reflect on how much L.A. was not a home for her, and how she and Jack often talked of leaving. It was her protests which kept them there.

And, what about friends? How many did she really have? Bill was never a friend. He was her boss and her sex partner, but he was never really a friend. Why, she thought, did I ever go to bed with him? What attraction had there been? She couldn't think of one.

She had women friends, but none who were close. With the exception of her sister in Phoenix, there was no "soul sister" she could confide and trust with her innermost thoughts and secrets.

Someone once told her that every woman should have a man who they could call their best friend. Lynda couldn't think of anyone in her life who fit that description — anyone that is, but Jack. She feared she'd lost not only her lover, but her best friend as well.

Three more women joined the party at the table next to hers. Minutes later, she scooted her chair in to allow yet another person to join the group. When the cocktail waitress came by, it was evident by their conversation they were regulars, or possibly worked at this restaurant.

Lynda gestured to the waitress and ordered another glass of wine. She opened a book she purchased at a remote train station in Montana during a brief stop. The novel was a mystery involving Scotland Yard's finest. It was rather boring, but the dialog brought back fond memories of England.

She'd read only a few pages when a person whom she surmised to be the guest of honor arrived at the table next to her's. She was blonde and Lynda's age, or possibly a couple years younger. Beautiful in a rather plain sort of way, she wore little, if any, make-up, and was casually dressed in jeans and a plain, white top.

But, it wasn't her appearance that attracted Lynda's attention. She was sitting close enough to the group to be able to listen to their conversation if she cared to. It didn't interest her, but when this woman showed up and the group seemed so collectively delighted to see her, Lynda turned to see what the interest was. She then heard the woman speak for the first time.

"Tis as I expected, it tis!" the woman said. "A fine lot ya are, the whole lot of ya!"

The words made Lynda smile. She wanted to ask what part of England the stranger was from, but instead turned back to her book. She managed to read a page or two in the next ten minutes, sitting there with her back to the group and listening to their laughter and the woman's accent.

Apparently some of them worked together, and when the manager came out and told the guest of honor she was welcome to return to her job at the restaurant whenever she chose, the story became complete. When the manager made a remark about kangaroos, Lynda ascertained the woman's nationality.

Lynda had just ordered her third glass of wine and was starting to get interested in her book, when something caught her ear.

"... and what about Jack, the world traveler," said one of the girls.

Lynda nearly knocked over her glass. She tried to take a drink, but noticed her hands were shaking, and she spilled some of her wine. The women's conversation fell quieter. She heard bits and pieces then, nothing substantial enough to come to a definite conclusion.

"I acted a bit of the naggin' wife, I did. Treated him terrible," said the Australian woman. " ... and he up an left." Lynda heard her say.

The tone of the conversation changed as well. Gone was the laughter, and when someone spoke to the Australian, it was with respectfulness. "You still have a couple of days, don't you? He still might come back," Lynda heard someone say.

Lynda was having a hard time believing this was happening. She was straining to hear some words which would invalidate what she was thinking and the coincidence of what she was hearing.

"You could always fly to L.A. before flying home to Sydney and Hogga Wogga, or whatever it is," said another girl.

The laughter from the last statement was in sharp contrast to the empty hurt which Lynda felt. She sat in a daze, her stomach feeling as though she'd consumed two and a half glasses of battery acid, not wine. The pain was rising in her chest as she listened further.

"It's bloody Wagga Wagga, is what it is, eh!" said the Australian. "I reckon I got another two days here to sit round the kitchen waitin', I do. And, I reckon I might just have to create a bit of a layover in Los Angeles." The conversation changed, back to the laughter filled one cultivated before.

Lynda waited until the party was breaking up before turning around. She saw the Australian girl for what she really was. Listening closely, she learned the woman's name was Yolanda. She was younger than Lynda had first thought, possibly as much as five years younger than herself. She was about five-six, tan, trim and athletic looking. She was beautiful, and exactly the kind of woman Jack would fall for.

Enough of the conversation was heard to be sure of several things. First and foremost, the person named Jack was her Jack. At one point, one of the women asked the Australian if she knew his last name. The question brought more laughs and later seriousness, as the response to the question reflected a mood of tenderness and melancholy.

Lynda learned Jack was here, possibly sitting at this very table. He'd met this beautiful waitress with the mysteriously lilting accent. More had happened, and she could only begin to imagine. Knowing Jack, he would have moved very slowly, possibly too slowly for the Aussie. She also knew there were some problems — some rift which halted their high speed romance. As quick and as short as the romance was, Lynda was convinced it was far from over. The fact remained the Australian was returning home, and the return was permanent.

The women all left, along with most of the after work crowd. Lynda sat quietly at the table, stunned by the events. What did she expect? She reflected upon all the beautiful women she'd seen in Europe, and shook her head at her stupidity and blindness.

"Can I get you anything more?" came a voice to her left.

She looked up from where she sat to see a waitress hovering over her shoulder. "No, just the check, please."

As the waitress started to turn, Lynda stopped her. "Excuse me," she added. "The woman who was having the party here, ah the blonde from Australia, I believe. She used to work here, isn't that right?"

"Yeah, she did. I never really got to know her very well though. I've only been working here a few of weeks. She was in graduate school, or something."

Working at a law firm, Lynda learned that people would often tell you everything you wanted to know and more if you kept quiet and listened. It always amazed her. "Oh?" she said.

"Yeah. I think she was only in Corvallis for a couple of terms or something, not a long time. I know everyone sure liked her," speaking as if she'd already left town.

"She's gorgeous. Probably left a trail of broken hearts," said Lynda.

"Yeah, you're probably right. I know she met some guy here she fell head over heels in love with, or at least that's what it sounded like."

"Really?"

"Yeah," the waitress replied with the word she used to start almost every sentence. "Some guy who was traveling around the world without getting on an airplane. I talked to him about it one day. It was pretty cool. He gave me the web address for the newspaper he writes for in California. I can't wait to read about it."

If there was any doubt in Lynda's mind, it was now gone.

"He's on to bigger and better things?" asked Lynda, her response sounding more like a statement than a question.

"Yeah, I guess," the waitress paused, as if wondering if he'd really in fact left town, or wondering if there was some place bigger and better than Corvallis, Oregon. "Ya know, ah ... I got a feelin' he'll be back. He spent a lot of time here, right over there at that table," she said, pointing to a small, secluded table near the corner of the building. "His eyes lit up whenever she came to work or waited on him. Yeah, I think he might just come back."

The Australian said she had two more days. As Lynda's waitress left to get her check, she thought to herself. Two more days. What's two more days? I've got no job, and I don't consider L.A. my home.

"Yeah," she said aloud, unknowingly picking up the waitress's habit. "What's two more days?"

****

"Emeryville," the loudspeaker announced. There followed the customary message about allowing people to get on and off the train, and that those wishing to smoke would have ten minutes to do so.

Jack looked out the window of his small, efficient roomette in one of the sleeping cars, checking his watch as he did so. Last night, he noticed his wristwatch was stuck on 5:30. Looking at the watch now, he realized the futility of the timepiece and the last few days.

Just beyond the station he could see a hotel. He hadn't slept well for reasons he wished to ignore, and the mere sight of the hotel made him sleepy. He stared at the building, and with every second he sat staring, he knew he was closer to being home. Then he thought, Where is home?

"You have to open the door!" said Jack, rather frantically.

"But sir, the train is leaving!"

"I don't care. I have to get off!" He reached past the conductor and turned the handle on the door. Jack stepped off the train, his bags dragging along beside him. He wondered if in his haste he might have left something in his room. If that was the case, it was too late. He watched the rear end of the last car quietly disappear to the south.

He was 600 miles away from the City of Los Angeles — 9 or 10 hours away from a city he called home simply because he worked, slept and ate there. He stood in the same spot for nearly five minutes before turning to lug his bags through the station. The hotel was only a couple hundred yards away, but a series of pedestrian overpasses almost tripled the distance.

He checked in for one night and then limped back to the station. There, he bought a one-way ticket for Albany, Oregon, to depart the next day. Once in Albany, he'd either rent a car or take a taxi to Corvallis. It wasn't home, but it's where he wanted to be.

There were no sleepers available, so the next morning Jack made do with a first-class reserved seat for the trip north. Luckily, the car he was assigned to was only half full. No one occupied the seat next to him, and a mere fifty miles out of Emeryville, with the train speeding through open country and northward towards Oregon, he fell asleep.

He dreamed of his eight, wonderful days in Corvallis....

****

Jack had arrived in Corvallis from Portland without a plan. From the window of his motel room on the bank of the Willamette River, he could see the slow moving river working its way north to join the Columbia and eventually ease its way into the Pacific Ocean. Across the river was a golf course, complete with colorful dressed players intent on perfecting a game impossible to play perfectly.

When Jack attended school in Corvallis, the golf course was simply farm land. The motel he was staying in did not exist then, and a bike and walking path along the rivers edge was but a thought in some city planners mind.

That first night, he went to a neighboring restaurant for dinner. He'd asked the waitress to bring him a telephone book while he enjoyed an after dinner cup of coffee. Trying to remember names of school friends and acquaintances, he searched the white pages. Corvallis is a small town with a population of about 80,000, but it seemed many of his friends had, like himself, moved on after college.

He noticed an ad for an insurance agency on the cover of the phone book, listing the name of father and sons peddling term life and auto insurance policies since 1952. He recognized one of the names as that of a man whose wife was a friend of Jack's wife. He wondered if the Paul Craviotto of Craviotto & Sons Insurance, was still married.

The second day, he went for a walk. It was late morning, and as he passed a restaurant on the bike and walking path, he noticed a woman struggling to open a large umbrella over one of the outside tables. It was something he could not help but notice. The woman's back faced him as he walked a short distance away. Leaning over the table and wrestling with the mechanism, her short dress was hiked up another four or five inches. She had great legs.

He opened a small gate leading onto the restaurants outside deck. "Would you like some help?"

"Oh," she said, startled to find someone standing next to her. "Ga-day. I could do with a bit of help, I could."

God, she's an English woman, he said to himself, enjoying the accent. Jack reached over, and after some manipulation, forced the push button holding the umbrella down to release. He pushed up on the ribs of the structure, and the bright, blue covering bloomed out over their heads.

She thanked him, telling him to, "carry on." He was too enthralled with her beauty and accent to really hear all of her words. He remembered thinking as he turned away, how her blue eyes seemed to sparkle in the bright, morning sunlight.

He'd just stepped onto the path when he looked back, hoping to see her struggling with one of the other umbrellas, hoping to get another look at her legs.

As he looked over his shoulder, she looked over her's at him. They both smiled, somewhat embarrassingly. He walked another twenty feet, thinking of the song by Buck Owens, the lyrics proclaiming, "... I was looking back to see if you were looking back to see, if I was looking back to see if you were looking back at me."

He turned abruptly and started back to the cafe's deck. She stood there watching him now, knowing something was on his mind. Wondering what it was, yet innately knowing.

Yolanda had lived in Corvallis for nine months. She'd come to the United States on an exchange program between an agricultural research center in her town and Oregon State University. Her father and brothers operated a large sheep station outside of Wagga Wagga, a town in New South Wales, Australia, on the Murrumbidgee River. She would return to work on her family's station, or ranch as Americans called them, in less than a fortnight.

While attending school, Yolanda took a job as a waitress on a lark, thinking it would allow her to meet people and overcome the homesickness she felt. She'd made many friends — friends whom she hoped to someday see again.

There were a few interested men, but the interest was rather one-sided. Although there was no man back home who held her heart, she was happy and content with being single. Besides, she didn't want life to be complicated by a long distance relationship.

But now, here was this handsome, seemingly kind-hearted man walking towards her. It was as if it were all happening in slow motion. She was neither ready or eager for his attention, yet she was happily anticipating what would happen.

"Are you open yet, or would it be possible to order a cup of coffee?" he asked, deflating her brief, romantic image.

"I reckon the coffee's on. Have a seat if ya care to," she replied.

The restaurant was not due to open for an hour. Yolanda arrived earlier than scheduled, as was her habit. She'd do the necessary set-up work, put on a pot of coffee and relax at a table with a cup. Once the restaurant opened, she would work at a frantic pace for two hours, and later leave to attend classes.

She brought Jack a cup of coffee, commenting on its freshness and that she herself had yet to enjoy a cup. She set the cup down on the table in front of him.

"I'm not very good at this, but ah ... and, maybe I shouldn't ask," he said, looking away for a moment. "Would you have a drink or a cup of coffee with me sometime?" Jack sheepishly asked.

"I reckon I would if I knew you." Yolanda wanted to say yes — even intended to just say yes — but some inner caution made her reply with a vague maybe.

Jack didn't believe in love at first sight, but he desperately wanted to hang around for awhile. "If you said yes, well, then you'd know me," he smiled.

"Yer a puzzlin' sort, ya are, and the coffee smells good. I've got a few more chores ta do, then I'll come round ta join ya for a few minutes."

She went back in the kitchen, shaking her head in disbelief at what she'd said to the stranger. Why didn't she just say yes, she thought to herself, instead of trying to explain it?

David, the owner and manager, was pouring himself a cup of coffee when she approached. "I'll miss your coffee in the morning," he said.

"I'm pleased ya like it. Say, would it be a bother if I sat down with that man out there for a few minutes. I've got the whole lot ready to open." She knew he'd say yes, but she was stalling for time. She didn't want to return too quickly and seem too anxious.

A few minutes later she was sitting across the table from Jack. They introduced themselves to each other, Jack asking what part of England she was from, it being a mistaken identity now common to her. They talked about her home, and what it was like. He told her of his journey, and how it was about to end.

When it was time for her to go back to work, Jack said he might come back and have lunch, asking her if she worked all afternoon. She told him she got off at 2:30.

Her father had taught her to be bold. Growing up on a sheep station with three brothers and the nearest neighbor over 15 kilometers away, necessitated being confident and taking measures into your own hands. Boldness with sheep and the vagaries of rural life was different however, than boldness with a man. "If ya could manage without tucker until then, well, I'd be hungry myself, I reckon," she surprisingly found herself saying.

Yolanda made a lot of mistakes that day in her efforts to serve people. She constantly felt as if she was a step behind in everything she did. She gave the wrong change twice, forgot to change the paper roll in the credit card machine, and spilled a glass of wine. Luckily, Robin, the other waitress, was able to take up the slack and help whenever necessary.

She found herself constantly thinking of the man she had just met. She briefly worried he might not return, but quickly set aside those thoughts. No, he'd return. The look on his face when she told him she would have lunch with him after work, was like that of a six-year-old boy on Christmas morning.

She also imagined the strangest things as she bumped around waiting tables, trying to undo mistakes amid lapses of concentration. She knew her father would like him. She thought of how her mother would like him too. Her brothers would tease and harass him at first, all in a good-natured way. She felt he would handle her brothers just fine, and by nightfall, a stranger would see a family of four brothers instead of three.

The end of her shift finally came, and she went outside where Robin was working. She'd told him a single man was seated outside, and Yolanda had peeked to happily see him sitting at a small table off by himself. She walked over, and he got up from the table. The moment was awkward for her, and she was nervous. She extended her hand, instantly thinking how dumb can I be. He doesn't want to shake hands.

He took her hand and reached out for the other one as well. They stood there facing each other for a moment or two, their hands still comfortably held together as one. He asked where she'd like to go for lunch, or if she preferred, they could eat right here.

Yolanda missed two classes that afternoon. It was the first time since arriving in Corvallis that she'd missed a class. She hardly thought about it. They ate lunch and enjoyed a couple of drinks. They talked for hours.

It was approaching 5:00 p.m., when he asked, "So, I know this may sound strange, but I was going to ask you to have dinner with me before you left for Australia."

"You'll be leaving before I shall," she interrupted.

"Maybe. I don't know. But, well, why don't we have dinner tonight?"

"We just finished eating." She was teasing him now. As relaxed as their conversation was, he seemed uncomfortable when asking her to dinner.

"We could meet somewhere, if you'd prefer. There's a restaurant right next to my motel that seems pretty good," Jack offered.

She knew where he was staying by now, and knew the restaurant he was speaking of. She wanted to play a little harder to get, but found herself incapable of the effort.

They kissed for the first time that night, a rather awkward kiss in the parking lot of the restaurant just before she got in her car to drive home. The awkward attempt was quickly followed by a kiss which was longer, more exploratory and relaxed. That kiss was followed by another and another. To her, the affection felt as though it belonged. She had a strange sensation of being home again.

"I should go," Jack said to her, his arms around her in such a way as to suggest his intent was to stay. "But, I want to see you tomorrow. If tomorrow is as good as today, well then, I must warn you, I'll want to see you the next day as well."

They saw each other for the next eight days in a row. On the fifth day of their relationship they made love to each other at her home. That same day, he left the motel and took up residence at her small apartment.

Yolanda's duties at the university were all but over, and luckily she had no exams. Just the same, she felt it necessary to visit campus one day and explain to several professors how busy she was with preparing to move home. One professor actually commented on how happy she looked. "Going home must agree with you. You look so radiantly happy," he had said.

Jack and Yolanda's time together was marked by a lot of love making and many hours of just talking. He told her about his discovery of Lynda's affair. She related an account of a love affair she'd had in Australia. Her relationships were all ancient history, buried a long time ago. She silently wished his love affair had dissolved more than a mere six months ago.

The first time they made love, he told her he could easily fall in love with her. He asked her if she was comfortable with that. She hadn't answered right away, and in fact didn't answer until after they had spent all of their lust and energy. They were lying naked on the bed, the comforter long ago having fallen to the floor. It was warm outside, and her upstairs apartment was not insulated very well. A small fan, swinging left and right, hummed the same tune over and over from a night stand in the corner.

"I've loved you since the moment you turned around and started on yer walkabout back to where I was standing on the veranda there," she said. She touched the corner of her mouth with her tongue in a nervous gesture as she awaited his reply to such a defenseless, open statement. She could taste the saltiness of sweat that was a mixture of both his and hers.

It was well into their whirlwind, eight day romance when Jack told Yolanda about the money. It was something he'd avoided discussing, for reasons he could not explain to himself. The omission was bothering him, making him feel as if he were hiding something extremely important to their future. Having just finished her work shift, they were walking along the path by the river.

"There's something I need to talk to you about," he said, changing the subject from what they were discussing. Seeing a look of concern come over her face, he added, "It's not a big deal, really. It's just something I've needed to tell you ... something that's always taken a back seat to more important things."

They kept walking, but he could feel the rhythm in her walk change slightly, their steps now not so much in sync as they'd been just seconds before. He debated whether or not he should make something up, something trivial and of no consequence.

"I've told you about Lynda and her boyfriend, the guy that's old enough to be her father. What I didn't tell you is that, well, they have been following me around the world. Chasing me, actually."

Yolanda stopped walking. This was just too good of a relationship for it to end with the man of her dreams turning out to be a criminal, or perhaps something even worse. "What did you do?" the words coming out much more accusingly than she intended.

Jack laughed. "Oh, you're so cute when you get a look of concern!" he laughed again. "I didn't do anything really. It's more like something very lucky happened to me."

She was still frozen to the spot of ground where she'd stopped, so he stopped and explained. "I won the California lottery. I won a whole bunch of money, more than I could ever spend in a lifetime."

He explained the e-mail offer he'd sent Lynda the day he boarded the *Hanjin Amsterdam* almost six months ago. He related Dan's message upon his arrival in Hong Kong, as well as Lynda's reply to his offer of a return flight to Los Angeles.

"The money doesn't mean anything to me. It's very important you understand that. I don't want luxury yachts or airplanes. I don't want a butler or fast cars. I just want to live each and every day to its fullest. I want Monday to be Monday, and not the first of five days before the weekend arrives, a weekend and two days of peace before it's Monday all over again and I'm looking forward to Friday."

"I've asked you before, but well, I hope yer not muckin' about with me now. Do you still love er', Jack Gillette? Out with it, if ya do."

"Yes, of course I still love her," he said, knowing instantly he'd answered too quickly, and answered with the wrong response. He quickly added, "But, the important thing is I'm no longer in love with her. I suppose in time I could even learn to forgive her, but our relationship as lovers, and as a couple, well ... that's over. It's taken awhile, but I'm okay with it now."

"Do you have her e-mail address?"

Jack nodded yes.

"If the money means nothing, and ya don't hate her ... e-mail her and tell her you'll give her the half you promised. Be done with it."

"But, she has to catch me to get half, and I'm almost home."

"But, ya just told me you wanted her to catch you, that you were originally going to wait somewhere in China ... wait for her and then go on together!"

"That was before my friend Dan e-mailed me about her and her boss," he quickly replied.

Yolanda was becoming worried and upset with each exchange of words. They were still standing there on the bloody footpath where this conversation began. Was this relationship the sort she feared? Was he still hung up on this Sheila who'd carried on with someone behind his back? The last few days she'd been happier than she'd ever remembered being in her life. She knew in her heart this man was the right one for her, but was she the right one for him?

"I don't understand. You say you love me, yet you say you still love her. You tell me you made a promise to er', yet now you dislike her so much you'll not be straight with er', and you'll not keep your promise."

He was wondering why he'd ever broached the subject. "Listen to me," he said, putting his hands on her shoulders. "I love you very much. Each day we spend together, I fall deeper and deeper in love with you. We've both got a lot to go through together ... our relationship is so young. If we can work everything out, I'd like it to work out so we spend the rest of our lives together. I feel that strongly about us. I love you that much."

"But, I'm going home, Jack! You're going back to Los Angeles where she'll be. You told me once that your trip changed you. What if it changed her too ... changed her for the better? Then what? I'm in Wagga Wagga whilst you're with her. I'm sorry, but I don't believe absence makes the heart grow fonder. All it does is make the bloody memory grow dimmer."

She turned to walk away. He was forced to let go of her shoulders to keep her from struggling to get away. He walked after her, talking with her, and trying to get her to understand. After prolonged pleadings from him she said she did, but her words rang hollow.

Jack entertained thoughts of moving to Australia, much as Yolanda thought of moving to Los Angeles. But, neither the negatives or the positives of such a relocation were discussed. It was ironic, as they walked back to the apartment, that they were thinking the same thing — thinking they should have gone slower — thinking they should have been more realistic.

Jack had one more story to write for the newspaper, and that evening he tried in vain to write it from Yolanda's computer at her kitchen table. It proved to be an impossible task. His heart wasn't in the piece, and it was difficult to concentrate. He wanted to work on his relationship with her. He wanted to somehow patch up the holes he'd put in it earlier in the day.

At 9:00 p.m. he gave up, saying he needed to find an internet hook-up. Yolanda used the internet facilities at the university, and her home computer was not on-line. He'd hoped she would ask to go along, but she made no effort to. He walked a few blocks from the apartment to a Kinko's copier store. Renting a Mac, he sat down and started working with no idea of what he would write.

Fuck it, he finally said to himself. It's not like they're going to fire me.

The Golden Age Of Travel

I have always dreamed of traveling to distant lands and traveling around the world — far away places with strange sounding names. I have accomplished that, or at least I will have after my final 1000 mile train ride from Oregon to Los Angeles.

I've seen more of the world than the average person. Yet, when I look at a map or globe and visually stick pins in all of the places I've been — I've experienced such a small part of this earth.

I'm blessed to have been able to travel. As this trip quickly comes to an end, I realize how blessed I am to have traveled at the very end of what I term, "The Golden Age of Travel." I fear those days, like so much water under the bridge, are irrevocably gone forever.

There was a time during the Golden Age, when a person would seek out places not experienced by other travelers. The only people they would encounter on their journey would be the natives of that land. Most, if not all of those places are a thing of the past.

In the years that followed, the wanderer would search for cultures living in a different, bygone age. Comforts would be few, and western influence minimal. Those goals were replaced with journeys to countries or cities where there were no McDonald's, Burger Kings or Kentucky Fried Chicken restaurants. Locations lacking this commercialism are quickly becoming a thing of the past as well. There is a Starbucks in Shanghai, and I attended the opening night of The Outback Steakhouse in Beijing.

Just a few years ago, a traveler traveling from western to eastern Europe by train, would feel the train come to a halt at the border. This cease in forward movement always seemed to happen at one or two in the morning. Armed border guards, their machine pistols slung over their shoulder would storm through the corridors of the rail cars. Passports would be checked and re-checked.

Flashlights would blink in the night, lighting up sleepy, but tense faces, and making comparisons to bad passport photos all the more ridiculous.

The border guard's hand would move to his belt, brushing against the butt of his holstered pistol. From a holster of a different type he would draw a metal contraption, and with rapid, aggressive hammering he would stamp the traveler's passport once, twice, and sometimes three times. It was all rather terrifying in an exciting, somewhat safe sort of way.

Today, the train doesn't even slow down, and the passport is rarely stamped. A trip to Europe and seven different countries may only reap one small, measly stamp from the airport of arrival.

Beginning in January of 2002, another vestige of the Golden Age disappeared. The Eurodollar replaced a great share of Europe's varied currency.

One of the great thrills of travel was to land in a foreign country, go through customs and proceed to a currency exchange. Through the small window opening, the traveler would pass familiar looking currency or travelers checks. Hands like a card dealer's would flit around behind the glass. Strange colors would become visible, disappearing just as quickly and replaced by some other unidentifiable color, shape or design. In an instant, money was pushed back through the window.

The line behind you would surge forward, and you'd step aside to marvel at the notes in your hand. Instead of seeing Jefferson's or George Washington's familiar face, you'd see the Minister of Something-Or-Other or the Duke of Here-And-There. The smile that would come over the face of the traveler at that moment is now gone forever.

And, there are so many people traveling today. So many in fact, that we categorize them as tourists, travelers, backpackers, day-trippers or wanderers. Beyond that are the extremists, intent upon scaling some distant mountain top or rafting down a river the guidebooks all claim to be impassable.

Rick Steves, Michael Palen and others of that ilk combine with publishers like Lonely Planet, The Rough Guide *and* Let's Go. *They all tell you the same thing, that is, they tell you where to go so you will be comfortable and somewhat familiar with your surroundings.*

A reader will never come across a passage written by one of these authors or publications which says, in effect; "I've never been to this place, and I haven't a clue what it's like. But I suggest you go there. If you live through it, (and the traveler probably would), don't write and tell me about it."

The days of exploration are gone. Someone has already been there and is more than willing to share their opinion of it.

Today, most people fly in an insulated, air-conditioned cocoon with vistas of blue sky and even more blue sky. They check out of a Hilton Hotel in Pittsburgh and check into a Sheraton in Frankfurt. The remote for the televisions all work the same.

Thanks to the Chunnel, you can drive from England to France. What's more terrifying is, the reverse is also possible. No one goes anywhere without a reservation and a cell phone. A postcard is archaic — send an e-mail. For the news, pick up a <u>USA Today</u> in either an Asian or European edition. Or, check out one of the many English language channels on the television in your hotel room.

I once overheard a person say; "No, we don't care for Mexico. You can't drink the water and nobody speaks English." There are people who travel to foreign lands secretly hoping for something different, and upon arrival are disappointed that familiar comforts and luxuries are not available to them.

Ultimately, the entrepreneurs and developers arrive. Western appointments in the form of restaurants and hotel chains follow. The tourist is bathed in familiarity — but, it is often the same tourist who complained about the lack of familiarity that now complains because the land is too commercialized.

I will continue to travel because it is who I am.

I'll always try to stay at the small, personable bed and breakfast or pensione hotel.

I'll hope to be comfortable in what I find are unfamiliar surroundings.

I'll revel at meeting the people of the land rather than seeing a landmark.

The Golden Age of Travel is over, or at the very least, seeing its last days.

I'm thankful I had a chance to experience a small part of it. I'm thankful my dreams came true.

Happy Trails,

Jack

After a cursory and thoughtless spelling and grammatical review, he e-mailed the piece. Walking slowly back to Yolanda's apartment, he felt as if he were treading water, the sight of land slipping further and further away as the tide and current took him out to sea.

Was she right? Should he just e-mail Lynda and cough up the fifteen million? The money didn't mean anything to him, and for a moment he thought it might have been better to have never won. Lynda would still been cheating on him however, and he would never have taken the trip or met Yolanda.

She was reading when he returned. "You were away a bit longer than I'd thought," she said matter-of-factly.

He stood before her as she sat in a chair in the small living room of the apartment. Boxes were stacked here and there, more boxes packed now than before. He reached down and took her hand, helping her to stand before him. He kissed her lightly on the forehead, and then they passionately embraced and kissed one another.

"I'm sorry if I upset you," he said.

She put her fingers on his lips to quiet him, but he took her hand, kissed the tips of her fingers, and went on, "You are what I want, and with you is where I want to be. We both have things we need to resolve, ah ... especially me. And it's possible things might not work out for us. But I want to put my heart, soul, and energy into trying to make us work."

"Oh Jack," she cooed. "It's all happened so fast, has it not? Maybe too fast."

"No ...."

She interrupted. "Yes, it's all happened too fast. Six months ago you were happy with someone else. Ya need more time than that. Go home to L.A. Try an sort things out a bit. Maybe we could meet for Christmas somewhere. If we still feel the same then, well ..., we can carry on."

"No. Please don't give up on this so easily."

"I'm not giving up. I just don't want to get involved with someone who isn't ready. And, I'm leaving soon. Don't know when exactly, but I'll be returning home. And you, I just don't think yer ready."

They talked well into the night. They both cried and held each other, but they didn't make love again.

Yolanda departed for the university early the next morning, leaving Jack sitting at the kitchen table. Hurting with the pain of their conflict, he wrote her a long letter. He left the tear stained paper and her extra key on the kitchen table, and forced himself to walk out the door. The relinquished key, followed by the lock clicking when he pulled the apartment door closed, made him think how irrevocable so many of the little things in life were. A word here or there, an action or reaction, or sometimes just a simple gesture seemed so final and conclusive — forever changing the future.

He rode silently in a taxi to Albany, thinking how his heart ached at the beginning of this trip, and how it once again ached as he neared its conclusion. He'd attempted to convince Yolanda his relationship with Lynda was over, yet he knew the possibility of their relationship being regained intensely bothered her.

"You were my friend before ye were me lover," she had said. "An see how quickly it changed. All ya bloody had to do was turn around an walk into my arms."

As he stood alone on the platform of the Albany, Oregon Amtrak station, his magical relationship with Yolanda hung in the balance. She hadn't exactly thrown him out, but she said it was best if he left.

****

Returning to Albany from California, Jack rented a car. He drove the thirty-odd miles to Corvallis. The weather had cooled dramatically during his three day absence. It was still comfortable, and he always felt October in the Willamette Valley was the best time of the year. The leaves on the trees were changing in a rainbow of colors, the smell of harvested crops hung in the air, and the cool night air seemed to make the mildly warm days that much more enjoyable.

As he drove, he hoped and prayed for a positive reunion. He knew he'd been wrong to just leave without personally saying goodbye to her, but he couldn't bear the hurt it was sure to bring.

He knocked on the door several times, each time a little louder, but to no avail. It was 4:00 p.m. She was no longer working at the restaurant, and Jack remembered her saying she was all but finished at the university as well. He left his car at the apartment and walked along the leaf strewn sidewalks, shuffling his feet purposely to create a path through the tinder-dry leaves that in some places were over four inches deep.

If you get back to your apartment, if you recognize the rental car, if you "reckon" I've gone to the restaurant — just follow my trail through the leaves, he daydreamed.

Entering the small restaurant, Jack saw no one he knew or recognized. He walked through the dining area and opened the swinging doors of the kitchen, peeking inside. He heard the voice before his eyes made contact, and once that occurred he strolled in.

"Well, if it isn't my old friend the world traveler," said the restaurant's owner David Andrews, setting down several boxes on a stainless topped table. They shook hands.

"I don't suppose Yolanda's around, is she?" asked Jack.

"She told me goodbye a couple of days ago, but I don't remember exactly when she was leaving town," David replied, looking around for a moment before shouting, "Chris!"

After the cook named Chris poked his head out of a walk-in refrigerator, David nodded towards the boxes with no verbal instructions, as if the nod itself was sufficient direction.

"Has Yolanda left town yet, or is she still hangin' round somewhere?" David asked the cook, asking him as if she might be sitting in the cooler reading a book.

When Chris simply shrugged his shoulders and disappeared behind the door, David turned to Jack and repeated the gesture.

"I thought she had another week or so before she'd have everything wrapped up at school?" questioned Jack.

David shrugged his shoulders again in response.

They talked for a few minutes, David changing the subject and asking Jack about some of the beers he'd experienced while circling the globe. When another employee showed up for work in the small kitchen, David and Jack went out to the bar. The owner invited him to try one of the new micro-beers on tap. Jack declined, opting instead for a Heineken.

Thirty minutes passed. Jack was becoming anxious talking of everything except where Yolanda might be. The bartender didn't know, and the waitress was new, having been hired as Yolanda's replacement.

Seeing Robin, one of Yolanda's co-workers enter the restaurant, he excused himself and met her as she approached the bar. "Hey, how are you?" Before waiting for much of a reply, he asked, "Have you seen Yolanda around anywhere?"

"Oh!" she said, sounding startled. She took him by the arm and steered him a few feet away from the bar, and out of earshot of those sitting there.

"You don't know?" she inquired.

"Know what? Is something wrong?"

"Jack, she left this morning. Cassy and one of her friends from school drove her up to Portland to catch a plane to San Francisco. From there, she plans to fly back to Australia."

"Ah shit." Jack slumped onto a stool at a nearby table. "I've screwed this up too," he said to no one.

Robin put her hand on his shoulder. "She told me you guys had a spat about something, but I didn't think it was any big deal. In fact, I kinda thought she might go to Los Angeles to see you before she flew back home. I know it involved changing her ticket and all, but I know she was thinking about it."

"Really? You think that was her plan?," the news temporarily picking up his spirits. "If so, she'd be there tonight, and now I'm here," he said, instantly slumping back into a dark mood. "Do you know where she'll be staying?"

Robin did not have any more information to add, and told him the next contact she expected was an e-mail from Yolanda after she arrived in Australia. She admitted Yolanda's plan to fly to Los Angeles was a long shot — that her initial efforts to change her ticket were met with monetary penalties and hassles.

"When did she decide to go home?"

"Oh, I'm not sure exactly, but I know it was quite a spur of the moment decision. I think her original ticket had her leaving sometime next week."

Robin excused herself, saying she needed to begin her work shift. By way of the bartender, another beer was put down on the table where he was half standing and half perched on a stool for support from Robin's bad news.

Standing there, he wondered if he should fly home. His home telephone was disconnected, and anyone calling the newspaper would be told he no longer worked there. The problem with her contacting him aside, there was no guarantee she would even go to Los Angeles.

As Jack considered flying to Australia himself, he absentmindedly glanced over and through the windows to the outside patio area. From where he stood he could see his favorite table, the small two-top sitting at the far corner next to an outdoor potted palm. It was the table where he first sat with Yolanda.

In a state of shock, he quickly picked up his beer and moved to another table. It simply could not be possible. From his new vantage point he took a step to his right in order to see the outside table which now commanded one hundred percent of his attention.

He was thankful the bar and the outside area were rapidly filling up with people getting off work. He paid his bill and walked a few feet towards the dining room, keeping people between him and those sitting outside.

She was sitting at the table in such a way that her back was, for the most part, turned toward him. He could see only part of her profile, but what he could see was enough. He was relieved to know she would have needed to completely turn around to see him at the bar where he'd sat with David.

He walked into a portion of the restaurant where he was in a position to fully see her through the window. When she took a drink and briefly looked around while setting it back on the table, he was sure. When it looked as if she might look through the window and directly at him, he ducked down slightly, a woman at a nearby table looking at him in a strange, bewildered way.

Jack walked back to the safety of the bar. The swinging doors leading into the kitchen were just a few feet away and out of Lynda's line of sight. He was sweating nervously, a trickle of the cold liquid running down from his armpit and along his side. He needed to get away from this place.

As he pushed open the swinging doors to enter the kitchen, his mind reeled with ideas of how to get to Los Angeles or San Francisco as soon as possible. Although he didn't harbor much hope he would catch up with Yolanda in either city, his thoughts were more about not making contact with Lynda than making contact with Yolanda.

Safely through the door and starting to walk through the kitchen, Jack spotted the service entrance leading to the alley. He abruptly stopped and turned, colliding with the cook named Chris. "Sorry," he said, walking back towards the swinging doors and the dangers of recognition which lie on the patio. He walked through the bar and out onto the patio.

Her back was to him, and he would have been able to walk right up behind her without detection. If he walked to the street and turned right, she probably would not see him. Even turning left, she would have to look up at just the right instant. Jack's last remaining options flashed before him in a matter of seconds, but his direction never wavered.

He walked to where she sat, brushing against her as he made his way to the opposite side of the small, round table. "May I?" he asked politely, as he pulled out the chair, not waiting for a reply.

She didn't even so much as flinch. A knowing smile on her face, and a half-full bottle of wine on the table, suggested she'd been there for some time. Next to the bottle of Chardonnay, was an empty, unused wine glass. She slid the glass in front of him, and picked up the bottle.

"Or, would you prefer a beer?," she asked, stopping sort of pouring anything in Jack's proffered glass.

"No, I'll have a glass of wine."

He looked at her closely, as her eyes followed the stream of wine filling up the glass. She looked good. She was tan and healthy looking. A paperback novel, some sort of mystery, lay on the table in front of her.

With the glass in his hand, he offered a silent toast, and took a sip of wine.

"So, how did you find me?"

"You forget. You found me," she said coyly.

"So, you didn't see me standing inside a few minutes ago?" Jack asked.

"No, I didn't. I had a feeling you might show up, but I wasn't sure. When I got here an hour or so ago, I did a lot of rubbernecking for the first fifteen minutes. But, after that I just sat here and read, sort of letting things happen as they will ... sorta leaving it all to fate."

"Where's Bill?"

She took a deep breath, the sureness on her face diminishing only slightly.

"Jack, I can't ask you to forgive me. It's too much to ask of you or anyone. All I can do is tell you I made a very bad mistake, an idiotic mistake, and I'm sorry. It was so long, long ago ... then ... well, I didn't even think about hurting you, or any of the consequences. I want you to know that. I look back at it, and I can't believe that person was me."

He started to say something, but she cut him off.

"Let me finish, please. Then, you can throw the glass of wine in my face if you like and walk away. I couldn't blame you, but please, let me finish ... it's something I've been thinking about for months." She paused for a drink of her wine, and for a moment felt she had nothing more to say. Then, she heard herself speaking again.

"You might think I'm a money hungry bitch. Well, I really don't care about the money. It's become more than that, something much more personal."

"So, you're pissed off at me?" he asked incredulously.

"Oh no, not at all. In fact, just the opposite. I'll never forget you, and even if you did throw that glass of wine in my face, I would forgive you. I'll not remember you that way. I refuse to remember you that way." She paused for a moment, looking at him fondly before continuing. "In so many, many ways, Jack Gillette, you are so blind. Yet, in so many ways you are so, what's the word ... ah, omnipotent? Is that the right word?"

"If you're trying to flatter me, yes I guess that's the correct word. But, before you go on, I'll pay you, Lynda. I'll live up to my end of the deal, if that's what you're getting at."

"Jack, listen to me. I don't care. Sure, I'd expect you to pay me five hundred thousand, simply because I went around the world without getting on an airplane. I also followed your route as closely as possible. But as for the other ... well, if you've got better things to do with it ... if you want it all for yourself, then so be it."

They sat there for a few moments, staring at each other. Their conversation had only lasted a few minutes, but they both looked tired from the effort.

"Jack, I'm not mad at you. I'm thankful you were in my life. I've always begged you to just let me be me. When I began this trip, I hated traveling alone and playing your game to your rules. I think I might have even hated you for that at one time.

"But, I later discovered you weren't trying to make me be alone. You were giving me the gift of learning how to be myself, by myself. You were teaching me in your own special way how to be myself without the comfortable and mutually supporting influences I took for granted. You were teaching me how to do those things without you, without my work or L.A., and even how to do them without Bill.

"I found out who I am. I found out I am so very, very much like you. The canker is, I found out too late for us."

"I'm sorry, I ...."

She stopped him again. "Don't be sorry. Be glad. You should be happy, I know I am. And, I've got nobody. You've got a beautiful new woman. By the way, I love her accent."

He sat back in his chair. He truly smiled for the first time since sitting down. "How do you know all of this? This cafe, this spot, this table, and specifically, Yolanda?"

"I was here yesterday afternoon. They had a party for her over there," pointing to where they'd been seated. I was sitting at the table right next to them, and I overheard them talking about this wonderful man who was traveling around the world without getting on an airplane. I literally choked on my glass of wine."

Lynda was smiling now too, the tension of their first meeting subsiding like the volume of wine in the bottle.

"It really is a small world, isn't it?" sighed Jack.

"Yes Jack, it is. And, I can't believe I've gone completely around it."

"Well, technically, you haven't. You still have a thousand or so miles to go. Of course, you could hop on a plane now, it's sort of a moot point. I'll keep our deal, a flight home or otherwise. Thirty million dollars is way too much money for me. All I could ask or hope for is that you would do something good with your half."

"I'll not be flying anywhere. I've come this far, and I'll be damned if I'm not going to finish," she replied.

They reminisced about the trip, sharing some of their experiences. At one point, he inquired about Bill, and how far he'd traveled.

She didn't tell him about Bill beating her. They were having too much fun, enjoying the moment of their reunion far too much for that sort of subject. They had started discussing Yolanda when she asked, "And, what are you intending to do about her?"

"I don't know. I really don't. She may be in L.A. looking for me at this very moment." He went on to explain the situation, telling her of the differences they'd had and how Yolanda was afraid he would go back to her.

"I wouldn't let you come back to me. Not that I haven't entertained the thought, but no, we've got to go our own separate ways. You need to do the things you've always wanted to do. I know you're not done traveling, by any means. But, if you want my opinion on what you should do, I'll give it to you," she said.

She stopped then, actually waiting for his reaction, and displaying a new side of her personality. In the past, when she said she would give you her opinion, it meant she would give it to you whether you wanted to hear it or not.

"Okay, I'll bite. What should I do?"

"Go there. Go to her. Don't always think everything will just happen, and the end result will be what was meant to be. That's all well and good for awhile, but some things you have to go after. And, don't make the poor girl jump through a bunch of hoops thinking that if she does, then she really loves you. Just go and find out if she can love you. Go, and find out if you can love her."

They ordered another bottle of wine, and shared something to eat. Robin became their waitress, and she was giving Jack some odd looks as if to say, "You toss one off at the airport and pick up another just like that!"

The sun went down and it became colder. Lynda pulled a sweater over her shoulders, telling Jack she should get back to her hotel. "We could travel together to Eugene if you like," she said. "I've got a rental car."

"I've got one as well," laughed Jack.

They sat and looked at each other, neither of them speaking. He silently recalled all of their good times together, knowing in his heart she was completely forgiven. She silently thought of how much she still loved this man, and wondered for the b-zillionth time how she could ever have thrown his love away.

"I could turn my car in," said Lynda, as she signed the credit card bill.

"Why don't I turn mine in. You can drive. We'll go down highway ninety-nine, remember that road ... goes through all the farm country. And, it goes right by the Eugene airport just north of town. You could drop me off there," he said, smiling at her.

She reached across the table, taking both of his hands in hers, pulling them to her face. She kissed the back his hands, holding them to her lips to linger for a few seconds before lowering them to the table.

"I'm proud of you. Send me a postcard from Sydney. It's a place I want to go someday."

*****

Epilogue

Lynda Turner rode a train from Eugene, Oregon to Los Angeles, California. She circled the globe without ever getting on an airplane. She was back in her apartment only three days when she presented the manager with a hand written, thirty-day notice of her intent to vacate.

She threw away, sold, or gave away almost everything she owned. What remained fit in the back of her car. She drove to Phoenix, where her sister lived, and after four days, arranged to have her car sold as well.

She flew from Phoenix to Denver, then on to Washington, DC. With all of her worldly possessions packed in just three bags, she caught a flight to Madrid, Spain.

Once in Madrid, she put an ad in the newspaper. Her Spanish was passable, if not perfect. She knew it would improve with time. She advertised English language lessons for business people, specializing in those who were in the field of law.

After thirty days, she had more than enough clients. It was rewarding work, and she enjoyed it. The work kept her busy, yet gave her plenty of time for herself. In the next year and a half she traveled to Morocco, Portugal, France and Italy.

She stayed in touch through e-mail with Ian, the man she met on her tour of the Great Wall Of China. After over a year of correspondence, he flew to Madrid and spent a week with her. Thirty days later, she flew to Britain.

She is currently living alone in Barcelona. She works only on occasion, and travels extensively. She is planning a solo trip to South America and the Patagonia Region of that continent.

****

William Hugh Davidson spent a month in Stockholm before flying back to Los Angeles. Shortly after arriving home, he was arrested and indited on charges of racketeering, fraud, and embezzlement.

After serving a mere fifteen months of a three year sentence at Pleasant Valley State Prison in Ione, California, he returned to Stockholm and a woman he met there. Fifty years old and slightly overweight, she owns a massage parlor.

****

Miguel Diaz Rodriguez, Bill Davidson's gardener, went to the Wells Fargo bank in Palm Springs and withdrew the entire balance of his account. The total amount was $172,457.34. He and his family currently live outside of Guadalajara, in a small village where both Miguel and his wife were raised. Together, they operate a children's preschool. Miguel has a large area where he gardens and grows vegetables.

****

Michael, the taxi driver who drove Jack to the California State Lottery Commission's offices in Sacramento, never made it to New Zealand. He died of AIDS and liver failure while Jack was traveling through Russia. He was 46 years of age.

With money provided by Jack, and with the assistance of Dan and the *South Beach Register*, Michael's sister traveled to Auckland, New Zealand. She roamed around for a week before deciding upon a place called Talaga Bay, located on the eastern shore of the north island.

She thought her brother would have liked the place she selected. He would have been at peace there. She scattered his ashes on a small deserted beach.

****

Bobby McGrath got out of the bar business. After selling McGrath's in Newport Beach, he moved to St. Andrews, Scotland. He opened a small coffee shop where he also offers e-mail and internet services. Located three blocks from the first tee of The Old Course, Bobby plays three rounds of golf a week and carries a 10 handicap.

****

Jack kept his promise to Dan and Rebecca. The following Spring, Dan and his wife traveled to Montana. They looked at various properties, finally deciding upon a small, 200 acre ranch outside of Billings.

They tore down an existing manufactured home and built a modest 4-bedroom house. They leased out most of the land to neighboring ranchers for cattle grazing.

Rebecca gave birth to a girl shortly after their initial trip to Montana. They named her Veruska. She is pregnant again and will soon give birth to a son. They will name him Jackie.

Dan wrote a novel. Then, he wrote another. He is currently working on his third novel, a western.

ABOUT THE AUTHOR

Bob Pedersen traveled around the world without ever boarding an airplane. He has written numerous articles detailing his journeys. *Bon Voyage* is his first novel. He lives in Eugene, Oregon, and travels overseas as often as possible.